6.95

GW01564339

A DICTIONARY OF BANKING

A DICTIONARY OF BANKING

F. E. PERRY
LL.B., F.I.B.

MACDONALD AND EVANS

MACDONALD & EVANS LTD
Estover Road, Plymouth PL6 7PZ

First published 1979

© F. E. Perry 1979

ISBN 0 7121 0428 3

This book is copyright and may not be reproduced in whole or in part (except for the purpose of review) without the express permission of the publishers in writing

Text set in 8/9 pt VIP Times, printed and bound in Great Britain at The Pitman Press, Bath

PREFACE

One certain quality required from a banker today is adaptability. Not only does his work change as fresh services are devised, but also there are many changes in the language which he uses. There are many sources of new business words. The flow of legislation provides some of them; for example, the Consumer Credit Act has introduced a host of new terms to us. The ever-diversifying business of banking demands from some an ability to deal with technical descriptions in management, personnel, marketing, accountancy or foreign trade.

Current affairs are a never-failing source of new words and phrases. The oil crisis introduced "recycling facilities", inflation produced "index-linked". There is a continual gestation of the business slang at which the City of London is so good, viz. "corset", "topping-up clause", "Swiss roundabout", "tombstone", terms which are used by the financial editors usually with an assumption that all their readers understand them.

So there is a need for a new dictionary of banking for bankers and students of banking; a dictionary which will concentrate on the provision of quick information for busy men. I hope that this will prove to be such a work. It contains little historical matter and no derivations. There is, however, a comprehensive cross-reference system. Alternative meanings are included only when they have some significance for bankers—in that term we must include economists, accountants, statisticians, marketing experts, foreign dealers, and many others along with the branch bankers. In brief, then, this Dictionary is intended principally for the use of branch managers and their staffs and for students of the banking industry. It is also hoped that it will be of use to the men in the specialised departments both at home and abroad, and in particular to our colleagues in the Common Market countries. Indeed, I very much hope that as our links with the continental bankers develop this Dictionary will be able to reflect the inflow of fresh words and phrases which is sure to take place.

As a modest first step along this road readers will notice a number of French and German banking and financial terms in this present work. These are displayed (with definitions) along with the English words and phrases in strict alphabetical order but in italics.

I have to thank many friends and colleagues for their advice and help, in particular Mr. G. I. Lipscombe, Assistant Editor of the *Lloyds Bank Review*, who suggested many words and phrases from current and topical sources; and Mr. A. J. W. Watson, Manager in the in the International Banking Division, Treasurer's Department, of National Westminster Bank, Ltd. who supplied definitions of the colloquial phrases and specialised terms of the foreign exchange markets. The French and German banking words and phrases are the result of the advice and help given to me by Dr. Kurt Steuber, Stellv. Direktor bei der Generaldirektion des Schweizerischen Bankverein, Basel, and Mr. A. E. Ford, a Deputy Manager in the Swiss Bank Corporation, London. Mr. D. W. Edge, formerly Treasurer, National Westminster Bank, Ltd. was good enough to supply me with a list of money market terms and, finally, Mr. J. C. Stephens, Chief Accountant of Lloyds Bank Ltd. subjected the entire work to a close criticism, making very many corrections and suggestions which were of the greatest value.

To all these gentlemen I offer my deepest thanks. I also acknowledge with gratitude the kind permission of the Swiss Bank Corporation to translate from their publications *Das Bank-Fachwort* and *Petit dictionnaire financier et bancaire* and to use them as source material.

London, 1979   F. E. Perry

ACKNOWLEDGMENTS

The author acknowledges the helpful information derived from the following books and periodicals:
Introduction to English Law. P. S. James. 9th edn. Butterworth, 1976. *Modern Real Property.* G. C. Cheshire. 12th edn. Butterworth, 1976. *New English Dictionary.* Collins, 1971. *Dictionary of Banking.* W. Thomson, ed. F. R. Ryder and D. B. Jenkins, 14th edn. Pitman, 1974. *A Dictionary of Economics and Commerce.* J. L. Hanson. Macdonald & Evans, 1977. *Business Terms, Phrases and Abbreviations.* ed. D. W. Fiddes. 14th edn. Pitman, 1971. *Save and Prosper Book of Money.* ed. Margaret Allen. Collins, 1974. *Essentials of Mercantile Law.* K. Smith and D. J. Keenan. 4th edn. Pitman, 1977. *Compact French-English Dictionary.* 8th edn. Cassell, 1968. *Contemporary German-English Dictionary.* Collins, 1971. *Compact Latin-English Dictionary.* 3rd edn. Cassell, 1966. *Finance of International Trade.* A. J. W. Watson. Institute of Bankers, 1976. *Das Bank-Fachwort.* Swiss Bank Corporation. *Petit dictionnaire financier et bancaire.* Swiss Bank Corporation, 1971. *Economic Alphabet.* M. Becket. Flame Books, 1976. *Journal of the Institute of Bankers. The Bankers' Magazine. The Banker.*

CONTENTS

PREFACE v

DICTIONARY 1

APPENDIX I 275
Uniform Customs and Practice
for Documentary Credits,
1974 Revision

APPENDIX II 287
Uniform Rules for Collections

A

A1 at Lloyd's. *See* Lloyd's Register of Shipping *under* Lloyd's.

Abandonner. To settle a matter on the Bourse by the payment of an agreed premium; to buy or sell where the transaction is at a premium.

Abandonnieren. Closing out a transaction on a stock exchange by the payment of a previously agreed premium.

Abate. To reduce, diminish, less, deduct.

Abattement à la Base. That part of income considered as an essential minimum and thus not subject to tax.

Abdecken. To clear a debt off by repayment.

Abgrenzungsposten. *See* Actifs Transitoires, Passifs Transitoires.

Ab Initio. From the beginning.

Abkommen. Agreement.

À Bon Compte. At a low estimate.

À Bon Marché. Cheaply.

Abonnement. Subscription.

Abrasion. A rubbing or scraping; the wear and tear on coins in universal use.

Absatzfeld, Absatzmarkt. Market.

Abschlag. The difference, usually expressed as a percentage, between a nominal or par value, and a lower value.

Abschlagsdividende. An interim dividend.

Abschluss, Abschlusszettel. Bargain, transaction.

Abschnitt. *See* Coupon.

Abschreibung. *See* Depreciation.

Absolute Title. The best type of title which can be granted under the registered land system. It gives the holder an indefeasible title against all the world. In the case of freehold land, the grant of an absolute title indicates an undisputed chain of title culminating in the present holder. An absolute title can be given to an owner of leasehold land only if the relative freehold title is already indicated as registered, thus proving the lessor's right to grant the head lease, or after ten years in which the proprietor, or successive proprietors, have been in possession.

Absorption. The result of the amalgamation of a small company with a large one, as a result of which the smaller company is incorporated into an existing business structure in such a way as to leave little of its original identity traceable.

Abstract of Title. An epitome of the deeds and documents making up the chain of title, prepared by a vendor's solicitor on a sale, when he has to show a good root of title at least fifteen years old and a clear title from then until the time of sale. The abstract therefore begins with the document which is the good root, and summarises it and the subsequent documents as shortly as possible; it mentions also those documents which are necessary to show a clear chain of title, but which are not usually handed to a purchaser, such as probate, letters of administration, marriage certificate and death certificate. The abstract is not itself part of the title. *See also* Marked Abstract.

Abtretung. The giving up or yielding of a right, a retirement, surrender or assignment.

Abwertung. *See* Devaluation.

Abzahlungsgeschäft. Hire purchase business.

Abzahlungskauf. Buying by instalments or on hire purchase.

Accelerated Depreciation. An arrangement whereby a business is allowed for tax purposes to depreciate a new machine over a period shorter than its working life, often with a much heavier depreciation allowance in its first year than in subsequent years.

Acceptance. The signification by the drawee of a bill of exchange of his assent to the order of the drawer. The acceptance must be written on the bill, usually on the face of it, and must be signed by the drawee. His signature alone is sufficient, but usually the word "accepted" is seen. If the bill is payable after sight, the drawee must add the date of sighting to his acceptance. The word is also used to describe the bill after it has been accepted. In the case of sale of goods, the buyer is deemed to have accepted the goods when he intimates to the seller that he has accepted them; or when the goods have been delivered to him, and he does any act in relation to them which is inconsistent with the ownership of the seller; or when after the lapse of a reasonable time, he retains the goods without intimating to the seller that he has rejected them. *See also* General Acceptance; Qualified Acceptance.

Acceptance Commission. A charge made by a banker or an accepting house for the use of its name as an acceptor on bills of exchange.

Acceptance Credit. A credit which stipulates the drawing of term bills which will be accepted by the issuing bank or by the customer.

Acceptance for Honour. Where a bill of exchange has been protested for dishonour by non-acceptance, or for better security, and is not overdue, any person, not being a party already liable thereon, may, with the consent of the holder, intervene and accept the bill *supra* protest, for the honour of any party liable thereon, or for the honour of the person for whose account the bill is drawn. A bill may be accepted for honour for part only of the sum for which it is drawn. An acceptance for honour *supra* protest in order to be valid must (1) be written on the bill, and indicate that it is an acceptance for honour; (2) be signed by the acceptor for honour. Where an acceptance for honour does not expressly state for whose honour it is made, it is deemed to be an acceptance for the honour of the drawer. Where a bill payable after sight is accepted for honour, its maturity is calculated from the date of the noting for non-acceptance, and not from the date of the acceptance for honour.

Acceptation. *See* Acceptance.

Acceptation Bancaire. *See* Acceptance Credit.

Accepting House. A banking house which specialises in accepting bills drawn upon it under credit established by or in favour of approved customers. The three qualities usually given as characteristic of an accepting house (or merchant bank) is that a substantial part of the business of the house shall consist of accepting bills to finance trade, that the bills once accepted command the finest discount rates on the market, and that the acceptances are freely taken by the Bank of England.

Accepting Houses Committee. A body representing seventeen of the most important merchant banks. Membership of the Accepting House Committee confers the facility of discounting commercial bills at the Bank of England at the finest rate. Every member has direct access to the Bank on any matter at any time.

Acceptor. *See* Acceptance; Drawee.

Access. The credit card system run jointly by Lloyds, Midland, National Westminster and Williams & Glyn's banks. The card is issued free and can be used in over 100,000 places in the U.K. and through the American Interbank Card Association (Mastercharge) link at over 1·6 m places world wide. Purchases of any value may be made provided the total outstanding at any one time does not exceed the personal credit limit granted to the cardholder. If purchases are settled within twenty-five days of the date of the statement on which they first appear no interest is charged, but any amounts left outstanding beyond that time attract interest of 2% per month from the statement date. Cash advances, which bear interest from the day they are taken until the date they are repaid, are available at the branches of the participating banks but at the time of writing are restricted to £50 at the request of H.M. Government.

Accommodation Bill. A bill to which a person adds his name to oblige or accommodate another person, without receiving consideration for so doing, i.e. as a surety or guarantor.

Accompagnateur. A punter, a speculator.

Accord (Fr.). An agreement.

Accord and Satisfaction. Where one party to a contract has fulfilled his side of the bargain, but the other has not, the first party may release the second party either under seal or in consideration of receiving some goods or service other than that specified in the original contract. The accord is the agreement to discharge the original obligation, the satisfaction is the consideration which supports the agreement.

Accord de Clearing. An agreement between two countries on the settlement of debts and credits between them, arising from their commercial and financial

transactions. A central office in each country handles the payments. Where the service of payments has been decentralised, this function is assigned in part to banks mutually agreed upon.
Accord de Paiement. An agreement between two or more countries regulating the transfers or payments between them.
Account. A reckoning, counting, computation; a statement of receipts and expenditure showing the balance; a register of debits and credits. In commerce, a statement showing the amount owing for goods, services, etc.; on the Stock Exchange, the time elapsing between one settlement day and the next; in banking, the current, deposit, foreign currency, loan, savings or other account maintained by a bank for a customer. A *Current Account* is one running from day to day on which cheques are paid and to which credits are paid in. No interest is usually allowed. Overdrafts may be taken on current accounts. No cheques are normally paid to the debit of a *Deposit Account* which is always maintained in credit. The balance is repayable at seven or fourteen days or after a fixed term. Interest is paid at deposit rate. A *Savings Account* is similar except that it is meant for the accumulation of smaller sums, and withdrawals up to a certain amount may be made on production of the savings book at branches other than the one maintaining the account, in addition to the normal duty on the bank to repay the balance plus any accrued interest at the account-maintaining branch. *See also* Open Account.
Accountancy. The keeping of books of account: the process of analysing, sorting under various heads, and recording the receipts and payments of a business or organisational undertaking.
Accountant. A person trained to post book entries and to balance books or to prepare balance sheets periodically: an auditor who inspects the books and records of a person or company as a check that they have been properly maintained: the title of a senior bank officer in a branch or head office.
Account Day. *See* Pay Day.
Account Payee. Words which may be added to the crossing on a cheque for greater safety. The phrase is an indication to the collecting banker that if he collects the proceeds of the cheque for anyone other than the named payee he may later face an action for conversion, brought by the payee. The addition does not prohibit transfer or affect the negotiability of the cheque.
Account Sales. An account sent by a trader to the consignor of goods, showing details of the goods and the net prices obtained after deduction of all the expenses of sale; an account sent to a principal by an agent who has sold goods at public auction on his behalf.
Account Stated. An account between two parties which consists of items which have been expressly or impliedly agreed between the parties as entries which have properly appeared on the account. Any balance showing is likewise agreed as correct.
Accreditif. An instruction given by one bank to another bank on the order of a third party, to hold at the disposition of the latter, or another beneficiary, a sum of money, under certain conditions. The sum is paid wholly or partially on the simple request of the beneficiary and after delivery of specified documents. A revocable credit imports no firm undertaking by the bank, but an irrevocable credit cannot be modified or revoked without the consent of all contracting parties. When an irrevocable credit is sent by one bank to another, the latter is not liable on it unless it has itself confirmed it. *See also* Documentary Credit.
Accreditif Confirmé, Accreditif non Confirmé. See above.
Accrued Interest. Interest which has accumulated, but which has not yet been paid over.
Acheter ou Vendre Dont. On the *Bourse*, the name describing a type of operation at a premium, where the premium is included in the quotation. An example would be "85 *dt.* 5", *i.e.* the price of 85 includes a premium of 5.
À Compte. On account, in part payment.
Acquerer. A buyer of something of value.
Acquisition. *See* Take-over Bid.
Acte de Défaut de Biens. A document establishing, after a bankruptcy or foreclosure, the unsecured amount of a claim, which becomes as from that time unenforceable.
Actif. An asset, assets.
Actif Circulant. Current assets.

Actif Réalisable. Liquid assets.
Actifs Transitoires. Accounting entries used to make adjustments between one financial year and another; expenditure arising in the current accounting year, but which concern the coming year; or receipts received in the current year for matters to be dealt with in the coming year.
Action. Anything done or performed; a civil proceeding instituted in a court of law. (*Fr.*) A share in a limited company.
Action au Porteur. Bearer share.
Action de Priorité. Preference share, preferred share, preferred stock.
Action Gratuite. Bonus share.
Actionnaire. A shareholder.
Action Nominative. Registered share.
Action of Debt. An action brought to recover a sum of money.
Action Ordinaire. Ordinary share.
Action Privilégiée. See *Action de Priorité.*
Action Privilégiée Cumulative. Cumulative preference share.
Action sans Valuer Nominal. Share of no par value.
Action Souscrite. Paid-up share.
Active. Continually employed, busy, characterised by action, work, or the performance of business.
Active Circulation. That part of the note issue of a country which is in circulation at any given time.
Active Debt. A debt owed to a person.
Active Market. A market in which there is much buying and selling; of the Stock Exchange, stock or shares having frequent and regular dealings, so that would-be buyers may be assured of obtaining the amounts they want.
Active Partner. A partner who takes an active interest in the management of the business and who is fully liable for the debts of the partnership.
Act of Bankruptcy. An act which, when committed by a debtor, may lead to a petition for bankruptcy being presented to the court, either by a creditor, or by the debtor himself. The petition must follow the act of bankruptcy within three months. There are ten acts of bankruptcy. They are (under the Bankruptcy Act 1914): (1) If a debtor makes a conveyance or assignment of his property to a trustee or trustees for the benefit of his creditors generally. (2) If a debtor makes a fraudulent gift, conveyance, transfer or delivery of some or all of his property. ("Fraudulent" here means with intent to defeat or delay creditors.) (3) If a debtor makes any conveyance or transfer of any or all his property, or creates any charge upon it, which would be void as a fraudulent preference if he were adjudged bankrupt. (4) If with intent to defeat or delay his creditors a debtor flees the country, or being out of England, remains out of England, or leaves his house or otherwise absents himself, or keeps house. (5) If execution against a debtor has been levied by seizure of his goods under process in any court action, or in any civil proceeding in the High Court, and the goods have been either sold or held by the sheriff for twenty-one days. (6) If the debtor files in the court a declaration of his inability to pay his debts, or presents a bankruptcy petition against himself. (7) If, having had a bankruptcy notice served upon him by a creditor who has obtained a court order against him, the debtor has not, within ten days after service of the notice, complied with its terms or satisfied the court that he has a counterclaim equal to or exceeding the amount of the judgment debt ordered to be paid, which he could not set up in the action in which the judgment was obtained. (8) If the debtor gives notice to any of his creditors that he has suspended, or is about to suspend, payment of his debts. (9) (under the Insolvency Act 1976) If a debtor, against whom an administration order has been made, fails to observe the conditions of the order, the court may substitute for it a receiving order against the debtor, in which case he shall be deemed to have committed an act of bankruptcy at the time the receiving order is made. (10) (under the Criminal Justice Act 1972) Where a person has caused loss or damage to property exceeding £15,000, the Crown Court may make a criminal bankruptcy order against such a person, who is then to be treated as a debtor who has committed an act of bankruptcy on the date on which the order is made. See also Administration Order; Assignment; Fraudulent Conveyance; Fraudulent Preference; Keeping House; Petition.
Act of God. The operation of uncontrollable natural forces in causing an event, *e.g.* tempest, earthquake, lightning,

which cause exceptional and unforeseeable damage. No individual or insurance company is liable for such damage.

Actuaire. An actuary (*q.v. below*).

Actuary. An officer of a mercantile or insurance company, skilled in statistics, especially on the expectancy of life and the average proportion of losses by time and other accidents: a senior officer in a savings bank.

Ademption. A taking away, the revocation of a grant or bequest, the destruction of something subject to a specific bequest between the time the will is executed and the death of the testator.

Ad Hoc. "For this", for a special purpose, for a particular occasion.

Ad Interim. In the meanwhile.

Adjudication Order. An order made by the court declaring a debtor bankrupt. The effect of the order is to vest the estate of the debtor in a trustee, who will wind it up for the benefit of the creditors.

Adjustable Peg. A flexible system of fixing exchange rates where a rate is allowed to vary within certain narrowly defined limits. *See also* Crawling Peg; Peg.

Administrateur. A company director.

Administration. The act of administering, the executive part of a government or a large business organisation; dispensation; direction; the management and distribution of the estate of an intestate.

Administration Order. An order made by the court for the summary administration of the estate of a debtor who is unable to pay the amount of a County Court judgment against him, and who has prepared and submitted a list of all his debts which shows that his total indebtedness does not exceed £300.

Administrator. A person appointed by law to wind up the estate of a person who dies intestate, or who leaves a will nominating an executor who predeceases him or refuses or is unable or unfit to act. He is very often the next of kin. There are a number of specialised terms to define different types of administrator.

Administrator *ad Litem.* An administrator of a deceased person's estate appointed for the purpose of defending the interest of that estate in a legal action.

Administrator *cum Testamento Annexo.* Where the deceased has left a will but no executor has been appointed it is necessary for an administrator to be appointed. As the administrator has the terms of the will to guide him in his administration he is given a grant of administration with the will annexed.

Administrator *de Bonis Non.* Where an administrator dies before completing his task of administration, or an executor dies in similar circumstances without appointing an executor, the court will appoint an administrator *de bonis non administratis*, for which the above term is a contraction, to complete the task.

Administrator *Durante Absentia.* An administrator appointed to act during the absence abroad of the previously appointed administrator.

Administrator *Durante Minore Aetate.* A temporary administrator, appointed to act during the minority of the executor or of the person entitled to a grant of administration.

Administrator *Pendente Lite.* An administrator appointed to administer the estate until any lawsuit respecting the validity of the will is brought.

Admission of Age. *See* Age Admitted.

Ad Referendum. For further consideration.

Ad Valorem. According to the value, generally in connection, with taxes or duties.

Advance. Payment beforehand, a loan; accommodation made available by a moneylender, by an employer, or by a banker to a customer by way of overdraft, loan, discount or credit card; a part payment made to a consignor of goods by a merchant or an agent on receipt of the relevant invoice and bill of lading; a payment beforehand by a publisher to an author on account of royalties expected to be earned; an early payment of salary to a clerk who will be on holiday on the day when salaries are to be paid.

Advance Freight. Money paid beforehand in respect of the transportation of goods, especially by water.

Advancement. A payment made by a trustee out of trust funds to a beneficiary for some long-term provision for his betterment, such as an investment which will help him to build up his career; a payment made by a testator during his lifetime of a sum of money to a beneficiary under his will. *See also* Hotchpot.

Advance Note. A draft on the owner of a ship, usually for one month's wages, issued by the ship's captain to a seaman on his signing the Articles of Agreement. The intention is to make it possible for the seaman to make some provision for those he is going to leave behind him, but as a precaution against the seaman failing to join the ship the advance note is expressed to be payable to the person named in the note three days after the ship has sailed.

Adverse. Acting in a contrary direction, opposite in position, unfortunate, unfavourable.

Adverse Balance. An overdrawn balance. As applied to the balance of trade, it means an excess of imports (for which payment has to be made) over exports (for which payment is received).

Adverse Possession. The enjoyment or use of property, with or without the tacit knowledge of the real owner, a use which becomes absolute if no objection has been raised during twenty years by the real owner.

Adverse Report. An unfavourable report on a person or a project.

Adverse Variance. A variance where the discrepancy is to the disadvantage of the organisation, as when actual profits fall short of budgeted profits.

Advice. Intelligence, information, counsel, opinion as to a course of action from a lawyer to his client, a doctor to his patient, a bank manager to his customer: commercial information conveyed by letter by which one party advises another of something done, or about to be done, on his account. Advice on the investment which a customer might make should not be given by a bank manager, but the opinion of a stockbroker should be obtained. Information as to the existing holdings of the customer, and his financial circumstances, must be given to the broker together with an intimation as to whether the customer desires primarily security of investment or a chance of capital appreciation. The broker will make a number of suggestions which will be passed on to the customer, who will make the final selection.

Advice Note. A letter informing the recipient of some particular transaction done or about to be done, in which he has an interest, such as the arrival or despatch of shipments, goods, or documents of title to goods, or the payment of accounts. *See also* Credit Advice; Letter of Advice.

Advise Fate. *See* Special Clearance.

Advisory Funds. Funds left with a bank by a customer for investment on his behalf, after consultation. Such funds are held in large amounts by Swiss banks, and their use for investment in Eurobonds assists the ability of the bank to place new issues. Also known as Discretionary or In-House funds.

Advowson. The right of presenting or nominating a clergyman to a vacant benefice.

Affaire. A business matter.

Affaire à Demi. The carrying out in common of business transactions by two banks, profits or losses being equally shared.

Affaire à Term. Business to be concluded over a period of time.

Affaire au Comptant. A matter for immediate payment.

Affaire de Garantie. A covering operation.

Affaire en Consortium. A business operation carried out in common by several banks which are united for this purpose in an association which may be either temporary or permanent.

Affaire Nette. The sale or purchase of documentary titles through the agency of a bank at no cost, commission being already incorporated in the rate.

Affaires. Business.

Affidavit. A voluntary written affirmation sworn to before a person qualified to administer an oath, such as a solicitor who has been appointed a Commissioner for Oaths, a consul or a notary public. The affidavit may be admitted as evidence in a court of law.

Affiliate. To receive into fellowship, to unite a society, association or firm with another, but without loss of identity; a company which associates with another, generally as its subsidiary.

À Fond. Thoroughly.

A Fortiori. With greater reason.

After-Acquired Property. Property coming to the bankrupt after the date of the adjudication order. This is property which should be reported to the trustee in bankruptcy, but there is statutory protection for any person dealing with the bankrupt *bona fide* and for value in respect of such property, whether real or personal, provided the transaction is completed before the trustee intervenes (Bankruptcy Act 1914, s.47(1)).

After Sight. *See* Sight.

Age Admitted. An endorsement on a life assurance policy, or on a separate note attached to it, to indicate that the assurance company is satisfied that the assured's age was correctly stated on the form of application for the policy, or that it has been since rectified. The assurance company calculates the premium from the statement of age by the assured, and does not check the age until it is asked to pay over the policy moneys. Then a birth certificate must be produced, and if the age is wrong a deduction may be made from the proceeds. To avoid this the banker who is holding a life policy as security prefers to make sure that the company has admitted that the age has been correctly stated.

Agence. An agency.

Agency. The office or business of an agent; a place of business, a commercial organisation; the relationship between a principal and an agent, i.e. between a bank in one country and its correspondent bank in another; a shop or office of good repute which supplies basic banking services for a bank in a place where that bank is not represented, having daily communication with a branch of the bank.

Agenda. Things to be done, engagements to be kept, a list of business to be transacted, especially at a company meeting.

Agenda Paper. The document on which is listed the various items of business which are to be considered at a meeting.

Agent. One entrusted with the business of another, one who is employed to represent his principal and to make contracts on his behalf. Responsibility for such contracts will fall on the principal as long as the agent keeps within the powers conferred on him by his principal. *See also* Del Credere Agent; Estate Agent; Export Agent; Forwarding Agent; General Agent; Import Agent; Insurance Agent; Mercantile Agent; Special Agent; Transfer Agent; Travel Agent.

Agent de Change. A stockbroker, an official member of the Paris *Bourse*.

Aggravated Damages. Damages awarded to a plaintiff who has suffered more than ordinary loss.

Aggregate. To collect together, to bring into a mass or whole, a sum or assemblage of particulars, the total; composed of individuals forming an association.

Aggregation. The act of combining together, the addition of total gifts to a beneficiary for the purposes of Capital Transfer Tax, or the addition of gifts to a beneficiary during the lifetime of the donor to the benefit received under the will of the same testator for a like purpose; any combination of assets or benefits for the purpose of income or other tax.

Agio. The difference in value between one kind of currency and another; money-changing; the charge for changing notes for cash, or one kind of money for another; the difference in value between metallic money and its paper equivalent; the difference, usually expressed as a percentage, between nominal or par value, and a higher price.

Agreement. A coming into accord, mutual understanding, *consensus ad idem*; a contract duly executed and legally binding; an understanding which is not intended to have legal consequences. *See also* Cancellable Agreement; Conditional Sale Agreement; Consumer Credit Agreement; Consumer Hire Agreement; Credit-token Agreement; Debtor-creditor Agreement; Debtor-creditor-supplier Agreement; Executed Agreement; Exempt Agreement; Hire-purchase Agreement; Modifying Agreement; Multiple Agreement; Non-commercial Agreement; Personal Credit Agreement; Regulated Agreement; Restricted-use Credit Agreement; Small Agreement; Unexecuted Agreement.

Agricultural Charge. A fixed charge upon the farming stock and other agricultural assets belonging to a farmer, whether a tenant or an owner, at the date of the charge or a floating charge upon the farming stock and other agricultural assets from time to time belonging to the farmer or both. Such a charge would form a security for a banker providing agricultural short-term credit, but it is invalid if the farmer, being insolvent at the time of creation, goes bankrupt within three months. Agricultural charges have to be registered, within seven days, with the Agricultural Credits Superintendent at the Land Registry, and this publicity can result in a restriction of the farmer's credit. Very few are now registered each year.

Agricultural Credit Banks. Co-operative societies which on the continent finance agriculture and have been responsible for much development in rural areas.

Agricultural Credit Corporation (A.C.C.). An organisation to help farmers at the limit of their bank accommodations. In approved cases the A.C.C. will guarantee the farmer's bank overdraft provided the farmer agrees that, if the guarantee is called upon, any securities held by the bank are thereafter to be held for the A.C.C.

Agricultural Development and Advisory Service (A.D.A.S.). A body formed in 1971 to give farm management advice. It replaced the National Agricultural Advisory Service, a technical and advisory service of the Ministry of Agriculture which for more than a quarter of a century had given free advice to the farming community, and was respected and trusted by farmers. But in later years the increased pace of technical and scientific development in farming has resulted in specialisation of farming systems to a degree never before seen. As a result there have emerged large, highly capitalised farm businesses, requiring a greater depth of advice at both technical and management level. The replacement of N.A.A.S. by a state extension service such as A.D.A.S. represents a change in governmental policy and will tend to result in the absorption of the activities of the A.D.A.S. adviser into a conventional Civil Service structure.

Agricultural Finance Federation. An organisation sponsored by the National Farmers' Union to assist farmers to obtain bank credit, by offering to guarantee advances made to finance a programme of agreed improvements on the farm. A condition is that the farmer shall accept specialist advice on the best way of carrying out these improvements. The government will meet up to three-quarters of any sums which the Federation has to pay to banks in cases where its guarantee is called upon.

Agricultural Mortgage Corporation. A corporation formed in 1929 to provide facilities whereby farmers could obtain long-term loans at reasonably favourable rates, secured by first mortgages on their farms, for periods of between five and sixty years. Repayments are made by equal half-yearly instalments of capital and interest over up to forty years if the loan has been used for improvements, or over up to sixty years if the loan was to assist in the purchase of the farm. To make these loans the corporation obtains funds partly from shareholders and partly from the issue of a debenture stock, secured by a charge on all its property and assets. The government has made the debenture stock additionally attractive to investors by guaranteeing it to the extent of twelve million pounds. The share capital of this corporation is provided by the U.K. clearing banks and the Bank of England.

Air Waybill. A form of waybill used as a receipt for the goods and evidencing the contract between the sender and the airline for the carriage of goods: the equivalent of a consignment note.

Akkreditiv. See Accreditif.

Aktie. Share, stock.

Aktien Bank. Joint stock bank.

Aktienbuch, Aktienregister. Share register.

Aktiengesellschaft. Joint stock company.

Aktienhandel. Stock-jobbing.

Aktienindex. A share index giving a report of share prices for shares or groups of shares on the *Börse*. It offers a useful set of comparative quotations.

Aktienkurs. Share price rate.

Aktienmantel. The share structure of a company which is practically in liquidation. It is against German law to make deals in such shares.

Aktiensplit. See Splitting.

Aktienzertifikat. Share certificate.

Aktionärbrief. A letter from the management of a company to the shareholders, twice or four times yearly, giving them information as to the progress of the business.

Aktiven. Assets.

Aktivgeschäfte. Entries arising from the business of the bank and appearing on the assets side of the balance sheet.

Aktuar. Actuary.

Akzept. Acceptance, bill of exchange accepted by the drawee.

Akzeptant. Acceptor.

Akzeptkredit. See Acceptance Credit.

All-Moneys Debenture. A mortgage debenture containing both fixed and floating charges securing any sums owing to the bank by the company at any time on any account.

Allocation. *See* Allotment.

Allonge. A slip of paper attached to a bill of exchange for the purpose of receiving indorsements when the back of the bill is already full of indorsements so that there is no room on the bill for any more. An allonge becomes an integral part of the bill to which it is attached.

Allotment. A distribution of shares in a public company among the persons who have applied for shares on a printed form of application, supplied by the company, and have paid a proportion of the price of the shares as a deposit. The amount of a new issue allotted to syndicate members by the managing bank. *See also* Instalment Allotment.

Allotment Letter. A letter sent to an applicant for an issue of shares, stock or bonds on offer to the public, informing him of the amount or number allotted to him and specifying the instalments of the balance of payment together with the dates on which they should be made. The letter is usually in the form of a certificate which is renounceable up to a certain date. The shareholder may accept or renounce his allocation by signing an appropriate form printed on the back of the certificate. If he renounces he may do so in favour of another person, who should sign the form of acceptance, or he may sell his rights through a broker. After the given date the certificate becomes the evidence of title to the holding in the usual manner.

Allotment Note. An authority, signed by a seaman, addressed to the master of the ship on which he is serving, directing that part or all of his wages shall be paid to his wife and/or family, or to a bank.

Alloy. To mix with anything base or inferior, to mix with a baser metal; an amalgam; the standard of purity, the quality of gold or silver; in coinage, the addition to a more precious metal of a baser but more hard-wearing metal.

Alteration of Bill. Where a bill or acceptance is materially altered without the assent of all parties liable on the bill, the bill is avoided except as against a party who has himself authorised or assented to the alteration, and subsequent indorsers. If a bill has been materially altered, but the alteration is not apparent, and the bill is in the hands of a holder in due course, such holder may avail himself of the bill as if it had not been altered, and may enforce payment of it according to its original tenor. The following are *Material alterations*: any alteration of the date, the sum payable, the time of payment, the place of payment and, where a bill has been accepted generally, the addition of a place of payment without the acceptor's assent.

Alte Rechnung. The last accounting period, now closed.

Alternative Cost. *See* Opportunity Cost.

Amalgamation. The union or merging of two or more firms or companies to form one new business. Amalgamation is one way for achieving expansion of business; thus the British clearing banks have reached their present size and position partly by the opening of new branches, and partly by amalgamation of banks. Amalgamation is associated with economies of large-scale provision of services, and with obtaining a larger share of the market.

American-Type Share Certificate. A certificate which has many of the characteristics of a bearer bond, but which is not a negotiable instrument because it does not give to a new owner any better title than the previous owner had. The name of the registered holder appears on the face of the document and a blank form of transfer is printed on the back. Usually the registered holder signs the form of transfer and this allows the certificate to pass from hand to hand like a bearer bond, delivery transferring title. Unlike a bearer bond, however, there are no coupons, and the dividend is sent to the registered holder, from whom the owner must claim it. The owner can get himself registered by completing the back of the form; then he will get dividends, notices, etc., sent direct to him, but the certificate will have lost its readily negotiable characteristic. *See also* Marking Names.

Amortir. To repay a debt partly or in full.

Amortisation. The act, or the right, of

alienating lands in mortmain, that is, of transferring lands in perpetuity to a charitable body or to an ecclesiastical authority; the redemption of bonds or loans by annual payment from a sinking fund. Payments into the sinking fund must be such as to make possible regular paying off of all bonds due to be redeemed plus the payment of all the interest due on bonds still outstanding.

Amortissement. A writing down in the value of balance sheet entries by a debit to profit and loss account in consideration of wear and tear and the depreciation in value of assets. Often the reductions are carried to the liabilities side of the balance sheet by way of adjusting entries. The word is also used for the repayment of a debt, whether on the repayment date, or by a drawing by lot, or by redemption of a certain number of bonds on the market.

Amortissement Cumulatif. Repayment of a loan by annual instalments, the interest no longer payable on that part of the loan already repaid accumulating each year towards the capital repayment.

Ancillary. Giving help to, auxiliary, subordinate.

Ancillary Credit Business. For the purposes of the Consumer Credit Act 1974, any business so far as it comprises or relates to credit brokerage, debt-adjusting, debt-counselling, debt-collecting or the operation of a credit reference agency.

Angebot. Offer, quotation, tender.

Angebot und Nachfrage. Supply and demand.

Anlage. Plant, investment.

Anlagefonds. See Investment Trust; Unit Trust.

Anlagekapital. Business capital.

Anlagepapiere. Investment stocks or shares.

Anlageplan. An investment plan to acquire a shareholding through regular purchases by instalment over a given period of time.

Anlagepolitik. The strategy of investment with regard to the degree of risk taken and how it can be minimised.

Anlagervermögen. Investment in the basic means of production; financing of stocks, retail sales, transport, etc., and those fixed assets which will lead to further profits, *e.g.* land and buildings, machinery, plant, equipment, etc. In the balance sheet these assets are shown subject to a charge for depreciation costs.

Anlagesparheft. An investment savings account, differing from an ordinary savings account by reason of a higher interest rate coupled with a more restricted right of withdrawal.

Anleihe. A loan.

Annahme von Wechsein. See Akzept.

Annual General Meeting. A yearly meeting between the shareholders of a company and the directors, so that the shareholders may be given a general knowledge of the progress of the company and have an opportunity to ask questions. Formal business transacted on this occasion includes the adoption of the accounts, the confirmation of the proposed dividend, the election of directors and the appointment of auditors. In the U.K. such a meeting must be held at least once in every calendar year and not more than fifteen months after the last preceding general meeting. Some relaxation in the rules is allowed to a newly-incorporated company—the company need not hold an annual general meeting in the year of its incorporation or in the following year provided that it is held within eighteen months of the company's incorporation.

Annual Return. Every company having a share capital shall, at least once in every year, make a return containing details as to the address of the registered office of the company, the situation of the register of members and debenture-holders, a summary of share capital and debentures, particulars of any indebtedness, a list of past and present members, and particulars of directors and secretaries. This information, together with a copy of the company's latest balance sheet, is to be sent to the Registrar of Companies.

Annuitant. A person in receipt of an annuity.

Annuität. A yearly charge for interest on, and repayment of, a fixed capital debt.

Annuité. The sum paid out annually for interest and partial repayment of a debt: if the yearly sum is of a fixed amount, the capital repayment will increase regularly as the interest service falls. *See also* Annuity.

Annuity. A sum of money paid quarterly, half-yearly or yearly: an investment insuring fixed annual payments. *See also* Deferred Annuity; Immediate Annuity; Joint Annuity; Life Annuity; Perpetual Annuity; Temporary Annuity; Terminable Annuity; Tontine Annuity.

Annuity Certain. One to continue for an agreed period of time.

Annulation. Annulment, revocation, cancellation: in the case of the loss of certificates or deeds of title, the legal procedure prescribed in such a case.

Anrecht. A right of a shareholder to participate in a new issue.

Anspruch. Claim.

Answer on a Cheque. When a cheque is returned unpaid it is a rule of the London Bankers' Clearing House that an answer should be written on an unpaid article. These answers fall into two groups; those where payment is refused for a technical reason, and those where dishonour is due to lack of funds. In the second case there is some risk to the banker if he does not exercise every care in checking the correctness of the return and the appropriateness of the answer, which must be such as to safeguard as far as possible the reputation of the customer. The customary answer where funds have proved inadequate is "Refer to Drawer", which has for many years been considered safe: now, however, there is a tendency to consider it as capable of carrying a defamatory meaning. The bank must be ready, therefore, to prove that these words are true in substance and in fact.

Antecedent. Going before in time, prior, anterior.

Antecedent Negotiations. For the purposes of the Consumer Credit Act 1974 these are any negotiations with the debtor or hirer (1) conducted by the creditor or owner in relation to the making of any regulated agreement; or (2) conducted by a credit-broker in relation to goods sold or proposed to be sold by the credit-broker to the creditor before forming the subject-matter of a debtor–creditor–supplier agreement within section 12(*a*) of the Act; or (3) conducted by the supplier in relation to a transaction financed or proposed to be financed by a debtor–creditor–supplier agreement within section 12(*b*) or (*c*) of the Act.

Antecessor. A previous possessor.

Antedate. A date preceding the actual date. To date before the true time, to precede, to anticipate.

Antedated Cheque. A bill of exchange is not invalid by reason only of the fact that it is antedated. However, a banker receiving a cheque antedated by six months or more for payment would regard it as "stale", and would return it unpaid unless he could get the confirmation of the drawer to pay it (some banks operate on a twelve-month basis). A cheque can also be "stale" for the purposes of negotiation. No time has been set by statute for this, but it is thought that a period of ten–twelve days after the date of the cheque will be enough to make it stale. A holder taking a cheque in negotiation cannot claim to be a holder in due course if the cheque is stale. He has to take the bill "complete and regular on the face of it". A cheque which is stale is not "regular".

Anteil. Share, dividend, interest.

Anteilschein. See Part Sociale.

Ante Omnia. First and foremost; before anything.

Anticipatory Credit. *See* Pre-finance Credit.

Anweisung. Instruction, order, remittance, draft, cheque.

Anziehen. A rise in prices, *e.g.* on the Stock Exchange.

"A" Ordinary Shares. *See* Non-voting Shares.

A Posteriori. From effect to cause.

Application Form. Any form on which a person desiring something is obliged to fill in details under the headings specified on the form.

Application Form for a Banking Account (*e.g.* company account, partnership account, account for an unincorporated association). A form which, when filled in by the prospective customer and returned to the bank, will give the bank full particulars of the applicant together with specimen signatures and instructions as to how the account is to be operated. A bank issuing application forms may take the opportunity to insert clauses designed to improve its legal position *vis-à-vis* the customer, *e.g.* in a form of application for a partnership account or a joint account, the imposition of joint and several liability; in the latter, an agreement that the balance of the account shall be paid to the survivor.

Application Form for Delegation of

Authority. This is in effect a principal's mandate to his agent, which will define precisely the powers which the agent is to have, in particular, whether he is to have power to negotiate overdrafts and charge securities on behalf of his principal.

Application Form for Shares. *See* Allotment Letter.

Applikationskurs. Closing rates on the stock exchange, which will be used by dealers when quoting rates for buying and selling commission.

Appointment of New Trustee. If a sole trustee dies, reference must be made to the trust instrument—it may contain directions as to the appointment of new trustees in such a circumstance. If not, the executor of the last trustee may act, or may appoint new trustees. In cases of difficulty and as a last resort, the court has power to appoint a new trustee or new trustees.

Apport. Contribution, share; the make-up of the capital of a limited company by reference to the type or source of contribution; the subscriptions of shareholders to a new company in exchange for shares.

Apportion. To mete out in just proportions; to divide in suitable proportion.

Appreciation. The setting of a value upon, a just estimate; a rise in value, as of stocks or shares, or a life policy held as security as further premiums are paid; a rise in prices generally through the effects of inflation; a rise in property values through a scarcity of available property, whether temporary or semi-permanent.

Appropriation. The act of setting apart for a purpose; anything thus set apart. The assignment of funds for a special purpose or use; the allocation of funds to be disbursed out of public money.

Appropriation Account. The account which shows how the annual profit of a company is divided up between dividend, reserves, pension funds, etc.

Appropriation of Goods. An act identifying goods with a contract.

Appropriation of Payments. The act of a customer who, when paying in a credit to his account, specifies the debit against which it is to be set. If the customer does not so appropriate, the banker is free to do so, and may appropriate the credit in discharge or partial discharge of the customer's indebtedness to the bank.

Appropriation under the Rule in Clayton's Case. *See* Clayton's Case.

A Priori. From cause to effect.

À Propos de. Concerning.

Aptitude. Natural capacity or general fitness for certain types of work, faculty for learning, talent.

Aptitude Tests. Tests carried out by organisations employing staff to try to match up the talents of the employee with the job he is to do. In banks, such tests should clearly indicate the most promising career pattern for a recruit, particularly whether he has any marked advantage in social "polish", or any specialised knowledge which would qualify him for a particular department.

Arab Currency-related Unit (Arcru). A "basket" of currencies linked to the currencies of twelve Arab countries (Algeria, Bahrain, Egypt, Iraq, Kuwait, Lebanon, Libya, Oman, Qatar, Saudi Arabia, Syria and United Arab Emirates). Devised in 1974, the Arcru unit was worth one U.S. dollar. Subsequently the value was calculated by eliminating the two currencies which showed the greater strength against the dollar since the base date, plus the two which proved the weakest, and then taking an average of the performance of the rest.

Arbitrage. A term formerly used to describe the activities of dealers in foreign exchange, when cross-dealing in various currencies quoted at differing rates in differing financial centres, with a view to making a profit. Now often used to describe the activities of bank customers who are able to switch money between a bank and a secondary market profitably for themselves. *See also* Compound Arbitrage; Direct Arbitrage; Hard Arbitrage; Reverse Arbitrage; Soft Arbitrage.

Arbitration. The referring of a dispute between employers and employees to an impartial body for a decision; the referring of a dispute in a commercial matter to a third party who will act as a judge, a procedure which is usually quicker and cheaper for the disputing parties than recourse to a court of law. The disputing parties agree to abide by the decision of the arbitrator, whose written findings are known as an *award*.

Argent. Money.

Argent à Terme. Bank deposits repayable at a term as opposed to those repayable on demand, the term deposits commanding a higher rate of interest.

Argent au Jour le Jour. Money repayable at call, overnight money.

Argent à Vue. Bank deposits repayable on demand.

Argent Comptant. Ready money, cash down.

Arithmetic Mean. An average, calculated by the division of the total of items by the number of the items.

Arrangement with Creditors or Members. A person or a company unable to pay debts due may propose an arrangement with creditors as an alternative to bankruptcy or liquidation. In the case of a debtor he may call his creditors together and offer to pay so much in the pound in full satisfaction of what he owes them, perhaps by instalments (A *Composition with Creditors*). The advantage of this arrangement for the creditors is that it allows them the full benefits of the total assets of the debtor, without the legal and court fees which would be deductible if he were made bankrupt. If the creditors concur the agreement may be drawn up and sealed. If so it is a *Deed of Arrangement* which must be registered at the Department of Trade within seven days of its execution, failing which it is void. The deed must be executed by the debtor and by all those creditors who agree to it. All the creditors may not agree. Those who do not are called *Dissenting Creditors*. After the registration there is allowed a period of twenty-one days for the deed to receive the assent of a majority in value and number of the creditors. If these assents are not forthcoming the deed is void. Within twenty-eight days from the registration, a trustee of the deed (perhaps one of the creditors or a solicitor or accountant) must file with the Department of Trade a statutory declaration to the effect that the requisite majority of the creditors have assented to the deed. Once creditors have assented to the deed, they are bound by it. Dissenting creditors are not so bound and may petition for the debtor's bankruptcy. Alternatively the debtor may offer to transfer all his property to a trustee to be administered for the benefit of his creditors. This arrangement, if sanctioned, will also keep the debtor out of the bankruptcy court. If the terms of the settlement are drawn up and sealed the deed is called a *Deed of Assignment for the Benefit of Creditors* and again comes under the rules for Deeds of Arrangement. The assignment is an Act of Bankruptcy. In the case of a limited company, where a compromise or arrangement between a company and its creditors or members is proposed, an order for a meeting of the creditors or members may be issued by the court on the application of the company, a creditor, a member or, if the company is being wound up, the liquidator. The proposals need the assent of a majority in number and three-quarters in value; if the necessary majorities are obtained the scheme then goes before the court for sanction, and if sanctioned becomes binding on all concerned. Any conveyance or assignment by a company of all its property to trustees for the benefit of all its creditors is void to all intents.

Arrear. The state of being behindhand; that which is overdue, unpaid or unsatisfied.

Arrears Certificate (or Deferred Interest Warrant). A certificate issued where interest is unpaid, certifying the amount unpaid and incorporating a statement as to the time or method of eventual payment.

Arrest. The detention of a ship in a port.

Arrest. (*Ger.*) Official embargo or distraint upon any valuable property.

Arrestment. A seizure of property by legal authority, an attachment of goods through court process; (in Scottish law) the process by which a creditor detains the effects of his debtor, which are in the hands of third parties, until money owing to him is paid. *See also* Attachment.

Articles of Association. In a limited company, the document setting out the rules which will govern the internal conduct of the company, and dealing with such matters as the transmission and forfeiture of shares, the powers and duties of directors, proceedings at general meetings, the voting of members, etc. Articles of Association may be altered by special resolution of the company. A public company limited by shares need not draft its own Articles, but if it does not do so it is deemed to have adopted "Table A" (*q.v.*). The Articles will specify who is empowered to exercise the company's borrowing powers on its behalf. Usually the Articles will provide that the directors may exercise the company's borrowing powers; often, however, the company imposes a top limit beyond which the directors may not borrow on behalf of the company without its prior sanction in general or special meeting. A borrowing *ultra vires* the directors can be ratified by the company, but the European Communities Act 1972 has enacted that a person acting in good faith is not affected by restrictions in the Articles on transactions decided upon by the directors. The exact interpretation of this change has still to be worked out by the English courts.

Articles of Partnership. The clauses and conditions of the agreement between partners defining the rights and duties of the partners as between themselves, expressed in writing. There is no statutory requirement that such clauses and conditions should be recorded and they do not affect the liability of the partnership to third parties.

Asked. The price demanded by the seller.

Assainissment. A financial or technical reorganisation.

Assay. Trial, test, examination; the analysis of the amount of metal in ores or coins.

Assay Master. An officer appointed to assay bullion and coin.

Assekurant. Underwriter.

Assent. (1) The agreement of the holder of stocks or bonds to some change in the conditions or terms of issue, in particular where the original obligations of a foreign government have not been honoured on a bond issue and the holder has been offered new and less favourable terms of payment. (2) A document executed by the personal representative of a deceased person, which vests the legal estate in the devisee. It must be in writing, must be signed by the personal representative, and must name the person in whose favour it is expressed to be. This person may be the personal representative himself, but an assent is still necessary to constitute him the beneficial owner. The only time when no assent is necessary is when the land is to be sold following the death of the previous owner. Then the personal representative may execute a conveyance direct to the purchaser.

Assented Bonds. Bonds for which a plan of financial re-organisation or of adjusted repayment has been approved by the bondholder.

Assessment for Tax. The official estimate of the tax which an individual has to pay; evaluations for the purpose of taxation. This assessment is made from the taxpayer's annual return, so covering the amount of income from every source. Under Schedule A assessment will cover income from property rents, under Schedule B from woodlands, under Schedule D from interest not taxed at source and from trades, businesses and professions, and under Schedule E from earnings and pensions. A normal assessment is one made by reference to the taxpayer's annual return. A provisional assessment is one made on incomplete knowledge, such as where the annual return has not been made; this is usually based on the figures of the previous year. An additional assessment is one made to correct a previous assessment.

Asset Deficiency. When market value of assets is low, so that the assets are currently worth less than they cost, or less than money borrowed to buy them; when debts cannot be fully paid in a liquidation.

Assets. Goods sufficient to satisfy a testator's debts and bequests; the effects of an insolvent debtor; all the property of a person or company which may be liable for outstanding debts; property in general.

Asset Stripping. Buying a company cheaply for the purpose of making a profit by selling its assets. Such an opportunity will arise when a company is trading at a loss, or making poor profits although its asset values are high.

Asset Value. What the assets will actually realise when they are sold.

Assignation. An assignment, writ or subpoena; an authority to pay to order similar to a bill of exchange, where the title is passed by indorsement; a contract by which a debtor or a holder is authorised to remit to an assignee, for the account of the assignor, a sum of money or documents of title, etc. which the assignor has authority to collect in his own name; a deed of conveyance in favour of an assignee.

Assignation du Trésor. A Treasury Bill.

Assignee. The person to whom assignment of any right or personal property is made.

Assignment. The act of assigning, allotment, allocation, legal transfer of a right or property; the instrument by which such transfer is effected; the right or property transferred.

Assignment for the Benefit of Creditors. *See* Arrangement with Creditors or Members.

Assignment of Debts. The transfer of a right to receive payment under an existing obligation from the original beneficiary (the assignor) to a third party (the assignee). Future debts can be assigned only in equity. If made for valuable consideration such equitable assignments are equivalent to contracts to assign and will be enforced by the court. Existing debts may be assigned at law or in equity. A legal assignment is one which is absolute (not purporting to be by way of charge only) and in writing under the hand of the assignor; notice of the assignment must be given to the debtor. The lending banker will insist on a legal assignment of an existing debt. The assignment must be absolute and may take the form either of an irrevocable order or letter addressed to the debtor, or a mortgage assigning the debt absolutely, subject to a right of redemption. Notice must be given to the debtor at once and he should be asked to confirm the amount, state whether any counter-claims exist (to which the assignment would be postponed) and to confirm that there is no prior charge. The debtor should acknowledge the receipt of notice and undertake to remit the payment to the bank. The assignment should be of the debt only, for a document which purports to transfer the property in goods as well as to assign their proceeds is a bill of sale and must be registered as such. If the assignment be executed by a limited company, it should be registered at Companies House within twenty-one days after the date of its execution.

Assignment of Life Policy. The transfer of a right to receive the financial benefit under a policy of life assurance from the assured (the assignor) to a third party (the assignee). The proceeds of the life policy may be assigned at law or in equity. A legal assignment is one made in writing, usually by a separate instrument, but possibly also by endorsement on the policy itself. Written notice of the assignment must be given to the assurance company, and the date of receipt of the notice by the company regulates the priority of the claim. The assurance company receiving notice must acknowledge its receipt in writing.

Assignor. The person making an assignment of any right or personal property to another.

Assigns. Persons to whom an assignment of any right or personal property is made—the plural form of "assignee".

Associate. A partner or colleague; a member of an association or institution. For the purposes of the Consumer Credit Act 1974 "associate" shall be construed in accordance with section 184 of the Act.

Associated Companies. An alternative to an amalgamation or the setting up of a holding company. Associated companies usually have an interlocking directorate so that some influence can be brought to bear to ensure that the companies pursue similar policies. However, it is not essential to have some directors in common provided that the investing company participates in commercial and financial decisions, but it will, of course, frequently be represented on the board of its associate company (who must not be a subsidiary). Participation should take the form of (1) a partnership in a joint venture or consortium or (2) a long-term and substantial interest (not normally less than 20% of the equity) on the part of the investing company, so that, taking into account the disposition of the other shareholdings, it is able to exert a significant interest.

Association. *See* Unincorporated Association.

Association Clause. The clause in the Memorandum of Association by which the original members agree to take up the number of shares written against their names.

Association des Banques et Banquiers, *11 Avenue de la Porte-Neuve, Boîte Postale 13, Luxembourg.* An association of banks and bankers in the Duchy of Luxembourg, formed for the purpose of protecting and developing the professional interests of its members. To achieve this end the association seeks (1) to establish permanent contact between its members in such a way as to facilitate the study of all questions affecting their activities; (2) to study legal questions of interest to the banks; (3) to promote among its members the establishment of agreements which will facilitate their professional work. The association was founded in 1945.

Association Européenne de Libre Exchange (A.E.L.E). See European Free Trade Association.

Association Francaise des Banques (A.F.B.). The *Association Professionnelle des Banques*—which took the name of *Association Francaise des Banques* (French Bankers' Association) in April 1976—replaced in 1941 the *Union Syndicale des Banquiers de Paris et de la Province*, an association whose function, as far back as the end of the last century, was both to examine problems of banking or financial technique and to act as intermediary between the members of the banking industry in their relationships with public authorities or international organisations. The Act of 13 June 1941 on the organisation of the banking industry made the Association official. Its members include all banks (*banques de dépôts, banques d'affaires*, long- and medium-term credit banks), except for banks or credit institutions with a special legal status (*banques populaires, caisses de crédit agricole, Crédit National, Crédit Foncier de France*, etc.). In accordance with its statutes—approved by the *Conseil National du Crédit*—the Association is governed by a board composed of twenty-one members representing the different types of bankers and appointed by the General Assembly of the Association members. The board elects a Chairman who is assisted by a Delegate General appointed by the *Conseil National du Crédit*. The Association's functions are defined by the Act in very general terms. In particular, it acts as the compulsory intermediary between banks and supervising bodies—the *Conseil National du Crédit*, the *Commission de Contrôle des Banques*, the Bank of France and the Ministry of Finance. In this capacity the Association must make recommendations on banks' applications for registration on the official list and on any decision of a general nature taken with a view to regulating and improving the banking industry. It may act as referee in disputes arising between members of the banking industry. However, the law only gives an incomplete picture of its real functions. The Association's sphere of competence in fact includes the following areas: members' representation with public authorities, harmonisation of banking techniques, reviews of fiscal, statutory or legal problems raised by the banking industry and members' information on issues of common interest, training of banks' staff and industrial relations (including negotiation of collective agreement and wage agreements).

Association of International Bond Dealers (A.I.B.D.). This association was founded in 1969 for the purpose of establishing uniform market practices. It now has a membership of over 350 banks, all of which are active in the issuing and secondary markets.

Associé. Partner.

Assurance. See Insurance.

Assureur. See Underwriter.

At a Discount. See Discount.

At a Premium. See Premium.

At Call. A phrase indicating the condition of repayment on which money is lent by a banker, namely that it is to be repaid immediately upon demand (especially in connection with bank loans to the discount houses in the City of London).

At Par. In the case of stock or shares, a quotation at a time when the nominal and market values are identical.

At Short Notice. A phrase indicating the condition of repayment on which money is lent by a banker, namely, that it is to be repaid seven or fourteen days after demand (especially in connection with bank loans to the discount houses in the City of London).

At Sight. See Sight Bill.

Attachment. The seizure of money or goods to secure a debt or demand; the writ or precept by which such apprehension or seizure is effected. *See also Fieri Facias*; Garnishee Order; Garnishee Summons.

Attest. To testify, especially in a formal manner, to vouch for, to bear witness, to put a person on his oath.

Attestation. A formal witnessing, especially of a signature. *See also* Will; Witness.

Attested Copy. A true copy of an original document, certified as such by a witness by a declaration to that effect written on the copy and signed by him.

Attorn. To assign or transfer, to recognise a new owner.

Attorney. A lawyer, a solicitor, one legally authorised by another to transact business, an agent, a deputy. *See also* Power of Attorney.

Attornment. The recognition and acknowledgement of a legal relationship such as landlord and tenant or principal and agent—*e.g.*, as where under the terms of a bank mortgage the mortgagor attorns (or acknowledges himself as) tenant of the mortgagee at a rent, or where in a produce advance a bank sends a delivery order, signed by the customer and accompanied by the warehousekeeper's existing receipt for goods in his warehouse, to the warehouse keeper, who will thereupon send a new receipt to the bank by which the warehousekeeper attorns to the bank (*i.e.* acknowledges that he now holds the goods on the bank's behalf).

Attribution (*Fr.*). The allocation of a new issue, when applications are wholly or partly satisfied.

Au Contraire. On the contrary.

Au Courant. In the stream, well-informed.

Auction. A public sale by a person licensed for that purpose, whereby the object to be sold is secured by the maker of the highest offer or bid; to sell by auction. Auctions are governed by conditions printed in the catalogues of sale binding both seller and purchaser. Where goods are put up for sale by auction in lots, each lot is *prima facie* deemed to be the subject of a separate contract of sale. A sale by auction is complete when the auctioneer announces its completion by the fall of the hammer, or in other customary manner. *See also* Dutch Auction.

Auctioneer. A person licensed to sell property by public auction. Up to the fall of the hammer he is the agent of the seller; thereafter he is agent for both seller and buyer and binds both parties by his actions. Where a sale is expressly notified to be subject to a reserve price, the auctioneer cannot sell below that price, but must withdraw the article. Where there is no such notification the auctioneer is still entitled to refuse any bid.

Au Detail. Retail.

Audi Alteram Partem. Give both sides a fair hearing.

Audit. An examination by qualified persons of the books and accounts of a business, public office or undertaking to prevent or discover fraud or inaccuracy on the part of the persons keeping them; to make such an examination. The audit should take place at regular intervals, *e.g.* yearly.

Auditor. One who audits books and accounts. The auditors of a company are primarily responsible for making an independent investigation into the affairs of the company and for reporting thereon to the shareholders. They must be members of a body of established and qualified accountants. At the conclusion of the audit the auditors must append to the company's profit and loss account and balance sheet a statement to the effect that they have received all the information they required and that in their opinion the figures they have seen represent a true and fair view of the company's affairs. If they find that they cannot do this they must qualify their report accordingly.

Au Fait. Well-informed, having expert knowledge.

Aufgeld. Premium.

Aufsichsrat. Board of directors.

Auftrag. Order.

Aufwertung. A rise in valuations to offset depreciation or an increased provision for an expected loss; a general rise in balance sheet figures which have hitherto been recorded at under their real worth.

Au Mieux. At the best possible rate, for a stock order which is to be executed immediately.

Ausfuhr. Export.

Ausgabe. Issue, expenditure.

Ausgabepreis. Issue price.

Ausgeleihenen. Outstanding.

Ausland Investition. Foreign investment.

Auslosungen. Redemptions of bonds by way of lot.

Ausschlussrecht. The right of a member

of an issue syndicate on a public subscription to reserve a certain part of the issue for itself.

Ausschuttung. Counting out, paying out, by dividend or under a scheme of participation.

Aussenstände. Arrears, outstanding debts.

Ausserbörslicher Handel. Unofficial business in stocks and shares conducted outside the exchange or after business hours.

Aussteller. Drawer of a bill or cheque.

Auszahlungsberechtigung. Authorisation of payment to be made for overseas trade.

Authorised Banks. Banks authorised by the Treasury to act under the Exchange Control Act 1947 as dealers in foreign currencies and gold, and themselves to authorise certain dealings in foreign exchange by their customers.

Authorised Capital. That sum mentioned in the Memorandum of Association of a limited company as being the amount which the company is authorised to raise.

Authorised Depositary. A person or institution authorised by an order of the Treasury to keep bearer securities in safe custody and to hold foreign stocks on behalf of the owners. The term arose under the Exchange Control Act 1947, and includes banks, members of the Stock Exchange, solicitors practising in the United Kingdom, and certain other financial institutions.

Authorised Investments. Investments which the trustees of a fund may make because they are sanctioned either by a statute or by the instrument setting up the trust.

Autofinancement. Financing investments from the undistributed profits of an enterprise.

Automated Real-time Investments Exchange Ltd. (Ariel). A company jointly owned by the accepting houses, operating a computer-based block trading system suitable for large-scale dealing in U.K. securities directly between institutional investors. It started operations in 1974 and has provided savings for its subscribers, who pay no jobber's turn and make a saving of about 50% of the stockbroker's commission on a deal of similar size. It has, furthermore, made it possible for subscribers to deal in stocks in a volume which would have been too great to be available in the market, thus providing liquidity.

Automatisierung. Automation.

Aval, Pour Aval, Bon pour Aval, Avalkredit. A guarantee under continental law that a party to a bill will meet his responsibility if called upon, often undertaken by banks who sign or stamp their name under the phrase *Pour Aval* or *Bon pour Aval*. The matter is dealt with in three Articles of the League of Nations Unifications of Laws on Bills of Exchange:

Article 30

Payment of a bill of exchange may be guaranteed by an *aval* as to the whole or part of its amount. This guarantee may be given by a third person or even by a person who has signed as a party to the bill.

Article 31

The *aval* is given either on the bill itself or on an allonge.

It is expressed by the words "good as aval" ("*bon pour aval*") or by any other equivalent formula. It is signed by the giver of the *aval*.

It is deemed to be constituted by the mere signature of the giver of the *aval* placed on the face of the bill, except in the case of the signature of the drawee or of the drawer. An *aval* must specify for whose account it is given. In default of this, it is deemed to be given for the drawer.

Article 32

The giver of an *aval* is bound in the same manner as the person for whom he has become guarantor. His undertaking is valid even when the liability which he has guaranteed is inoperative for any reason other than defect of form. He has, when he pays a bill of exchange, the rights arising out of the bill of exchange against the person guaranteed and against those who are liable to the latter on the bill of exchange.

The *aval* is not recognised as such under English law and banks do not endorse bills in this manner unless for a special reason, and then only when there is complete confidence in the customer and against a suitable indemnity. The *aval* should indicate on whose behalf it has been given. It should be written as "*Pour Aval*" or "*Bon pour Aval*" on behalf of . . . . ., and should be properly signed on behalf of the bank. It should be recorded in the bank's books in a similar manner to an acceptance. The customer on whose behalf it is given must have obtained any necessary Exchange Control approval for payment at maturity. In view of the U.K.'s closer links with the continent of Europe, it may be that appropriate legislation will be introduced to clarify the position.

Avarie. Damage sustained by a vessel or its cargo.

Average. A number or quantity intermediate to several different numbers or quantities; a mean; the rate, proportion, degree, quantity or number generally prevailing; ordinary, normal; the apportionment of loss arising from damage to ship or cargo at sea as between the parties interested. *See also* General Average; Particular Average. **To Average Out.** To calculate an average, to divide proportionately to the number involved, to take as a mean rate.

Average Adjuster. One who calculates the proportions which are to be borne by the owner of a ship and by the owners of the cargo respectively of any losses which result from sacrifices which have been made to preserve the safety of the ship or cargo.

Average Balance. The figure resulting from a mathematical calculation, whereby the balance of an account is recorded daily for a given period and then totalled and divided by the number of days in the period.

Average Bond. A bond obtained by the master of a ship which has incurred a general average loss from the consignee of the cargo, before delivery is made to them, under which they agree to pay their proportion of the general average as soon as it has been ascertained.

Average Clause. A clause in a marine insurance policy stipulating that certain articles shall be free from average, unless general, and that others shall be free from average, unless general, under a certain percentage. The clause is also becoming more commonly used in fire policies.

Average Cleared Credit Balance. The average balance on a credit account, adjusted for uncleared effects, used as the basis of an allowance made against the cost of keeping a current account before the commission charge is ascertained.

Average Cost. The total cost of production incurred by a company or firm in a given period of time, divided by the number of units of output.

Average Life. The maturity of a total borrowing after taking into account purchases by the borrower's sinking fund.

Average Revenue. The total income received by a company or firm in a given period of time, divided by the number of units of output.

Average Settlement Day. *See* Factoring.

Averaging. A system on a stock exchange whereby a speculator increases his purchases or sales as a result of price movements of the stocks or shares in order to average out the purchase or sale prices. Thus a "bull" averages by purchasing more stock if the price falls, a "bear" by selling more stock if the price rises. *See also* Bear; Bull.

Avertissement Formel. See Notice.

Avoir. A credit, a bank deposit.

Avoir à Terme. A fixed term bank deposit, which carries an interest rate higher than, for example, a deposit repayable on demand, which may be at short or medium term.

Avoirs Bloques. Accounts, usually of non-residents, from which transfers may be made only under certain conditions, or which are totally blocked. *See also* Blocked Currency.

À Vue. On sight or demand.

Award. The written decision of an arbitrator. *See also* Arbitration.

B

Back Bond. A deed by which a party holding a title acknowledges that he holds it in trust for a certain purpose.

Back Freight. The charge for the return of goods not accepted at the port of delivery.

Backing Support. Gold or silver securities as support for a country's note issue.

Back-to-Back Credit. This is a description of the procedure where a customer of the bank, acting as a middle-man, has had a documentary credit opened in his favour by the foreign importer of his goods. On the strength and security of this credit the customer's bank agrees to open a credit for the benefit of the original supplier of the goods. The two credits are put "back to back", the one being issued on the security of the other. It is necessary to ensure that the documents called for under the second credit will satisfy the requirements of the first credit. The middle-man's invoices are substituted for those of the seller and the ultimate buyer must not find out the identity of the seller. If he did he would deal direct with him on subsequent occasions.

Back-to-Back Loan. Accommodation devised to avoid exchange risks, sometimes arranged within a multi-national enterprise by way of "netting" procedures, which can give rise on occasion to tax benefits, *e.g.* a Dutch company might need sterling for an outward investment in U.K.: a British company might need guilders for a similar operation in Holland. Each company funds the other's enterprise in its own country. While tax and exchange control problems can usually be surmounted, an interest rate differential often poses difficult questions.

Backwardation. A consideration paid by a seller of stock on the London Stock Exchange for the right to postpone delivery for a time.

Bad and Doubtful Debts. Debts which are bad are those which are not recoverable. Accordingly they are written off as losses. Doubtful debts are those of which the recovery, in full or in part, is uncertain. These are provided for by sums set aside out of profits. As evidence of this a bank balance sheet will show an item "Advances to Customers, less provision".

Bail Bond. (1) A bond given to the court in order to secure the release of a vessel under arrest. The warrant, nailed to the vessel's mast, is usually issued to obtain redress for damage to port facilities by a vessel. The bond is released after the money is paid.
(2) A bond given by a person who is being bailed and his surety.

Bailee. One to whom goods are entrusted for safe keeping or for a specific purpose.

Bailment. The delivery of goods to a person in trust on the terms that the goods will be returned when the purpose for which they were bailed has been effected; a contract whereby one person leaves property in the custody of another, the bailee, on the terms that he is to have it back when he wants it, and in the meantime the bailee is responsible for its safe keeping.

Bailor. One who entrusts goods to another for a specific purpose, such as safe keeping.

Bail Out. A term sometimes informally used in banking to indicate security, or a source of repayment.

Baisse. Contraction in the prices or quotations for shares, securities, goods, etc.; a slump, a fall in prices generally.

Baissier. A speculator who sells shares, securities, etc., which he hopes to buy back later at a lower price; a bear.

Balance. In book-keeping, the difference between the debit and credit sides of an account; cash in hand, or payment still due.

Balance Certificate. A document received by a shareholder when he has sold a portion only of shares represented by a share certificate.

Balance Commerciale. *See* Balance of Trade.

Balance des Capitaux. The world-wide

balance of account for a country as a result of capital movements at short or long term in or out of the country.

Balance des Paiements. *See* Balance of Payments.

Balance des Revenus. A periodic account showing the balances of all credits or debts of a country as a result of international payments, but excluding the movement of capital as shown in the capital balance account. In this account will be found all the credits and debits which give rise to the balance of trade including visible and invisible imports and exports.

Balance of Payments. The total of transactions with foreign countries in trade, services or capital, contained in the balance of revenue and balance of capital of a country.

Balance of Trade. The difference between the cost of the imports and exports of a country.

Balance Sheet. A statement of the assets and liabilities of a trading concern at any particular point in time, usually at the end of the last day in the financial year of the trading concern. *See also* Consolidated Balance Sheet.

Balance Sheet Ratios. Various ratios in balance sheets are used to give information and to assist control. In a bank's balance sheet the most important ratios are the cash ratio, the liquidity ratio, the reserve assets ratio and the lending ratio. In businesses other than banks other ratios are important. The *Liquidity Ratio* is the relationship between those assets of the business which are in cash or can quickly be turned into cash (including the unused part of an overdraft facility) and amounts due to be paid, such as trade creditors, current tax, hire purchase, and bank interest and repayment instalments; others are *gross profit as a percentage of turnover*, *net profit as a percentage of gross profit*, *credit taken* (creditors compared with purchases), *credit given* (debtors compared with turnover) and *rate of stock turnover* (average stock compared with cost of turnover—"cost of turnover" is the sales turnover less the gross profit). *See also* Cash Ratio; Lending Ratio; Liquidity Ratio; Prudential Ratios; Reserve Assets Ratio; Solvency Ratio.

Balance Ticket. A temporary document issued by a company to the broker handling a sale of shares representing part only of a greater number of shares evidenced by a share certificate. The new certificate for the unsold shares is later obtained by surrender of the balance ticket.

Balancing the Books. A periodical closing-up of accounts by bringing down a balance to bring the totals of debit and credit sides into agreement; the adjustments of ledger accounts by traders to ascertain the profit or loss made in a period.

Bancomat. A cash dispenser.

Bandbreite. The spread within which foreign exchange rates in a regulated system may move.

Bank. An establishment which deals in money, receiving it on deposit from customers, honouring customer's drawings against such deposits on demand, collecting cheques for customers and lending or investing surplus deposits until they are required for repayment. A statutory definition of a bank in the United Kingdom is awaited. *See also* Agricultural Credit Banks; Authorised Banks; British Overseas Banks; Central Bank; Clearing Bank; Commonwealth Banks; Correspondent Bank; Deposit Bank; Drive-in Bank; *Familien bank*; Foreign Banks; Industrial Bank; Investment Bank; Joint Stock Bank; Land Bank; Listed Bank; Merchant Banks; Mobile Bank; Penny Bank; Piggy Bank; Private Bank; Savings Bank; *Universalbank*.

Bankakzept. Bank Acceptance Credit.

Bank Bill. A bill bearing the indorsement of a bank.

Bank Book. A passbook in which a customer's dealings with his bank are recorded.

Bank Charges. The commission debited by a bank to the customer's current account for the service of keeping his account, plus the interest, if any, on accommodation enjoyed by the customer.

Bank Charter. A deed, instrument, or Act of Parliament incorporating a banking company.

Bank Credit. The amount of new credit or money created by the action of banks in granting loans or overdrafts to their customers.

Bank Deposits. The total amounts standing to the credit of all customers of all banks in a country.

Bank Draft. *See* Bankers' Draft.

Bankenerklärung. Certificate by a bank in respect of foreign-owned securities.

Bankers' Automated Clearing Services. *See* Credit Clearing.

Bankers' Clearing House. *See* Clearing House.

Bankers' Draft. A draft drawn by a branch of a bank on the bank's Head Office or City office. As this is sure to be paid when presented it is acceptable anywhere as equivalent to cash. Such a draft does not satisfy the definition of a bill of exchange because it is not "drawn by one person on another". However, there is statutory protection for the paying banker (in respect of a crossed or open draft) under the Stamp Act 1853, s.19, and the Cheques Act 1957, s.1, and (in respect of a crossed draft) under the Bills of Exchange Act 1882, s.80, (as extended by the Cheques Act 1957, s. 5), and for the collecting banker under the Cheques Act 1957, s.4.

Banker's Lien. A general lien enjoyed by the banker over such of his borrowing customer's property as comes into his hands in the ordinary course of his business as a banker. It is an exceptional lien in that it has a right of sale after reasonable notice to the customer. A banker's lien has been described as an implied pledge. Both the type of property and the reason it was handed to the banker are critical factors. The usual sort of property over which a banker has a lien consists of negotiable securities such as bills of exchange, promissory notes, or coupons. Cheques paid in for collection are very common types of valuable paper which may become subject to a lien. Where the property is handed to him for a particular purpose, however, the banker has no lien. Thus he has none over security handed to him for the purpose of selling it through a stockbroker, or property handed to him for safe custody.

Bankers' Order. A written order from a customer to his banker authorising him to make a series of periodic payments on his behalf.

Bankers' Payment. Any order or draft drawn upon any bank in the U.K. by a branch of that bank in favour of another bank and used for the purpose of settling some account between the two banks, such as a special presentation.

Bankers' Reference. *See* Status Enquiry.

Bank for International Settlements (B.I.S.). A bank established at Basle in 1930 to implement the reparation payments to be made by Germany following the First World War. All the European central banks contributed to its establishment and were represented on its board. When reparation payments lapsed it maintained itself in existence by doing a small amount of commercial business. Its importance increased in 1950 when it became banker to the European Payments Union, in 1954 when it became banker to the European Coal and Steel Community, and in the 1960s when it became the centre for central bank co-operation.

Bank for Reconstruction and Development. *See* International Bank for Reconstruction and Development.

Bankgeheimnis. The bank's duty of secrecy as to the affairs of its customers.

Bank Giro. The name given in British banks to the system of credit transfers, standing orders and direct debiting when the National Giro was established in 1968; on the continent, any system between banks which allows for the settlement of mutual debts, without the use of cash, but by means of balance payments or set-offs administered by a central authority or clearing house.

Bank Holiday. A day on which banks are closed for business by statute or proclamation.

Bank Hours. The hours during which a bank is open to the public for business. These change from time to time and vary according to the place and circumstances. Thus normally hours in the United Kingdom are from 9.00 or 9.30 a.m. until 3.00 or 3.30 p.m., but some branches may open in the evenings on certain weekdays, and some branches are open at all times where there is a 24 hour demand, such as at an airport. Most Scottish banks close in the lunch hour. Clearing banks do not open on Saturdays. Some sub-branches open only on certain days each week. In foreign countries where there is a hot climate banks may close at the time of the afternoon siesta, opening earlier in the morning and closing later in the evening. Bank hours are determined by a compromise between the needs of the bank and the convenience of the customers.

Bank Interest. The interest allowed on money deposited with a bank; the interest charged on an overdraft, loan or accommodation.

Bank Interest Certificate. A certificate issued by a bank to a borrowing customer stating the amount of interest paid by him on his bank advance, so that he may include this information in his tax claim. Before such a certificate can be issued the interest charged must have been actually paid by the customer and taken into bank profits.

Bank Notes. Promissory notes issued by a bank of issue, payable to bearer on demand.

Bank of England Bill. A bill eligible for discount at the Bank of England. The bill must bear two good British names, one of which must be the acceptor. The other may be a discount house.

Bank of Issue. A bank authorised by the central legislative body to issue its own notes payable to bearer on demand, such an issue forming the currency of the country. The Bank of England is the sole bank of issue in England and Wales.

Bank Rate. The advertised minimum rate at which the Bank of England was prepared to discount approved bills of exchange. Bank Rate was used by the central government as a means of controlling the money demand and checking the growth of inflation until 16 October 1972, when it was superseded by minimum lending rate.

Bank Return. A weekly statement issued by the Bank of England in accordance with the provisions of the Bank Charter Act 1844, disclosing its financial position for the information of the public.

Bankrott. Bankruptcy.

Bankrupt. An insolvent person who has been adjudicated bankrupt by the court. He is then deprived of nearly all his legal powers, his estate passing into the hands of a Trustee in Bankruptcy. *See also* Undischarged Bankrupt.

Bankrupt Partner. The bankruptcy of a partner will postpone his liability for the debts of the firm to his private debts; his private creditors will receive payment in full before any of the creditors of the firm receive anything (but *see* Joint and Several Liability). The partnership is not necessarily also bankrupt, because there may be other partners who are solvent. Subject to any provision in the partnership deed, the partner relationship is brought to an end by the bankruptcy of one partner, and his share in the partnership assets will have to be calculated and brought into his private estate.

Bankruptcy. The state of being bankrupt. This is brought about by a petition against the debtor, which may be made by an unpaid judgment creditor or by the insolvent person himself, founded upon an available act of bankruptcy committed by the debtor. *See* Act of Bankruptcy. Thereupon the court makes a receiving order. A general meeting of creditors is held, following which the court appoints a day for the public examination of the debtor. As a result of this hearing the debtor is adjudicated bankrupt; thereupon the assets of the bankrupt rest in a trustee and become divisible amongst his creditors. *See also* Trustee in Bankruptcy.

Bankruptcy Notice. A creditor who has sued a debtor in a court and has received a judgment in his favour may then cause a bankruptcy notice to be issued against the debtor, stating the amount of the debt and calling upon him to pay in ten days. If the debtor does not comply (and if he has not entered a counterclaim for at least the amount stated in the notice) within the allotted time, he has committed an act of bankruptcy, on which a petition for his bankruptcy may be based.

Bankruptcy Petition. *See* Petition.

Bank Statement. A mechanised or computerised statement supplied by banks to their customers, showing some details of the customer's debit and credit transactions, and his balance.

Banque Agréée. A bank having delegated authority from a central bank to authorisé foreign exchange transactions.

Banque Centrale. See Central Bank.

Banque d'Affaires. A bank engaged in financing business operations on a long term basis and taking an equity participation in the businesses so financed; a merchant bank.

Banque de Clearing, Banque de Compensation. See Clearing Bank.

Banque de Virement. A clearing bank.

Banque sous Forme de Société par Actions. *See* Joint Stock Bank.

Banque Universelle. A credit institution, usually a large bank, in a position to supply its clients over the complete range of banking services.

Bar. A dealer's term for £1,000,000 transacted on the interbank market.

Bar. (*Ger.*) Ready.

Barclaycard. A credit card introduced in 1966 by Barclays Bank. There is no entrance fee for new cardholders but a credit limit for each individual is imposed, ranging from £100–£500. The control by the government on the amount of cash withdrawn. The cardholder receives a monthly statement. If the amount outstanding is paid within twenty-five days there is no interest charge. If credit is taken, minimum monthly repayments of 5% or £5 per month, whichever is the greater, are required. The charge on the outstanding debt is at 2% per month. Barclaycard also acts as a cheque card.

Bare Münze. Face value.

Bare Trustee. *See* Naked Trustee.

Bargain. An agreement between two persons concerning a sale; an advantageous purchase; the thing bought or sold; a transaction in stocks or shares.

Barge. A code word formerly used to authenticate a customer's cheque on reference by the paying cashier to the ledger keeper while the customer waited in ignorance. The word, given orally, meant "He has the money".

Bargeld. Ready money, cash.

Barkauf. Cash purchase.

Barratry. Any unlawful acts wilfully committed by the master or crew of a vessel by which the interests of the shipowner are damaged.

Barreserve. Immediate cash holdings available for investment should a favourable opportunity arise; cash reserves.

Barring the Entail. The conversion of an estate tail by a tenant-in-tail into a fee simple by a deed called a disentailing assurance, with the consequence that the tenant may then freely dispose of the estate, if he so wishes, thus defeating the rights of his issue and of the persons whose estates are to take effect after the determination of the entailed interest or in defeasance of it.

Barschaft. Ready money.

Barter. The exchange of goods for goods; a swap.

Bartransaktion. Cash transaction.

Barzahlen. To pay cash.

Barzahlung. Cash payment.

Base Fee. An estate in fee simple into which an estate tail is converted, where the issue in tail are barred, but persons claiming estates by way of remainder or otherwise are not barred.

Base Rate. The basic lending rate of a bank or financial institution, on which its lending rates and deposit interest rates are founded. Each bank is free to fix its own base rate as it thinks best, but in practice none varies by very much from Bank of England minimum lending rate. In a recent development the direct link between base rate and seven-day deposit rate has been broken, and deposit rate is now fixed independently.

Base Year. A year chosen as a base for a series of index numbers such as, for example, the General Index of Retail Prices. The selected year is usually given an index number of 100, so that subsequent indices may be readily represented as percentage rises or falls.

Baukredit. Advances for new building or structural alterations secured by a mortgage registered on the Land Register.

Bazaar. An oriental market place; a shop where miscellaneous articles are sold; a sale of work where donated articles are sold for charitable purposes.

Bear. A speculator on the Stock Exchange who anticipates a fall in the value of a certain security and therefore sells stocks which he does not possess in the hope of buying them back more cheaply at a later date, thus making a profit.

Bearer. The person in possession of a bill or note which is payable to bearer. A bill is payable to bearer which is expressed to be so payable, or one on which the only or last indorsement is an indorsement in blank. *See* Indorsement in Blank. A bill or cheque payable to bearer requires no indorsement. Title passes by simple delivery, coupled with an intention to transfer title.

Bearer Bill, Bearer Note. A bill of exchange, cheque or promissory note which is expressed to be payable to the bearer thereof, or a bill of exchange which is indorsed in blank.

Bearer Bond. A bond which is payable to bearer and one in respect of which no register of owners is kept by the company concerned. It has attached to it a series of coupons, which are torn off at the right time and sent forward as evidence of the bondholder's right to receive the interest or dividend. A bearer bond is a negotiable instrument —that is, title passes by simple delivery coupled with an intention to transfer. The transferee must take in good faith and for value, and without notice of any defect in the title of the transferor. Bearer bonds have to be kept in the possession of an Authorised Depositary, *e.g.* a banker, stockbroker, solicitor, etc.

Bearer Cheque. *See* Bearer Bill.

Bearer Note. *See* Bearer Bill.

Bearer Scrip. A temporary document issued as evidence of title by a government or company making a new issue until such time as all instalments have been paid, when the bearer scrip is exchanged for a bearer bond or for registered bonds or certificates. The bearer scrip is a negotiable instrument.

Bed and Breakfast Deal. The practice, now restricted, of selling stock which has fallen in value on one evening and buying it back on the next morning, for the purpose of establishing a tax loss to offset against capital profits.

Bedarf. Need, demand, requirement, supply.

Behauptet. Stabilising, holding firm, *e.g.* a rate which has been moving up or down settles in one position.

Bei Sicht. At sight.

Belehnungs Grenze. Secured limits, up to which figure advances may be made.

Belfast Gazette. See Gazette.

Bénéfice. See Profit.

Bénéfices d'Exploitation. Trading profits.

Bénéfices Nets. Net profit.

Bénéfices non Distribués. Retained profits.

Beneficial Owner. A person entitled absolutely to the benefit of any property, real or personal, of which the legal title is held by a trustee. Certain covenants for title are implied where the vendor conveys as beneficial owner (and in fact possesses that status) and the conveyance is for value. They are (1) that the vendor has a good right to convey; (2) that the purchaser shall have quiet possession; (3) that the property is free from incumbrances; (4) that the vendor will do everything which is right and possible to perfect the title, should that prove necessary.

Bénéficiare de Change. The payee of a bill of exchange.

Beneficiary. One who benefits from the act of another; a person named in a will as a legatee or devisee.

Benelux. The name of the customs union between Belgium, the Netherlands, and Luxembourg, established shortly after the Second World War.

Bequest. A gift or legacy of personal property under a will, especially to a public body or institute.

Bergung. Salvage.

Berne Union. An international association with about thirty members representing credit insurance institutions in twenty-four countries, known as the Union d'Assurance des Credits Internationaux, established in 1934. Its main function is the study of export credit insurance techniques and in recent years it has concentrated on working towards a common policy in credit insurance with a view to avoiding a "credit war" between exporters in different countries. Credit insurers wish to discourage abnormally long credit or competition in credit giving, and to this end the Berne Union has a "five year understanding" by which members agree not to insure transactions involving more than five years post-shipment supplier credit except in very special circumstances, which have to be reported to the Union. The long-term credit (financial guarantee) is, of course, not supplier credit, but rather buyer credit, and falls outside the scope of the "five year understanding".

Berth. The space at a wharf or quay allotted to a ship for loading or unloading.

Berthage. The charge for the use of a berth.

Berth Bill of Lading. A bill of lading issued by the master of a steamship belonging to a regular transport line.

Besserungschein. A deed embodying rights of creditors which will be settled if the position of the debtor improves.

Bestand. Stock, balance.

Bestätigtes Akkreditiv. A confirmed documentary credit.

Bestens. At the best rate obtainable.
Betrieb. Management, working, trade, plant.
Betriebsdirektor. Managing director.
Betriebsforschung. See Operational Research.
Betriebsgewinn. Trading profit.
Betriebsjahr. Financial year.
Betriebskapital. Working capital.
Betriebskosten. Working expenses, overheads.
Betriebskredit. Credit for industrial production.
Betriebspersonal. Staff.
Betriebsspesen. Working expenses, overheads.
Betterment. Improvement; enhanced value of property, as a result of local improvements; tax levied by the Land Commission on the development value of land.
Bezogener. Drawee.
Bezugsrecht. The right of existing shareholders in a limited company to participate in a new capital issue in proportion to their existing holdings.
Bid. To offer a price; the offer of a price, especially at auctions.
Bid Price. A price quoted by a jobber on the Stock Exchange at which he will buy stocks or shares on offer (*see also* Offered Price); or a price quoted by the management company of a unit trust at which they will buy sub-units of the trust (*see also* Offer Price).
Biens de Consommation. Economic goods satisfying current demand, consumer goods. *See also* Consumer Spending.
Biens de Consommation Durable. Consumer goods with a life of more than three years, *e.g.* cars, furniture, household equipment, etc.
Biens d'Équipement, Biens de Production. Goods used in the production of other goods such as machines and industrial installations of all kinds; capital goods.
Big Four. Barclays, Lloyds, Midland and National Westminster Banks.
Big Ticket Leasing. The leasing of big, expensive items, such as aircraft, computers or process plant, costing millions of pounds.
Bilan, Bilanz. Balance sheet, schedule.
Bilan Consolidé. See Consolidated Balance Sheet.
Bilan des Mouvements. The tabular presentation of the sources and uses made of funds of an undertaking during any given financial year.

Bilateral. Two-sided, of a treaty or agreement drawn up by two parties; imposing mutual or reciprocal obligations.
Bilateral Contract. One in which both parties undertake mutual duties which are enforceable at law.
Bilateral Trade Agreement. A trade agreement between two countries. Each country must balance its receipts and payments with each other country and this must be done at the lower level of the country importing the smaller amount.
Bill Broker. A merchant who buys and sells bills of exchange. Bill brokers are more commonly termed discount houses. Discount houses are an important part of the short term money market, one of their importance functions being to provide a source of first class bills for bankers. They are tenderers for Treasury Bills and they also deal in short-dated Government Bonds. They act as the channel through which the Bank of England controls the amount of money in the financial system of the country. *See also* Bill of Exchange; Discount; Treasury Bills.
Billet à Ordre. Evidence of a debt, in the form of a promissory note.
Billets de Banque. Banknotes.
Bill for Collection. A bill of exchange drawn by an exporter, usually at a term, on an importer overseas, and brought by the exporter to his bank with a request to collect the proceeds. The bank sends the bill to its agent in the foreign town where the importer lives and has the bill presented for acceptance, or payment, or both. It then brings back the proceeds, converts them into the home currency, and credits the customer's account. If such a bill has documents of title attached, it is called a documentary bill; if not, a clean bill. The customer must instruct the bank whether documents are to be released against acceptance by the importer (D/A) or only against payment (D/P).
Bill for Negotiation. A bill of exchange drawn by an exporter at a term on an importer overseas, brought by the exporter to his bank with a request to negotiate it, that is, discount it. If the bank agrees to buy the bill it will pay the customer the face value of the bill less discount, with recourse. The bill will in many cases be drawn in a foreign cur-

rency. The banker may ask for security to be deposited in support of the transaction. Once the banker has bought the bill he is collecting it for himself. *See also* Recourse.

Billig. Cheap.

Bill in a Set. A foreign bill drawn in several copies, identical except that each is numbered and contains a reference to the other parts. They are sent for safety by separate mails. The drawee accepts only one copy of the bill.

Bill of Entry. A written statement by a merchant, concerning the nature and value of goods exported or imported, for the use of the customs house. Goods for export are "entered outwards", for import "entered inwards". When the collector of customs duties is satisfied that this statement is correct (a "perfect entry") he signs it. The signed bill authorises the shipping or unloading of the goods to which the bill refers.

Bill of Exchange. An unconditional order in writing, addressed by one person to another, and signed by the person giving it, requesting the person to whom it is addressed to pay on demand, or at a fixed or determinable future time, a sum certain in money to, or to the order of, a specified person, or to bearer. A bill of exchange is the most commonly used method of obtaining payment in international trade. *See also* Accommodation Bill; Bank Bill; Bank of England Bill; Bearer Bill; Clean Bill; Commercial Bill; Corporation Bills; Documentary Bill; Eligible Bill; Fine Bank Bill; First Class Bill; Foreign Bill; House Bill; Ineligible Bill; Inland Bill; Interest Clause Bill; Long Bill; Made Bill; Order Bill; Original Bill; Pre-finance Bill; Re-finance Bill; Renewal Bill; Short Bill; Sight Bill; Sola Bill; Term Bill; Trade Bill; Usance Bill.

Bill of Imprest. An order entitling the bearer to have money paid in advance.

Bill of Lading. A receipt for goods received for carriage to a stated destination, signed by or on behalf of the master of a ship. The bill is also a negotiable document of title to the goods, transferable by indorsement, but is not a negotiable instrument in the true sense. It is furthermore evidence of the contract of carriage. Normally bills of lading are issued in sets of three and a fourth copy is retained by the ship's master.

Bill of Sale. A document given as security for a loan or debt whereby the debtor assigns personal chattels to the lender. It authorises seizure and sale in cases of non-payment, and must be registered at the Central Office of the Supreme Court within seven days after its execution. A bill of sale may be absolute (equivalent to an out-and-out transfer), or conditional by way of mortgage. Banks do not accept this type of security; possession remains with the borrower and there can be no control over the security. The assignment of a book debt is not a bill of sale, but a document which purports to transfer the property in goods as well as to assign their proceeds is a bill of sale and must be registered as such. *See also* Ship Bill of Sale.

Bill of Sight. A temporary authority issued by the Customs House authorising the landing of goods for examination, in cases where the importer is not certain of the exact description of goods consigned to him.

Bill Rate. The discount rate on bills of exchange, varying according to the quality of the bill to be discounted.

Bills Discounted. *See* Discount. *See also* Tap Bills; Tender Bills.

Bimetallism. A system whereby coins made from two different metals, gold and silver, circulate side by side in a country. The fluctuating value of one metal in terms of the other causes difficulty, and in this country the system was abandoned in 1816 when a Coinage Act was passed establishing a gold standard.

Black *Bourse*. An illegal exchange market.

Black List. A list of uncreditworthy people issued for the private guidance of traders and lenders: a list of customers in difficulties issued by a bank manager to his staff.

Blank Cheque. A cheque signed by the drawer, but having no details filled in.

Blanket Policy. An insurance policy by the terms of which an underwriter accepts liability for a fixed figure for a certain time, adjustments of the premium paid being made when it is known exactly what the shipment was worth. This type of policy is used when similar goods are sent in consignments on a number of different voyages.

Blank Indorsement. *See* Indorsement in Blank.

Blankocheck. A cheque with an important particular, such as the amount, not yet filled in.

Blankoindossament. *See* Indorsement in Blank.

Blankokredit. A credit without a limit to be observed by the beneficiary.

Blankowechsel. A bill of exchange with an important particular, such as the amount or the maturity date, not yet filled in.

Blank Transfer. A transfer of stock or shares with the name of the transferee left blank, sometimes used when shares are mortgaged as security for a debt. If repayment is not forthcoming the lender may then fill in his own name as transferee, date the transfer, have it stamped, and send it to the company for registration of the shares in his own name as owner. This procedure should not be used where a transfer has to be under seal, because such a transfer is a deed and takes effect from the date of its delivery. If on that day the deed is not complete, the blanks can only be filled in subsequently by the transferor, or by his authority which itself must be under seal. A further point is that stamping must be done within thirty days after execution; late stamping attracts a penalty.

Blocked Currency. Currency of a country which by government decree can be used only for purchases within the country, thus reserving all the advantages of trade to residents of that country. As a further refinement the blocked currency may itself be divided into various categories to be used only for various purposes, *e.g.* tourist disbursements. The price of blocked currency is at a discount on that of the free currency.

Bloc Sterling. *See* Scheduled Territories.

Blue Book. A government publication, so called because it is issued in blue covers, dealing with such matters as the reports of Royal Commissions, or being a more detailed account of a matter formerly dealt with in a White Paper.

Blue Button. An authorised clerk of the London Stock Exchange.

Blue Chip. A term used to describe the ordinary shares of first class industrial companies.

Bon. Correct, sound, fitting, profitable; voucher, warrant, bond, draft, bill.

Bona Fide. In good faith.

Bona Vacantia. Unclaimed goods. When a person dies leaving no relatives in the category entitled to inherit the estate passes to the Crown.

Bond. A legal engagement in writing to pay a certain sum of money or to fulfil certain conditions; a certificate of ownership of capital lent to a government, municipality, etc.; a surety demanded by Customs authorities from persons holding dutiable goods, on which duty still has to be paid. *See also* Assented Bonds; Bail Bond; British Savings Bonds; Convertible Bond; Drawn Bond; Equipment Bond; Floating Rate Bond; Foreign Bond; Income Bond; Local Authority Bonds; Mortgage Bond; Non-assented Bonds; Straight Bonds. **In Bond.** In a bonded store.

Bond-Creditor. A creditor secured by bond.

Bonded. Placed in bond, mortgaged.

Bonded Goods. Goods stored, under care of Customs House officers, in warehouses until the duty is paid.

Bonded Warehouse. A Customs store for bonded goods.

Bon de Jouissance. A document, as a general rule with no nominal value, which gives a right to a share in the net proceeds of the realisation of the assets of a liquidated company; eventually also to a preferential right to subscribe to a new issue. In the case of a financial re-organisation, this document can have the character of a *bon de récuperation* (*q.v.*).

Bon de Livraison. A temporary certificate issued on payment for a share issue, to be replaced in due course by a definitive certificate; a document accompanying goods.

Bon de Récuperation. A document similar to a *bon de jouissance* (*q.v.*) which allows a creditor to recover his losses if the debtor has a recovery in his fortunes.

Bond-Holder. A person holding a bond or bonds granted by a private person, a company, or a government.

Bond-Holder's Register. The name of a trade paper published on the second and fourth Tuesday in each month, containing information of interest to bond-holders and holders of scrip securities, such as details of dividends and drawings pending.

Bon du Trésor. Treasury bond.

Bond-Washing. Now illegal in the United Kingdom, this is the device of selling securities *cum. div.* at a higher price, and re-purchasing them later *ex. div.* at a lower price to avoid paying tax on dividend.

Bon Marché. Cheap.

Bonne Livraison. Good delivery, according to commercial custom.

Bons. A name given to certain French documents which bear the phrase *"bon pour x francs"*—good for *x* francs.

Bons de Caisse. Cash obligations.

Bonus. Something over and above what is due; a premium given for a privilege, or in addition to interest for a loan; a gratuity over and above a fixed salary or wages.

Bonus Ausgabe. Scrip, or capitalisation issue.

Bonus Certificate. A statement received by an insurance policy holder from the insurance company on the occasion of a division of its profits, to inform him of the amount accruing to him, usually to be added to and payable with the sum assured under the policy.

Bonus Issue. An issue of stock or shares by a company which finds that its shares have appreciated so much as a result of past profitable trading that they are becoming difficult for small investors to buy on the Stock Exchange because of their cost; or where it is desired to finance expansion from reserves built up in the past out of undistributed profits; or where after a period of inflation there has been considerable appreciation of the company's real capital in monetary terms. In any of these cases it is desirable to bring the company's issued capital more into line with the capital it employs. The bonus issue will usually be allocated to shareholders proportionately to their existing holdings.

Book Debts. The amount owing to a trading concern for goods sold. *See also* Assignment of Debts.

Book Entry. An accounting entry passed merely for purposes of book adjustment.

Book-Keeping. The art or practice of keeping accounts; the record of commercial transactions of merchants or others in a set of books kept for the purpose.

Book Value. The value of company assets as displayed in the balance sheet.

Boom. A period of increasing confidence in the economic affairs of a country, when production is increasing, unemployment decreasing and wages rising. An increased speculative demand for stock exchange securities will lead to a general rise in their prices.

Borrowing Powers. The legal ability of an individual, a limited company, or an organisation to borrow money. A minor has no power to borrow and if he is allowed to do so cannot legally be compelled to repay. A limited company is an artificial person whose borrowing powers are defined in its Memorandum of Association. These powers may be exercised by the directors of the company or by the company in general meeting—information as to these matters, and as to any limits imposed, will be found in the Articles of Association or, if there are no Articles, in Table A of the Companies Act under which the company is incorporated. Organisations not having a separate legal entity, such as unincorporated associations, have no power to borrow. Individuals acting in an official capacity, such as trustees or personal representatives, have no power to borrow unless authority is contained in a trust instrument, a statute or a testamentary document. The borrowing powers of an agent must be strictly defined in the principal's mandate. The borrowing powers of building societies and local authorities are defined in statutes. The borrowing powers of a statutory body are as defined in the statute creating it. *See also Ultra Vires.*

Börse. Stock exchange.

Börsenbrief. Periodic bulletins from an information service giving details of the progress and prospects on the stock exchange.

Börseneinfuhrung. Introduction to the *Börse*, granting of a quotation.

Börsenmakler. Stock Broker.

Börsenspekulant. Punter, speculator.

Bottomry Bond. A document by which the master of a ship charges the keel or bottom of the ship (and thus the ship in its entirety) as security for the repayment of a loan, such repayment being dependent upon the safe arrival of the ship at its destination. Such a bond may be effected where urgent repairs are necessary in the course of a ship's journey, or for refitting.

Bought Day Book. A ledger containing a list of all items bought by a business.

Bought Note. The contract note supplied by a stockbroker to his client, detailing the particulars of a purchase made for him.

"Bouncing". In common parlance, dishonouring a cheque for want of funds.

Bourse. A continental term for a money market or a stock exchange; an international clearing house for the settlement of balances of trade.

Boursicoteur. Speculator, punter.

Bracket. Groups of banks involved in a new issue. First comes the lead-manager, then the co-managers, the special underwriters (if any), underwriters and other selling group members. In each bracket banks are listed either alphabetically or according to their commitments.

Branch Clearing. The operation within a large bank whereby the collection of cheques between the branches of the bank is organised through a department in the Head Office of the bank.

Branch Credit. A credit paid in by a customer for his account at a branch of the bank other than the one where he keeps his account.

Brassage. *See* Mintage.

Breach of Trust. The act of a trustee who does not observe the conditions laid down in the deed or will under which he is appointed, such as the investment of trust monies in an improper manner.

Breach of Warranty of Authority. An agent contracting on behalf of his principal with a third party by implication warrants that he has the necessary authority to make the contract. If this is not the case, he may be personally sued by the third party for breach of warranty of authority.

Breaking an Account. The cessation of operations on a running account, leaving a balance outstanding. A fresh account may be opened for subsequent transactions. This is done to prevent the operation of the Rule in Clayton's Case, as, for example, upon the death of a partner where the partnership account is overdrawn, or on the death of a guarantor, where the account of the principal debtor is overdrawn, and recourse against the deceased's estate is to be preserved.

Breaking Bulk. Opening a consignment for the purpose of selling part of it, or to take a sample.

Break-up Value. The value of a company's assets when it is viewed as a "gone concern"; the value at current stock exchange prices of the holdings of an investment or unit trust.

Bretton Woods Conference. A meeting under the auspices of the United Nations at Bretton Woods, New Hampshire, United States of America, in 1944, to set up some degree of co-operation in matters of international trade and payments and to devise a satisfactory international monetary system to be operated after the end of the Second World War. The particular objectives hoped to be achieved were stable exchange rates and free convertibility of currencies for the development of multi-lateral trade. Both the British and American Treasuries had prepared plans for attaining these ends and a compromise solution was adopted which contained elements of both. Two important results of this conference were the establishment of the International Monetary Fund, and of the World Bank (the International Bank for Reconstruction and Development).

Brevet. Patent, certificate.

Bridging Advance. A short-term advance to a customer pending the receipt by him of funds from another source. Very frequently this is in connection with a change of house. The customer is selling one house and buying another. The money for the house being bought is often required before the money comes in for the house being sold and the banker is asked to "bridge" the gap.

Brief. (*Ger.*) The rate at which securities, foreign bills, etc. are offered.

British Bankers' Association. An association formed in 1919, for the benefit of British banks whose principal business and head offices were in the United Kingdom, and British banks whose principal business was outside the United Kingdom and who were at that time members of the British Overseas Banks Association. The membership was widened in 1972 to include all recognised banks operating in the United Kingdom, whether British or foreign, including the discount houses. This step was inspired in part by the forthcoming British entry into the European Economic Community and the need to facilitate liaison with the banking industries of other member states, whose representative associations were organised on a similar basis. The Association is the British member of the European Economic Community Banking Federation.

British Export Houses Association (B.E.H.A.). An organisation to advance the interests of its members, who consist of factors engaged in the business of the export trade, advancing money against debts owing from abroad and themselves undertaking the collection of such debts; confirming houses; and finance houses interested in export finance.

British Overseas Banks. British banks originally set up in the nineteenth century to provide banking facilities for settlers and traders in the colonies, but having their headquarters in London. In some countries their branches have been subjected to restriction in the course of the countries' development and in others they have been taken over, and considerable adaptation has been necessary, particularly in the building up of foreign currency deposits and in participation in the money markets.

British Overseas Banks Association. An association formed in 1917, for the benefit of British banks carrying on business in the then British Empire and in other countries outside the Empire, but having their head offices in London.

British Savings Bonds. Defence Bonds were issued during the last war as a form of investment, between government marketable securities and National Saving Certificates, for the small saver. After the war it was felt that a more appropriate name for a peace-time issue would be National Development Bonds, and these were followed by British Savings Bonds, which were first issued in 1968. They are sold in units of £5 and currently bear interest at $9\frac{1}{2}\%$. They are issued for five years, at the end of which time a bonus of 4% is added. There is a maximum holding per person of £10,000 on each issue. The interest is paid twice yearly without tax deduction.

Broker. An agent, a factor, a middleman; a person employed in the negotiation of commercial transactions between other parties in the interests of one of them. *See also* Bill Broker; Deposit Broker; Foreign Exchange Broker; Government Broker; Insurance Broker; Produce Broker; Stockbroker.

Brokerage. The commission charged by a broker for carrying out the instructions of his client, *e.g.* to buy or sell shares.

Broker's Contract Note. *See* Contract Note.

Bronze Coins. Coins of the lower denominations are of bronze: the alloy consists of ninety-five parts of pure copper, four parts of tin, and one part of zinc. The bronze coins of the United Kingdom consist of $\frac{1}{2}$ penny, 1 penny, and 2 pence. These are legal tender up to 20 pence.

Bruchzins. The amount of interest to be calculated for a broken period.

Brut, Brutto. Gross, without deduction of commission, tax, expenses, etc.

Bubble. Excessive and unjustified speculation in the shares or stock of a doubtful company as a result of which the value of the shares is grossly inflated far beyond their real value. Anything unsubstantial or unreal, a fraud, a swindling project, a "get rich quick" scheme. *See* South Sea Bubble.

Buch. A book.

Buchgeld. Bank or Giro deposits readily convertible at any time into notes and coin.

Buchgewinn. A notional profit by upward revaluation of book entries.

Buchverlust. A notional loss by downward revaluation of book entries.

Buchwert. A book or nominal value of an asset in the balance sheet.

Bucket Shop. Originally an office for gambling in grain or stocks for small amounts; the place of business of an outside broker who does not belong to any recognised stock exchange and who carries on risky and highly speculative business with questionable integrity.

Budget. The annual statement made by the Chancellor of the Exchequer in which he estimates the expected revenues and expenditure of the forthcoming year; a plan for systematic spending; a financial programme for an ensuing fiscal year. Its purpose is to provide an orderly administration of the financial affairs of an establishment to ensure their proper correlation and achieve the most desirable results. It involves an examination of the past, taking stock of the present and setting priorities for future action. It is thus a report, an estimate and a proposal compounded into one.

Budget Account. A scheme to allow a customer to even out the regular payments which he has to make. He gives the details of his usual outgoings to a bank which totals the annual cost, opens a budget account for the customer, and issues him with a special budget account cheque book. Thereafter the bank will debit the customer's ordinary current account and credit the budget account with a monthly sum representing one-twelfth of the annual cost. The service costs a few pounds per year. Also, a system of credit-trading operated by some big department stores by which the customer pays so much each month and in return obtains credit for a multiple of the sum. A service charge is built into the scheme.

Budgetary Control. The determination in advance of the financial requirement of a business in respect of expenditure anticipated and income necessary to meet the expenditure, and a subsequent comparison of the budgeted figures with actual costs and performances. Once a business target has been set, the next thing to do is to compare performance figures with target figures. This measure of performance will help management to find out the variances and the reasons for them. A continuous monitoring will help to determine how realistic or unrealistic the forecast is, and the adequacy or inadequacy of the machinery for carrying out the plan. *See also* Variance.

Building Agreement. A contract between a builder and the owner of a piece of land whereby the builder undertakes to build houses or flats on the land to meet certain specified standards, and the owner undertakes to grant a lease to each purchaser of a completed house, etc.

Building Lease. A lease of land by the freeholder for a term of years, usually 99 years, but sometimes 999 years, to a builder at a fixed ground rent. The builder undertakes to build houses upon this land and when he has done so he sells the houses to purchasers and subleases the individual plots to the individual buyers at a price together with an increased ground rent. The right to receive the improved ground rents for the term of the lease may subsequently be sold to a finance company.

Building Societies. Societies existing to provide long-term loans for the acquisition of homes on the security of the houses and land so bought. In this capacity they are non-profit making bodies and their interest rates are loosely linked with money rates. To gather the funds which they need the societies must offer a rate sufficient to bring in the funds. If money is difficult to get, interest rates offered will have to be raised and this in turn will mean that mortgage rates will also have to go up. The first building societies were called *Terminating Societies*, because they were composed of groups of members who paid fixed monthly sums, so accumulating funds which were used to buy land and build houses on it for the members. When everyone had eventually acquired a house the society was dissolved. Such societies did not borrow, and therefore had only the funds paid in by members. About 1850 a relaxation of this rigid link between the investing and borrowing aspects of membership permitted the emergence of the *Permanent Building Society*. Funds were now borrowed, not only from members who were saving for the express purpose of buying a house, but also from those who had savings to invest. Modern building societies maintain share accounts and deposit accounts, and run subscription schemes and saving schemes linked with life assurance. The Registrar of Building Societies is the Chief Registrar of Friendly Societies. He is concerned to protect the interests of depositors, who may invest in share accounts or deposit accounts. All building societies are regulated by the Building Societies Act 1962. Nearly all the bigger societies are members of the Building Societies Association, which makes recommendations on interest rates to be offered to investors and charged to borrowers, and imposes certain conditions of membership such as the maintenance of minimum liquid resources in cash and securities which member societies should hold.

Bulk Buying. Buying in large quantities and therefore more cheaply.

Bulk Cargo. A ship's cargo such as oil or

grain which is not in separate bags or bales.

Bull. A speculator on the Stock Exchange who anticipates a rise in the value of a certain security and therefore buys such stocks, not intending to pay for the purchase, but hoping to sell them later, at a profit, before the settlement date.

Bullet. A straight debt issue without a sinking fund.

Bulletin de Versement. *See* Credit Slip.

Bullion. Gold or silver in bars or in specie. The term is also used to describe quantities of gold, silver or copper coins when measured by weight.

Bullion Points. *See* Specie Points.

Bundesverband Deutscher Banken e.v. *Postfach 10 02 46, 5000 Köln 1.* An association for the preservation and protection of the interests of German banks in general. In particular its objectives are: (1) consultation with groups of members on all questions touching and affecting them, and the giving of instruction on technical matters; (2) consultation with and support for the decision-making bodies in German banks in affairs concerning them; (3) the dissemination of information about professional standards and prospects; (4) the fostering of good relations with banking groups in other countries.

Buoyancy. In an inflationary period, a tendency for stocks and shares to increase in price; revenue from taxation which is increasing as the result of rising prices and wages.

Burden. That which is borne or carried; the interest charges which a person or a business is paying on money borrowed; the taxation which is incurred; (on a country) the cost of servicing that part of the National Debt which is owed to other countries or to the International Monetary Fund; the weight of cargo a ship may carry; an encumbrance or restriction on property.

Bureau de Change. (*Fr.*) A bank or office where foreign money is dealt in and exchanged; a foreign exchange office.

Bürgschaft. The contractual obligation of a surety towards a creditor of a third party (the principal debtor) for the repayment of a debt. *See also* Guarantee.

Bürgschaftsgenossenschaft. An association with the objective of helping its members, mostly small traders and shop-keepers, by granting loans to assist them in their commitments.

Bürgschaftskredit. Credit given against no concrete security, but covered by the undertakings of one or more sureties.

Business. Employment, occupation, trade, profession, work, concern, province; commercial, industrial or professional affairs, buying and selling, bargaining; a particular matter demanding attention; a commercial establishment; a shop with stock, fixtures, etc. It is provided in the Consumer Credit Act 1974 that a person is not to be treated as carrying on a particular type of business merely because occasionally he enters into transactions belonging to a business of that type.

Business Day. *See* Non-Business Day; Working Day.

Business Development Loan. A type of loan designed to meet the needs of smaller business for extended credit with planned and agreed repayments, which include interest charges. It is available in the range of £2,000–£100,000, for expenditure on property purchase or extension, the purchase of plant, machinery or vehicles, the purchase of a business or professional practice, or by way of additional working capital for a new or existing business, or any other approved project. A term of from one to five years is usual, or in exceptional cases up to fifteen years. The term is phased on an appraisal of the profit flow and the expected life of any assets purchased with the proceeds of the loan. Interest is added to the initial amount of the loan and the total amount repaid in equal monthly instalments over the agreed period of the loan. The borrower is normally required to have life cover to the amount of the loan.

Business Hours. Fixed hours of work or for transaction of business in a shop, office, etc.

Business Names. Where in a business partners or a company trade under a name different from their own they are using a business name. In the case of a company the name used may apply to some separate or distinct activity of the company and a banking account may be opened in a name which differs from that registered by the company. In the case of partners a descriptive title may be used to indicate the nature of the business, or originally true surnames may be retained for the sake of goodwill although partners may die and new partners may enter the business. A sole trader also may be trading under a name which is not his surname. In the United Kingdom certain business names need registration. *See* Registration of Business Names.

Buyer Credit. An arrangement whereby an exporter negotiates a contract with an overseas buyer on a cash basis, the latter finding up to 20% of the contract price and negotiating a separate loan from a U.K. bank for the balance owing to the exporter. The U.K. bank obtains an unconditional guarantee from the Export Credits Guarantee Department in respect of the principal and interest due from the buyer. These facilities are usually found for larger contracts (over £2 million), for which the repayment period can be as long as ten years, but can be made available for contracts of £850,000 and upwards. Buyer credit is drawn after shipment and repays the pre-shipment finance which can be made available when the contract is for £1 million or more.

Buyer's Market. A condition of markets in which goods are plentiful and there is little demand for them, so that the buyer can make his own terms.

Buying In. If a seller of securities on the Stock Exchange has not delivered them to the purchaser by the proper time, they may be "bought in" by an official of the Stock Exchange for delivery to the purchaser and any loss, charge, or expense thereby incurred must be borne by the seller.

Bye-law. A local law made by a subordinate authority such as a corporation, town council, etc.

C

Cable Transfer. *See* Telegraphic Transfer.

Caisse d'Épargne. See Savings Bank.

Call. A demand by a company to shareholders for payment of an instalment, or the balance due on shares. This may refer to the period of flotation of a company, when the shareholders are usually asked to pay a certain portion of the capital on allotment and the remainder on call, or to any other time when a company, in need of more capital, calls up some or all of the uncalled capital on partly paid shares: a Stock Exchange term. *See also* Option.

Callgeld. Day to day money.

Call Money. Money lent to bill brokers by bankers and others at interest on the terms that it is repayable "at call" or on demand.

Call of More Option. *See* Option.

Call Option. *See* Option.

Call Rate. The rate of interest applicable to call money or to deposits repayable on demand and not subject to notice.

Cambiste. A foreign exchange dealer.

Cancellable Agreement. A regulated agreement which may be cancelled by the debtor or hirer in certain circumstances, such as where the debtor or hirer signs the agreement on premises which are not those of the creditor.

Cancellation. A crossing out or an obliteration. A cheque is cancelled by the writing of the initials of the cancelling clerk in the paying bank across the signature of the drawer, or by perforation of the date on which payment is made, or by a stamp. A bill of exchange other than a cheque is cancelled by the cancellation of the acceptor's signature. A bond or similar document is cancelled by writing across it the word "cancelled" or by defacing it. A will is cancelled by revocation by the testator. *See also* Revocation of Will.

Canon Law. The law of the church.

Canvassing. Soliciting support, votes, contributions; for the purposes of the Consumer Credit Act 1974, the soliciting of another person, the consumer, into a regulated agreement as debtor or hirer, by oral persuasion, during a visit by the canvasser to a place which is not the business premises of the creditor, without having been asked to do so (see sections 48 and 153).

Capacity. Power of containing or receiving, power to absorb; ability, scope; relative position, character or office; legal qualification. Capacity to incur liability as a party to a bill is co-extensive with capacity to contract.

Capital. Money used to run a business, often raised by an issue of shares; sums of invested money; the amount of money used or available to carry on a concern. *See also* Authorised Capital; Circulating Capital; Fixed Capital; Floating Capital; Free Capital; Issued Capital; Liquid Capital; Paid-up Capital; Share Capital; Subscribed Capital; Working Capital.

Capital Allowances. Deductions allowed in a tax assessment for sums expended on certain capital equipment used in a business or profession. The allowances have to be specifically claimed.

Capital Authorisé. See Authorised Capital.

Capital de Dotation. Founding capital, wholly in the hands of the state, and allocated by it to a public enterprise.

Capital de Fondation. Share capital, public money sunk into the flotation of a company.

Capital d'Exploitation, Capital de Roulement. See Working Capital.

Capital Element. That portion of an annuity repayment considered to be repayment of capital and thus not chargeable to tax.

Capital Émis. See Issued Capital.

Capital Gains Tax. Originally a tax to penalise any profits made from buying and re-selling stocks and shares and land within 12 months, it is not now confined to land and stocks and shares, nor to a twelve-month period except in the case of gilt-edged securities. These short-term gains are treated as unearned income and are assessable to income tax, being based on the excess of the proceeds of disposal over the cost of acquisition, *or* the value on 6 April 1965. They must therefore be included in the income tax return. At present the tax is at the rate of 30% on the amount of the gain. Alternatively, half the gain can be charged to income tax as investment income. Where total proceeds do not exceed £1,000, exemption is allowed. The tax does not apply to private residences, private cars, small gifts, etc. Within the tax year gains and losses are aggregated. Any net loss may be carried forward and set against gains made in future years.

Capitalisation. Using a given rate of interest, the theoretical estimation of the capital amount representing the total sum lent or the periodic revenue; the stock exchange value of a company obtained by multiplying the share quotation by the number of issued shares.

Capitalisation of Profits. The conversion of retained profits into paid-up capital by a bonus share issue.

Capitalised Value. The value of an asset calculated by reference to its current annual earnings at the prevailing rate of interest.

Capitalism. The economic system of employing capital to produce wealth; a form of economic, social and industrial organisation of society involving ownership, control and direction of production by privately owned business organisations.

Capital Redemption Reserve Fund. A reserve fund to be established by a company limited by shares which issues redeemable preference shares. In cases where such shares are redeemed otherwise than out of the proceeds of a fresh issue, there shall out of profits which would otherwise have been available for dividend be transferred to a reserve fund, to be called the "capital redemption reserve fund", a sum equal to the nominal amount of the shares redeemed, this fund to be regarded as equivalent to paid-up share capital of the company.

Capital Redemption Yield. The profit made by holding a dated stock until redemption; the difference between the purchase price paid and the proceeds received on redemption at par. It is usually expressed as a rate per cent, arrived at by dividing this figure by the number of years to redemption.

Capital Transfer Tax (C.T.T.). C.T.T., which was introduced by the Finance Act 1975, is payable on any chargeable transfer of value, whether money or goods, which reduces the estate of the transferor and is intended to benefit someone else. The new tax replaces estate duty, which no longer applies. It bites when the total chargeable transfers during life, or at death, exceed £25,000 It is cumulative and the rates are assessed on the total value of the gifts made over the years. Liability arises at the time when the property is handed over, whether outright or to trustees. It applies on death when property passes to others and on trust property when the person entitled to the income from the property dies. Property held on discretionary trusts is also affected. There are two different rates of tax—one for lifetime transfers and the other for transfers after death. Lifetime transfers of up to £300,000 are charged at a lower rate of tax than death transfers, although the tax increases progressively with the value of the amount transferred. Up to £100,000, the lifetime rate is only half the death rate. Above £300,000, all rates are the same. A donor of a gift in a lifetime which attracts the lower rate must survive three years after making the gift, or an excess death transfer is payable. Exemptions apply to (1) Gifts in any one year up to a value of £2,000. (2) Transfers between husband and wife. (3) Gifts of up to £2,500 in consideration of marriage if neither party is related to the donor, or £1,000 if not. Each parent may give £5,000 to a son or daughter on their marriage. (4) All lifetime gifts to charity made more than a year before death. (5) Gifts for national purposes. (6) Gifts to local authorities. (7) Certain assets, including reversionary interests, some overseas pensions, some classes of annuities and, in some cases, savings, by people domiciled in the Channel Islands or the Isle of Man. (8) Legacies to one's spouse, if one's estate goes wholly to the spouse. C.T.T. is payable, however, on the death of the survivor. (9) Normal expenditure transfers. (10) Gifts to political parties.

Capitation. A poll tax.

Capitaux Errants, Fugitifs, Migrateurs. See Hot Money.

Card Index. A system of filing particulars by the use of loose cards arranged in a container.

Carnet. A book, a notebook. In the U.K. the term is used to describe the document by which exemption is obtained from the immediate payment of Customs dues.

Carnet de Banque. A pass-book.

Carnet de Chèques. A cheque-book.

Carnet d'Épargne. A savings account pass-book in the name of a particular person, or inscribed to the bearer, issued by a bank, in which a record is kept of payments in, drawings out, and interest allowed. The savings bank account is used principally for the deposit of money and not for the settlement of sums due, as with other bank accounts.

Carriage. Carrying, transporting, conveyance, especially of merchandise; the cost of conveying; the manner of carrying.

Carriage Forward. (Of goods) to be paid for on arrival.

Carrying Over Day. On the Stock Exchange, the name for the first day of settlement.

Carry Over. On the Stock Exchange, to continue a bargain for another account, to postpone the settlement of an account from one settling day to another.

Carte Chèque. See Cheque Card; Eurocheque Scheme.

Carte de Credit. See Credit Card.

Cartel. An agreement among manufacturers to keep the price of their products at an artificially high level; an industrial combination for the purpose of regulating price and amount of product.

Case Law. The law built up by judges from their case decisions.

Case of Need. The person whose name may be included in a bill of exchange by a drawer or by any indorser, so that such person may act as a "referee in case of need"—that is, he can be contacted by the holder if the bill is dishonoured by non-acceptance or non-payment, and will then arrange for payment at maturity.

Cash. Generally considered to be made up by banknotes and coin plus deposits at the deposit banks but a wider use of the word may include not only cash but those things which can readily be turned into cash, such as any readily negotiable paper (*e.g.* bills, drafts, bonds, etc.).

Cash Account. A book-keeping account recording the payments in and out of cash, the balance on the account being the balance of cash in hand.

Cash Bonus. A sum in cash given over and above any fixed amount of salary or wages; a share of the profits of a life assurance company paid to the assured in cash, in place of being used to increase the amount ultimately payable, or to reduce the amount of the premium.

Cash Book. A book containing a record of all cash transactions in and out.

Cash Card. Cards issued to customers of large banks to enable them to obtain cash at any time of the day or night from a machine called a cash dispenser. The cash card has punched holes and is fed into the machine for electronic checking, after which the machine delivers a packet of notes, usually £10 worth.

Cash Discount. Discount allowed on a bill not yet due, in consideration of immediate payment; a deduction from the invoice price of goods in return for payment within a stipulated time.

Cash Dispenser. A machine used by banks both in the outer wall of the bank, and inside the office but available to the public, to supplement the work of the cashiers. The machine pays against a cash card, which it retains so as to initiate a debit to the customer's account. The cash card is then returned to the customer. *See also* Cash Card.

Cash Flow. The gross trading profit of a business, including provision for depreciation of fixed capital, but not including the cost of replacing normal stocks of materials required in the business and work in progress. The provisions for stock appreciation in times of rapid inflation can account for considerable sums and as a result it is possible for a company showing good profits nevertheless to be in difficulties when it comes to paying tax, dividends or wages. A good cash flow, properly budgeted forward, will ensure that a company always has enough ready cash to meet its current obligations. *See also* Discounted Cash Flow; Gross Cash Flow; Net Cash Flow.

Cash Flow *Actualisé*. *See* Discounted Cash Flow.

Cash on Delivery (C.O.D.). A service provided by the Post Office where the purchaser of mail order goods pays the postman.

Cash Point. The name of a computerised cash dispenser which can handle variable amounts of cash. It returns the cash card to the customer at the time of operation. *See also* Service Till.

Cash Ratio. The amount of cash held in a bank's tills or as a balance at the Bank of England, expressed as a percentage of the total of customers' balances held on current or deposit account. Formerly maintained in the U.K. at 8% it is, since Competition and Credit Control, at a lower figure, usually between 5%–7%.

Casting. The act of adding or totalling figures; addition of figures.

Catchment Area. By analogy with the area in which water collects to form a river, the physical area of the country which contains the new staff which a bank needs to recruit; or the area from which a branch bank will draw its business. The establishment of a new branch, for example, must take into consideration the factors which will bring customers in, such as position of the branch, the local shopping facilities, the population figure, housing, industry and commerce, and competitors.

Caution. In registered land, a way of protecting certain interests of a lender or interested party by lodging a notice at the Land Registry; the name of the notice so lodged. Thus a pending action affecting the land would be the subject of a caution.

Caution. (Fr.) A guarantee of the debt contracted by another person.

Cautionary Obligation. The name given in Scotland to a guarantee.

Cautionnement. Security, guarantee.

Caution Solidaire. A guarantee which can be called upon before the principal debtor and, should the occasion arise, even before realisation of any security.

Caveat. A warning, a caution; a legal process to stop procedure.

Caveat Emptor. "Let the buyer beware". The seller is not obliged to volunteer information about the property being sold, although he must answer relevant questions truthfully.

Cédant. One who transfers a credit or a claim to a third party.

Cedel. A clearing system for the Eurocurrency market, based in Luxemburg and owned by several European banks.

Cédule. See Payroll Tax.

Cédule Hypothécaire. A personal credit guaranteed by real security.

Ceiling. The upper limit of production, wages, prices, etc.; a borrowing limit for a customer maintained at the Head Office or regional or area office of a bank, being somewhat above that recorded at the branch and agreed with the customer.

Central Bank. The bank in any country which is authorised by the government of the country to control the amount of credit in the country, to supervise the operations of the commercial banks, to carry out the business of the government and to maintain its accounts, to control the note issue and the country's reserves, and to preserve the value of the country's currency on the foreign exchanges.

Certificat. See Certificate.

Certificat de Copropriété. A document certifying a holding in a unit trust.

Certificat d'Entrepôt. The document of title to goods in a bonded warehouse.

Certificat de Trust. A certificate issued by an unit trust company.

Certificat d'Origine. See Certificate of Origin.

Certificate. A written testimony to the truth of a fact. *See also* Bank Interest Certificate; Definitive Certificate; Provisional Certificate; Quality Certificate; Scrip; Share Certificate; Stock Certificate; Ullage Certificate; Veterinary Certificate; Zoological Certificate.

Certificated Bankrupt. A person who has been made bankrupt but who subsequently obtains his discharge from the court, together with a certificate to the effect that his bankruptcy was caused by misfortune without any misconduct on his behalf.

Certificate of Bonds. A certificate issued to a holder of registered bonds particularising the bonds which are registered in his name.

Certificate of Charge. A sealed certificate issued by the Land Registry when a lender registers a charge on registered land. It has the original charge, signed by the borrower, stitched inside it. As evidence of title it takes the place of the land certificate, which is withdrawn during the currency of the charge.

Certificate of Deposit. Evidence of a deposit with a bank repayable on a fixed date. It is a fully negotiable bearer document transferable by delivery. To ensure the marketability of the certificates there needs to be what is called a "secondary" market, that is, somewhere where the holder of the certificate can sell it if he so wishes. This secondary market is provided by the discount houses and the banks in the inter-bank market. *See also* Dollar Certificate of Deposit; Sterling Certificate of Deposit; "Straight" Deposit.

Certificate of Existence (Life Certificate). A certificate issued by a banker or solicitor to the effect that a customer or client was communicated with on a certain day and that a reply was obtained, or that he/she was visited and seen on that day. Such certificates are often required by companies paying annuities, as proof that the beneficiary is still alive.

Certificate of Fair Rent. A certificate issued by a rent officer to a person who wishes to build, let, or convert premises which, when let, will be subject to the provisions of the Rent Acts. The certificate is not a final estimate of the rent which will be obtainable, but is intended to be an indication of the economic return to be expected.

Certificate of Incorporation. A certificate granted by the Registrar cf Companies to a company just formed, after completion of certain necessary formalities, stating that the company has been duly registered and is now incorporated under the Companies Acts. Before the granting of this certificate the company has no legal power to conduct business or to maintain a banking account. The banker should inspect this certificate and note the particulars in his records.

Certificate of Inspection. A shipping document certifying the condition of perishable goods in a cargo as at the date of their dispatch.

Certificate of Insurance. A certificate issued by an insurance broker as evidence that a marine insurance has been effected. Such a certificate is not acceptable to a buyer under a C.I.F. contract because the right of the insured cannot be transferred by indorsement and delivery of a certificate, but only of the policy of insurance.

Certificate of Mortgage or Sale of Ship. A document issued by the registrar of the port at which a ship is registered to a registered owner who wishes to mortgage or sell the ship (or any share of it) to any person in any country other than the one in which the port of registry is situate, in order to enable him to do so.

Certificate of Origin. A certificate issued and signed by Chambers of Commerce confirming the place of growth, production or manufacture of goods. *See also* Negative Certificate of Origin.

Certificate of Posting. A certificate issued by a post office for a small charge to evidence the posting of a letter or packet.

Certificate of Protest. The official document given by a notary public evidencing the dishonour by non-acceptance or non-payment of a bill of exchange. Such a certificate is accepted as proof of dishonour in a court of law. A protest must contain a copy of the bill, and must be signed by the notary making it, and must specify (1) the person at whose request the bill is protested; (2) the place and date of protest, the cause or reason for protesting the bill, the demand made, and the answer given, if any, or the fact that the drawee or acceptor could not be found.

Certificate of Registration. A document issued by the Registrar of Companies evidencing conclusively that any mortgage or charge given by a limited company, and requiring registration under the provisions of the Companies Act 1948, has been so registered.

Certificate of Search. A document issued by the Registrar of a Charges or Land Register giving the result of a search made in the register in respect of certain properties or names at the request of a lender against such property, or other interested party. Such a certificate is also issued in respect of certain local land charges by local authorities.

Certificate of Survey. A document issued by a Port Surveying Officer in respect of the outward appearance and condition of goods discharged from a vessel.

Certificate of Tax. *See* Tax Certificate.

Certificate of Tax Deposit. This certificate is obtainable from the Inland Revenue for a minimum of £2,000, and pays interest at a tax-free rate which is altered from time to time to accord with money market rates and which is substantially higher on certificates used to pay tax than on deposits withdrawn for cash. Certificates of Tax Deposit may be used to pay income tax (other than P.A.Y.E.), corporation tax, capital gains tax, and capital transfer tax.

Certificate to Commence Business. A document issued by the Registrar of Companies to a public company in evidence that all necessary formalities have been completed and that the public company now has official permission to commence trading. A private company requires no such certificate.

Certified Cheque. See Marked Cheque.

Certified Transfer. A stock or share transfer form which has been marked in the margin with the words "certificate lodged" by the Registrar of a company as evidence that the certificate for the stock or shares dealt with have been delivered to the Registrar's office. The certificate may be by rubber stamp, usually initialled or signed by an authorised company officer. The device is commonly used where part only of a holding has been sold and therefore the certificate has to be split.

Certiorari. An order at the discretion of the court which, if granted, operates to bring before the High Court for review any case decided or pending in an inferior court.

Cesser. A ceasing of liability; a ceasing of payment by a tenant.

Cession. (*Fr.*) The transfer of a right, more especially of a credit, to a third person.

Cessionaire. The person who acquires credits or rights transferred by an assignor.

Cession des Biens. Conveyancing.

Cestui Que Trust. The person for whose benefit trust property is administered.

Cestui Que Use. The person on whose behalf land is held.

Cestui Que Vie. The person whose life span has been appointed as a measure of the duration of the benefit of property enjoyed by another.

Ceteris Paribus. All other things being equal.

Chain of Representation. The mere naming of a man as executor in a will does not bind him to accept the duty, but usually (where the executor is a private person) the relationship is one based on friendship and trust. Because of this if B, an executor, dies before completing the winding-up of A's estate, and B has named his executor as C, C will deal with B's estate and will also finish the administration of A's estate. Although perhaps A did not know C, he knew and trusted B, and B knew and trusted C. This is a "chain" of executorship or representation.

Chain of Title. In the proof of title to land, the sequence of deeds and documents from the good root of title to the holding deed.

Chamber. A place where a legislative assembly meets; the assembly itself; a hall of justice; an association of persons for the promotion of some common object. *See also* Upper Chamber.

Chamber of Agriculture. A board or committee appointed to promote the interests of agriculture in a district.

Chamber of Commerce. An association of businessmen formed to protect their commercial and trading interests in one particular area.

Chamber of Deputies. The French legislative assembly, the equivalent of the House of Commons.

Chamber of Shipping. An association of ship owners to promote their interests, particularly in respect of changes in the law or the passing of new statutes which would affect them.

Change. (*Fr.*) Monetary change; exchange of one money for another; the rate of exchange.

Change of User. Town and Country Planning legislation in the U.K. provided that any proposed development of the land—any change in the way the land was going to be used—must have the permission of the local authority. "Development" includes "the making of any material change in the use of buildings". Thus turning a house into a shop, or dividing the house into flats, requires permission. If development is carried out without permission, the local authority may within four years serve an enforcement order on the owner of the land, requiring the land to be restored to its original condition.

Charge. An office, duty or care; to debit to; to ask a price for; to take a pledge, mortgage or assignment of security belonging to a borrowing customer.

Chargeable Assets. Assets which are not exempt from capital gains tax.

Charge by way of Legal Mortgage. *See* Legal Mortgage.

Charge Certificate. *See* Certificate of Charge.

Charge for Credit. For the purpose of the Consumer Credit Act 1974, the sum total of interest, etc., which a debtor will pay for a credit facility.

Charges. In banking, the total cost of keeping the customer's account, traditionally divided into commission and interest on overdraft, and debited to the account quarterly or half-yearly; a bundle of cheques presented for payment by one bank, being a member of the Clearing House, to another through the medium of the House; mortgages, pledges or assignments over property given by customers to banks as security against accommodation; for tax purposes, reductions in income of taxpayers which operate to reduce the amount of tax payable. Charges on income for tax purposes must be legal charges such as an annual payment by the taxpayer which he is committed to making by his signature on a legal document, *e.g.* an annual payment under a deed of covenant.

Charges Forward. Charges attracted by goods to be paid by the buyer on receipt of the goods.

Charges Register. *See* Land Certificate.

Charging Order. An order obtained from the court by a judgment creditor charging property of the debtor with the amount of the debt. The effect of the order is to stop all transactions in respect of the property so charged for six months. If by that time the debtor has not paid, the creditor can get an order for sale from the court and take the benefit of the property.

Charitable Company. A company formed for the purpose of promoting art, science, religion, charity or any other like object, not involving the acquisition of gain by the company or by its individual members.

Charitable Trust. A trust for the relief of poverty, for the advancement of education or religion, or for the benefit of the community in some other way.

Charity. As respects England and Wales, a charity which is registered under the Charities Act 1960, or any exempt charity within the meaning of that Act; as respects Scotland and Northern Ireland, an institution or other organisation established for charitable purposes only.

Charte. *See* Charter.

Charter. An instrument in writing granted by Parliament or by the Sovereign, incorporating a certain company or institution, or conferring certain rights or privileges; a formal document confirming privileges, titles or rights; the hiring of a vessel; to hire, as a ship. *See also* Demise Charter; Time Charter; Voyage Charter.

Chartered Accountant. One qualified under the regulations of the Institute of Accountants in England and Wales, or in Scotland.

Chartered Bank. A banking company incorporated under a charter granted by the Crown.

Chartered Company. A company deriving its authority to carry on business, not from the Companies Acts, but from a special charter granted by the Crown.

Chartered Institute of Public Finance and Accountancy (C.I.P.F.A.). An association of treasurers and financial officers of British public and local authorities. An important section of its work, which is to promote the best interests of its members and to maintain a high standard, is carried on by its Loans Bureau which channels funds from commercial, industrial and private lenders to those local authorities desiring to borrow, and also directs funds from local authorities having cash surpluses to those looking for a loan. The Bureau keeps in close touch with the rates and trends in the interbank market and in other sterling markets.

Charter Party. A contract between the owners of a ship and the charterer, whereby the vessel is hired to, or placed at the disposal of, the charterer for a certain voyage or for a certain time, for the conveyance of goods.

Charter Party Bill of Lading. A bill of lading which is subject to the terms and conditions of the charter party.

Chattels. All property other than freehold land.

Chattels Personal. Goods, furniture and other articles capable of complete transfer by delivery, and, when separately assigned, fixtures and growing crops as soon as severed from the ground.

Chattels Real. Leasehold property.

Cheap Money. Money which can be borrowed at a low rate of interest.

Checkkarte. *See* Cheque Card.

Check Ledger. The daily machining or writing of all cheques and credits on a check ledger sheet, the items then being called back against the ledger postings as a check on accuracy. The cheque ledger list also carried from day to day the calculation of the ledger balance. In later mechanised systems this was done on Extract Cards. In modern bank accountancy the computer has rendered both check ledger sheets and extract cards obsolete.

Check Rechnung. Assets in a bank which can be made available at any time, particularly through the use of cheques; a cheque account.

Cheque. A bill of exchange payable on demand, drawn on a banker. *See also* Antedated Cheque; Bearer Bill; Blank Cheque; Crossed Cheque; Marked Cheque; Open Cheque; Order Cheque; Stopped Cheque; Travel Cheques.

Cheque as an Assignment of Funds. In England a cheque does not operate as an assignment of funds, but in Scotland, where the drawee of a bill has in his hands funds available for the payment of it, the bill operates as an assignment of the sum for which it is drawn in favour of the holder, from the time when the bill is presented to the drawee. Thus, if the balance of an account is not sufficient to pay a bill or cheque, nevertheless the presentation of the instrument operates to assign the available funds. Thus when the instrument is returned unpaid, the balance must on the same day be transferred to an "Attached Funds" account.

Chèque Barré. *See* Crossed Cheque.

Cheque Book. A book of cheque forms, usually containing ten, twenty-five or sixty cheque forms, issued by a bank to a current account customer.

Cheque Book Register. A record of cheque books issued to individual customers maintained by a bank.

Cheque Card. A piece of plastic about 85 mm by 54 mm, bearing (in the U.K.) an amount of £50, the name of the bank, the name and signature of the customer, the sorting code number of the branch maintaining his account, the card number and the expiry date. It is renewed yearly. The issuing bank undertakes that any cheque not exceeding £50 will be honoured as long as the cheque has been signed in the presence of the payee, is drawn on a bank cheque form whose code number agrees with the code number on the card, and is authenticated by a signature which agrees with the specimen signature on the card. The cheque must be drawn before the expiry date of the card, and the card number must be written on the reverse of the cheque. The extension of the use of the cheque card abroad relates only to the encashment of cheques up to £30 twice daily at banks participating in the scheme. On the Continent the British cheque card is not a guarantee for buying goods from a continental retailer, as it is in Britain. There a uniform cheque and cheque card is being developed under the Eurocheque scheme. The card, headed "Eurocheque", is sold to customers by the banks for a nominal sum, and then enables the holder to draw cash up to a limit of 300 Swiss francs (about £70) from bank branches, and also acts as a guarantee up to the same limit at hotels and stores on the Continent. Both the cheque and the card are slightly different from those individual banks used to issue before the advent of the Eurocheque scheme. United Kingdom banks have yet to decide whether they will become full members of Eurocheque and start issuing uniform cheques and cheque guarantee cards. Meanwhile, continentals are restricted in the United Kingdom to using their cheque cards for cash at banks.

Chèque de Voyage. *See* Travel Cheques.

Cheque Rate. The cost in one country of the purchase of a cheque or sight draft drawn in the currency of another country.

Chief Rent. A perpetual rent charge to which freehold land may be subject. In default of payment the owner of the chief rent has a right of re-entry upon the land.

Chiffre d'Affaires. Turnover.

Chose in Action. A right enforceable in a court of law.

Chose in Possession. A sum of money or a good in the actual possession of the owner.

Circular Letter of Credit. *See* Letter of Credit.

Circulating Capital. Property bought with the intention that it shall be resold over a short period at a profit. Such property is completely changed in form or used up in the preparation of a new product. Thus, in a manufacturing company, cash is converted into new materials, which are made up into finished goods, which are sold for cash.

Circulating Medium. Money such as banknotes, etc., used as a means of exchange in commerce.

Circulation. The act of moving round, motion in a circle; the extent of sale of a newspaper, etc.; the money circulating in a country. *See also* Active Circulation; Restricted Circulation.

Cite. To quote, to allege as an authority, to quote as an instance, to refer to; to summon to appear in court.

City. A collective description of the financial institutions of the City of London.

City Code. The published rules of the Panel on Take-overs and Mergers.

Claim. A real or supposed right; a title; in taxation, a claim for an allowance, normally made by inserting the appropriate particulars in the annual tax return, or for a refund of tax, as where dividends form part of the income and the total of the personal allowances exceeds earnings plus any other untaxed income. Part or all of the tax deducted from interest will then be repayable on claim.

Claim Form. An inter-branch form used when one branch claims upon another for a sum due as a result of some customer transaction, *e.g.* for an unpaid cheque.

Clause à Ordre. The phrase "or to his order" written after the name of the beneficiary on a document of title, allowing him to transfer it by indorsement.

Clause de Change. A clause in a contract stipulating that the sum due at payment date shall be of an equivalent value to the sum at the contract date, in order to guard against devaluation.

Clause Négative. A clause in an agreement forbidding a debtor to undertake a specific transaction, *e.g.* the giving of a mortgage or other security.

Clause-Or. A stipulation that a debt is repayable in gold, or by reference to the value of gold.

Clausing. A statement on the face of a bill of exchange giving details of the transaction in respect of which the bill is drawn.

Claw Back. A term used originally to describe a refund of tax due to the taxpayer; more recently, a recovery by the Inland Revenue of tax relief formerly granted, notably in the case of certain family allowances and in some cases of early surrender or conversion of life policies.

Clayton's Case: *Devaynes* v. *Noble* **(1816).** This important old case has left two lessons: (1) Where a debtor keeps two or more accounts with a creditor, and pays such creditor a sum of money in reduction, the debtor has the right to allocate or appropriate his payment to such account as he may choose. If the debtor does not exercise this right of appropriation, the creditor is free to do so. (2) The Rule in Clayton's Case is of great importance to bankers, and its operation is frequently guarded against in bank forms of charge. The rule is as follows: *"In a running account payments in are presumed to be appropriated to payments out in the order in which the items occur."* In a credit account, therefore, credits are paid in before debits are paid, and the money paid into the bank is regarded as being available to meet the debits in date order. In an overdrawn account the credits paid in are similarly allocated towards repayment of the debits and therefore in reduction of the overdraft. This reduction is often concealed by the payment of fresh debits. To avoid the operation of the Rule an overdrawn account must be ruled off on notice of certain events (notice of a second mortgage, notice of death of a partner, expiry of notice of termination of a guarantee) to protect the bank's position. A new account must be opened to continue the customer's business and will normally be maintained in credit. The overdrawn balance of the old account is left as it stands and must not be taken into account in the working of the new account. If the overdrawn account is not broken in this way (and if any form of charge does not guard against the risk), as the running account continues to operate, credits as they are paid in are deemed to repay the old overdraft (which was secured, or in respect of which there was a claim against a guarantor or his estate, or a deceased partner's private estate), while fresh debits as they are paid gradually build up a new overdraft which is not secured, or in respect of which there is no claim against a person or his estate.

Clean. Free of attached material or of derogatory factors or information; work which is free from error; documents which are in order and require no correction or special supervision; a staff or customer record showing no undesirable features.

Clean Bill. A bill which has no documents of title attached.

Clean Bill of Lading. A bill of lading free from any clause or indication suggesting damage to the goods covered.

Clean Credit. A credit opened by a banker which provides for the payment by the banker of bills drawn upon him, such bills having no supporting documents attached. *See also* Clean Bill.

Clean Rate. A dealer's term for a rate on a deposit where no certificate of deposit has been issued.

Clearance. Completion of the formalities and procedure before a ship or an aircraft may leave; of a bill or cheque, the obtaining of money in place of the bill or cheque; of goods, the performance of duties and formalities which are necessary before goods can be dispatched or allowed to enter, *e.g.* customs duties.

Clear Days. Days reckoned exclusively of those on which a notice is given and those on which some event, in respect of which the notice was issued, takes place.

Clearing. Presenting a cheque or draft for payment through the banking machinery set up for this purpose, that is, through the London Bankers' Clearing House; the process whereby the amount of a cheque or draft is transferred from the drawer's bank to the payee's bank. *See also* Credit Clearing; Town Clearing. **In Clearing.** The cheques received each morning by branches from the clearing house. The branch inspects each cheque to confirm that the signature of the drawer is genuine and that the cheque is otherwise in order. If one has to be returned unpaid for any reason it is mailed direct to the collecting bank and should arrive there on the morning of the fourth day after it has been paid in (or the sixth day if a weekend has intervened). An unpaid claim form debiting the collecting bank is passed through the General Clearing and ultimately finds its way to the collecting bank, which will have sent the returned cheque back to its customer and debited his account with it. **Out Clearing.** Cheques which are paid in at any branch are collected throughout the day. Cheques drawn on the same branch are dealt with at the branch, but the remainder (comprising cheques drawn on other branches of the same bank and cheques drawn on other banks in the U.K.) are sorted into bundles according to the banks they are drawn on and are posted at the end of the day to the clearing office in London of the collecting bank. *Clearingabkommen.* An agreement between two states for mutual set-off of debts resulting from financial and business transactions between them. Administration is handled by central departments in each country, delegation of much of the work being handled by authorised banks.

Clearing Bancaire. The settlement of reciprocal debts between banks. *See also* Clearing House.

Clearing Bank. A bank which clears customers' cheques drawn on other banks through a central clearing house; a bank which is a member of a central clearing organisation. In this country there are nine members of the London Bankers' Clearing House—Bank of England, Barclays Bank, Central Trustee Savings Bank, Co-operative Bank, Coutts & Co., Lloyds Bank, Midland Bank, National Westminster Bank, and Williams and Glyn's Bank.

Clearing des Valeurs. The setting-off by a central department of credits in money or share-holdings.

Clearing House. The London Bankers' Clearing House is in Lombard Street, where it has been situated since its origin in the 1770s. Representatives of each clearing bank attend there each business day to exchange bills of exchange, cheques, etc., drawn upon each other, and to settle for them. The clearings are divided into the *Town Clearing* and the *General Clearing*.

Clearing House Automated Payments System (C.H.A.P.S.). A proposal for automating part of the existing Town Clearing by taking out the larger amounts and automating them through computer terminals to be installed in the branches concerned. This is a long-term project, at the time of writing still under discussion.

Clients' Accounts. Current or deposit accounts in the name of a solicitor at a bank, in the title of which account the word "client" appears. Under the Solicitors' Accounts Rules, money held for clients must be kept separate from the solicitor's personal or office accounts. They should not become overdrawn. There is no set-off between clients' accounts and personal or office accounts.

Clipping. *See* Milling.

Close Company. A company which is under the control of up to five persons, some or all of whom may be directors, except companies not resident in the United Kingdom, companies controlled by the Crown, and registered industrial and provident societies.

Closed Indent. An order from a buyer overseas, placed through an agent, but naming the manufacturer who is to supply the goods.

Close Out. The action taken by foreign exchange dealers to complete a forward contract in the event that the counterparty finds himself unable to fulfil his obligations under it.

Closing. Concluding, coming to an end, final.

Closing an Account. Paying the balance of an account, after all entries have been passed, to a customer or to someone entitled to receive it on his behalf or on behalf of his creditors. The account may be closed at the request of the customer, or of the bank, or by operation of law. The banker must obtain the return of any unused cheque forms. An account may be closed by the banker because of its unsatisfactory conduct by the customer; if so an adequate period of notice must be given by the banker. If the customer refuses to close his account, but continues to pay in for its credit, the banker should nominate a day at least ten days in the future, advising the customer accordingly, on which the account shall be closed. On that day he should send a cheque for the balance to the customer and may thereafter return cheques with the answer "account closed". If the customer persists in paying in credits at other branches of the bank, or at other banks, the banker should pass these credits to a suspense account until the customer accepts the situation. The balance may then be returned to him.

Closing Entries. The entries which close off standing accounts at the times when the books are balanced.

Closing Prices. The final prices quoted on a market at the end of the trading for the day, especially those on a stock exchange.

Clôture. The closing of the books for the balance sheet and profit and loss accounts to be struck.

Club. *See* Unincorporated Association.

Club Insurance. *See* Mutual Insurance.

Code Number. (1) An integral part of the P.A.Y.E. system of tax deduction. The net allowances, less any untaxed interest, of any taxpayer are listed on a notice of coding and the net total is given a code number by reference to a list of allowances at various levels. An employer is thereby enabled to look up the appropriate code number for any employee in the tax tables issued to him and so to discover the correct amount of tax to be deducted weekly or monthly and subsequently handed over to the Collector of Taxes. A code number generally consists of the first two figures of the total net allowances followed by the letter H (signifying personal allowance appropriate to a married person), or L (signifying personal allowance appropriate to a single person). There is also provision for letters P (lower age allowance) and V (higher age allowance). An employee wishing to conceal his or her status may on request be allocated the letter T, which gives an employer no information on the subject. (2) The number by which a branch bank authenticates a telephoned message to its head office or to another branch of the bank.

Codicil. An additional document varying the terms of a will or revoking part of it. The codicil must be signed by the testator and witnessed in a similar fashion to the execution of a will.

Coin. A piece of metal stamped and current as money; money, especially coined money; to mint or stamp, as money; to acquire money rapidly, to invent, to fabricate; to make counterfeit money.

Coinage. The act of coining; the pieces coined; the monetary system in use.

Coin of the Realm. The authorised coinage of a country.

Collateral. Subsidiary, concurrent, subordinate; additional security, security deposited by a third party, as opposed to primary security deposited by the borrower. In America the word has the same meaning as our word "security".

Collecting Banker. The banker who collects for his customer's account the proceeds of bills and cheques which have been paid in to him for that purpose. If the customer has a faulty title to such a cheque, or no title at all (as where he has obtained it by fraud) the collecting banker may be sued by the true owner for the tort of conversion. The collecting banker can look to statutory protection against this claim so long as he has collected the cheque(s) in question in good faith, without negligence, and for a customer.

Collection. The receipt, transmission and presentment for payment to a paying agent or banker of a bill, draft, cheque or other instrument by a collecting banker for a customer, and the subsequent direction of the resulting funds into the customer's account. *See also* Special Clearance.

Co-Manager. Bank ranking next after the lead manager in the marketing of a new issue.

Combine. A permanent or temporary association of two or more firms or companies for business purposes; an association of persons formed to control the course of trade, especially in relation to prices; a cartel, a trust.

Combined Transport. The carriage of goods by at least two modes of transport.

Comme il faut. Correct, proper.

Commerce. Trade, traffic, buying and selling, the interchange of commodities between nations or individuals, all services which exist to assist the carrying on of trade, such as banking, insurance and transport.

Commerce de Transit. Trade between two countries passing through an intermediary in a third country.

Commercial Bill. A bill drawn against a commercial transaction. The expression is also used to cover all bills other than Treasury bills.

Commercial Intelligence Department. A department in a bank or large organisation which provides information for customers or traders on the conditions of trade in various countries, or provides reports on buyers at home or overseas.

Commercial Invoice. One which describes the goods, price and shipping terms.

Commission. An allowance made to a factor or agent; a percentage, a charge. *See also* Acceptance Commission; Exchange Commission.

Commission Agent. A person who buys and sells goods for another, receiving a percentage for the contracts he has arranged.

Commission de Transfert. The charge paid by the recipient of a payment made abroad.

Commissioner for Oaths. A solicitor legally authorised to administer oaths.

Commission on Current Accounts. A charge made by bankers keeping current accounts which do not maintain a sufficiently profitable average cleared credit balance.

Commission sur le Chiffres d'Affaires. Bank commission based on the use made of an account.

Committee. A board elected or deputed to examine, consider and report on any business referred to them; the executive body of an unincorporated society.

Committee of Inspection. A committee appointed by resolution of creditors for the purpose of superintending the administration of a bankrupt's property by the trustee, or of a company's winding-up by the liquidator.

Committee of London Clearing Bankers. A body consisting of the Chairmen of the Clearing Banks which constitutes a forum for discussion of matters of common interest, which acts as a medium for the circulation downwards to the clearing banks of governmental directives and instructions, and which also communicates upwards to the Treasury any requests, suggestions or recommendations which the committee members as representatives of their banking organisations may wish to make.

Committee to Review the Functioning of Financial Institutions, 54 Parliament Street, London S.W.1. A committee to enquire into the role and functioning of the financial institutions of the City of London, under the chairmanship of the former Prime Minister, Sir Harold Wilson. The membership, announced on 6 January 1977, was taken equally from the City, industry, the trade unions, and academics, and numbers seventeen in all. The committee is in response to the demands of the *Tribune* left-wing Socialist group that banking and insurance institutions should be nationalised. It will consider the possible extension of the public sector as well as the provision of funds for trade and industry, and may deem it necessary to define investment priorities for financial institutions.

Common Carrier. A transport organisation obliged by law to carry any goods offered to them at a reasonable charge for delivery to any destination served by the carrier. The goods had to be delivered in an undamaged state; if they were damaged the negligence of the carrier was assumed.

Common Law. The unification, by the itinerant justices of Henry II, of the varying systems of law prevailing in different parts of the country into a single coherent and consistent body of rules. Common law is sometimes contrasted with Equity, a system of law developed in the Court of Chancery based on principles of fairness and justice, or with statute law, which is law passed by Parliament.

Common Market. An association of European states formed for commercial and political reasons. Its aims are a common currency, the abolition of customs duties, the setting up of a common agricultural policy, and freedom for citizens of member states to travel without restriction within the Community. The U.K. joined the Common Market nations, known as the European Economic Community, in 1973. The Community consists of West Germany, France, Belgium, Italy, the Netherlands, Luxembourg, Denmark, Eire and the United Kingdom.

Commonwealth Banks. Canadian and Australian banks having offices in London, but with headquarters abroad.

Commorientes. The name of a presumption of law, in cases where two or more persons die in circumstances which make it uncertain who was the last to die, that the deaths occurred in order of seniority.

Communauté Economique Européen (C.E.E.). See Common Market.

Company. A number of persons associated together by interest or for carrying on business, a corporation. A limited company incorporated under the Companies Acts must have a Memorandum and Articles of Association. The Memorandum contains, in its objects, a list of the legal powers of the company. The Articles are a collection of rules for the internal conduct of the company. A certificate of incorporation, issued by the Registrar of Companies, is the legal birth certificate of the company. In the case of public companies, a trading certificate is also required. When a company wishes to borrow from its banker, a resolution should be passed by the directors or by the company in general meeting, whichever is appropriate, authorising the advance and naming the security to be offered, and a copy of this resolution should be furnished to the banker. The company exists in law as a being in its own right. Limited companies are built around the principle of limited liability. A shareholder in a limited company can lose the value of his shares, but beyond that he has no liability for the debts of the company. *See also* Close Company; Holding Company; Limited Company; One-man Company; Parent Company; Private Company; Public Company; Statutory Company; Subsidiary Company; Trading Company; Unlimited Company; Unregistered Company.

Company Limited by Guarantee. A company in which the liability of the shareholders for the debts of the company is limited to the amount they guarantee to pay in the event of the company's being wound up. *See also* Limited Company; Registration of Charges.

Company Limited by Shares. A company in which the liability of the shareholders for the debts of the company is limited to the amount of their shareholding.

Company Meetings. *See* Annual General Meeting; Extraordinary General Meeting; Statutory Meeting.

Compensatory Damages. Damages awarded to compensate a plaintiff for his loss.

Competition and Credit Control (C.C.C.). The name of a document produced in May 1971, by the Bank of

England, setting out a new system of financial control which would allow freer competition between the banks, while at the same time allowing the authorities to exercise a comprehensive control over the national credit. All banks were to be included in the scheme, the merchant and overseas banks along with the clearing banks. Some measure of competition was also to be introduced into the discount houses' bidding for Treasury bills. The basic policy points were put into operation as from September 1971. These were (1) Quantitative directives to the banks would end. (2) Banks and discount houses would abandon their mutual agreements on various rates so as to allow for freer competition and their greater efficiency. (3) Bank overdraft, loan and seven-day deposit rates were no longer to be linked with Bank Rate (now replaced by minimum lending rate), but each bank would calculate them by reference to its own "base" rate, which it would vary as it wished. (4) Instead of keeping a liquidity ratio of 28%, banks would maintain day by day a uniform minimum reserve asset ratio of 12½% of its eligible liabilities. Cash in tills was no longer to count as a reserve asset. (5) Reserve assets and special deposits would be calculated as percentages of eligible liabilities. (6) London Clearing Banks must keep about 1½% of their eligible liabilities in cash at the Bank of England. *See also* Eligible Liabilities; Qualitative Directives; Quantitative Directives; Reserve Assets; Special Deposits. A similar scheme with a reserve asset ratio of 10% was applied to deposit taking finance houses.

Composition. The adjustment of a debt, etc., by compensation mutually agreed upon by debtor and creditor; the amount so accepted.

Composition with Creditors. A payment by a debtor of some or all of the debts owing, by instalments or on deferred terms. Such an arrangement must be agreed to by the creditors. A liquidator may make a similar arrangement with company creditors. *See also* Arrangement with Creditors or Members.

Compos Mentis. Of sound mind.

Compound Arbitrage. Dealings in foreign currencies involving more than one centre when a free market exists in foreign exchange.

Compound Interest. Interest on the principal and also on the added interest as it falls due. A banker paying interest on deposit should always credit it to the current account, if there is one.

Compound Settlement. *See* Settled Land.

Comprehensive Policy. One covering all risks except Acts of God.

Comptabilité de Gestion. Management accountancy.

Comptable. See Accountant.

Comptant. For immediate payment, a transaction for cash.

Compte. See Account.

Compte Ancien. A closed current account.

Compte Courant. A current account on which the account holder may draw his money whenever he wants it.

Compte d'Accord. An account managed by a bank for a foreign correspondent domiciled in a country with which a system of regulated payments is in force.

Compte de Chèque. A banking account for which a cheque book has been issued.

Compte de Pertes et Profits. Profit and loss account.

Compte Joint, Conjoint. See Joint Account.

Compte Nouveau. New account; the present currency of a running account, as opposed to an old account already closed.

Compte Provisoire. An account held by a bank in the name of a foreign correspondent on which are recorded those transactions which, because of the regulations in force in the correspondent's country, cannot be authorised by exchange control.

Compte Rendu. An account rendered, a detailed account, especially of a meeting, lecture, etc.

Compte-Salaire. A bank account of an employee to which the employer regularly pays his salary direct. The salaried account presents most of the characteristics of the ordinary current account (withdrawals, standing orders, cheques, etc.), some banks additionally allowing overdrafts.

Compulsory Liquidation or Winding-up. The winding-up by the court of a company's affairs. A petition for winding-up may be presented by a creditor, the company itself, a contributory, or the Department of Trade where there is fraud. The company may be wound up (1) where it has by special resolution resolved that the company be wound up by the court; (2) where default is made in delivering the statutory report to the Registrar or in holding the statutory meeting; (3) where the company does not commence its business within a year from its incorporation or suspends its business for a whole year; (4) where the number of members is reduced, in the case of a private company, below two, or in the case of any other company, below seven; (5) where the company is unable to pay its debts; (6) where the court is of the opinion that it is just and equitable that the company should be wound up. The court hears the winding-up petition and may make a winding-up order. The winding-up commences at the date of the petition. The Official Receiver becomes provisional liquidator until some other liquidator is appointed. Creditors must prove their debts by affidavit, giving particulars of the debt and stating whether it is secured or not.

Condition. A stipulation, an agreement, a term of the contract; that on which anything depends; in land law, the specification of some event which, if it takes place during the time for which an estate has already been limited to continue, will bring that estate to an end.

Conditional Acceptance. See Qualified Acceptance.

Conditional Indorsement. An indorsement where the indorser has attached a condition to his indorsement. Such a condition may be disregarded by the paying banker. As between indorser and indorsee the condition is valid and if the indorsee received the proceeds of the bill without the condition being fulfilled, he would have no claim to the money.

Conditional Order. A conditional order upon a banker to pay a certain sum on the fulfilment of a condition, very often that a receipt on the back of the draft shall be signed. Where this condition is clearly stated on the draft, and is addressed to the banker, the draft is not an "unconditional order" and hence not a bill of exchange. Accordingly the banker loses any statutory protection applicable to a bill of exchange, and will only consent to deal with such orders if the customer will give him an indemnity. Even then, the banker does his best to discourage the practice. There is protection for the paying banker under the Cheques Act 1957, s.1, for crossed or open conditional orders or, for crossed orders only, under the Bills of Exchange Act 1882, s.8 (as extended by the Cheques Act 1957, s.5), and for the collecting banker under the Cheques Act 1957, s.4.

Conditional Sale Agreement. An agreement for the sale of goods or land under which the purchase price or part of it is payable by instalments, and the property in the goods or land is to remain in the seller (notwithstanding that the buyer is to be in possession of the goods or land) until such conditions as to the payment of instalments or otherwise as may be specified in the agreement are fulfilled.

Condition Precedent. A stipulation that some event must occur before a contract becomes fixed and binding.

Conditions of Sale. The terms and conditions upon which goods are to be sold at public auction.

Condition Subsequent. The making of a contract conditional upon the happening or the non-happening of a specified event at a later date—e.g. the contract between banker and new customer is made subject to a condition subsequent that a reference satisfactory to the banker shall duly be obtained; in land law, where a condition is annexed to a conveyance, providing that, in case a particular event does or does not happen, or if the grantor or the grantee does or does not do any particular act, the interest shall be defeated—e.g. a grant of land to X "on condition that he never sells out of the family".

Confidential Invoice Factoring. See Factoring.

Confirmed Credit. A credit which is opened by a bank in the importer's country in favour of an exporter in another country is notified to the exporter through a bank in his own country. If this bank adds its confirmation to the notification the exporter will enjoy the benefit of a confirmed credit. Not only has the issuing bank undertaken to pay the exporter against the specified documents, but also a bank in his own country has given a definite undertaking, either that the provisions for payment and acceptance will be duly fulfilled or, in the case of a credit available by negotiation of drafts, that such drafts will be duly negotiated by the confirming bank without recourse to the drawer. The bank thus confirming a credit will charge the opening banker an additional commission.

Confirming House. An agent in one country for a buyer in another country. His function is to assist in the trouble-free shipment of the goods purchased by the overseas buyer and to pay for them promptly.

Connaissement. See Bill of Lading.

Conseil d'Administration. Board of Directors.

Conseil de Prud'hommes. Board of Arbitration.

Consensus ad Idem. See Agreement.

Consideration. The price paid. The term has been defined in relation to the law of contract as "some right, interest, profit or benefit accruing to one party, or some forbearance, detriment, loss, or responsibility given, suffered or undertaking by the other".

Consign. To give, transfer or deliver in a formal manner, to entrust goods to a carrier for transport by rail, air or sea.

Consignee. The person to whom goods are consigned.

Consignment. The act of consigning, the goods consigned.

Consignment Note. A form describing and particularising goods to be sent by rail, addressed by the consignor to the railway company, requesting and authorising it to deliver the goods to the named consignee at the address stated.

Consignor. The person who consigns goods.

Consolidate. To form into a compact and solid mass, to strengthen, to bring into close union, to combine.

Consolidated Annuities, Consols. British Government securities, consolidated into a single stock in 1751, bearing interest at 3% (now 2½%).

Consolidated Balance Sheet. The balance sheet of a parent company, in which are found figures of the parent company itself plus all the reserves, balances on profit and loss accounts, and fixed and floating assets and liabilities of all the subsidiaries, shown in total with no particulars and no breakdown. All unrealised profits on inter-group trading, and all inter-company balances, are eliminated before the figures are grossed up. The consolidated balance sheet will show details of minority interests, and these will also appear in the consolidated profit and loss account. If the cost of the shares acquired by the parent company exceeds the share of net assets acquired this will give rise to a figure for goodwill on acquisition: if the cost is less, to a capital reserve. *See also* Group Accounts.

Consolidated Fund. A national fund for the payment of certain public charges, first formed in 1786 by consolidating the aggregate, general and South Sea funds, to which the Irish Exchequer was added in 1816; now the fund of the National Exchequer into which is paid revenue from Customs and Excise, Income Tax, succession duty, etc.

Consolidation of Mortgages. Where one mortgagor has given several mortgages on different properties to the same lender, he is entitled to redeem any one of them without at the same time repaying the amounts owing on other mortgages. This may not suit the lender, who may find that the mortgage best secured is redeemed first, leaving him with less desirable security for the other mortgages. He may therefore insist, at the time of making the loans, or any of them, on retaining the right to consolidate—that is, he may refuse to allow the borrower to redeem any one mortgage without at the same time redeeming all the others. Such a right usually appears in any bank's form of mortgage, but it is a right which has to be expressly given in the mortgage deeds, or in one of them.

Consolider. To turn a floating debt into a fixed debt at the longest possible term.

Consols. See Consolidated Annuities.

Consommateur. See Consumer.

Consortium. An agreement between several countries or large organisations for mutual assistance and joint action, especially in financial matters; an association of large or international banks for the purpose of financing major undertakings. Such consortia arrange, manage and underwrite international bond issues, assist with mergers and

Constructive Trust. ...acquisitions involving companies in different countries, provide financial advice to multi-national companies, and arrange and syndicate term loans needed to finance major projects on a world-wide basis.

Constructive Trust. A trust imposed by law independently of any person's intention.

Consular Invoice. An invoice issued in differing formats by different countries, to be legalised by the consul of the importing country and required by the Customs of that country to confirm such details as the origin of the goods.

Consumer. The one who, or that which, consumes or uses up; the purchaser of an article; for the purpose of the Consumer Credit Act 1974, any individual or unincorporated body to whom credit is extended under a regulated agreement.

Consumer Credit. Credit from banks, usually by way of personal loan, or hire-purchase finance. In the U.K. comprehensive safeguards for the credit consumer were provided by the Consumer Credit Act 1974. The act is principally concerned with credit transactions up to £5,000, in the personal sector only. Bank lending comes within the scope of the Act, as well as hire purchase and credit sale agreements, credit cards, private loans and mortgages. The true cost of a facility must in all cases be disclosed, and written agreements will be required—it is now clear that this will not apply to overdrafts. Certainly many security forms will have to be re-written. The act is coming into force by stages as regulations are published.

Consumer Credit Agreement. A personal credit agreement by which the creditor provides the debtor with credit not exceeding £5,000.

Consumer Hire Agreement. An agreement made by a person with an individual (the "hirer") for the bailment of (or in Scotland the hiring of) goods to be hired, being an agreement which (1) is not a hire-purchase agreement, and (2) is capable of subsisting for more than three months, and (3) does not require the hirer to make payments exceeding £5,000.

Consumer Spending. The current expenditure of individuals including purchases of so-called "consumer durable" articles such as television, radios, washing machines and machinery for use in the home.

Container Bill of Lading. A bill of lading issued by a container operator; a document which in itself is not a bill of lading, *e.g.* a forwarder's receipt evidencing the dispatch of goods in one container in a groupage shipment.

Contango. The charge made by a stockbroker on the Stock Exchange for allowing a bull transaction to be carried over to the next settlement.

Contango Day. The first of the Stock Exchange settling days, and the day on which arrangements are made for the carrying over of transactions to the next account. Also known as *Carrying Over Day*, *Continuation Day* or *Making Up Day*.

Contemnor. One who is held to be in contempt of court.

Contemptuous Damages. Damages of a trifling amount where a plaintiff's claim, though proved, has little merit; an expression of the court's opinion of the plaintiff's worth.

Contingency Plan. A plan to deal with a chance event, a possibility. Thus at branch level there should be a contingency plan to deal with a shortage of staff through sickness, if staff departments can provide no relief, by which the duties will be re-arranged among the available staff. At the corporate level the bank, or any company, should have plans to meet any contingencies which can be envisaged, but particularly one for financial emergencies. Companies should estimate ahead their working capital resources and cash flow levels, and should then provide for the possibility of unexpected shortfalls. Their contingency plans might in this case include a reduction in planned output with a corresponding reduction in staff, the use of uncommitted reserves, liquidation, or perhaps sale and release of some assets, factoring of debts, etc.

Contingent. Liable to happen, but not certain to do so.

Contingent. (*Fr.*) *See* Quota.

Contingent Account. An account to provide for unforeseen or uncertain liabilities.

Contingent Annuity. An annuity which is payable only in the event of the happening of some uncertain event.

Contingent d'Importation. Import quota.

Contingent Interest. An interest in property which will become vested only upon the happening of an uncertain event, *e.g.* the interest of a minor who is left under a will or settlement a capital sum provided that he or she attains majority.

Contingent Liability. A liability which can exist definitely only upon the happening of some uncertain event, *e.g.* the liability of an endorser upon a bill of exchange, or of a guarantor upon the guarantee which he has given.

Contingent Remainder. A reversionary interest where the passing of the benefit is made to depend upon the happening of an uncertain event, *e.g.* the attaining by the remainderman of his twenty-fifth birthday. If he dies before that day, the benefit passes to some other person.

Continuation Day. *See* Contango Day.

Continuing Security. A security taken to secure an account which fluctuates or changes from day to day, as for example, a current account. The security will then be good to secure the "ultimate balance" on the account. A form of guarantee/indemnity, for example, will expressly state that it is a continuing security: if this were not done the guarantee would be good for the balance on the day the guarantee was taken, but would thereafter be subject to the operation of the Rule in Clayton's Case, to the detriment of the bank, as the current account continued to operate.

Conto Suo. The account of a foreign bank held in the books of an indigenous bank in the currency of the latter. *See also Vostro* Account.

Contract. An agreement between bargaining parties, which is intended to be legally enforceable. The parties must be of full contractual capacity. Where a special formality is required by law (*e.g.* writing), that formality must be complied with. To be enforceable at law, a contract must either be supported by consideration, or be under seal. *See also* Bilateral Contract; Executed Contract; Executory Contract; Open Contract; Simple Contract; Specialty Contract; Standard Contract; Unilateral Contract.

Contract Note. When an order to buy or sell any stock or shares on the Stock Exchange has been complied with, the broker sends a contract note to the client giving particulars of the transaction and its cost or proceeds.

Contractual Saving. Money saved as a result of agreed deductions from wage or salary payments, *e.g.* the S.A.Y.E. scheme.

Contrat. *See* Contract.

Contributory. A person who, as an existing or past member of a company, is liable in certain circumstances to contribute to the assets of the company if it is wound up. This liability exists only in respect of the amount unpaid on shares held or amount guaranteed.

Contributory Negligence. *See* Negligence.

Contributory Negligence of Plaintiff. Where a defendant is found negligent, the damages he will have to pay may be reduced if it is found that the plaintiff was also negligent, and that his negligence contributed in some part to the loss or damage complained of. This doctrine is well known in the case of collisions between vehicles or ships, but was not applied to banking until 1971, because prior to that the relevant statute—the Law Reform (Contributory Negligence) Act 1945—was thought to apply only to actions for negligence, whereas the banker is sued for conversion. In that year, however, this view was modified, and since then a customer may be partly liable, in cases where a banker is found to be negligent, if he has by his actions contributed to the loss—as, for example, by recklessly issuing blank signed cheque forms, or by failing to exercise proper supervision over his clerk or agent.

Contributory Pension. A pension paid to a worker on his retirement, towards which he, and his employer, have contributed during the employee's working life. The amount of the pension depends upon the number of contributions paid and upon the average salary over a number of years, or upon the final salary.

Control. To regulate, to check, to restrain; authority or power; any test or check, especially in an experiment, to provide a standard for future experiments; in a bank, a system of listing and detailing all debits and credits passing through an office in the course of a day's work, whether handwritten or machined by a control machine, or based on a system which photographs each voucher as it passes through the machine. *See also* Proofing Machine.

Contrôle Budgétaire. *See* Budgetary Control.

Contrôle de Production. Process control.

Contrôle de Qualité. Quality control.

Contrôle des Changes. Exchange control.

Controller. One who controls; a public functionary appointed to oversee the accounts of others. For the purposes of the Consumer Credit Act 1974, "controller", in relation to a body corporate, means a person (1) in accordance with whose directions or instructions the directors of the body corporate or of another body corporate which is its controller (or any of them) are accustomed to act, or (2) who, either alone or with any associate or associates, is entitled to exercise, or control the exercise of, one third or more of the voting power at any general meeting of the body corporate or of another body corporate which is its controller.

Controlling Interest. The interest held in a company by a person or by another firm or company who/which holds shares in it carrying at least 51% of the voting rights.

Controls. Regulations imposed by government in economic and political fields, usually most rigorous in time of war, when rationing and direction of labour may be imposed. In peace-time there may be exchange control, import restrictions, control of investment, prices and wages control, directives to lending banks, and town and country planning restrictions.

Convention. (*Fr.*) An agreement for the uniform application of certain rules, for example, those by which commission is calculated.

Conversion. A tort committed when one person wrongfully interferes with the property of another in such a way as to show that he denies or is indifferent to the title of that other. It is no defence that the tort is committed innocently. Any banker who collects a cheque for a customer who has a defective title or no title to it commits conversion when he credits the proceeds to his customer's account, and renders himself liable to an action in conversion by the true owner of the cheque. Against this risk he has the statutory protection contained in section 4 of the Cheques Act 1957, if he can comply with the conditions therein, to collect in good faith, for a customer, and without negligence. The word is also used to indicate an operation whereby a Government which has issued stock carrying a high rate of interest is able to repay it on maturity (if interest rates are then lower) by offering in its place a new stock carrying a lower rate of interest, possibly with the inducement of a bonus to the stockholder who exercises his option to convert his holding into the lower paid stock.

Conversion. (*Fr.*) The transformation of a repudiated or time-expired loan stock into a new loan issue. The holder of such stock who does not wish to convert into the new issue in general has the option to demand repayment.

Conversion Forcée. An obligatory conversion of an old stock into a new one, where holders who do not wish to convert are not given the option to demand repayment.

Conversion Rights. The rights of holders of government stocks to convert into a stock with a lower interest rate of return where some preference or inducement is attached to the offer (as described above), or the rights of debenture holders where there is a provision that within a specified period they may convert them into the ordinary shares of the company. *See also* Convertible Stocks or Securities.

Conversion Stocks. Government stocks which have been offered to holders of other stocks, due for repayment, as an alternative to receiving cash payments.

Convertibilité. *See* Convertibility.

Convertibility. A state of affairs where traders in goods and services between countries can make or receive payments in their own currencies at a rate of exchange fixed within narrow limits. Convertibility is associated with an absence of exchange restrictions and can be sustained only by countries with satisfactory balances of payments.

Convertible. Exchangeable for another kind of thing. When used of a currency it indicates that the currency is freely exchangeable into any other currency.

Convertible Bond. A bond which, on demand by the bearer, can be exchanged for a holding in shares.

Convertible Paper Currency. Paper money which can be exchanged for metal to its face value at the central bank on demand.

Convertible Stocks or Securities. (1) Securities which may readily be turned into cash. (2) Securities having the right to transfer from one form of holding to another, *e.g.* fixed interest securities that are exchangeable at a later date into ordinary shares on pre-determined terms.

Conveyance. The act of conveying real property from one person to another; the deed by which it is transferred. *See also* Voluntary Conveyance.

Conveyance on Sale. Every instrument, and every decree or order of any court or of any commissioners, whereby any property, or any estate or interest in any property, upon the sale thereof is transferred to or vested in a purchaser, or any other person on his behalf or by his direction.

Conveyancing. The act or profession of drawing up deeds for the conveyance of real property.

Co-ownership. The ownership of property by more than one person. Such co-ownership may be by co-parceners, tenants in common, or joint tenants.

Co-parceners. Co-heirs to whom land devolved where a tenant in fee simple or a tenant in tail died intestate leaving only female heirs, whereupon the females succeeded jointly to the estate. This method of inheritance was abolished in 1925, and co-parcenary can now arise only in the case of entailed interests.

Co-partnership. A system of management by which employees are entitled to a voice in the management of a concern and a share in any profits.

Copyhold. A tenure of land where the tenant's right is evidence by a copy of the rolls made by the steward of his lord's court; property held by such tenure. In the U.K. copyhold was converted into freehold with effect from the beginning of 1926.

Copyright. The exclusive right of the author of a literary or artistic production, or his heirs, to publish or sell copies of his works. This right endures for the term of the author's life and for fifty years thereafter.

Coram Judice. In the presence of the judge, before the court.

Corbeille. The environs of the *Bourse* where members are to be found during the sittings to carry through their bargains; the old name for the *Parquet. See also* Coulisse.

Corner. To buy up the whole existing stock of a commodity in order to raise or control the price of it; to establish a monopoly.

Corporation. A united body; the authorities of a town or city; a legal, municipal, mercantile or professional association authorised to act, plead or sue as a single person, governed by its own bye-laws, and electing its office bearers from its own body; a company or association for commercial or other purposes, created by an Act of Parliament or by a charter granted by the Crown.

Corporation Aggregate. One consisting of many persons, as, for example, a corporation of a town.

Corporation Bills. Under the Local Government Act 1972, which came into force on 1 April 1974, local authorities, subject to rate income and Treasury consent, may issue bills for periods not exceeding twelve months. Corporation bills up to *six months* qualify as reserve assets for United Kingdom banks, and are eligible for re-discount at the Bank of England.

Corporation Sole. One consisting of a single individual and his successors, *e.g.* a bishop.

Corporation Tax. A tax payable by a company. In the U.K. there is a single tax on company profits and income, including capital gains, which applies to all transactions of any particular company. The tax is at a single rate on all profits wherever arising, whether distributed or undistributed. In the case of "smaller" companies (companies with profits below a certain figure), however, a lower rate is payable.

Corporeal. Tangible, visible, physical.

Corporeal Hereditaments. Tangible, visible property, such as land itself and houses built on it, which may be passed on to one's heirs; hence, an interest in land possession, a right to enjoy the possession of land. *See also* Incorporeal Hereditaments.

Corpus Iuris. The body of the law.

Correspondent Bank. A bank in one country which acts when so required for a bank in another country. The relationship is one of agency. The choice of the correspondent bank may depend on its position, or on the amount of business

Corset. A system of non-interest-bearing special deposits related to increases in the bank's interest-bearing eligible liabilities, introduced in December 1973. Banks were to be penalised by the imposition of such special deposits if the growth in their interest-bearing liabilities exceeded 8% in the first half of 1974. The corset was renewed for a further six months on progressively easier terms for the banks, and was finally discontinued in March 1975. Its effect has been to re-impose quantitative controls without actually calling them that. Thus the system of Competition and Credit Control was preserved in name. The Bank of England reserved the right to re-impose the "corset" at any time, using a new base, and this was in fact done early in 1977.

Cost. The price charged or paid for anything, expenditure of any kind; the evaluation in money terms of the resources, time and labour which have gone into a product. *See also* Distributive Cost; Factor Cost; Fixed Cost; Marginal Cost; Opportunity Cost; Prime Costs; Real Cost; Retail Cost; Wholesale Cost.

Cost Accounting. A system of accounting in which the cost of production at all stages of manufacture is calculated in order to show where useful economy is possible. It is also used as a basis for pricing.

Cost Allocation. The assignment of costs to stages in the productive sequence in the proportions in which they have attracted them.

Cost and Freight (C. & F.). A contractual term indicating that the price quoted to the buyer includes transit costs. The cost of insurance must be paid by the buyer.

Costing. The system of calculating cost of production. *See also* Theory of Comparative Costs.

Cost, Insurance, Freight (C.I.F.). A contractual term indicating that the price quoted to the buyer includes transit costs and insurance.

Cost of Living. *See* General Index of Retail Prices.

Cost of Living Bonus. An addition to basic pay made by reference to the General Index of Retail Prices.

Cost of Production Theory. The theory that the price of an article depends upon the cost of material and labour used in making it, plus a profit margin. The theory approaches the problem from the supply side and does not explain why the price of finished goods should rise long after the goods were made.

Cost Price. The wholesale, as opposed to the retail, price.

Cost Push Theory of Inflation. The theory that rises in wages and in other manufacturing costs lead, after a time lag, to price rises, which in turn lead, after a further time lag, to further rises in wages.

Costs. The expenses of a law suit.

Cost Unit. The amount or quantity of goods upon which a cost assessment can conveniently be made.

Cotation. On the *Bourse*, acceptance of an application for a quotation.

Coulisse. The old name given to the unofficial market on the Paris stock exchange or *Bourse*. At the present time the name has all but disappeared, following the amalgamation of the two markets.

Council for Mutual Economic Assistance (Comecon). A body composed of the Russian bloc countries and including the Soviet Union, Bulgaria and Rumania, with Cuba and Yugoslavia as associate members. There is a joint convertible currency backed by gold.

Count. To number, to reckon; a charge in an indictment.

Counter. The opposite, the contrary; a raised bench across which goods are sold; the fixture in a bank which divides the office space from the public space, across which customers pay in and draw out. **Over the Counter.** *See Marché Hors Cote.* **Under the Counter.** Goods in short supply offered to privileged customers at an enhanced price.

Counter-claim. A claim set up by the defendant in a suit to counter that of the plaintiff.

Counterfeit. To coin, to imitate in base metal; forged, made in imitation with intent to be passed off as genuine.

Counterfeit Coin. Coin not authorised by the state. It may be detected by its appearance, its malleability, and its tone when thrown down, which will be dull. Silver or gold coins lend themselves to counterfeiting because of their intrinsic value, but modern cupro-nickel coins do not.

Counterfeit Note. A forged banknote.

Counter-foil. A perforated slip attached to a cheque, receipt, dividend, interest warrant, share certificate, etc., retained by the issuer, on which to note particulars of the instrument issued. The word is used in a specialised sense in the case of dividend and interest payments.

Counter-Indemnity. An indemnity given by a customer to his banker when the latter has given an indemnity to a third party at the customer's request.

Countermand. An order contrary to or revoking a previous order.

Countermand of Payment. An order to a banker from a customer to stop payment of a cheque which the customer has issued. The customer may give this over the telephone but must subsequently confirm in writing. The bank must be told the number of the cheque, and preferably also the date, amount, and name of the payee.

Countermark. An additional mark for identification or certification, put upon goods or safe custody articles belonging to several persons that they may not be opened except in the presence of all; the mark of the Goldsmith's Company to attest the quality of the metal.

Counterpart. A correspondent part, a duplicate or copy; one of two corresponding copies of an instrument, especially the copy of a lease, signed by the lessee, received by the lessor.

Countersign. To attest the correctness of a document by adding an additional signature, to ratify, as where a company customer may instruct its bankers to honour its cheques if signed by a director and countersigned by the secretary.

Countervailing Credit. An old name for a "back to back" credit. The countervailing credit is the "prime" credit, or the first credit to be opened.

Counting House. The room or office in business houses set aside for the keeping of accounts.

Coupon. A detachable certificate for the payment of interest on bonds. When the time for the payment of interest has arrived the appropriate coupon must be cut off and presented for payment to the bond-issuing authority. A banker is responsible for doing this on his customer's behalf where he is the authorised depositary of his customer's bonds. *See also* High Coupon.

Couponbogen. *See* Coupon Sheet.

Coupon Sheet. A sheet of coupons issued with, and usually attached to, a bearer bond so that each coupon may be cut off and forwarded for payment of interest at the right time.

Coupures. The unit shares which together make up an issue.

Cours. Quotation on the *Bourse*, market value.

Cours d'Application. The quoted rates on the *Bourse* which are applied by the broker to the purchases and sales of his clients.

Cours de la Clôture. After a session of the *Bourse*, the last rate at which a bargain was struck, for any given stock; the closing rate.

Cours de la Demande. On the *Bourse*, the rate at which stocks and shares are bid.

Cours de l'Offre. On the *Bourse*, the rate at which stocks and shares are offered; the offer or asking rate.

Cours d'Emission. The price at which a new issue is offered.

Cours d'Intervention. On the *Bourse*, the rate whose level is affected by the intervention of parties interested in influencing the *Bourse* quotation of any particular stock.

Cours d'Ouverture. The opening price of any stock on the *Bourse*.

Cours du Change. Exchange rate.

Cours Libre. The rate as determined by supply and demand, a free rate.

Cours Officiel. The official exchange rate.

Courtage. Commission, brokerage.

Courtage-Konvention. An agreement as to the uniform handling of certain transactions by banks.

Courtier. Stock exchange broker.

Courtier en Valeurs Mobilières. An intermediary in transactions on the *Bourse*, particularly *coulisse* brokers of the Paris *Bourse*, as opposed to the official members of the *Bourse*, who were admitted to the floor of the House. These brokers have in general become either approved members or approved agents. *See also* Half Commission Man.

Court Terme. Short term, one month up to one year.

Coût. *See* Cost.

Coût, Assurance, Frêt (C.A.F.). Cost, insurance, freight (C.I.F.) (*q.v.*).

Coût de la Vie. Cost of living.

Coûte que Coûte. Cost what it may.

Coût par Facteur de Production. See Factor Cost.

Couvert. Covered, secured, guaranteed.

Couverture des Billets en Circulation. The gold reserves of the central bank of issue, stocks of foreign currency held in support of the note issue; today in practice a satisfactory relation between the total of the convertible resources for settling international payments and the total of the banknotes in circulation. *See also* Reserve.

Covenant. A mutual and solemn agreement, a contract, a compact, a written agreement; to agree to do a certain thing, *e.g.* to make periodic payments to a charity; any promise touching and concerning land that is contained in a tenancy agreement made otherwise than by deed. *See also* Deed of Covenant.

Cover. To be enough to defray; to protect by insurance; sufficient funds to meet a liability or insure against loss; security deposited by a customer at a bank against a borrowing; a deposit of cash or marketable securities by a client with a broker, to protect him against loss.

Cover for Dividend. The profit available for distribution by way of dividend. If the profit is twice the sum actually paid out by way of dividend the dividend is said to be "twice covered". Both amounts are usually quoted after corporation tax, but the dividend is taken before deduction of income tax.

Cover Note. A document issued by an insurance company indemnifying the insured person against any damage or loss suffered in the interval between the acceptance of the proposal and the issue of the insurance policy.

Crawling Peg. A proposed method of adjustments to the system of fixed international currency parities which were established following the Bretton Woods agreement of 1944. It was recognised that some countries might experience considerable strains by holding too long to a parity which was becoming untenable. The crawling peg would make for small and frequent adjustments which would seem less drastic and would upset the system to a lesser degree. The adjustments would be automatic, and would, it was claimed, prevent speculators jobbing against a currency. In the end it seemed more logical to let currencies find their own level. It could be said that where a currency is floating the crawling peg is operating every day.

Créance Inscrite au Livre de la Dette. The cover provided for a state loan. It is not evidenced by a document of title, but is merely inscribed in the record of public debt.

Créancier. Creditor.

Credit. A reputation for solvency; the time given for payment of goods sold on trust; trust reposed with regard to property handed over on the promise of payment at a future time; anything due to any person; the side of an account in which payment is entered, opposed to debit; an entry on this side of a payment received. For the purposes of the Consumer Credit Act 1974 "credit" includes a cash loan, and any other form of financial accommodation. Where credit is provided otherwise than in sterling it shall be treated for the purposes of the Act as provided in sterling of an equivalent amount. *See also* Branch Credit; Buyer Credit; Clean Credit; Fixed-sum Credit; Letter of Credit; Payroll Credit; Running Account Credit; Supplier Credit.

Credit Advice. An arrangement between banks whereby a customer can cash cheques at another branch or bank from the one where he keeps his account; a notification from a bank to a customer advising him of the receipt of a payment which has been placed to the credit of his account.

Crédit à la Consommation. Credit allowed to the purchaser of a consumer article. *See also* Consumer Credit.

Crédit à la Production. Trading credit, credit used in the business of the borrower to finance the expansion of production.

Credit Bank. *See* Agricultural Credit Bank.

Credit Brokerage. The effecting of introductions of (1) individuals desiring to obtain credit, or (2) individuals desiring to obtain credit to finance the acquisition or provision of dwellings occupied or to be occupied by themselves or their relatives, and prepared to offer the security of land, or (3) individuals desiring to obtain goods on hire, to businesses likely to be able to meet these requirements, or to other credit-brokers.

Crédit-Cadre. Credit granted to finance a line of exports up to a certain maximum, usually made available to the government or the central bank of the importing country. Favourable conditions are granted both in respect of the term and the repayment: the credit is essentially intended to assist the purchase of the means of production by countries already in a fair stage of development.

Credit Card. A piece of plastic about 85 mm by 54 mm, bearing the name and computer number of the holder and the period of availability. The holder must sign it. The best known cards in the U.K. are Barclaycard, Access, Diners' Club and American Express. With the credit card, goods can be bought in a shop, petrol bought at a service station, hotel bills paid, air fares met, etc., in many parts of the world. The retailer sends in his account to the card company, which sends monthly statements out to each card holder. Interest starts to run, currently at 2% per month, between twenty-five and sixty days after the statement is sent out. Diners' Club and American Express charge an entrance fee, but allow unlimited credit, to be paid for on receipt of the account (unless a loan is agreed). Access and Barclaycard have no entrance fee, but impose a credit limit of £100–£500.

Credit Clearing. The system of clearing was extended to credits in 1960, and it now handles credit transfers, standing order payments, etc., all brought together under the heading of money transfer services. The *Bankers' Automated Clearing Services* are part of the Credit Clearing, although entries passing through B.A.C.S. are not included in statistics for either debit or credit clearing. The computer processes magnetic tapes containing details of standing orders, bank Giro credits, payroll credits and automated items, prepared and sent to the Clearing House by the clearing banks and by company customers who have their own computers. (B.A.C.S. is located at Edgware but there is a facility for delivery of tapes to a centre in the City.)

Crédit Construction. Credit for the finance of new building, secured by an entry in the land registry giving a charge on real security. Once the building is completed, the credit is funded by a mortgage.

Crédit d'Acceptation. See Acceptance Credit.

Crédit d'Aval. See Aval.

Crédit de Cautionnement. Credit granted against no primary security but covered by one or more guarantees.

Crédit de Courrier. Very short term credit, for example for one or two days, repayment being by return of post.

Crédit de Rembours. An acceptance credit financing imported goods against the security of a bill of lading.

Crédit de Transfert. See Credit-Cadre.

Crédit d'Exploitation. See Credit à la Production.

Crédit Documentaire. See Documentary Credit.

Crédit en Blanc. See Crédit Personnel.

Créditeur. See Creditor.

Crédit Garanti par Cession de Créances. Credit granted against the security of an assignment of monies due. The assignment is notified to the debtor.

Crédit Hypothécaire. Credit granted against the security of real property.

Crédit Immobilier. See Credit Hypothécaire.

Credit Insurance. A means of insuring the payment of commercial debts against the risk of non-payment by the buyer because of his insolvency, or for some other reason.

Credit Limit. For the purposes of the Consumer Credit Act 1974, the maximum debit balance which, under the credit agreement, is allowed to stand on an account during a given period (disregarding any term of the agreement allowing that maximum to be exceeded merely temporarily). *See* section 10 of the Act.

Crédit Lombard. A loan secured by a charge on easily negotiable security (stock exchange securities or goods).

Crédit Mobilier. See Crédit Réel.

Credit Note. A document sent to a person advising him that his account is credited with a stated amount in respect of goods returned, or when any discount or allowance is made, or when there has been overpayment.

Creditor. One to whom a debt is due. A

banker is a creditor when a current account is overdrawn, the customer is a creditor when a current account is in credit. For the purposes of the Consumer Credit Act 1974, "creditor" means the person providing credit under a consumer credit agreement or the person to whom his rights and duties under the agreement have passed by assignment or operation of law, and, in relation to a prospective consumer credit agreement, includes the prospective creditor. *See also* Debtor; Sundry Creditors.

Creditor's Voluntary Winding-Up. *See* Voluntary Liquidation.

Crédit Personnel. Credit granted unsecured: the character of the borrower is of the essence.

Credit Rating. An opinion as to the credit-worthiness of a trader, obtained by a party who is thinking of entering into a contract with the trader, or may be supplying goods to him. The opinion may be obtained, through the inquirer's bank, from the trader's bank, or the trader may give trade references, or the inquirer may use the services of a special inquiry agent, or he may consult a register published by an established inquiry and credit rating agency.

Crédit Réel. Credit granted against the security of real or personal property.

Credit Reference Agency. For the purposes of the Consumer Credit Act 1974, a person carrying on a business comprising the furnishing of persons with information relevant to the financial standing of individuals, being information collected by the agency for that purpose.

Crédit Saisonnier. Credit for working capital at short term granted in the course of the year to meet a temporary peak in the financial demands of a business; seasonal credit.

Credit-Sale Agreement. An agreement to sell with a term which provides that payment shall be made by instalments. The property in the goods passes at once to the buyer.

Credit Slip (or Paying-in Slip). The form which is filled in to accompany the cash, bills of exchange and cheques which are paid in by a customer to the credit of his account. Each slip should show the name of the account, its computerised number and the date on which the payment in is made. It should list and particularise the detailed items making up the total and should be made out in duplicate and signed or initialled by the customer or his agent. The duplicate should be stamped with the name of the bank and the date and be returned to the customer as a receipt. A credit slip evidencing a payment from a third-party source may be advised to the customer through the post. After they have passed through the customer's account, credit slips should be retained with the customer's vouchers and may be returned to him with his statement.

Credit Squeeze. The name given to a period of credit restriction, when banks are directed to lend only to certain classes of borrowers (qualitative controls) and hire-purchase is made more difficult by the imposition of higher down payments and shorter periods of repayment. Banks may be subjected to special deposits.

Credit Stand-by. Credit, carrying certain specific conditions, put at the disposal of members of the International Monetary Fund who have already exhausted their normal credit resources with this organisation.

Credit Status. *See* Credit Rating.

Credit Token. For the purposes of the Consumer Credit Act 1974, a credit token is a card, check, voucher, coupon, stamp, form, booklet or other document or thing given to an individual by a person carrying on a consumer credit business, who undertakes (1) that on the production of it he will supply cash, goods and services (or any of them) on credit, or (2) that where, on the production of it to a third party, the third party supplies cash, goods and services (or any of them) he will pay the third party for them, in return for payment to him by the individual.

Credit-Token Agreement. A regulated agreement for the provision of credit in connection with the use of a credit token.

Credit Transfer. A system by which any person is enabled to pay in money at any branch of any clearing bank for the account of another person having an account at any other branch of any clearing bank.

Credit Union. A system, popular in North America, by which people with a common bond—membership of the same club, church, tenants' association or trade union—can collaborate to put their savings into a joint fund. Members can then apply to borrow from the fund and make repayments at an annual interest rate of no more than 12%. Northern Ireland has laws which provide for credit unions, but the rest of the United Kingdom does not. There are more than 400 credit unions in Northern Ireland and Eire. The credit union movement came to Britain in 1964, but legal problems have restricted their total to fifty. Under existing legislation they may become a limited company, or come under the Registrar of Friendly Societies, or stay unincorporated. As a limited company the credit union must have permanent officials liable for debts, but most credit unions keep down costs by not having permanent officials. Under the Registrar a credit union could lend only against security provided by the borrower or a third party. Being unincorporated means that many people would hesitate to trust their money to an organisation which is subject to no safeguards or supervision. The National Consumer Council has been pressing Parliament for the last two years to pass legislation which will "give credit unions a legal identity of their own, permit them to make unsecured loans in certain circumstances and provide the framework within which these can be registered and properly supervised". No Bill to this effect has yet appeared, but the government has committed itself to pass suitable legislation when time permits, and it is now expected that this matter will be dealt with in the draft clauses on the Licensing and Supervision of Deposit-Taking Institutions, expected later this year (1978).

Critical Path. In considering the implementation of a new project it is naturally desirable to find the quickest and cheapest way to the required end. It is often possible to reduce to tabular form the various options open, taking into account the stages through which work must pass. Some of these stages may depend on the fulfilment of conditions defined in earlier stages, some may depend on the availability of material or staff at the critical time; cost will always be a relevant consideration. When all the material factors have been reduced to plan form, stage by stage, it may be seen that there are a number of options open to achieve the desired end. The critical path through the data assembled will be one of a number of possible alternatives, but it will be that which offers the quickest, best, and cheapest way of attaining the defined objective.

Cross-Border Leasing. Leasing to a concern in another country not through a subsidiary in that country, but directly.

Crossed Cheque. A cheque bearing across its face an addition of the words "and company" or any abbreviations thereof between two parallel transverse lines, with or without the words "not negotiable"; or two parallel transverse lines simply, with or without the words "not negotiable" (a general crossing); or a cheque bearing across its face an addition of the name of a banker, with or without the words "not negotiable" (a special crossing). A crossed cheque must be collected through a banking account and cannot be cashed across a counter. The crossing therefore constitutes a protection for the drawer, who should always cross cheques which he is intending to send through the post, as a precaution against the cheque falling into wrong hands. *See also* Not Negotiable.

Cross-Firing. Where one person draws a cheque in favour of another, or upon his own account at another bank, and at the same time a similar cheque is drawn by the other person in favour of the first, or by the first on his other account, for the credit of the first account. If the banker mistakenly allows drawings against uncleared effects, the cross-firing will inevitably increase in the amounts for which the cheques are drawn, and will continue until one branch returns a cheque unpaid. At that time the other account will, because of the debiting of the returned cheque, show an overdraft, which will be difficult or impossible to recover. Sometimes the process involves more than two accounts.

Cross Guarantees. Security given for a loan to a parent company or to any subsidiary in a group, which takes the form of a guarantee from each of the other companies in the group. Cross guarantees are particularly appropriate where the banker is lending to more than one company. In the event of a liquidation, the banker will be able to prove against each company for the amount of its individual debt, plus the total of its guarantees on account of all other companies.

Cross Rates. The rates of exchange arrived at by expressing the quotations for any two currencies in terms of a third.

Crown. A coin of the value of 25p, formerly a five-shilling piece; any of several foreign coins.

Crownhold. A tenure of land established by the Leasehold Reform Act 1967 to denote land which has been compulsorily acquired by the Land Commission and regranted by the Crown subject to statutory restrictions.

Cube Cutting. A fraud practised usually by a shipping agent or a manufacturer. The cubic capacity of a cargo is underestimated to the shipping line (so there is less to pay) and over-estimated to the exporter (so he pays more).

Cui Bono. "Who gains by it?"

Cum. With.

Cum Div. Together with the dividend about to be paid. The buyer of stocks or shares sold *"cum div."* takes the benefit of the dividend about to be distributed.

Cum Drawing. When bonds are sold near the time when a periodical drawing is about to take place, there is always a chance that one or more of the bonds included in the sale will fall to be repaid, at par, or at a premium. When such bonds are sold *"cum* drawing", any advantages gained or profit made from such a drawing accrues to the buyer.

Cum Rights. Shares sold *"cum* rights" pass to the buyer not only the shares but also any rights attaching to them, *e.g.* a right to take up further issues.

Cumulative Preference Shares. Those where a deficiency one year is made up later if subsequent yearly profits permit.

Cupro-Nickel. An amalgam of three-quarter parts of copper to one-quarter part of nickel. Post-war currency has been cupro-nickel in place of the earlier silver currency, which has now become too expensive to maintain. The intrinsic value of a cupro-nickel coin is minimal.

Currency. The time during which anything is current, the state of being in use; the circulating medium by which purchases and sales are made; money, gold, silver and copper; banknotes, bills of exchange, cheques. *See also* Foreign Currency; Hard Currency.

Currency Bonds. Bonds issued in a foreign country and repayable in the currency of that country.

Currency of a Bill of Exchange. The period which a bill of exchange has to run before its maturity.

Current Account. *See* Account.

Current Assets. *See* Liquid Assets.

Current Balance. The balance of visible and invisible items in international trade, but not including any movements of capital.

Current Cost Accounting. *See* Inflation Accounting.

Current Liabilities. Debts arising in the normal course of a business which are due for payment within the next twelve months, such as debts due to trade and hire purchase creditors, amounts due to the bank, and taxation payable. In the case of hire purchase creditors, an alternative is to show the liability as a deduction from the asset, even though the ownership has not yet passed to the hirer. Also called *Short-Term Liabilities.*

Curtesy. *See* Tenant by the Curtesy.

Curtilage. The courtyard or land adjacent to a dwelling house and reckoned as forming one enclosure with it; the ground which is used for the comfortable enjoyment of a house or other building, although it has not been marked off or enclosed in any way.

Custodian Trustee. A trustee who takes charge of the property of a trust and is responsible for its safe keeping.

Custom. Fashion, usage, habit, business patronage; long-established practice or usage, which may have the force of law; a source of law; toll, tax or tribute.

Custom Duties. Taxes, levied chiefly on imported goods, but occasionally on some exports.

Customer. As there is no statutory definition of a customer, reliance must be placed on case law definitions. These include (1) "To make a person a customer of the bank there must be either a current or deposit account, or some similar relation." (2) "The relationship of banker and customer begins as soon as money or a cheque is paid in and the bank accepts it and is prepared to open an account." (3) "The word 'customer' signifies a relationship in which duration is not of the essence. A person whose money has been accepted by the banker on the footing that he undertakes to honour cheques up to the amount standing to his credit is a customer of the bank irrespective of whether his connection is of short or long duration." The question of whether a person is a customer in the period between his first contact with the bank and the receipt of the final letter authenticating the reference introduction is not free from doubt. If the reference is satisfactory the person is a customer and probably always has been: if it is not, and no other satisfactory reference can be supplied, the banker will probably decide not to proceed. In this case the person is not a customer and never has been. If in this interval the banker has collected a cheque for the person, he may be at risk, for he cannot claim the statutory protection of section 4 of the Cheques Act 1957.

Custom House. The office or place where payment is made of duties on imports and exports.

Cycle. A regularly recurring succession of events or phenomena, or the period of time occupied by such a succession; applied to fluctuations in a national economy to mean alternating periods of prosperity and depression which are to some extent predictable.

Cycle Économique. See Trade Cycle.

Cy-Près **Doctrine.** The principle that where the terms of a trust, as set out by a testator or a settlor, cannot be exactly adhered to for some reason, then the courts shall have power to order that these shall be carried out "as nearly as possible". The doctrine is particularly important in cases of bequests to charity, where the original charity has been changed, taken over, or amalgamated with another, or where the state has made itself responsible for the ends formerly served by the charity.

D

d'Accord. Agreed.

Dachgesellschaft. Holding company.

Damage. Any injury or harm to person, property or reputation; a loss incurred; the value of an injury done. *See also* Direct Damage; Proximate Damage; Remote Damage.

Damages. Legal compensation in money paid to an injured party on the basis that, as far as money can do it, he shall be placed in the same position as he was in before the act complained of occurred. Damages are a common law remedy. They are claimed by an injured party as of right. *See also* Aggravated Damages; Compensatory Damages; Contemptuous Damages; Exemplary Damages; Nominal Damages; Substantial Damages.

Danske Bankforening, Den. The Danish banks, with very few and minor exceptions, are organised in the Danish Bankers' Association, Amaliegade 7, Copenhagen. This attends to their interests as far as parliament, the government and the public authorities are concerned. An example of this is the co-operation with the National Bank (the central bank), where agreements on monetary policy are made between the National Bank and the Danish Bankers' Association. The more advanced training of bankers is also attended to by the Association.

Darlehen. The lending of a specified amount at a fixed term with provision for repayment in one sum on the due date, or by fixed instalments.

Data Processing. The handling of accounting or other information by a computer.

Date. The period or time of an event; the time when a writing was executed, especially a deed. A deed must be "signed, sealed and delivered", and thus takes effect from the date of its delivery, whatever may be the date of its execution, or indeed if no date is stated. A bill of exchange is not invalid by reason that it is not dated. Any holder may insert the true date of issue or acceptance and the bill shall be payable accordingly. Any holder may insert the true date of issue on a cheque. This right lasts for a reasonable time only. The date on a bill or cheque is a material part of it, and any alteration to it requires the concurrence of all parties liable on it, otherwise the bill is void except as against anyone who made the alteration or agreed to it, and indorsers subsequent to him. *See also* Antedate; International Date Line; Postdate.

Date d'Échéance. Maturity date.

Date de Livraison. Delivery date.

Dated Stock. Gilt-edged stock issued by the government having a date by which it will be repaid. Where there are two dates, as in the case of Treasury $8\frac{1}{2}$% 1984–1986, the stock may be redeemed at any time between the dates stated.

Datenverarbeitung. Data processing.

Days of Grace. Three days formerly added on to the maturity date of a bill of exchange (other than one payable on demand or at sight) for the benefit of the acceptor. Days of grace were abolished by the Banking and Financial Dealings Act 1971.

Day-to-Day Money. Sums of money lent by banks to the discount houses and stockbrokers overnight. Such loans may be renewed from one day to another if both parties are agreeable.

Dead Stock. Unsaleable goods left on hand.

Dead Weight. That weight of a ship's cargo which brings the ship down to the Plimsoll mark, at which point the ship is fully laden.

Dead Money. Money which can only be borrowed at a high rate of interest.

Dealer. A trader, a merchant; a dealer in foreign exchange; on the Stock Exchange, the jobber who deals in stocks and shares.

Debenture. An acknowledgment of indebtedness, usually given by an incorporated company, often under seal, and frequently including a charge on the assets of the company. It may be a registered debenture or one payable to a bearer. *See also* All-moneys Debenture; Fixed Debenture; Floating Debenture; Income Debenture; Irredeemable Debenture; Mortgage Debenture; Naked Debenture; Redeemable Debenture; Sandwich Debenture; Secured Debenture; Simple Debenture.

Debenture Holder. The holder of a debenture, whether registered or payable to bearer.

Debenture Stock. A debenture which is expressed as part of a total debt. Certificates of debenture stock may be for any amount.

Debouché. An outlet, a market for goods.

Debt. Something owed to another, a liability, an obligation. A chose in action which is capable of being assigned by the creditor to some other person. The assignment must be in writing and must apply to the whole of the debt. The debtor must be notified. *See also* Action of Debt; Active Debt; Bad and Doubtful Debts; Floating Debt; Funded Debt; National Debt; Straight Debt.

Debt-Adjusting. For the purposes of the Consumer Credit Act 1974, negotiating with the creditor or owner, on behalf of the debtor or hirer, terms for the discharge of a debt, or taking over, in return for payments by the debtor or hirer, his obligation to discharge a debt.

Debt Collecting. For the purposes of the Consumer Credit Act 1974, the taking of steps to procure payment of debts due under consumer credit agreements or consumer hire agreements.

Debt Conversion. *See* Conversion.

Debt-Counselling. For the purposes of the Consumer Credit Act 1974, the giving of advice to debtors or hirers about the liquidation of any debt due under consumer credit or consumer hire agreements.

Debtor. One who owes money, or is under some obligation, to another; the debit side of an account. For the purposes of the Consumer Credit Act 1974, "debtor" means the individual receiving credit under a consumer credit agreement or the person to whom his rights and duties under the agreement have passed by assignment or operation of law, and in relation to a prospective consumer credit agreement includes the prospective debtor. *See also* Sundry Debtors.

Debtor–Creditor Agreement. A regulated consumer credit agreement being (1) a restricted-use credit agreement which falls within section 11 (1) (*b*) but is not made by the creditor under pre-existing arrangements, or in the contemplation of future arrangements, between himself and the supplier; or (2) a restricted-use credit agreement which falls within section 11(1) (*c*); or (3) an unrestricted-use credit agreement which is not made by the creditor under pre-existing arrangements between himself and a person (the "supplier") other than the debtor in the knowledge that the credit is to be used to finance a transaction between the debtor and the supplier.

Debtor–Creditor–Supplier Agreement. A regulated consumer credit agreement being (1) a restricted-use credit agreement which falls within section 11 (1) (*a*); or (2) a restricted-use credit agreement which falls within section 11(1) (*b*) and is made by the creditor under pre-existing arrangements, or in contemplation of future arrangements, between himself and the supplier; or (3) an unrestricted-use credit agreement which is made by the creditor under pre-existing arrangements between himself and a person (the "supplier") other than the debtor in the knowledge that the credit is to be used to finance a transaction between the debtor and the supplier.

Deceased Partner. Subject to any agreement between the partners, the death of one of them dissolves the partnership. The surviving partner(s) must wind up the firm; usually, however, the partnership deed will provide that, notwithstanding the death of a partner, the business will be carried on. The share of the deceased partner must be ascertained and paid over to his personal representatives. If the firm's bank account is overdrawn it should be ruled off on notification of the death, to retain the liability of the deceased partner's estate for the debt.

Deceit. The tort of fraudulent misrepresentation (*q.v.*).

Decimal Coinage. A system of coinage in which the standard unit of currency is divided into 100 sub-units.

Decimal System. A system of weights and measures in which the values proceed by multiples of ten. This system is in use on the Continent of Europe. Metrication is in the process of adoption in the

U.K. following upon the decision to become part of the E.E.C. Decimal currency was introduced in the U.K. in 1971. The pound sterling is now divided into 100 pence. The decimal coins consist of ½p, 1p, 2p (bronze), 5p, 10p, and 50p (cupro-nickel). *See also* Metric System.

Deckung. Collateral.

Deckungsgeschäft. A stock exchange transaction to cover a commitment already made.

Découvert. A debit position on the stock exchange where a bear has sold shares which he now has to cover at a higher price; an advance which has risen above the sanction granted or is in excess of the security value; an overdraft.

De Diem in Diem. From day to day.

Dédit. The penalty which has to be paid on withdrawal from a contract.

Deed. A written document under seal, evidencing a legal transaction; an instrument containing the terms of a contract, and sealed as a formality. A deed must be signed, sealed and delivered by the parties to it. The date of delivery is the effective date of the deed.

Deed of Arrangement. *See* Arrangement with Creditors or Members.

Deed of Assignment. *See* Arrangement with Creditors or Members.

Deed of Covenant. An agreement under seal by a contributor to a charitable, etc., association that he will subscribe a fixed sum annually for seven years. Such associations, if approved by the Inland Revenue, are then enabled to reclaim the tax paid by the contributor on these subscriptions.

Deed of Gift. A document under seal effecting the conveyance of property by way of gift.

Deed of Partnership. The agreement between partners recorded under seal. The deed will record the terms and conditions of the partnership, the ratios in which profits are to be shared, whether the business is to continue after the death, bankruptcy, etc. of a partner, and so on.

Deed of Postponement. Where a bank is asked to lend money to a company and finds on examination of the balance sheet that a director has made a loan to the company, it may feel that, if the director has his loan repaid by the company during the currency of the bank advance, then the company will be by that amount less able to repay the bank. The bank may therefore make it a condition of granting the accommodation that a deed of postponement be executed, by which the director undertakes not to accept repayment before the bank has been repaid, and the company similarly undertakes not to make repayment to the director. A clause may be inserted that in the event of the liquidation of the company the director will claim as an unsecured creditor, but will hand any dividend received to the bank.

Deed of Reconveyance. Where there has been a legal mortgage of land as security for a loan which the customer has now repaid, the property must be reconveyed. This can be simply done by the completion by the bank, under seal, of a form of receipt which will have been incorporated on the back of the bank's form of legal mortgage. This will operate, without more, to re-transfer the legal estate to the customer. Sometimes, however, a more formal alternative is requested—the deed of reconveyance—by which the bank acknowledges under seal the repayment of the debt and re-transfers the legal estate in the land back to the customer, the mortgage being extinguished.

Deed of Settlement. A deed made in consideration of marriage, for the benefit of the wife and/or any issue of the marriage; a deed, or will, or other instrument under which any land or other property stands for the time being limited in some way, *e.g.* in trust for any person by way of succession, or limited to, or in trust for, a married women. *See also* Settled Land.

Deed Poll. A deed made by one person only, so called because the paper is cut or polled evenly, and not indented.

De Facto. In fact, actually.

Defamation. The publication of a statement which tends to lower a person in the estimation of right-thinking members of the community generally. Spoken defamation is slander, written defamation is libel. There are three special defences to an action for defamation—privilege, justification, and fair comment. In certain cases an offer of amends, coupled with an apology, will entitle the defendant to some relief.

Default. Fault, neglect, defect, failure to

appear in a law-court when summoned, failure to account for money held in trust, failure to repay a loan or an overdraft as promised. *See also* Judgment by Default.

Default Notice. For the purpose of the Consumer Credit Act 1974, a notice in a prescribed form, to be served on a debtor or hirer before a creditor or owner can become entitled, by reason of any breach by the debtor or hirer of a regulated agreement, to terminate the agreement, or to enforce any security, or to recover possession of goods or land, etc.

Defeasance. A condition relating to a deed and incorporated in it, which being performed renders the deed void; the act of annulling a contract.

Defence Bonds. *See* British Savings Bonds.

Defender. Scots law term for *Defendant*.

Deferred. Put off, postponed.

Deferred Annuity. An annuity which does not begin to operate until after a certain period.

Deferred Charges. Prepaid items for a period greater than the current accounting period, so that there is a balance of value to be carried forward to the subsequent accounting period, *e.g.* where rates are paid in advance, or a railway season ticket purchased for a year instead of for three months.

Deferred Interest Warrant. *See* Arrears Certificate.

Deferred Shares. Shares postponed to ordinary shares: they receive a dividend only if the dividend on the ordinary shares reaches a certain level. These are sometimes called *Management* or *Founder's* shares, and are created to remunerate the founders or promoters of a company. When company profits are good the return from deferred shares may be very considerable.

Deficiency Advances. Advances from the Bank of England to the Government when there are insufficient credit balances in the revenue accounts to meet permanent charges, such as the periodic dividends due on Government stocks.

Definitive Bond or Certificate. Where on an issue of bonds or shares payment is being made by instalments, and a provisional certificate or scrip has been issued as temporary evidence of title, such a temporary document will be exchanged, when payment has been completed, for the final or definitive bond or certificate.

Defizit. Shortage, deficit.

Deflation. An attempt by the government of a country to reduce a rate of inflation with its pressures on costs and manufacturers by taking measures to reduce demand, but maintaining the supply of goods so that prices should stop rising and even start to come down; any process in the manipulation of a currency designed to raise the value of money in terms of prices; a reduction in the issue of paper money. The success of a deflationary policy may depend on the causes of the inflation, and may furthermore be affected by political rather than economic considerations. The primary cause of inflation may be higher costs of raw materials, or increased labour costs. Militant trade unions may succeed in their claims to the point where unit costs are increased by short time working, or where wages rise faster than productivity: the State may be spending too much money on providing lavish social security benefits or maintaining an uneconomic standard of living for its populace by borrowing abroad (while its credit remains good). Theoretically, if the cause of inflation is greatly increased raw material costs, the State should re-value its currency; if the cause is a disproportionate rise in wages the state should impose an incomes policy. Measures taken to reduce demand can only bottle up demand temporarily; when the restrictions are removed demand will burst out again.

Defunct Company. A company which has ceased to do business, and which has had its name struck off the register of companies.

Dégressiv. Failing: falling away.

Dégrèvent Fiscal pour Double Imposition. Double taxation relief.

De Iure. In law, rightfully.

Délai de Presentation. The late production of documents for exchange or payment.

Délai de Réclamation. Delay due to the presentation to a purchaser of shares which have formal defects; a notice of complaint.

Del Credere, Delkredere. Provision for probable losses on sundry debtors; an element of risk factor incorporated in a charge.

Del Credere Agent. An agent who guarantees to his principal that third parties with whom he contracts on behalf of his principal will always meet their obligations to the principal: if they do not, he will himself make the deficiency good.

Delegated Authority. The agent to whom authority has been delegated by his principal may not further delegate. He must do the work himself. There are some common law exceptions to this rule. An agent may delegate if an express or implied agreement to that effect exists; where delegation is necessary for the proper performance of the work; where there is a trade usage to sanction the delegation; or if there is a sudden emergency necessitating delegation. Executors may delegate amongst themselves, *i.e.* one alone may sign cheques for the executors, but all trustees must sign. A trustee may, however, by statutory authority employ an agent, whether a solicitor, banker, stockbroker or other person, to transact any business or to do any act required to be done in the execution of the trust, or may by power of attorney delegate for not longer than twelve months the execution of duties and powers vested in him to any person except his only other co-trustee (unless a trust corporation). A trustee may delegate duties if so empowered by the instrument creating the trust.

Delegated Legislation. Power given by Parliament to be exercised at a later date by executive officers of the State. A comprehensive Act having a national impact may well need to come into force in stages, or may necessarily leave some details to be decided upon after further experience. As it would be impossible for Parliament to supervise these points and details itself it may pass an "enabling" Act laying down the principles of the legislative ends to be gained, leaving a Minister or a Department of State with statutory authority to devise schemes or make orders, rules or regulations.

Delegation. The act of assigning work, a duty, or a completion of an order, to another. The ability to delegate is an essential requisite of successful management.

Delegatus non Potest Delegare. A requirement in agency stemming from Roman law—he to whom work is entrusted may not entrust it to another.

Delivery. The act of delivering, transfer; the act of putting another in formal possession of property; the handing over of a deed to a grantee. Every contract on a bill, whether it be the drawer's, the acceptor's, or an endorser's, is incomplete and revocable, until delivery of the instrument in order to give effect thereto.

Delivery Note. A document accompanying the delivery of goods, particularising the items delivered, so that the consignee may check them.

Delivery of Bill or Cheque. Transfer of possession, actual or constructive, from one person to another. Ownership of a cheque or bill payable to "bearer" is transferred on delivery; of one payable to "order", by indorsement and delivery.

Delivery of Deed. A deed must be signed, sealed and delivered and until it is delivered it is ineffective.

Delivery Order. An order by the owner or holder of title to goods, addressed to a warehouse keeper, to the superintendent of a dock or wharf, or to a railway company, holding the goods, authorising and requesting him to deliver the goods, whether in whole or in part, to the bearer of the order, or to the party thereon named by indorsement. The beneficiary should at once take delivery of the goods, or obtain a receipt or warrant, or have his title registered, whichever is appropriate; if he does not, he runs the risk that a later delivery order will be issued and acted upon.

Delivery, Terms of. Indications as to whether consignor or consignee are to pay the delivery charges on goods consigned, *e.g.* carriage forward, carriage paid, C.I.F., F.O.B., etc.

De Mal en Pis. From bad to worse.

Demand. An authoritative claim or request; the desire to purchase or possess; a legal claim; the quantity of a product which will be bought at a particular price. **In Demand.** Much sought after. **On Demand.** At call, whenever requested.

Demand and Supply. A phrase used to denote the relation between consumption and production: if the demand exceeds the supply the price rises, and *vice versa*.

Demand Draft. A bill of exchange payable on demand; a cheque; a draft drawn by a banker on the Head Office of the bank at the request of a customer, and payable on demand. *See* Bankers' Draft.

Demand-Pull Theory of Inflation. Demand for goods and services exceeds the supply, which causes buyers to bid up the prices for such goods and services.

De Minimis non Curat Lex. The law does not concern itself with trivial matters.

Demise. To transfer or convey by lease or will; a transfer or conveyance by lease or will for a term of years or in fee simple; the granting of a lease.

Demise Charter. A charter party where the charterer of the ship makes all the arrangements for working it, hires the crew, etc., so that for the time being he is effectively the owner.

Demonetize. To deprive of its character as money; to withdraw (a metal) from currency; to diminish or deprive of monetary value.

Demurrage. The undue detention of a ship; compensation paid by freighters if goods cause delays to barges, ships or wagons for such delay, or by port authorities if there is unreasonable delay in berthing. There is usually a free period before the charge starts to operate.

Depenses. Disbursements.

De Pis en Pis. Worse and worse.

Deponent. One who gives evidence in court under oath, a witness, one whose disposition or written testimony is accepted as evidence in a trial; one who makes an affidavit to any statement of fact.

Déport. On the Stock Exchange, but also on the foreign exchange market, the extension for a "bear" operator of the time for payment until the next settlement day; a carrying over.

Deposit. To entrust, to lodge with anyone for safety or as a pledge; an earnest, a first instalment, a trust, a security. For the purposes of the Consumer Credit Act 1974, "deposit" means any sum payable by a debtor or hirer by way of deposit or down-payment, or credited or to be credited to him on account of any deposit or down-payment, whether the sum is to be or has been paid to the creditor or owner or any other person, or is to be or has been discharged by a payment of money or a transfer or delivery of goods or by any other means. *See also* Fixed Deposit; "Natural" Deposit; Notice Deposit; Sight Deposits; Special Deposits; "Straight" Deposit; Time Deposits.

Deposit Account. A bank account on which a rate of interest, quoted by reference to a base rate, is payable. Such accounts are normally repayable at seven or fourteen days' notice. A passbook or loose-leaf statement is issued periodically to the customer.

Deposit Bank. A bank taking money from customers on current, deposit or other accounts on the terms that the money is to be repaid on demand or at the end of an agreed term; usually confined to banks which take any sum on deposit, and do not specify any minimum amount.

Deposit Broker. Intermediaries who arrange for deposits to be placed with one bank or financial institution by another.

Depositen. Short or medium term money deposited at a bank.

Depositenheft. Deposit account book.

Deposit Insurance. The payment by banks of a sort of premium to a central fund whose resources would be used to repay depositors if they were in danger of losing their money on the failure of a bank. It is proposed that all deposit-taking institutions in the U.K. shall require a licence as a condition of doing business. Licences will be issued on a grading system—the higher up the grade a bank climbs the more confident its depositors. It is at the lowest level where the need of depositors for protection is greatest. The concept is a logical development of the work of the Lifeboat Committee, which has firmly established the principle that the funds of depositors should be protected. The only detail so far fixed is that insurance will be limited to deposits under £10,000, or the first £10,000 of larger deposits. *See also* Supervision of Banks.

Deposition. A written declaration (signed before a magistrate) by a witness who must later appear to testify in court.

Deposit Rate. The rate of interest paid by a bank on money on a deposit account.

Deposit Receipt. A receipt issued by bankers and others when money is lodged in a deposit account and no deposit passbook or statement is issued.

Deposit Society. A type of friendly society which encourages its members to open deposit accounts with it, such money to be used to supplement insurance benefits, and repayable on the retirement of the member.

Dépôt. Sums deposited with a bank on short or medium term; items deposited for safe custody.

Depotbank. *See* Deposit Bank.

Dépôt Collectif. Deposit of shares, bonds, etc., with a bank, the securities of the different customers of the bank being kept together, classified by categories, and without indication of the name of the owner of each share certificate.

Dépôt d'Actions d'Administrateur. The deposit of company shares by the directors of a limited company for the duration of their continuance in that capacity.

Dépôt de Change. A bill or note given by way of a guarantee, usually in the form of an I.O.U., which does not circulate but serves to assure a creditor that, if the debtor fails to fulfil his engagement, he can be sued on the note.

Dépôt Fermé. Articles of value deposited under seal for safe custody only.

Depotgebuhr. Yearly charge for safe custody and management of bills and securities passing through the bank's hands.

Depotgeld. Deposits at a term, *i.e.* left with the bank until an agreed fixed maturity date, so attracting a higher rate of interest.

Depotgeschaft. Safe keeping of securities at a bank, whether resulting from delivery of a single item to be held under management and supervision under open deposit, or from delivery of a bundle of securities, shares, etc., for exclusive safe custody in a closed deposit.

Dépôt Individuel. Deposit of shares, bonds, etc., with a bank, the securities being kept under the name of the individual customer and not placed in the same run with similar securities of other customers or of the bank itself.

Dépôt Joint. A joint account of which several persons can dispose individually and without limit (up to the balance of the account), even after the death of one of the joint account holders (by virtue of the "balance to survivor" clause).

Dépôt Ouvert. Shares, etc., left with a bank for management and control.

Depot-stimmrecht. The authority of the bank to handle the shares of its customers held under its management, which have been placed in the name of the bank.

Depotwechsel. Notes or bills, mostly I.O.U.s, which are not in general circulation but are held as additional security against a loan.

Depreciation. Of assets, a loss in value by wear and tear, obsolescence, etc., or normal deterioration in value which takes place during the life of an asset. This loss in value is recognised by a depreciation figure which may be calculated in a number of ways, of which two of the most common are the *Straight-Line Method* and the *Reducing Balance Method*. Under the first, a machine's final scrap value at the end of its life is estimated, and this figure is deducted from its original cost. The difference is divided by the estimated number of years of useful life. Under the second, a charge is made each year which is a flat percentage of the previous year's value figure. In this way the original cost is reduced over the period of years chosen to the estimated scrap value, but the annual depreciation figure will be very large to start with and very small to finish with. The merit of this system is said to be that it compensates for increasing costs of maintenance and repair as the machine gets older. These systems take for granted that the cost of a replacement asset is going to be the same as it originally was. This is not usually so, because inflation has lowered the purchasing power of the pound in the intervening years. A figure should therefore be allowed for the inflationary factor and applied additionally to the basic depreciation. *See also* Accelerated Depreciation; Excess Depreciation; Trade-weighted Depreciation.

Depreciation Allowance. A tax allowance to business concerns on the cost of new machinery, spread over a number of years. In some cases it is replaced by a capital allowance, in which case the whole benefit is received in the first year.

Depreciation of a Currency. Where exchange rates are floating, the value of a national currency will be determined by the demand for, and the supply of, that currency. If the demand is small, because the country is exporting less than it is importing, or because investors in that country are losing confidence in the stability of its currency, or both, the exchange rate will fall and the currency will depreciate.

Depression. A period of heavy unemployment, reduced business activity, and loss of confidence generally.

De Rigueur. Obligatory, indispensable.

Détacher, Detächieren. To separate or cut off the coupons from a bond.

Determinable Fee Simple. *See* Estate in Fee Simple.

Determination. Termination, conclusion, bringing to an end; settlement by a judicial decision. A debt due to a bank may be determined by a call on a guarantor, the appointment of a receiver under a debenture, or notice of the death, bankruptcy or liquidation of the customer, etc.

Detinue. The illegal retention of the chattels or property of another.

De Trop. Superfluous, out of place.

Dette. Debt.

Dette Consolidée. A long term commitment—for example, in the form of loans secured by bonds, mortgages, etc.

Dette Flottante. Short- to medium-term obligations of the State, for example in the form of short-term issues, Treasury bills, etc.

Devaluation. The reduction of the official par value of the legal unit of currency, in terms of the currencies of other countries. Devaluations become necessary when one country's costs are rising faster than those of other countries, so that it becomes increasingly difficult to keep its exports competitive. The strain on the currency is often made worse by the activities of international money dealers who transfer their holdings of the weak currency into a stronger currency, to avoid being caught with it after a devaluation, and thus intensify the weakness. Devaluations do not deal with the central problem, which is the lack of a country's competitiveness, but only with the symptom or effect of the problem. Devaluation can therefore be only a temporary palliative.

Devastavit. An act committed by a personal representative who has done something in his administration of the estate which is contrary to law. In such a case the personal representative will be personally liable unless he is relieved by the court.

Development of Land. *See* Change of User.

Devise. The act of bequeathing landed property by will.

Devise. (*Ger.*) A foreign bill of exchange.

Devisee. One to whom real property is left by will.

Devisen. Currency coming from overseas countries and payments forwarded to overseas countries; foreign exchange payments.

Devisenausländer. A person who will be considered for foreign exchange purposes as a non-resident.

Devisenbewirtschaftung, Devisenkontrolle. Exchange control, directed by the central authority.

Deviseninländer. A person who will be considered for foreign exchange purposes as a resident.

Devises. (*Fr.*) Foreign securities payable abroad.

Devolution. Transference or delegation of authority (as by Parliament to one of its committees); passage from one person to another; descent by inheritance; descent in natural succession. Thus real estate to which a deceased was entitled for an interest not ceasing on his death shall on his death, and notwithstanding any testamentary disposition thereof, devolve from time to time on the personal representative of the deceased.

Dezentralisierter Zahlungsuekehr. The traffic of foreign payments, supervised by the authorised banks, themselves under the direction of the central authority.

Diarising. The noting of points which need attention in the future. A banker will need to know the dates on which various instalments on an allotment letter are to be paid, the date on which a customer's life policy falls due for repayment, the days by which various returns must be made to Head Office, and many other matters. All these details can be listed under the relevant date on sheets of paper and sorted away in a filing system under months and days. Each morning a clerk will distribute around the office to the people who are going to attend to them the diary notes for the day. Diary notes should be made out for a few days before the actual or last possible dates.

Dictum de Dicto. A hearsay report.

Dienstleistungsbilanz. Invisible balance of trade.

Dies Non (*Juridicus*). A day on which the law courts do not sit; hence, a day on which no business can be transacted.

Difference. Disagreement, the amount by which one total fails to agree with another; on the stock exchange, payment or receipt by a speculator on settlement day of the difference between the price at which his bargain was recorded on the day of its transaction and the price on settlement day.

Differential. In wage payments, the difference between the payments made to one class of workers and another, or between the remuneration of employees in different industries, or that paid to different grades of employees in the same industry.

Differential Duties. Variable duties imposed on the same commodity coming from different countries.

Diners' Club. A credit card company originating in the U.S., in which National Westminster Bank has an interest. There is no specified credit limit.

Direct. Straightforward, immediate, in a straight line.

Direct Arbitrage. Dealings in foreign exchange which are confined to one centre.

Direct Cost. The cost of production in money terms.

Direct Damage. Damage which arises naturally from a breach of contract. Compensation may only be awarded in respect of a loss arising from the break of the contract itself.

Direct Debit. A direct claim made by a creditor on the customer's account, to be paid by the bank on each occasion. The customer must approve this arrangement before any transfers are made and he must authorise his banker to meet the claims. A single signed form will be enough to authorise the regular payments until further notice. The system, which is particularly suitable in the case of large creditors such as local authorities, gas and electricity boards, and insurance companies, permits of variations in the periodic claims, such as may be expected in the case of, say, index-linked assurance policies.

Directeur Générale. Managing director, general manager.

Direct Expense. All items of cost in the manufacture of a product which are essentially linked with any stage of the production process, as opposed to overhead costs which continue irrespective of production.

Directive. Tending to guide or advise; general orders from a supreme authority outlining procedure to be followed in the implementation of a new plan or policy; an instruction from the Bank of England to the lending banks imposing qualitative or quantitative limitations.

Direct Letter of Credit. *See* Letter of Credit.

Direct Production. The satisfaction by a person of all his economic wants entirely through his own efforts.

Direct Selling. Sales by producer directly to consumer, by-passing wholesaler, distributor and retailer.

Direct Tax. A tax levied directly on the taxpayer, *e.g.* income tax, as distinct from a tax levied on goods or services.

Director. A member of a board of managers in a large commercial business. In a limited company he is a member of the company appointed by his fellow-members to administer the company's affairs.

Director-General of Fair Trading. The Fair Trading Act 1973 was concerned with both competition and consumer protection, and created new machinery for the control of unfair business practices, and consolidated the old law on monopolies, mergers and restrictive trade practices. The Act provided for the appointment of the Director-General and charged him with the tasks of (1) keeping under review commercial activities relating to the supply of goods and services to consumers; (2) collecting information about activities which may adversely affect the economic interests of the consumer; (3) reviewing commercial activities in monopoly conditions; and (4) making appropriate recommendations on these matters to the Secretary of State for Trade. He is also obliged to take action with respect to courses of action detrimental to the interest of consumers. The Consumer Credit Act 1974 placed on him the duties of (1) administering the licensing system set up by the Act; (2) exercising the adjudicating functions conferred on him in relation to the issue, renewal, variation, suspension and revocation of licences; (3) generally superintending the working and enforcement of the Act, and regulations made under it; and (4) where necessary himself taking steps to enforce the Act and the regulations made under it. He must keep these matters under review and from time to time advise the Secretary of State of social and commercial developments in the United Kingdom and elsewhere relating to the provision of credit or bailment or (in Scotland) hiring of goods to individuals and related activities, and about the working and enforcement of the Act and regulations and orders made under it.

Director of Savings. An officer appointed under Part 5 of the Post Office Act 1969, under whose control the national savings facilities known as the National Savings Bank (previously the Post Office Savings Bank), the National Savings Stock Register (previously the Post Office Register of Stock), National Savings Certificates, Savings Bank Annuities and Insurances, and Premium Savings Bonds would be continued. As from October 1969, Savings Contracts were also issued through the Director of Savings.

Direktem Hypothekargeschäft. See Hypothekarkredit.

Dirigeant. See Executive.

Dirty Bill of Lading. A bill of lading marked or claused to show that the goods were received in a damaged condition.

Dirty Float. The essence of a floating currency is that the central bank shall not intervene either by buying or selling its own currency on the foreign exchange markets. However, the generally stated intention is to regard a floating rate of exchange as a temporary measure only, and to return to fixed parities when the currency has stabilised itself. A central bank may therefore look ahead to this time and push its currency to a level which it would like to see established by quiet intervention in the currency markets.

Disagio. The difference, usually expressed as a percentage, between nominal or par value and a lower price.

Discharge. To unload (from ship, vehicle, etc.); to get rid of; to dismiss from employment; to set free from a binding obligation; to pay off, to settle, to perform, to pay a debt; to release from a duty by the issue of a suitable document, *e.g.* an executor's discharge; an entry in a bank's books to show that an item of security or safe custody has been released to a customer or to a third party; the signature of a customer in a Boxes & Parcels Book or in a Night Safe Wallet Record Book.

Discharged Bankrupt. A bankrupt person who has received his discharge from the court. If his discharge is unconditional, his former debts are considered settled and no longer binding on him and he is free to make a fresh start in business. His discharge may be conditional, *e.g.* in respect of earnings or after-acquired property.

Discharged Bill. A bill of exchange is discharged when payment is made in due course by or on behalf of the drawee or acceptor; where the acceptor of a bill becomes the holder of it at or after its maturity; where the holder of a bill at or after its maturity unconditionally renounces his rights against the acceptor; or where a bill is intentionally cancelled by the holder or his agent. *See also* Cancellation.

Disclaimer. A renunciation, disavowel or repudiation. Thus a beneficiary under a will may disclaim it, or a trustee in bankruptcy may disclaim any asset in the bankrupt's estate which is burdened with onerous clauses.

Disclosure. *See* Secrecy.

Discount. To deduct a certain sum or rate per cent from an account or price; the deduction of a sum for payment in advance; the act of discounting; the rate of discount; the depreciation in value of an investment. The amount of deduction at an agreed rate per cent per annum, which is calculated when the holder of a term bill which has still a period to run before its maturity wishes to cash it immediately. There must be two good names on the bill, which must be in respect of a genuine trade transaction. Discount is usually worked at overdraft rate and represents a charge on the amount of the bill for the number of days to its maturity. *See also* Recourse. In the foreign exchange market, the forward margin applied to a currency which is cheaper forward than it is spot in terms of another currency. It is added to the spot rate. *See also* Cash Discount;

Trade Discount. At a Discount. Goods offered or bought at a reduction made as an inducement to an immediate sale; the market prices of bonds, shares or stock which are below the nominal value, so described.

Discount Broker. *See* Bill Broker.

Discounted Cash Flow. A way of comparing alternative capital projects by assessment of the present values of expected cash flows during the existence of each capital project.

Discount House. *See* Bill Broker.

Discount Market. The members of the Discount Houses Association together with those money brokers and traders who are recognised and approved by the Bank of England. The discount houses make their profits by absorbing surplus funds from the banking system and investing them mainly short-term, in a mixture of commercial and government paper. The market is at the centre of short-term money dealings.

Discretion. Prudence, discernment, liberty to act according to one's judgment.

Discretionary Funds. *See* Advisory Funds.

Discretionary Income. What remains out of a person's income when all his basic needs and commitments have been met.

Discretionary Limits. *See* Managers' Discretionary Limits.

Disentail. To break the entail of (an estate), the act of disentailing. *See* Barring the Entail.

Disentailing Assurance. *See* Barring the Entail.

Dishonour of a Bill. A bill of exchange may be dishonoured either by non-acceptance or non-payment. It is dishonoured by non-acceptance when the drawee of a bill refuses to accept it. It is dishonoured by non-payment when the acceptor fails to pay it on the due date. A cheque is dishonoured when it is returned unpaid by the banker on whom it is drawn.

Disinflation. The act or process of correcting an inflationary situation, but not to the extent of causing deflation. Disinflation is the concept of a target set by the authorities: deflation is one method which can be used to achieve that target.

Diskont. Interest deduction on a trade or redemption obligation not yet due, in particular by the purchase of a bill of exchange; discount.

Diskont à Forfait. The cost of discount by a bank of a bill of exchange on a foreign buyer of exported goods, without recourse on the seller.

Diskontgeschäft. The granting of credit by a bank through the purchase of a bill of exchange not yet due, subject to a deduction in respect of the time still to run; discount business.

Diskontpolitik. The policy of the central bank, as shown by its manipulation of the discount rate.

Diskontsatz. The rate of interest applied to the period between the date of discount of a bill of exchange and its due date.

Dispense. To divide out in parts; to administer, as laws; to excuse from, to grant a dispensation from a duty or obligation.

Dispensing Notice. For the purposes of the Consumer Credit Act 1974, an authority signed by a joint account holder waiving his/her right to receive separate current account bank statements.

Disponibilités. Liquid assets.

Disposable Income. Income left after all direct taxes have been deducted.

Disposition. The act of disposing, arrangement, guidance; conveyance of property.

Disseize. To deprive of an estate in freehold wrongfully.

Disseizin. Unlawful dispossession of freehold land.

Dissenting Creditor. *See* Arrangement with Creditors or Members.

Dissolution. Disintegration, termination (of marriage, partnership, etc.); dismissal of an assembly (as of Parliament before a general election).

Dissolution of Company. The termination of a company and its business by winding-up and striking off the register of companies.

Dissolution of Partnership. The ending of a partnership by expiration of an agreed term; or by notice by a partner; or by the death, bankruptcy or retirement of any partner; or by charge on a partner's share for a separate debt; or by the happening of an event which makes it unlawful to continue the partnership; or by an order of the court on application of a partner; or by the insolvency of the partnership; or by the completion of the purpose for which the partnership was established.

Distrain. To seize for debt, to take the personal chattels of, in order to satisfy a demand or enforce the performance of an act, to take possession of.

Distraint. The act of seizing goods for a debt.

Distress. The act of distraining, goods taken in distraint. *See also Distringas.*

Distributed Profits. Profits passed on to shareholders by way of dividend. Whether profits are distributed or retained for use in the business may be a factor in the level of tax imposed upon them.

Distribution. Apportionment, division; the apportionment of wealth among the various classes of the community; the allotment of goods by producers among consumers.

Distribution Expense. The cost of dispersion among consumers of a finished product; those expenses which are associated with the distribution of goods, *e.g.* warehousing facilities, carriage outwards, postage, packaging and containerisation.

Distributive Cost. The cost of getting the goods from the place where they are produced to the point of consumption.

District Land Registry. Following the decentralisation of the work of the Land Registry a number of district land registries were set up, each handling the registration of titles within its own district. A list of all counties, county boroughs and London boroughs, with the district land registries which serve them, can be obtained from the Land Registry.

Distringas. An old writ directing a sheriff or other officer to distrain. The writ was abolished in 1883, giving place to a *Notice in Lieu of Distringas*—a much simpler procedure which achieved the same end. The notice is used in connection with stocks and shares and a banker who has taken a mortgage of this type of security may file an affidavit at the Central Office of the Supreme Court, or at a District Registry on a notice in a specified form. It is then necessary to obtain an office copy of the affidavit and a duplicate of the filed notice, both authenticated by the Seal of the Central Office or the District Registry. The two documents are then served on the company, the effect being that the company must then give the banker eight days' warning before registering any transfer of the shares or paying a dividend to the registered holder. This interval will give the banker time to apply to the court for an injunction restraining the company from passing the transfer or paying the dividend. The method may be used where money is lent on the security of a mortgage of a reversionary interest in an estate comprising or including stocks and shares, as a check against any dealing by the trustees. It may also be used by the revenue authorities where they have any claim in respect of capital transfer tax against stocks and shares.

Dividend. (1) A payment made out of the profits of a company to the share- or stockholders. The payment may be at a fixed rate, as with preference shares (always assuming that profits permit), or at a variable rate, reflecting trading success, to the ordinary or "equity" shareholders. It may be omitted altogether if the company has made no profit, or insufficient profit, or is in trouble with its cash flow.

(2) A distribution by a trustee in bankruptcy paid to creditors in respect of realisation of the bankrupt's assets, or by a liquidator in respect of the realised assets of a company which is being wound up. *See also* Equalising the Dividend; Final Dividend; Interim Dividend; Passing the Dividend.

Dividend Counterfoil. The top portion of a dividend warrant, containing details of the gross amount and the rate and amount of income tax which the company will account for, which may be used by the recipient as a tax credit. Where the shareholder has authorised the company to pay the dividend direct to a bank for his credit, the dividend counterfoil will be used as a credit voucher.

Dividend Cover. The money needed for a dividend payment divided into the profits (after tax) of the company available for the payment.

Dividende. See Dividend.

Dividende Intérimaire. See Interim Dividend.

Dividendstop. Governmental limitation of the rate at which dividends may be paid; the imposition of a top limit on dividend rates.

Dividendenwerte. Document of value embodying the right to a share in the profits of a company; dividend.

Dividend Limitation. Restriction on any increase in dividend payments as a measure to check inflation.

Dividend Mandate. An authority from a shareholder to the company to send dividends on his shareholding direct to his bank for credit to his account.

Dividend Warrant. An order or warrant issued by a company and drawn on its bankers, authorising them to pay the dividend specified thereon to the stock or shareholder.

Dividend Yield. The yield on an industrial share dividend by the share price.

Divisionalisation. A method by which large banks can overcome the problems of communications and co-ordination which arise as the banks extend their range of services, their representation in their home countries or overseas, and their methods of obtaining, controlling and lending money. The bank's resources in personnel and material assets are concentrated in a division which becomes largely self-contained and is principally concentrated on the fulfilment of the designated task, *e.g.* Financial Services, Domestic Banking, or International Banking Divisions.

Division d'Action. See Splitting.

Docket. A summary of digest; a register of judgments; an alphabetical list of cases for trial; a similar summary of business to be dealt with by a committee or assembly; an indorsement of a letter or a document summarising the contents; a warrant certifying payment of duty issued by a customs house; a ticket or label showing the address of a package, etc.; to make an abstract, digest or summary of judgments and enter in a docket; to make an abstract or note of the contents of a document on the back.

Dock Warrant. A warrant issued by a dock company in respect of goods in their possession, specifying details of the goods, naming the ship in which they were imported, the consignee to whom they are addressed, and the date from which they were warehoused. If dock warrants are accepted by a banker as security, they should be endorsed by the customer and accompanied by a lien letter or a memorandum of deposit. A safer alternative is to have the goods transferred into the bank's name in the books of the dock company or, if the goods have been warehoused, the warehouse keeper.

Document. A written or printed paper containing information for the establishment of facts; to furnish with documents necessary to establish any fact, to prove by means of documents.

Documentary Bill. A bill which is supported by documents of title, such as bills of lading, invoices, insurance policies, etc.

Documentary Credit. The best method of financing overseas trade is for the contracting parties to insert in the contract for the sale of goods a provision that payment shall be made by a banker under the provisions of a documentary credit. Under this system a banker undertakes to pay the price of the goods, or accept a bill of exchange for the invoice amount, in return for the delivery to him by the exporter of the invoices and shipping documents, provided they are in conformity with the details advised by the importer to the bank. The nature of the undertaking varies according to whether the credit is revocable or irrevocable, or confirmed. The banker receives a small percentage commission. Frequently the documents are pledged to the banker as security. *See also* Acceptance Credit; Back-to-Back Credit; Confirmed Credit; Countervailing Credit; Irrevocable Credit; Negotiation Credit; Pre-finance Credit; Re-finance Credit; Reimbursement Credit; Revocable Credit; Revolving Credit; Shopping List Credit; Sight Credit; Term Credit; Transferable Credit.

Documents against Acceptance (D/A). *See* Bill for Collection.

Documents against Payment (D/P). *See* Bill for Collection.

Doit. See I.O.U.

Dokumentarinkasso. Cashing under a documentary credit; paying to an exporter the sum authorised by the buyer's bank against the shipping documents.

Dollar Certificate of Deposit. Certificates of deposit were introduced in the United States in 1961, and were so successful that similar dollar certificates were issued by New York banks on the London market five years later. A substantial market developed in these certificates, in which the discount houses obtained permission to deal. The dollars are obtained from the Euromarket. The certificates appeal to short-term holders of dollars who would like to invest a sum of dollars which is not large enough to be of interest to the Eurodollar market, or who do not know for certain how long they will wish to hold them. By investing them in dollar certificates of deposit they are certain to get the dollars back when they need them and in the meantime they enjoy a good rate of interest. Certificates are issued in multiples of $1,000, with a minimum of $25,000, for maturities of 30, 60, 90, 120, 150 and 180 days, 12 months, and several years.

Dollar Premium. Exchange control regulations in Britain restrict the purchase by residents of shares in foreign companies, property overseas, etc., so as to limit the flow of sterling going out of the country; therefore a premium has to be paid on top of the share or investment price. This premium is always quoted in dollars. *See* Investment Currency; Premium Stripping.

Domestic Banking. The normal course of business between banker and his customer (as opposed to "wholesale" banking), or the banking business in this country (as opposed to international or foreign banking).

Domestic Credit Expansion (D.C.E.). Bank and overseas lending to the public sector plus bank lending in sterling to the private and overseas sector plus changes in the public's holdings of notes and coin. The importance of D.C.E. is that when the domestic supply of money exceeds the domestic demand the excess tends to flow abroad. Sterling is sold in exchange for foreign currency bought and reserves have to be used, or the rate drops, or both.

Domestic Trade. *See* Trade.

Domicile, *Domizil.* The place where a person has his permanent residence or home; the place at which a bill of exchange is made payable.

Domiciled Bill. A bill whereupon the acceptor, at the time of accepting it, has specified a place, such as a bank, where the bill is to be payable.

Donatio Mortis Causa. A gift made in anticipation of, and conditional upon, the death of the donor, upon which estate duty was liable to be paid. Since the Finance Act 1975, however, these gifts are, in the U.K., subject to the capital transfer tax, which has replaced estate duty, while the phrase *donatio mortis causa* is now described as "a chargeable transfer of value which reduces the estate of the transferor and is intended to benefit someone else".

Donneur d'Ordre. An application for a documentary credit facility.

Dontgeschäft. See Acheter ou Vendre Dont.

Doppelbesteuerung. Double taxation.

Doppelbesteuerungsnachlass. Double taxation relief.

Doppelquittung. A receipt "twice over". It will be demanded when a receipt is required at two places at the same time; it is then said to be "twice valid for a single transaction".

Dormant. Sleeping, undeveloped, inactive, inoperative, in abeyance.

Dormant Account. Account which has not been used by the customer for a long time, so that the balance has remained unchanged. Such balances are eventually transferred from a branch to a central account, but this is for good administration only. The Statute of Limitations does not apply to dormant accounts, which may be claimed at any time.

Dormant Partner. One who has money invested in the firm, but takes no active part in it; he shares in the profits and is liable for the firm's debts.

Dotationskapital. State capital for the permanent provision for a public institution; endowment capital.

Douane. Customs. *En Douane.* In bond.

Double Entry. A system of book-keeping in which every transaction is entered twice, once on the credit side of the account that gives, and once on the debit side of the account that receives.

Double Option. *See* Option.

Double Prime. *See* Stellage.

Double Taxation Relief. A reciprocal arrangement between two countries which relieves the citizen of one country who has earned money in the other from having to pay tax on the income in both countries.

Doubtful Debts. *See* Bad and Doubtful Debts.

Dower. A widow's share of her husband's property; the portion a woman brings in marriage.

Dow-Jones Index. *See Indice* Dow Jones.

Down Payment. A deposit of part of the purchase price as evidence of good faith, an earnest; a deposit in connection with a hire purchase transaction.

Draft. The first outline of any scheme, writing or document; a rough sketch of work to be executed; a written order for the payment of money; a cheque or bill drawn, especially by a department or branch of a bank, upon its Head Office, or upon another of its branches. *See also* Bankers' Draft; Demand Draft; Foreign Draft.

Drain on the Reserves. A run on the stocks of foreign currency held by a country, which may become sufficiently serious to lead to a devaluation, or, in the case of a floating rate, an adverse movement which necessitates support by the central bank; an adverse influence on the liquid position of a company caused, *e.g.*, by inflation.

Draw. To picture or portray; to write a cheque, draft or order upon a banker.

Drawback. Money paid back, especially excise or import duty remitted or refunded on goods exported; a deduction, a rebate.

Draw Down. To take up part or all of an agreed standby facility—not normally applied to retail banking in the form of overdrafts, but more often found in connection with standby facilities in the wholesale market of £100,000 and upwards.

Drawee. The person on whom a bill is drawn. When he has accepted the bill he is known as the acceptor. The acceptor of a bill, by accepting it, engages that he will pay it according to the tenor of his acceptance, and cannot deny to a holder in due course (1) the existence of the drawer, the genuineness of his signature, and his capacity and authority to draw the bill; (2) in the case of a bill drawn to drawer's order, the then capacity of the drawer to indorse, but not the genuineness or validity of his indorsement; (3) in the case of a bill payable to the order of a third person, the existence of the payee and his then capacity to indorse, but not the genuineness or validity of his indorsement. The acceptor accepts a bill by signing his name across the face of it. *See also* Acceptance.

Drawer. The person who writes out and signs a cheque or a bill of exchange. By drawing the bill he engages that on presentation it will be accepted and paid according to its tenor, and if it is not he will compensate the holder or any indorser who is compelled to pay it, provided that the requisite proceedings on dishonour are taken. He cannot deny to a holder in due course the existence of the payee and his then capacity to indorse.

Drawing Account. A current account; an account used to record all sums drawn by a partner or business proprietor for his personal use.

Drawing Rights. *See* Special Drawing Rights.

Drawn Bond. A bond which has been drawn or selected for repayment upon a certain date.

Dresser le Bilan. To strike a balance sheet. *See also* Window Dressing.

Drive-in Bank. A branch office having a cashier so positioned that he/she may pay money to, or receive money from, a customer through the window of the customer's car.

Drive-in-Schalter. See Drive-in Bank.

Droit. Right, due, fee, law.

Droit à la Clientèle. See Goodwill.

Droit d'Auteurs. Copyright.

Droit de Douane. Customs duty.

Droit de Souscription. The right of a shareholder to participate in a new issue of capital, in proportion to his existing holding. This right is generally negotiable and can therefore be acquired and exercised by some person other than the shareholder; the right of a shareholder, during a certain period, to subscribe for shares of the issuing company at a fixed price.

Droit de Succession. Succession duty.

Droit de Timbre. Stamp duty.

Droits de Garde. Annual charges for safe custody and/or management.

Droits de Tirage Spéciaux (**D.T.S.**). *See* Special Drawing Rights.

Dual Control. The principle that two bank officers, one preferably being a senior, must together take some act such as entering the bank's strongroom; the system of keyholding to ensure this; the appointment of not less than two trustees to administer a trust.

Dubiose Debitoren. Doubtful debts.

Ducroire. See Del Credere.

Due Date of Bill. The date on which a bill of exchange is payable. This is on the last day of the time of payment as fixed by the bill, or, if that is a non-business day, on the succeeding business day. The time of payment as fixed by the bill is at a fixed and stated period after date or sight, or on or at a fixed period after the occurrence of a specified event which is certain to happen. A demand bill is payable on demand, or at sight, or on presentation. A cheque, unless post-dated, is payable on demand. A post-dated cheque is payable on or after its date.

Dumping. Selling goods in overseas markets at a cheaper rate than in the home market.

Duopoly. A situation where there are only two producers of a particular commodity.

Duplicate. A copy of an original document having equal binding force; a copy made in lieu of a document lost or destroyed; the second copy of a bill drawn in two parts. Where a bill has been lost before it is overdue, the person who was the holder of it may apply to the drawer to give him a duplicate bill, giving the drawer an indemnity if required.

Durable Goods. Goods which require replacement only at long intervals.

Durée. The term of a loan; the currency of a bill; the time before and up to the date of repayment.

Duress. Hardship, imprisonment or constraint, actual or threatened violence. If in an action on a bill it is admitted or proved that the acceptance, issue or subsequent negotiation of the bill is affected with fraud, duress, force or fear, or illegality, the burden of proof is shifted, unless and until the holder proves that, subsequent to the alleged fraud or illegality, value has in good faith been given for the bill.

Dutch Auction. A sale in which property is offered above its value, and the price gradually lowered until someone accepts an offer.

Duty of Secrecy. *See* Secrecy.

E

Earmark. Any distinctive mark or feature; to set a distinctive mark upon; to allocate for a particular purpose—used especially of the allocation of funds or of a balance on an account.

Earned Income. For tax purposes, income derived from paid employment, whether as an employee or as a self-employed person, as contrasted with *Unearned Income*.

Earned Income Relief. A fundamental distinction has always been made in U.K. taxation between earned and unearned income, the latter being taxed at a higher rate. Especial relief was given to earned income because it was the direct result of the personal labour of the taxpayer. With the introduction of unified tax, the earned income relief was abolished, a compensatory increase in personal allowances being given in lieu. It is still necessary to maintain the distinction, however, because the investment income surcharge which (with the higher rate tax) replaced surtax, is applicable only to unearned income.

Earnest. A pledge, an assurance of something to come. Money given by a buyer to a seller to bind an oral agreement between them.

Earning Assets. Those assets of a bank which earn an income for the bank, *i.e.* money at call and short notice, bills discounted, investments and advances.

Earnings Yield. The profit of a limited company in relation to the total of the ordinary share capital, after all charges have been paid.

Easement. A liberty, right or privilege, without profit, which one proprietor has in or through the estate of another, *e.g.*, a right of way, air, light, etc. An easement may be legal or equitable.

Écart. The difference between two quotations or two rates of interest.

E.C.G.D. Policy. A policy issued by the Export Credits Guarantee Department (*q.v.*), issued to exporters by the Department of Trade to give them cover against the insolvency or default of the overseas buyer and various other risks not ordinarily insurable. A charge on such a policy may be taken by a bank.

Échéance. The date of repayment of a loan, especially the annual date for coupon payment from a bond.

Econometrics. The use of statistical and mathematical methods in the evaluation and testing of economic theories.

Economic Growth. The rate of expansion in the volume of production of goods and services of a country, the rate at which the gross national product increases from one year to another.

Economic Planning. The allocation of the factors of production of a country following a decision as to the amount and kind of goods and services which shall be produced in an ensuing period.

Economics. The science which deals with the rules governing the production, distribution and consumption of the world's resources and the management of State income and expenditure in terms of money.

Économie. Saving, thrift.

Edinburgh Gazette. *See* Gazette.

Effects Not Cleared. *See* Uncleared Effects.

Effekten. Funds, stocks, etc., readily saleable or transferable, which are therefore peculiarly suitable for stock exchange business.

Effet. A bill or note; an action or operation.

Effet Commercial. A bill of exchange based upon a merchandise transaction.

Effet de Change. A bill or note which must comply with legal form, the principal types being a draft, in which the drawer undertakes that the payee will receive payment of a sum of money from the drawee, and an I.O.U., which is a promise to pay.

Effet de Change de Cautionnement. *See* Dépôt de Change.

Effet de Change de Garantie. *See* Dépôt de Change.

Effet de Change en Blanc. A bill lacking the amount, or possibly some other essential detail; a blank cheque.

Effet du Trésor. A Treasury bill.
Effet Financier. A bill of exchange other than one based upon a merchandise transaction.
Eigenkapital. Net worth of an undertaking.
Eigentumsübertragung. Conveyancing.
Eigentumsvorbehalt. The completion of the satisfaction of a sum due by various instalments agreeable to the seller.
Eigenwechsel. Promissory note.
Einfache Bürgschaft. A secondary guarantee which can only be called upon when the principal debtor can no longer maintain his repayments. See also *Bürgschaft.*
Einfuhr. Import.
Einführung an der Börse. The granting of a share price on the Stock Exchange.
Einführungsprospekt. Opening prospectus in prescribed form of share quotations.
Einkommen. Income.
Einlage. Deposit.
Einlageheft. Deposit book.
Einnahmereserven. Revenue reserves.
Einschlag. See *Disagio.*
Einschuss. Paid-up capital.
Einzelhandelspreis. Retail price.
Ejusdem Generis. Of the same kind or description.
Election. A choice. A legal doctrine where a person must choose between one of two courses, as where a plaintiff may elect to sue one or other of joint defendants, but cannot sue first one and then the other; or where a beneficiary under a will must choose one of two advantageous courses, but cannot take the benefit of both together.
Eligible Bill. A bank bill payable in the United Kingdom accepted by a British or Commonwealth bank whose name appears on a list published by the Bank of England, including the London and Scottish clearing banks, members of the Accepting Houses Committee, the larger British Overseas banks and those Commonwealth banks which have had branches in the City of London for many years, together with certain other banks and some Bank of England customers of long standing. These bills are eligible for re-discount at the Bank of England and qualify as reserve assets for United Kingdom banks up to a maximum of 2% of total eligible liabilities.
Eligible Liabilities. The sterling deposits of the banking system as a whole, excluding deposits having an original maturity of more than two years, plus any sterling resources gained by switching foreign currencies into sterling, and including promissory notes, bills and other negotiable paper, items in suspense and 60% of credit items in transmission. Interbank transactions and sterling certificates of deposit (both held and issued) are taken into the calculation of individual banks' liabilities on a net basis, irrespective of term. See also *Corset; Reserve Assets; Special Deposits.*
Elegit. The name of an old writ of execution chosen by a successful creditor-plaintiff to take possession of lands or property of the defendant for his own use until the sum awarded was paid. The modern practice is to obtain a charging order in respect of such land.
Emballage. Packing.
Embargo. A prohibition by authority upon the departure of vessels from ports under its jurisdiction; a complete suspension of foreign commerce or of a particular branch of foreign trade; an order forbidding the despatch of a certain class of goods, usually munitions, to a foreign country; a prohibition of any travel in or out of a country, whether by land, sea or air, as a result of an attempted coup.
Embassy Documents. Consular and legalised invoices required by certain importing countries' authorities.
Embezzlement. The fraudulent misappropriation by an employee to his own use of money or goods rightfully belonging to his employer.
Emblement. The produce of land sown or planted; growing crops annually produced by the labour of the cultivator, which belong to the tenant, though his lease may terminate before harvest, and in the event of his death fall to his executors; sometimes extended to the natural products of the soil.
Émetteur. Issuer.
Émission. The putting into circulation of money, banknotes, newly-issued shares or bonds, etc. See also *Nouvelle Émission.*
Emissionspreis. Offer price of a new issue.
Emissionsprospekt. An issue prospectus, in terms regulated by law, giving an opening account of expenses paid out and property held, in respect of a new loan.

Emissionssyndikat. A group of banks handling a new issue.

Emittent. The name of the bank or place where a new issue is being handled.

Emprunt. A loan, a medium or long term debt, generally at a fixed rate of interest, divided into units.

Emprunt à Lots, Emprunt à Primes. Lottery bonds carrying no interest, or only a low rate of interest, prizes being periodically allotted to specific bonds by drawings.

Emprunt Indexé. A loan where capital and interest are linked to an index of prices or to some basic value, with the aim of protecting the holder from loss through depreciation of money.

Encaissement Documentaire. Payment by a bank under a documentary credit against the documents of title to the goods.

Encumbrance. *See* Incumbrance.

Endorsement. *See* Indorsement.

Endowment Policy. A life assurance policy under the terms of which a fixed sum of money is payable at the end of a certain number of years if the insured has survived that long, *e.g.* payable at the age of sixty. Such policies may be with or without profits.

Endowment Profits. Profits made by banks from higher interest rates imposed as a matter of governmental policy.

Enfranchisement. The conversion of a copyhold into freehold on commutation of services due to the lord of the manor.

En Nom-Beteiligung. Participation in a syndicate handling a new issue, particularly by a bank whose name appears in the issue prospectus.

Enquiry (Status or Bankers'). *See* Status Enquiry.

Enschadigung. Indemnity, compensation.

En Soignant. A stock exchange order leaving discretion to buy or sell with the bank, which will take into consideration the current quotations rather than completing the order at any cost; thus the bank will not buy if prices are very high, or will not sell if prices are very low.

En Souffrance. Unpaid—as where, for example, one speaks of loans where the capital repayments, or the interest, are not paid punctually on the due date.

Entailed Interest. *See* Estate in Fee Tail.

Entered Inwards. *See* Bill of Entry.

Entered Outwards. *See* Bill of Entry.

En Train. In progress.

Entrepôt. A bonded warehouse; an intermediate warehouse for goods in transit. *See also* Re-export.

Entrepôt Hors Douane. *See* Bonded Warehouse.

Entrepreneur. A contractor, an organiser of trade or business, one who brings land, capital and labour together in pursuit of some defined commercial end.

Entreitien. *See* Maintenance.

Entry. The act of inscribing in a book; an item so entered; a credit or debit amount passed to a customer's account; the act of taking possession by setting foot upon land or tenements; the depositing of a document in the proper office; the formal placing on record. *See also* Double Entry; Single Entry.

En Ventre sa Mère. "In the belly of his mother"; the embryo conceived but not yet born. For the purpose of English land law, particularly in relation to the rule against perpetuities, this embryo counts as a life in being.

Épargne. Economy, thrift, savings.

Épargne à Primes. Savings on which the bank pays not only interest, but also, if certain conditions are fulfilled, a supplementary bonus.

Épargne Forcée. Forced savings, curtailment of expenses made necessary by State measures. The money saved is put at the disposal of the state, by way of loan, to serve certain ends, such as the payment of an increase in the old-age pension, for example.

E Pluribus Unum. "One out of many".

Equal Pay. Equal remuneration for both men and women for work of equal value; the removal of discrimination between men and women concerning pay and conditions of employment.

Equalising the Dividend. If necessary, supplementing a dividend payment from reserves, or reducing a possible dividend sum so as to permit a transfer to reserves, in order to maintain a dividend at a consistent and reliable level.

Équilibrer une Position. To balance one's commitments by the purchase or sale of shares, stock, bonds, foreign currencies, bills, goods or merchandise, etc.

Equipment Bond. On the Continent, railway company bonds secured by a charge on rolling stock.

Equitable Assignment. An assignment is a transfer by a creditor to an assignee of the right to receive a benefit (usually money) from a debtor. The requirements for a legal assignment were stated in the Law of Property Act 1925. The assignment must be absolute and not purporting to be by way of charge only; it must be in writing and notice of the assignment must be given to the debtor. If these conditions are satisfied the assignment passes, subject to prior equities, the legal right to the debt together with all legal remedies for non-payment. An assignment which does not satisfy all these statutory conditions is an equitable assignment. Bankers are concerned with assignment in three cases; bills of exchange, life policies, and book debts. In the case of bills of exchange, including cheques, the proceeds are assigned every time the bill, or cheque, is negotiated. In the cases of life policies and book debts, the banker is concerned because he commonly takes both these forms of security. *See also* Assignment.

Equitable Charge. *See* Equitable Mortgage.

Equitable Doctrine. A legal principle of belief stemming from equity, which offers a more just alternative to a common law principle.

Equitable Estate. The estate enjoyed by a beneficiary to whom come all the income and advantages of the estate, as opposed to the *Legal Estate*, which may be held by trustees who must negotiate any matters relating to the legal ownership of the estate, which they hold for the benefit of the owner of the equitable estate. A person may be both the legal estate owner and at the same time the owner of the equitable estate, as a person who owns the unencumbered house in which he lives.

Equitable Interest. An interest which before 1873 would have been enforceable only in a court of equity. Since then common law and equity have been administered side by side in the same courts, and equitable interest is one dependant not on common law but upon principles of equity.

Equitable Lien. A lien which most generally arises when a seller has passed property to a buyer before he has been paid. He becomes entitled to an equitable lien for the amount of the unpaid purchase money which is enforceable by a sale under the direction of the court.

Equitable Mortgage. A mortgage in which both possession and ownership of the security remain with the borrower.

Equitable Waste. A tenant for life under a settlement is nearly always unaccountable either for voluntary or permissive waste, and may therefore at common law open new mines or fell timber and sell it as absolute owner. In equity, however, wanton or extravagant acts of destruction, *e.g.* felling ornamental trees, will be restrained by an injunction coupled with an order to rehabilitate the premises. These acts are described as equitable waste because before 1873 they could be restrained only in a court of equity. Now, however, a tenant for life is by statute declared to have no right to commit equitable waste unless such a right can be construed from the instrument of creation.

Equity. Justice, fairness; a body of legal principles which slowly developed in England to remedy injustices due to a too rigorous application of the letter of the law, being administered until 1873 in the Chancery Division of the courts, but now having its administration merged with that of the common law.

Equity Capital for Industry (E.C.I.) (the Equity Bank). A fund raised in 1976 from various investing institutions (principally insurance companies and life offices, pension funds, and investment trusts) to be invested in fresh equity capital for quoted and unquoted small- to medium-sized industrial companies. The new institution met with mixed reactions from those who, it was hoped, would subscribe the capital, the main stumbling block being a doubt that there was a significant gap in the present lending system of finding capital for industry. Funds from banks and financial institutions were thought to be usually quite readily available to industry, although there have been criticisms of the major investing institutions for being too remote from manufacturing industry and too insensitive to its needs. Eventually the objects and advantages of E.C.I. were stated to be—

It would assist those recipients who would normally be too small for major institutions, and who could not turn to other sources of cash for some reason or other, *e.g.*, where a company is unable to make a rights issue because its shares are standing at or below par; or where a company needing equity capital cannot obtain it because it is highly geared. £40·9m capital has been raised for these purposes. Contrary to earlier indications, E.C.I. will not take an active role in the management of companies in which it invests.

Equity of a Company. *See* Ordinary Shares.

Equity of Redemption. The right allowed to a mortgagor to have a reasonable time within which to redeem his estate when mortgaged for a sum less than its worth; the right of a legal mortgagor of real or personal property to have his property re-transferred to him on repayment of the sum so secured.

Erbschaftssteuer. Succession duty.

Ergonomics. The study of the relationship between a worker's abilities and the work he does, with the objective of suiting the man to the work.

Ermächtigte Bank. See Authorised Banks.

Erneuerungsschein. See Talon.

Eröffnungskurs. The opening rate for any stock on a stock exchange.

Ersparnis. Saving economies.

Ertragsbilanz. The yearly position of a country engaged in international traffic, taking account of all outstanding demands and obligations, but excluding movements of capital.

Ertragsrechnung. Profit and loss account.

Ertragswert. The estimated value of an asset on the basis of present or future profits to be expected from it.

Escheat. The reverting of property to the lord of the fee, or to the Crown, or to the State, on the death of the owner intestate without heirs; property so reverting. This legal process was abolished in 1925, since when the same end has been achieved by the transfer to the Crown of the property as *bona vacantia*.

Escompte. Discount.

Escompte de Caisse. A percentage deduction allowed when an invoice is paid within a given time.

Escompter. To discount, to anticipate, to discount in anticipation (as on the stock exchange).

Escroc. A swindler.

Escrow. A deed, kept in the possession of a third person, which cannot be put into legal operation until the grantee has met certain conditions. When the conditions have been complied with, the document is then delivered to the grantee, and takes effect as a deed.

Eskomptieren. To discount, to take into account in advance, to bear in mind.

Esnecy. The right of the eldest daughter to make first choice in the division of property descending to daughters (coparceners) in default of male heirs.

Espèces. The total banknotes and coin in circulation in an economy.

Estate. Everything which a person possesses, the total of his goods, property and money; the length of time for which an interest in land will exist. *See also* Equitable Estate; Freehold Estate; Leasehold Estate; Legal Estate.

Estate Agent. An agent who arranges for the sale and purchase of houses and properties.

Estate Contract. A contract by an estate owner to create a legal estate, including a contract conferring either expressly or by statutory implication a valid option of purchase, a right of pre-emption, or any other like right. This in practice means a contract for the sale of a legal fee simple, an agreement for the grant of a term of years absolute, or an option to acquire either of these interests, *e.g.*, a tenant's option to renew a lease. Estate contracts are registrable as land charges in the sub-division C(IV); *see* Land Charges; Land Charges Register.

Estate Duty. *See* Capital Transfer Tax.

Estate for Life. An estate where land is limited to a tenant for his own lifetime, or for the lifetime of another person (*pur autre vie*).

Estate in Fee Simple. The word "fee" meant that the estate would endure until the owner died intestate, leaving no heir. If he left an heir the estate passed to him, and so on. "Simple" meant that the estate would pass to any heir and that the descent was not restricted to any particular class of heir. The doctrine of heirship (except in the case of an entailed interest) was abolished in 1925, since when the land no longer passes to the nearest heir, but on the death of its owner intestate is held by administrators on a trust for sale. Either the land, or the money for which it has been sold, now passes to the nearest relations, so that the fee simple is still an estate which is inheritable even if it has been converted into money. The *Fee Simple Absolute in Possession* is the highest type of land holding and the nearest to absolute ownership that it is possible to get. It is capable of lasting indefinitely. "Absolute" means "not subject to conditions" and "in possession" means in possession and enjoyment of the land itself or receiving the rents and profits from the land, or having the right to receive the same. A *Determinable Fee Simple* is one which, according to the express terms of its limitation, may be brought to an end by some happening or event before the completion of the full period for which it may possibly continue.

Estate in Fee Tail. An estate in land which continues to exist only so long as the original tenant or any of his descendants survive. Thus the right to interest is restricted to a class of heirs specially mentioned in the gift. (Also called *Estate Tail* or *Entailed Interest*.) *See also* Base Fee.

Estate Owner. A person or body of persons in whom an estate in land is vested. In the case of a fee simple absolute in possession the "estate owner" may be a beneficial owner entitled in his own right, a personal representative, a mortgagor, a tenant for life or trustees for sale. *See also* Settled Land.

Estate *Pur Autre Vie*. *See* Estate for Life.

Estate Tail. *See* Estate in Fee Tail.

Estimate. An assessment by an individual, firm or company of how much a certain job will cost. An assessment is not binding and the actual cost may be more or less.

Estoppel. Anything which prevents a person by his own acts or words from denying or confirming a fact, or the true validity of a document. Estoppel is given when a representation, overt or implied, which is meant to induce a certain course of conduct on the part of the person to whom the representation is made, is followed by an act or omission by that person as a result of the representation, such act or omission leading directly to loss or damage to such a person.

Estovers. The right enjoyed by a tenant to take wood from an estate, either for repairs or for fuel; any necessaries of life allowed by law; alimony.

Et Alia (*Et Al.*). And others.

Étalon-Or. A monetary system based on gold which was freely minted into gold coins of legal size and weight and accordingly enjoyed unlimited confidence while acting as the legal currency. The yellow metal was particularly useful for making payments abroad and acted as a regulator of exchange rates through the operation of the gold points. It fulfilled at one and the same time the functions of a measure of value, an instrument of exchange, and a means of saving. *See also* Gold Standard; Specie Points.

Etat. (Ge.) Budget.

État de Compte. Budget, stock-taking.

Et Hoc Genus Omne. And everything of this kind.

Et Sequens (Et Seq.). And the following.

Étude du Travail. Work study. *See* Time and Motion Study.

Eurobonds. International bonds issued in various currencies by Government concerns or big international companies. They may be in the form of bonds, debentures or convertible debentures. The Eurobond investor must be an owner of foreign currency held outside the country of the currency's origin. A secondary bond market has been established in which the Eurobond may be bought and sold. The Eurobond market is unique in having no material base and therefore in being unable to look to any government for support should its prices collapse.

Eurocard. A cheque card available for use in the *Eurocheque Scheme*; *see* Cheque Card.

Eurocheque Scheme. A scheme whereby holders of cheque cards can cash their personal cheques abroad for travel expenditure only. The extension of the use of the cheque card abroad relates only to the encashment of individual cheques up to £30 twice daily at banks participating in the scheme (nearly all European banks) and does not cover payments to hotels, restaurants and shops. Payment is made in the currency of the country. The continental Eurocheque is described under Cheque Card.

Euroclear. International clearing system for the settlement of transactions in securities, essentially Eurobonds. It is based in Brussels and is provided under contract by Morgan Guaranty for over a hundred banks which own it.

Eurocurrency. A term used to describe

deposits of currency, at first dollars, but also guilders, Swiss francs, sterling and deutschmarks, which are held by people who do not live in the country whose currency it is, and who keep the deposits in a third country. For example, a bank in France which received dollars from Spain (or any other country except the U.S.) would have some Eurodollars. These could be lent out at a good rate of interest to anyone wishing to borrow in that currency. The actual dollars would throughout remain in the U.S., but as the borrowers and lenders concluded their agreements various accounts in the U.S. would be credited and debited with the sums in question. There is a ready market for Eurocurrencies. The demand comes from banks and continental industrial firms. The main market for Eurosterling is in Paris, and for other Eurocurrencies in London.

Eurodollars. *See* Eurocurrency.

Europäische Freihandelszone. *See* European Free Trade Association (E.F.T.A.).

Europäische Wirtschaftgemeinschaft (E.W.G.). *See* Common Market.

European Composite Unit (Eurco). A weighted "basket" of the currencies of the nine countries of the E.E.C.

European Currency Unit (E.C.U.). A multiple-currency unit linked to the currencies of the six original E.E.C. members. The investor receives payment in whichever currency is the strongest, but at its old parity.

European Economic Community (E.E.C.). *See* Common Market.

European Free Trade Association (E.F.T.A.). An economic association of countries formed in 1960 with the object of achieving an area of free trade by the reduction of tariff barriers between them. The original members were the U.K., Denmark, Austria, Norway, Sweden, Switzerland and Portugal, later joined by Iceland and Finland. The abolition of all internal tariffs and trade quotas was achieved in a few years while the level of external tariffs remained as a matter for each individual country to determine. The intention was to compensate for a possible loss of trade with the then Common Market countries by an increase in trade between themselves. In 1972 the U.K. and Denmark left E.F.T.A. on joining the E.E.C.

European Investment Bank (E.I.B.). A bank formed in 1958 to assist economic development within the E.E.C., having its headquarters at Brussels. This is done by making or guaranteeing long-term loans which will further the balanced development of the Community. Loans of from £1m to £20m are normally made for from seven to twenty years against acceptable security or the guarantee of a member country. For smaller transactions the E.I.B. allocates a block sum to credit institutions (as, for example, the Industrial and Commercial Finance Corporation) and delegates the disbursement to them.

European Monetary Agreement. An agreement on the settlement in gold of outstanding debits and credits of the former European Payments Union when sterling and other West European currencies became fully convertible in 1959. With convertibility came a free and effective foreign exchange market, well equipped to handle the business of settling inter-European debts, and rendering the E.P.U. superfluous.

European Monetary Union. The proposed establishment of a common currency for the E.E.C. countries.

European Payments Union (E.P.U.). A scheme introduced in 1950 to encourage multilateral trade between the European countries, to work towards convertibility and to act as a clearing house for financial settlements within the group. Each country was allotted a quota, based on its share of world trade, of the initial reserves of $350 million, provided by the U.S.A. Surpluses and deficits between the fifteen member countries were recorded as debits or credits and there was a monthly settlement of net debit or credit positions, made in gold or U.S. dollars, or by entries to the members' credit balances. The scheme was handled by the Bank for International Settlements based in Basle. With the coming in 1959 of convertibility of sterling and other West European currencies the E.P.U. ceased to function, and its place was taken by the European Monetary Agreement.

European Unit of Account (E.U.A.). Dating from the mid-1970s, the E.U.A. is similar to the Special Drawing Right in that it is calculated as a "basket" of currencies, but by reference to the various currencies of the member states of the European Economic Community only. As it is based on floating rates it has itself a floating value. *See* Special Drawing Rights.

Évaluation. Estimate, assessment, appraisal.

Ex-. Former, out of or from, without.

Examination of Title. The checking of a person's claim to be the owner of a valuable asset, particularly in a bank, in connection with security. Whereas in some cases the mere production of the certificate or evidence of ownership is enough (as in the case of stock exchange security where an equitable charge is to be taken), in others a more searching check is made (as in the case of land). In this last case the examination of title is done by a solicitor, whether the land is unregistered or registered. Because the bank may need to sell the land, if the advance is not repaid, it must be sure that it has a good title to offer a possible purchaser: this in turn depends upon the title of its borrowing customer. *See* Land Certificate (for registered land); *Prima Facie* Check (of Deeds).

Ex Cathedra. Authoritatively.

Excédent. See Surplus.

Excess Depreciation. In addition to that for ordinary depreciation of currency. A diminution or lessening of the power of the monetary unit over the market, diminution being shown by a rise in prices.

Excess Liquidity. The maintenance by banks of a greater degree of liquidity than is normally prudentially desirable. Such high liquidity is unlikely to be voluntary: it usually arises from the reluctance of borrowers to come forward, either because of a lack of confidence or because of high interest rates.

Exchange. To give or receive in return for something else, to hand over for an equivalent in kind; exchanging of coins for their value in coins of the same or another country; the system by which goods or property are exchanged and debts settled, especially in different countries, without the transfer of money; the place where merchants, brokers, etc., meet to transact business. *See also* Bill of Exchange; Forward Exchange; Parities.

Exchange as per Indorsement. A clause put on a bill of exchange by the drawer to ensure that the importer pays an amount in his own currency which, when calculated at the rate of exchange quoted in the indorsement, will be equivalent to the sterling amount of the bill. The rate is inserted by the negotiating banker and represents his buying rate of exchange on the bill.

Exchange Broker. An agent operating on the foreign exchange market for principals who pay him commission.

Exchange Clause. A clause put on a bill of exchange drawn in sterling on a person abroad to establish the method of calculating the rate of exchange at which the bill is to be paid, so as to ensure that any exchange charges will be paid by the drawee, *e.g.* "Payable at the current rate of exchange for sight drafts on London", "Exchange as per indorsement", etc.

Exchange Commission. The charge made for exchanging sums in one currency for sums in another.

Exchange Control. A system of control by government operating through the central bank over scarce supplies of the currencies of other countries. The nationals of a country are allowed to obtain foreign currency only on application to the central bank and only for purposes approved by the government. In this way imports may be restricted to goods and commodities considered essential for the country's welfare, and foreign travel may be restricted to that designed to increase the country's export trade, to the exclusion of holiday-makers and tourists. Powers to approve applications may be delegated to authorised banks, and limits may be set to the extent of such delegation so that requests of a particular type or for larger sums must be forwarded to the central bank. Bank accounts may be designated resident or non-resident, the balances on the latter being freely transferable abroad. The purchase of foreign stocks or foreign properties may be forbidden or restricted by a requirement that such funds may come only from the proceeds of foreign currency resulting from sales of similar stocks or properties by nationals. The inadequacy of such investment currency itself creates a premium which is no part of official exchange control policy. There is also usually restriction on foreign business investment.

Exchange Equalisation Account. An account managed by the Bank of England on behalf of the Treasury, for the purpose of maintaining reasonable stability in the value of the pound sterling on the foreign exchanges. For that purpose the whole of the country's reserves of gold and foreign currency have been transferred to the account for the use of the managers as required. Since the floating of the pound the managers have been mostly concerned to prevent the rate from falling too steeply. This is effected by buying in sterling on the exchanges so as to increase the demand for it and so tend to raise the rate.

Exchange Rates. *See* Parities.

Exchequer. The State treasury, the government department dealing with the public revenue, finances or pecuniary resources.

Exchequer and Audit Department. A department charged with the function of authorising issues from the Exchequer and auditing and reporting to the House of Commons on all government expenditure.

Excise. A tax or duty on certain articles produced and consumed in a country; the branch of the Civil Service which collects and manages the excise duties, namely the Commissioners of Customs and Excise; a tax of any kind.

Excise Duties. Taxes on home-produced articles, as contrasted with customs duties, which are levied on imports.

Excise Licences. A tax on the enjoyment of certain services or facilities, *e.g.* television, motor vehicle, driving and dog licences.

***Ex* Coupon.** Bonds sold without the benefit of the next instalment of interest to be paid.

***Ex* Curia.** Out of court.

***Ex* Div.** Shares sold without the benefit of the current dividend shortly to be paid.

***Ex* Drawing.** Bonds sold without any benefit there may be from a drawing for repayment due to be made.

Execute. To carry into effect, to put into force; to perform what is required to give validity to any legal instrument, as by signing and sealing.

Executed Agreement. This means a document, signed by or on behalf of the parties, embodying the terms of a regulated agreement, or such of them as have been reduced to writing.

Executed Contract. One in which at least one party has actually performed his duties under the contract.

Executive. A body appointed to administer the affairs of a corporation, a company or a club; a high official of such a body; under the parliamentary system, members chosen from the legislature to carry into effect the laws of the country; one who is responsible for seeing that a certain part or aspect of the company's work is carried out.

Executive Currency Packs. A pack or assortment of low denomination currencies of a number of countries for travellers' use, so that they may be able to pay taxi fares, tip baggage handlers, etc., immediately on arrival at their destination. Packages contain currency worth £10 or £15. The countries covered in the scheme include Bahrain, Columbia, Hungary, Iran, Saudi Arabia, Thailand, Turkey and Venezuela. The packs are issued by British Airways in conjunction with a U.K. subsidiary of a group of foreign exchange companies.

Executor. A person appointed by a testator to pay his debts and to carry out the provisions of his will.

Executor and Trustee Corporation. Specialised companies attached to banks and other financial organisations which offer to act as personal representative or trustee. They have the advantage that, not being mortal as is a person, they can carry out their duties without any break. They will see to the deceased's funeral, agree and pay the capital transfer tax, obtain probate of his will, pay legacies, and act in the best interests of the beneficiaries. A will should contain a charging clause, empowering the bank to pass its fees to the debit of the estate. The corporation usually charges an acceptance fee on a percentage basis on the value of the estate as ascertained for capital transfer tax purposes, an annual fee for administration, which may include the judicious investment of trust funds, and a vacating fee on termination. It will act alone or jointly with a named executor.

Executor *de son Tort*. A person who without authority intermeddles in the estate of a deceased person.

Executor's Year. The period normally thought sufficient for an executor to deal with the estate of the deceased, pay capital transfer tax, debts and legacies, etc., and wind up the estate. More complicated estates, however, will require a longer time.

Executory Contract. One in which all the duties set out in the contract remain to be performed in the future.

Exekution. Distraint; compulsory regulations as on a stock exchange or in connection with foreign exchange business.

Exemplary Damages. Damages based on the principle of punishing the defendant rather than compensating the plaintiff (also known as Punitive or Vindictive Damages).

Exemplification. An attested copy of any proceedings in a court of record.

Exemplification of Probate. A duplicate copy of probate, issued by the court in cases where the original has been lost.

Exemplify. To illustrate by example, to manifest, to witness; to prove by an attested copy, to make an authenticated copy of.

Exempt Agreement. A consumer credit agreement where the creditor is a building society or a local authority which finances the purchase of land, or the provision of dwellings on land, against the security of a mortgage on the land; any debtor–creditor agreement secured by mortgage of land.

Exempted Dealers. Dealers, including banks, insurance companies and independent pension funds, who are authorised by the Department of Trade to buy and sell securities on their own behalf.

Exemption Clause. A clause in a contract which seeks to protect one party from being sued by the other for negligence, non-performance, damage or loss, etc. Bankers use them in documents of foreign trade, where the clause states that the bank accepts no liability for any loss, damage or delay, however caused, which is not directly due to the fault or negligence of its own employees, and in replies to status enquiries, which are stated to be given without responsibility on the part of the sender. Such a clause will be effective except where the information is given fraudulently. In general, however, an exemption clause may be narrowly interpreted by a court, and in each case it should be seen to be reasonable in the particular circumstances and as regards the particular parties; and, on a broader basis, not unreasonable from the point of view of the public at large.

Exercise. *See* Financial Year.

Ex Facie. Manifestly, on the face of it.

Ex Gratia. As a favour (not as a legal right).

Ex New. Shares sold without the benefit of new shares being issued to existing shareholders—that is, the seller reserves to himself the right to receive the new shares.

Ex Officio. By virtue of office, official.

Ex Parte. On one side only, one-sided.

Expectation of Life. The statistical basis of an assurance company's assessment of risk. Although it is not possible to say how long a man will live, it is possible to say how long a group of men, or women, will live from a given moment in time. Actuarial tables showing the expectation of life from different ages are compiled and regularly revised, and these form the basis of life assurance premium assessment.

Expenses. Outlay, cost, expenditure; the costs of an action. For tax purposes, deductions from income before tax is charged. Employed persons must satisfy the tax inspector that the expenses have been incurred wholly, exclusively, and necessarily in the performance of the duties of the employment. Self-employed persons must show that the expenses have been incurred wholly and exclusively for the purpose of the business.

Export. To send goods or produce out of a country, the act of exporting. *See also* Invisible Exports; Visible Exports.

Export Agent. An agent who arranges a contract between his principal, an exporter of goods or services, and a foreign buyer.

Exportation. *See* Export.

Exportation de Capital. The export of funds in various ways: for example, by the issue or sale of bonds or of foreign shares, by the granting of credit to overseas debtors, and by financing foreign branches or businesses.

Exportation Invisible. Invisible exports.

Exportation Visible. Visible exports.

Export Credits Guarantee Department (E.C.G.D.). A Government department which since 1919 has provided insurance cover for British exports abroad. The principal risks covered are the insolvency of the buyer, political restrictions delaying payment, the imposition of new import licensing restrictions in the buyer's country, war, and cancellation of a U.K. export licence. Over the years the types of policy available have broadened and diversified and the department now also provides in certain circumstances guarantees to banks lending to exporter-customers. Such guarantees cover short-, medium- and long-term finance. The Department now provides cover against cost escalation (where the contract is for £2m or over, and the manufacturing period 2 years or more); cover for investment abroad against appropriation, war risks and restrictions on remittances; and guarantees to assist in obtaining performance bonds. *See also* Buyer Credit; Supplier Credit.

Exporters' Yearbook. A source of information of documentary requirements for different countries.

Export Finance Companies. Specialists in providing and arranging finance on a non-recourse basis for capital and semi-capital goods. These companies can offer to arrange E.C.G.D. cover themselves or they can accept assignment of the exporter's policy and, with the larger contracts, can arrange and manage the finance on behalf of a syndicate of banks in Britain. Finance can be provided for single transactions, or for a series of orders, or as a "package deal" for a large project, or through a credit line negotiated with a bank in the buyer's country. Their services are thus similar to, and extended beyond, those provided by merchant banks. The export finance companies can also usually arrange finance for non-sterling contracts raising a proportion of the required finance overseas.

Export Houses. Specialists in handling goods destined for practically every market in the world, serving all kinds of companies from the largest to the smallest and financing entrepôt trade. They may be involved at any stage of a transaction between a manufacturer and overseas buyer, and their activities range from the promotion of sales to the collection of debts. Among the many combinations of services, the main ones undertaken are to buy and sell on their own account as principals or to act as agent for the manufacturer or overseas buyer. Their financial services include paying the manufacturer immediately on shipment, making arrangements for credit facilities on behalf of their clients where these are required, or as factors assuming the full responsibility for the collection of the debts. In the case of overseas firms engaged in importing direct from Britain, they will also act as "confirming houses", financing and confirming contracts on behalf of the buyer.

Exportrisikogarantie. A State guarantee, on payment of a fee, to an exporter against certain risks connected with the export of goods abroad (*e.g.* political upheavals, transport and preservation risks, etc.). *See also* Export Credits Guarantee Department (E.C.G.D.).

Export Specie Point. *See* Specie Points.

Exposé. An explanatory summary; a full account.

Ex Post Facto. After the deed is done, retrospective.

Exposure Draft. A draft of a proposed measure, whether Parliamentary or not, prepared for reading and criticism by those who will be affected by it. In this way, the views of all interested parties will be taken into account before preparation of the Bill or instruction in its final form.

Express Trust. A trust which is expressly created by the person who imposes it.

Ex **Quay.** Goods to be taken under the control of the purchaser as soon as they have been landed.

Ex **Rights.** *See Ex* New.

Ex **Ship.** A price quoted for goods on arrival at the port, not including costs of unloading and delivery to the premises of the purchaser.

External Account. Sterling accounts of non-resident customers maintained by banks in this country. Bank of England permission is required before credits in passed to these accounts, because once money is on them it can be transferred abroad, thus affecting the country's balance of payments position.

External Convertibility. A currency with limited convertibility for the people of the issuing country, but freely convertible among foreign holders.

External Debt. The amount of debt owing by one country to another.

External Loan. A public loan raised from sources abroad.

Extra Cost. *See* Marginal Cost.

Extract Cards. *See* Check Ledger.

Extra Judicium. Out of court.

Extraordinary General Meeting. A meeting of the shareholders of a company for discussion and transaction of special business. Such a meeting may be called by the directors, or by members who hold at least one-tenth of the paid-up capital of the company, provided such capital holding carries the right to vote at general meetings.

Extraordinary Resolution. One passed by a majority of not less than three-fourths of such members as vote in person or by proxy, at a general meeting of which notice specifying the intention to propose the resolution as an extraordinary resolution has been duly given.

Ex **Warehouse.** The price to be paid if the purchaser collects the goods himself from the warehouse in which they are stored.

F

Fabrication. Manufacturing.

Fabrication en grande série. Mass production.

Face Value. Apparent worth; the nominal amount shown on coins, banknotes, etc.; the nominal value of stocks or shares.

Facility. Ease, aptitude, ease of access; in banking, an overdraft or loan limit or some other banking service which has been made available for a customer.

Facility Letter. A letter from a lending bank to a borrowing customer, confirming the terms on which a loan has been agreed. Such a letter specifies the total sum to be lent, the rate of interest to be charged, the terms of repayment, and the security to be charged. It will also lay down certain conditions or covenants which have to be observed—*e.g.* balance sheet ratios, security margins, total borrowing from all sources, etc. For the purposes of the Consumer Credit Act 1974, it is a letter which sets out certain terms of an overdraft agreement in a prescribed manner.

Facsimile. An exact copy of handwriting, printing, picture, etc.

Facsimile Signature. A signature placed on a document by rubber stamp. Such facsimile signatures on cheques are not acceptable to banks unless a suitable indemnity is given, because there is no guarantee that they have been placed on the cheque with the authority of the signatory.

Factage. The cost of postage on small parcels or packets.

Factor. An agent, one who transacts business for another on commission; a mercantile agent having in the customary course of his business as such agent authority either to sell goods, or to consign goods for the purpose of sale, or to buy goods, or to raise money on the security of goods; a steward or agent of an estate. A factor has the goods he sells in his own possession and deals in his own name, although he is buying or selling for a principal. *See also* Mercantile Agent.

Factorage. The commission paid to a factor by his employer.

Factor Cost. The price of goods paid by the consumer, less any tax or duty included in the price.

Factoring. The factor operates by buying from his client, a trading company, their invoiced debts. The client has fulfilled an order, dispatched the goods, and now awaits payment. Some debtors are slow to pay up, some may never pay. Credit control in the trading company may be lax. The factor becomes responsible for all credit control, sales, accounting and debt collection. Thus companies are able to sell their outstanding book debts for cash. The selling company receives payment for the debts purchased on a calculated *"Average Settlement Day"*. The company passes its invoices to the factor as soon as it has made them out. The full factoring service comprises maintenance of the company's sales ledger, credit control over the company's customers, full protection against bad debts and collection from debtors. The combination of these services is sometimes called *Maturity Factoring*. If, in addition, the company is being financed ahead of the maturity date (up to 80% against the indebtedness showing in the sales ledger) then this is *Financed Factoring*. Factoring is *"Disclosed"* or *"Undisclosed"* according to whether the supplier has notified his customers that payment is to be made to the factor or not. At one time there was a feeling that factoring was not quite respectable (a feeling which did not survive the entry of the big banks into the business) and a supplier who did not wish his customers to know that he was using the services of a factor set up some kind of arrangement to disguise this fact. Disclosed factoring is now by far the most common arrangement. *See also* Invoice Discounting; Recourse Factoring.

Factum Est. "It is done".

Facture. *See* Invoice.

Faible. On the Stock Exchange, a tendency towards a downwards movement.

Failli. A bankrupt.

Faillite. Bankruptcy.

Failure. Cessation, deficiency, omission, non-performance, non-occurrence, breaking-down; insolvency, suspension of payment, bankruptcy or liquidation.

Faire des Économies. To save, retrench.

Fair Rent. Either the tenant or the landlord of a regulated tenancy may apply to a rent officer to decide what is a fair rent. If the parties after consultation with the rent officer cannot agree, the rent officer will determine a fair rent. There is an appeal to a rent assessment committee, whose decision is final. The fair rent, once determined, must be registered in a local public register. *See also* Certificate of Fair Rent.

Fair Wear and Tear. Normal depreciation of an asset over a period, not covered by insurance.

Fait Accompli. An accomplished fact.

Faktura. Invoice.

Fakturabetrag. Invoice amount.

Falligkeit. Maturity.

False Pretences. Wilful misrepresentation for an ulterior motive. Paying for goods with a cheque which the drawer knows is worthless, or the obtaining of money by the cashing of a cheque by pretending to be the payee, is obtaining goods or money by false pretences and may attract a prosecution. A customer who tricks a bank into lending money to him may render himself liable to penalties under the Theft Act 1968, section 16 (1), which applies to any person who by any deception dishonestly obtains for himself or another any pecuniary advantages.

Falsification of Accounts. The destruction, alteration, mutilation or falsification of any book, writing, security or account by any officer, clerk or employed person acting wilfully and with intent to defraud. This is a criminal act and can attract a term of imprisonment.

Familienbank. A network of branch banks in Germany, owned by Chase National Bank, offering consumer credit and ancillary services such as household budgeting, high-interest savings and current accounts, and two-tier interest rates and service fees.

Family Protection Policy. A life assurance policy which offers a large sum at an early date if the life assured dies, dropping to quite a small one at maturity, by which time the children have grown up and are not in such need of assistance.

Farm Development Loan. A type of loan available to sound, practical farmers for such purposes as buying stock, machinery and plant, and farm improvements. The loans are available for amounts up to £20,000. Interest is charged on the full amount of the loan for its full term, loan and interest being repayable in equal monthly instalments up to a period of five to seven years. The borrowing term will be fixed to take account of the expected life of any machinery and plant purchased with the proceeds of the loan.

Fate of a Cheque. Whether it is honoured or not.

Faustpfand. A pledge of moveable property, *e.g.*, documents of title, goods, etc., as security for a loan.

Faute de Mieux. For want of anything better.

Faux Pas. A tactless remark or action.

Favourable Variance. A variance where the discrepancy is to the advantage of the organisation.

Feasibility Study. An enquiry into whether a particular project is capable of being done, or is practical, or will be profitable. Such a study may be performed by a bank as a preliminary to seeking a new market, extending its branch structure, introducing a new service, embarking upon a new training system, etc.

Fédération Bancaire de la Communauté Économique Européenne. An instrument of common action of the professional banking associations to assist in attaining, within the sphere of banking activity, the European aims laid down by the Treaty of Rome, without prejudicing the maintenance and development of relations of member associations with the banking establishments of third party countries. The Federation is concerned to harmonise banking legislation in the E.E.C. countries and to secure general agreement in the rules relating to consumer credit. It is interested in the control of banking mergers and in securing a general agreement in matters concerning stock exchanges and public offers for sale. Other subjects of concern are value added tax and its operation as regards banks, the obtaining of a general standard for the structure of limited companies, the financing of small-and medium-sized enterprises by risk capital, and the creation of a community instrument for the financing of multi-national export trade.

Federführung. The combined management of a syndicated business.

Fee. Payment, wages, money, remuneration to a public officer or a professional man for the execution of official functions or for the performance of a professional service. *See also* Base Fee; Retaining Fee.

Fee Farm Rent. In some parts of the U.K. it is customary for a purchaser of a fee simple to enter into a covenant to pay a perpetual annual rentcharge, often called a fee farm rent or a chief rent, instead of paying a lump sum for the purchase. The vendor retains a right of re-entry in the case that the annual payment falls into arrears.

Fee Simple. *See* Estate in Fee Simple.

Fee Tail. *See* Estate in Fee Tail.

Feinheit. The proportion of pure metal in a gross alloy.

Feme Covert. A married women.

Feme Sole. An unmarried women, a spinster, a widow, a wife economically independent of her husband.

Ferme. Likely to improve, as, for example, in speaking of a tendency on the Stock Exchange.

Fest. Firm, as of a Stock Exchange rate.

Feste Schuld. A long-term debt consolidated in the form of bonds, mortgages, etc.

Festgelt. Money at a fixed term, deposited with a bank (usually short- or medium-term deposits).

Festverzinslich. A bond paying regular fixed interest.

Feuille de Coupons. A sheet of coupons.

Fiat. A formal demand, an authoritative order; the order or warrant of a judge or other constituted authority sanctioning or allowing certain processes.

Fiat Money. Paper money made legal tender by governmental decree.

Fiction. Something feigned, invented or imagined. *See also* Legal Fiction.

Fictitious Asset. An asset which has no present value, *e.g.* preliminary expenses when a company is being formed. The money has been spent and therefore has to appear somewhere, but it will be written out of the balance sheet as soon as possible.

Fictitious Payee. A non-existent payee, or an existing person named as payee who never had, and was never intended to have, any legal interest in the proceeds of a bill. In such a case the bill may be treated as payable to bearer. *See* Payee.

Fideicommissaire. Trustee.

Fidelity Guarantee. A guarantee by a person or insurance society that an employee will remain honest.

Fiduciary. Holding or held in trust.

Fiduciary Capacity. The capacity descriptive of a trustee.

Fiduciary Issue. An issue of notes by a bank without reserves of gold or silver behind them, but having their value sustained by a general public confidence. The fiduciary issue in the U.K. is backed by securities. An upward change in the amount, if persisting over two years, must receive the sanction of Parliament.

Fiduciary Loan. A loan made without security because of the confidence of the lender in the honour of the borrower.

Fiduciary Relationship. A relationship between two parties where in the nature of things one trusts and depends on the other, *e.g.* a ward and his/her guardian. In such a case the law demands a higher degree of care and responsibility from the dominant party.

Fiduziarisch. Of the nature of a trust.

Fief. An estate formerly held on condition of military service.

Fieri Facias (fi.fa.). A writ which may be issued on behalf of a judgment creditor, whereby the sheriff is authorised to seize goods of the debtor in satisfaction of a debt.

Filiale. Subsidiary.

Final Accounts. The calculations of the gross and net profits of a business for the year, and the distribution of the net profit, are dealt with in four different accounts, called the manufacturing account, the trading account, the profit and loss account, and the profit and loss appropriation account. Because these four accounts are made up only at the end of each trading period they are called the final accounts. A trading concern which buys goods for resale does not, of course, manufacture them and will not, therefore, keep a manufacturing account.

Final Dividend. The last dividend paid by a company to its shareholders in its financial year.

Finance. The science of controlling public revenue and expenditure; the management of money affairs; to raise money by negotiations; to subsidise. *See also* Front End Finance; Project Finance.

Finance Bill. (1) A Bill put before Parliament by the government of the day concerning the raising of finance, which after being passed becomes the Finance Act of the year.
(2) A bill drawn by a firm or company for the purpose of arranging a short-term loan. The bill is by arrangement drawn on another firm or on a bank or accepting house. When the bill is accepted it is discounted.

Finance Corporation for Industry (F.C.I.). A corporation set up to provide temporary or longer period finance for industrial concerns, to help them in redevelopment schemes and to assist them to work up to maximum efficiency. The corporation was merged with the Industrial and Commercial Finance Corporation in 1973 to form F.F.I., but continues to fulfil the role of a provider of finance for larger companies. Loans are between £1m and £15m for periods of seven to fifteen years. In 1975, F.F.I. raised a further £1,000m of private money to provide a new medium-term lending facility, to be handled by F.C.I., following government proposals for the regeneration of British industry.

Financed Factoring. *See* Factoring.

Finance for Industry (F.F.I.). A company formed in 1973 by the merger of F.C.I. and I.C.F.C. It is hoped that F.F.I., by lending substantial sums of money for up to fifteen years to companies in need of capital for industrial and commercial expansion, may play an important part in the rebuilding of British industry and may, indeed, become the country's major medium-term loans bank. F.F.I. is likely to be concerned in cases where large advances are needed for investment before profits can be seen, or with heavy programmes of capital re-equipment which must be spread over a number of years. In 1975, F.F.I. raised further large sums, partly by public issues of fixed interest stocks, and partly from its existing shareholders. These sources of funds, it was hoped, would enable F.F.I. to expand its lending by up to £1,000m over two years. These new funds are to be available mainly in the form of medium-term loans subject to strict criteria of commercial viability. However, high interest rates, a low demand for funds, and competition from the clearing banks, gave F.F.I. a slow start towards achieving its aims, and half way through 1976 only one-fifth of the target of £1,000m of advances had been achieved.

Finance House. *See* Hire Purchase Companies.

Finance House Base Rate. The Finance House Association is advised of the three-month inter-bank rate at 11 a.m. each day by inter-bank brokers. An average rate for the week is calculated each Friday, and on the last Friday of each month a further average of the previous eight weekly averages is calculated. This rate is rounded up to the nearest $\frac{1}{2}\%$, which rate will apply for the following months. *See also* Base Rate.

Finance Houses Association. An association of about thirty of the larger and better-known firms in Britain engaged in financing hire purchase transactions. Together they represent about 85% of all finance house business.

Finance Lease. A leasing contract providing for the lessee to pay the rental for a minimum non-cancellable period of time (the primary period) which suffices in total to amortise the lessor's capital outlay, incurred in the purchase of the asset which is to be leased. These rentals commonly include also an element of interest. The lessee always assumes the liability to maintain the equipment: a service agreement may be offered by the suppliers of the equipment. Where the asset is not fully amortised during the hire period, the lease is called an "operating lease" or a "rental contract". Also known as a *Full Payout Lease.*

Financement à Forfait. In export finance, the sale to a bank of long-term credits which the exporters have abroad.

Financement Externe. External liabilities.

Finances. The income of a state or person, resources, funds.

Financial Year. Any twelve-monthly period for which public, official or company accounts are made up. In Great

Britain it is the year from 1 April to the following 31 March, but for fiscal purposes it is the twelve months from 6 April of one year to 5 April of the year following (the tax year).

Finanzweichsel. An exchange transfer which is purely a financial one and not one based on a goods transaction.

Fine Bank Bill (or Prime Bank Bill). A bill drawn on, and accepted by, an accepting house or British bank with an unquestioned financial standing.

Fine Rate. The most favourable rate of interest charged to an undoubted borrower; the most favourable rate of discount to the seller of a fine bank bill.

Fire Insurance. A contract of indemnity by which an insurance company undertakes to make good any damage or loss by fire to buildings or property during a specified time.

Fire Policy. A policy guaranteeing compensation up to a stated limit in case of damage by fire.

Firm. A partnership or association of two or more persons for carrying on a business; the name, title or style under which a company transacts business; a commercial partnership. *See also* Business Names.

Firma. Firm.

Firmenwert. Goodwill.

Firm Offer. A definite offer to purchase specified property at a stated price.

First Class Bill. A good commercial bill which is self-liquidating on a short-term basis.

First Cost. The cost of production in money terms.

First Mortgage. A mortgage on a property which is not subject to any prior mortgage.

First of Exchange. Three bills of exchange drawn in connection with foreign trade are described as first, second or third of exchange respectively. A set may be of any number, but three is the most usual. *See also* Bill in a Set.

Fiscal. Pertaining to the public treasury or revenue.

Fiscal Drag. As money incomes increase the proportion of income paid in tax rises, because personal allowances, etc., are fixed. In inflationary times the real value of the fixed allowances decreases, until such time as they are increased. "Fiscal drag" is the amount, measured in real values, by which the allowances fall behind increasing tax. As a result the State takes in taxes a steadily increasing portion of incomes.

Fiscal Policy. The use of taxation in the Budget as a weapon of monetary policy.

Fiscal Year. The tax year or years of assessment in the U.K., ending on 5 April.

Fishing Expedition. A name sometimes given to the practice of making a status enquiry on a customer of a banker for varying amounts, with the object of ascertaining the extent of the customer's resources. A banker should not make an answer for more than one amount, which should be in connection with a genuine business transaction.

Fixed. Made firm, made permanent, established, secure, determined.

Fixed Assets. Those assets which have been acquired for the purpose of carrying on the business of a company and which will not be resold, but will be kept in permanent use until they wear out.

Fixed Capital. Items of property, equipment and machinery bought out of the paid-up capital. Fixed-capital items are meant to be used in the business of the company and to be kept for the whole of their working life. Their value should be progressively written off or depreciated in the company's books during their working life.

Fixed Charge. A periodic charge which has no relation to the amount of business done, an overhead charge, *e.g.* rent or rates; a charge for services rendered or work done, which has been established at a certain figure by agreement; a charge appearing in a mortgage debenture covering a company's land and buildings. Such a charge may also cover machinery, equipment, goodwill and even book debts.

Fixed Cost. The cost of a business which does not vary with output.

Fixed Debenture. A debenture charged on the fixed assets of a company, such as land.

Fixed Deposit. A deposit repayable on a pre-determined future date. Such transactions may be for periods ranging from overnight to five years. The interest rate applicable is also "fixed" for the full period of the transaction.

Fixed Loan. A loan repayable on a pre-determined future date. Such transactions may be for periods ranging from overnight to five years. The interest rate applicable is also "fixed" for the full period of the transaction.

Fixed-Sum Credit. For the purposes of the Consumer Credit Act 1974, a facility which is not a running-account credit, but which enables the debtor to receive credit (*e.g.* a loan).

Fixed Trust. A unit trust whose trust deed provides for a set list of security holdings for spreading risk over a period of ten to twenty years, with severe restrictions on the ability of the management to vary the investments.

Fixen. The sale of stock which the speculator does not possess, in the hope of buying it back later at a cheaper price; a "bear" operation.

Fixer. (*Ger.*) A "bear".

Fixings. *See* London Gold Market.

Fixtures. (1) Chattels which are so affixed to land or to a building as to become part of it, passing with the ownership of the land; furniture or fittings permanently fastened to the structure of a building.
(2) In international trade, a loan made for a fixed period of time and not repayable until the maturity date. Seven days fixed, one, two, three, four or six months, one year or annually up to five years, are common periods for fixtures. Loans may be in sterling or any other marketable currency on such terms.

Flat (or Running) Yield. The annual return derived from the interest or dividend on an investment, divided by the price and multiplied by 100.

Flexible Trust. A unit trust whose trust deed empowers the managers to vary or substitute the security holdings of the trust at their discretion, although usually restricting their choice to a given list.

Float. To set going, as a business company; to put into circulation; a sum of money kept on one side to meet small expenses or to assist in balancing a cashier's till; the action of a country's currency when it is allowed to find its own level on the foreign exchanges through the action of the laws of supply and demand.

Floatation, Flotation. The act of launching a commercial enterprise, especially a limited liability company; the launching of a new capital issue.

Floater. First-class bearer securities deposited with lending banks against overnight or call money.

Floating Assets. The assets of a company which are continually changing, *e.g.*, cash or stock.

Floating Capital. Money available for the carrying on of any business concern.

Floating Charge. A charge on the floating assets of a company, included in a debenture. The floating charge crystallises to affix itself to the assets on the day on which a receiver is appointed.

Floating Currency. A stable rate of exchange, defended by the country's central bank which buys its own currency unit when it is under pressure, can prove more costly to maintain than the country concerned is willing or able to afford. The home currency unit has to be paid for in foreign currencies which have been earned by exporting, and if the pressure is too great the out-drain will seriously endanger the country's reserves if it is allowed to continue. One remedy for this situation is devaluation: another is to allow the currency to float, that is, to find its own level on the foreign exchanges through the operation of the forces of supply and demand. This involves abandoning the Smithsonian Agreement but nevertheless many countries have taken this step. The stated intention is still to return to fixed parities once currencies have stabilised themselves at some level.

Floating Debenture. A debenture charged on the floating assets of a company, such as stock. Such a charge "crystallises" on the day on which a liquidator is appointed, and will then attach to whatever stock, etc., is available on that date.

Floating Debt. That part of the National Debt which consists of Treasury Bills, short-term Exchequer bonds, etc., and fluctuates according to circumstances; short-term loans or debts repayable at short notice.

Floating Money. Money in the hands of bankers and others at a time of excessive liquidity, for which no profitable use can quickly be found.

Floating Mortgage. *See* Floating Charge.

Floating Policy. A marine policy covering goods which may be widely spread over a district or area, or in whatever ship they may be.

Floating Population. Shifting population

whose movements are controlled by the fluatuating demand for labour, especially in sea-ports or industrial areas.

Floating Pound. The pound sterling left to find its own level on the foreign exchanges through the operation of the laws of supply and demand.

Floating Rate. A freely fluctuating rate of exchange.

Floating Rate Bond. A bond whose coupon is linked to prevailing market rates of interest. It remains relatively stable in price, not suffering capital gains or losses as interest rates rise or fall.

Floating Rate Stock. *See Valeur à Revenu Variable.*

Flotation. *See* Floatation.

Flottant. Floating.

Flow Chart. A visual representation, by means of a graph, chart or pictorial summary, of the steps in sequence through which a productive operation is progressing.

Fluchtkapital. *See* Hot Money.

Fluctuation. A rising and falling, a vacillation, irregular changes in degree; changes in the value of stocks and shares, or in the value of a country's unit of currency on the foreign exchanges; varying intensities of demand for a product.

Flussig. Liquid.

Folio. A page number in a book or ledger; the number of words (seventy-two or ninety) taken as a unit in computing the total number of words in a document; a page of manuscript.

Fondé de Pouvoir. *See* Proxy.

Fonds. Stock, funds, means. *See also Rentrer dans ses Fonds.*

Fonds Consolidés. Consols, consolidated funds.

Fonds d'Amortissement. Money put together, or to be put together for the repayment of a loan; a sinking fund.

Fonds de Placement. *See* Unit Trust; Investment Trust.

Fonds de Roulement. Liquid assets, assets immediately available (cash, bank balances) or realisable in a short time (negotiable stocks and shares, short-term investments, etc.); working capital.

Fonds de Tiers. Third party funds; funds of various kinds entrusted to a bank.

Fonds Publics. Government stocks. *Rentrerdansses Fonds.* To get one's money back.

For. (*Fr.*) The place where a legal action must be brought.

For Cash. A Stock Exchange phrase referring to transactions which must be paid for at the time they are made (also *For Money*).

Forderungsanmeldung. Form of application for approval and authorisation to make available foreign exchange in settlement of a payment due.

Foreclose. To prevent, to exclude, to deprive of the right to redeem a mortgage.

Foreclosure. The method by which the mortgagee acquires for himself land mortgaged to him, freed from the mortgagor's equity of redemption. Taking possession of an estate mortgaged to a lender, where repayment has not been made, and after a foreclosure order has been obtained.

Foreclosure Order. If the time fixed in the deed of mortgage for repayment has passed, and no repayment has been made, the lender may apply to the court for an order for foreclosure, so that he may appropriate the fee simple if the borrower still fails to pay. The court issues an order for foreclosure *nisi* which orders that the mortgagor shall lose his property unless he pays upon a certain date (usually six months later) specified. The order is then made absolute and this vests the fee simple absolute in the mortgagee and extinguishes his mortgage term and all subsequent mortgage terms.

Foreign. Situated outside a place or country, alien, subject to the law of another country.

Foreign Banks. Banks of foreign countries maintaining an office or offices in London but with their headquarters in their own country.

Foreign Bill. A bill drawn in the United Kingdom and payable abroad, or a bill drawn abroad and payable in the United Kingdom.

Foreign Bill for Collection. *See* Bill for Collection.

Foreign Bill for Negotiation. *See* Bill for Negotiation.

Foreign Bond. A security issued by a borrower in the national capital market of another country.

Foreign Currency. The money of any foreign country.

Foreign Currency Securities. Securities on which interest or dividends are payable in a foreign currency, and repayment of which will be made similarly.

Bank of England permission is required before a resident may purchase foreign currency securities.

Foreign Draft. A bill drawn in a foreign currency and payable abroad.

Foreign Exchange. The exchange of one country's currency for another; foreign currency generally.

Foreign Exchange Broker. A broker operating on the foreign exchange market for a principal, whether a financial institution, a bank, or a government.

Foreign Trade. Commerce carried on between merchants in different countries, resulting in demands for foreign currencies which affect the balance of trade of the countries concerned.

Forfaitieren. Acceptance by a bank of middle- and long-term bills of exchange on an overseas buyer, without recourse to the seller.

Forfeit. That which is lost through fault, crime, omission or neglect; a penalty, a fine, especially a stipulated sum to be paid in case of breach of contract.

Forfeit of Shares. The articles of association of a limited company may provide that where a call is made to the holder of a number of the company's partly-paid shares, and the shareholder fails to pay the call, the company may declare the shares forfeit.

Forfeiture. Deprivation, confiscation; the loss of the remainder of a leasehold term (subject to the court's decision) by a lessee for non-payment of rent.

Forged Banknotes. Unauthorised copies of the banknotes of a country, illegally put into circulation; counterfeit money.

Forged Indorsement. A forged signature by way of indorsement does not invalidate the bill, but where it purports to be a signature forming part of the chain of title to the bill it is ineffective to pass any title to the person who acquires the bill from the forger. But if the forged signature is unnecessary to the transfer of the title (as, *e.g.*, where it appears on a bearer bill) it may be ignored.

Forged Share Transfer. Signatures of customers on stock transfer forms taken in connection with a mortgage of stocks or shares to the bank as security should be made at the bank to avoid the risk of forgery. A bank forwarding a certificate and a stock transfer form to a company for registration is deemed to guarantee the genuineness of the signature on the stock transfer form.

Forged Signature. Where a signature on a bill is placed thereon without the authority of the person whose signature it purports to be, the forged or unauthorised signature is wholly inoperative. A forged signature cannot subsequently be ratified, but an unauthorised signature may so be. A banker paying a cheque having a forged signature cannot debit his customer's account with the amount of the cheque, unless the drawer is precluded from setting up the forgery. It is not a bill of exchange, as it is not signed by the person giving it.

Forgery. The act of counterfeiting a coin or document, or falsifying a document whether in a material particular or in the copying of another's signature, or illegally using another person's signature.

Formal Protest. A protest of a dishonoured bill of exchange, made by a notary public, as opposed to a householder's protest.

Forretnings Bankenes Felleskontor. A sister organisation to the Norwegian Bankers' Association, from which it was divided in 1955. Its activities consist of (1) keeping the banks abreast and adequately informed of all laws and administrative decisions that are of importance for their operations; (2) keeping the banks informed of court decisions of importance to their operations, including the publishing of summaries of court cases; (3) issuing advisory information and reports on legal, technical and general matters in the area of banking; (4) promoting the security, simplification and rationalisation of the banks' working routines and business methods, and implementing uniform rates and terms as and when desirable; (5) establishing and conducting joint measures for the safeguarding of the banks' various branches of activity, such as reporting systems for missing securities, control of giro accounts, debtor records, etc.; (6) conducting the banks' common advertising and public relations of whatever kind; (7) preparing and printing account loan documents, forms, schedules of fees, etc., which the banks need in their business; (8) keeping available for the members professional literature and periodicals of importance to the operations of the banks; (9) through membership of other institutions, furnishing the banks with information and results of research, which the banks need in their business.

Forschung. Research, investigation, discovery.

For the Account. A Stock Exchange phrase referring to transactions which are to be settled or paid for on the next account day or settling day.

Fortune Nationale. The total wealth of a country.

Forward. Onward in time; to promote, to re-address, to send out or despatch (of goods). *See also* Carriage Forward.

Forward Combination. An amalgamation between a company or a firm and the business which markets the company's product.

Forward Exchange. Buying or selling foreign currency in advance through the forward exchange market; the purchase or sale of foreign currency for delivery at a future date. *See also* Option Forward Rate; Swap.

Forwarding. Despatching merchandise, sending goods forward.

Forwarding Agent. An agent who undertakes the collection, forwarding, documentation and delivery of goods.

Forwarding Note. A note giving the description of goods, etc., and the name and address of the consignee, which is transmitted with the goods.

Forward Rate. The rate at which foreign currency can be bought or sold for delivery at a future time. *See also* Option Forward Rate; Swap.

Founders' Shares. *See* Deferred Shares.

Fournisseur. Dealer, supplier.

Fracht. Freight.

Frachtbrief. Consignment note.

Fractional Banking. A banking system where it is customary to keep a definite fixed ratio between total deposits and cash, or where such a ratio is imposed by law.

Frais de Cotation. Annual charge for the admission of stocks or shares to a quotation on the *Bourse*.

Frais de Dépôt. See Droits de Garde.

Frais Généraux. Overhead costs.

Frais de Vente. Selling costs.

Franchise. A privilege conferred by a government; the district to which such a privilege extends; the right to vote in elections; a percentage of the insured value of goods which an underwriter requires the owner of the cargo to cover himself; a sort of collaboration offered to small independent shops in which a manufacturing enterprise puts at the disposal of all the shops taking part in the scheme, for a remuneration (the franchise), a complete and uniform marketing programme. *See also* Enfranchisement.

Franco, Franko. Free of expense, at no charge.

Franco à Bord. See Free on Board.

Frank. To send or cause to be sent under an official privilege; the right to send letters through the post free of charge; the letter thus sent.

Franked Income. Revenue on which a tax has been paid and which therefore is free of liability to that tax in the hands of the recipient.

Franking Machine. A machine which stamps or franks envelopes with a symbol indicating that the postage has been paid.

Franko. See Franco.

Fraud. An act or course of deception deliberately practised to gain unlawful or unfair advantage; such deception directed to the detriment of another; a deception, a trick, trickery. In the U.K. the Theft Act 1968 makes it an offence for a person by any deception dishonestly to obtain, for himself or any other, any pecuniary advantage. The cases in which a pecuniary advantage is to be regarded as obtained for a person are cases where (1) any debt or charge for which he makes himself liable, or is, or may become liable (including one not legally enforceable) is reduced or in whole or in part evaded or deferred; (2) he is allowed to borrow by way of overdraft or to take out any policy of insurance or annuity contract, or obtains an improvement of the terms on which he is allowed to do so.

Fraudulent. Practising fraud, intended to deceive; in bankruptcy, having the intention to defeat or delay creditors.

Fraudulent Conveyance. A transfer of property by a debtor which has the effect of defeating or delaying creditors, even though made in good faith. A fraudulent conveyance is void and the transferee must return the property to the trustee in bankruptcy. A conveyance is not fraudulent if it has been made for valuable consideration in good faith. Evidence of a fraudulent intent might be the gratuitous character of the transfer or the receipt of a purely nominal consideration. *See also* Act of Bankruptcy.

Fraudulent Misrepresentation. The tort of deceit. It is committed when a person makes a false representation of fact, knowing it to be false, or without believing it to be true, or recklessly, careless whether it be true or false. There must be an intention on the part of the maker that it shall be acted upon by the person deceived, that person must in fact act upon it, and must as a result suffer some loss. The remedy for the injured party is a right to rescind the contract (if he discovers the fraud in time), and an action for damages on the tort. *See also* Fraud.

Fraudulent Preference. Any conveyance or transfer of money or property or charge thereon made by a debtor when insolvent in favour of a creditor (or of any person in trust for any creditor) with a view to giving such creditor (or any surety or guarantor for the debt to such creditor) an advantage over other creditors; paying one creditor in full or in part when all other creditors are not paid in full or proportionately. A fraudulent preference must be established by the trustee or liquidator. It must be a voluntary act on the part of the debtor, made entirely without pressure from the creditor. There must also be an intention to prefer, that is, the payment by the debtor must be deliberate and not accidental. *See also* Act of Bankruptcy.

Fraudulent Settlement. (1) A settlement made before and in consideration of marriage where the settlor is not at the time of making the settlement able to pay all his debts without the aid of the property comprised in the settlement, or (2) any covenant or contract made in consideration of marriage for the future settlement on, or for, the settlor's wife or children of any money or property wherein he had not at the date of his marriage any estate or interest. If the settlor is adjudged bankrupt, or compounds or arranges with his creditors, the court may refuse or suspend an order of discharge or refuse to approve a composition or arrangement, if it thinks the transaction was done in order to defeat creditors or was not justifiable, having regard to the state of the debtor's affairs, at the time when it was made.

Free. Not under restraint, not subject to restrictions, duties, etc.; gratuitous, liberal.

Free Alongside Ship. Delivered free on the dock or wharf.

Free Capital. Capital held in the form of cash and therefore available for transportation into any form of real capital. It is also a term now frequently used in connection with banks in the context of prudential ratios. Used in this way, it is usually taken to include reserves and subordinated loan stock less money tied up in property, equipment and trade investments. Cash in tills is sometimes also included in the formula.

Free Docks. A price quotation for goods by an exporter which includes the cost of the goods themselves plus the cost of transporting them to the docks where they will be loaded on board.

Freeholder. The possessor of a freehold estate.

Freehold Estate. An estate in land which is properly described as an estate in fee simple absolute in possession, signifying the highest type of land ownership which anyone can possess; the tenure of property in fee simple or fee tail. *See also* Estate in Fee Simple; Fee.

Free Market. A market where stallholders pay no tax; on the Stock Exchange, a market in shares which can be bought or sold without difficulty.

Free of All Average. A clause in a marine insurance policy meaning that claims for general or particular average cannot be recovered.

Free of Particular Average. A clause in a marine insurance policy meaning that claims for particular average cannot be recovered.

Free of Tax. *See* Tax Free.

Free on Board (F.O.B.). A contractual term indicating that the price quoted to the buyer is the price of the goods plus the cost of putting them on board the vessel which is to carry them. All freight charges and the cost of insurance must be paid by the buyer.

Free on Rail (F.O.R.). A contractual term indicating that the price quoted to the buyer is the price of the goods plus the cost of transporting them to the railway station from which the goods are to be despatched.

Free Port. A port where ships of all nations may load or unload free of duty.

Free Ship. A neutral ship, free from liability to capture.

Free Trade. The policy of unrestricted international trade; the free interchange of commodities without protective tariffs.

Freeze. *See* Frozen Assets; Wage Freeze.

Freier Kurs. A floating rate which is the result of demand and supply.

Freight. A charge made for the carriage of goods in a ship; the cargo itself; the sum paid for the hire of a ship or part of it.

Freight Car. A railway car used for goods.

Freight Collect/Freight Payable at Destination. An annotation to a bill of lading inserted by a shipper or shipping company to evidence that freight has not been paid, commonly associated with f.o.b. contracts where the buyer is responsible for payment of freight.

Freight Forward. The term to indicate that freight on goods is payable at the port of destination.

Freight Indemnity. A guarantee to a shipping line that freight charges will be paid, with the intention of obtaining the delivery of a bill of lading. It is mostly used where big companies having numerous contracts with a shipping company prefer to pay any freight due on a monthly basis rather than on each individual contract as and when it goes through. Pending the monthly settlement the shipping company is happy to accept a banker's indemnity for the amount of unpaid freight on any particular contract.

Freight Note. A document issued by a shipping company particularising the freight charge for a cargo.

Freight Paid. A clause stamped or marked on a bill of lading to indicate that the freight payable on the goods to which the bill refers has been paid. In a C.I.F. or C.A.F. contract it is essential for this point to be checked, for otherwise the shipping company will refuse to release the goods and the importer will have to pay the freight himself to get them.

Freigrenze. In international traffic with foreign countries, the limit below which no customs tolls or duties are payable. If this limit is crossed tax is levied on the whole amount.

Freiverkehr. Business in securities conducted outside the stock exchange; business in unquoted securities.

Fret. See Freight.

Friendly Society. A mutual insurance society in which the members subscribe for provident benefits, in particular, sickness, old age, endowment and death benefits, and provisions for widows and orphans. Although the National Health Service now meets most of the needs for which the original friendly societies were set up, they still continue to operate and have diversified to include industrial insurance, industrial, provident and building societies; trade unions; certified loan societies; and some superannuation and pension schemes. All are closely regulated by the Friendly Societies Acts 1896–1971.

Front End Finance. An international trade payment may be made by way of loan to the buyer by a U.K. bank in the case of large contracts, to assist the U.K. exporter, repayment being guaranteed by the Export Credits Guarantee Department, but such advances will seldom exceed 80% of the contract price. "Front End Finance" is a further loan from another source to help the buyer meet the direct cash payment that he must make, the commonest source of funds for this purpose being the Eurodollar market.

Frozen Assets, Frozen Balances, Frozen Credits. Assets, etc., temporarily blocked and impossible to realise for the time being, *e.g.* the bank balances of foreign banks in a country which is at war with the bank's country.

Frustration of Contract. The occurrence of events which have not been foreseen and which operate to make the continued observance of a contract, which is intended to last over a period of time, impossible. Such events are sickness, war, accident, the interference of third parties, or subsequent legislation which renders any further performance under the contract illegal.

Full Payout Lease. *See* Finance Lease.

Fully-Paid Shares. Shares where no call can be made on the holder, because the full value of the shares has been paid up in full.

Functional. Having a special purpose, pertaining to a duty or office.

Fund. Permanent stock or capital; an invested sum, the income of which is used for a set purpose; a store, an ample supply.

Funded Debenture Interest. Debenture interest which has, by agreement with the debenture holders, been paid not in cash but by way of further debentures.

Funded Debt. Government stock having no date for repayment, stock whose principal the government need not repay until it wishes. Sometimes called undated stocks, such securities have only an income yield, but no redemption yield.

Fundierte Schuld. *See* Funded Debt.

Funding. The act or process of establishing a funded debt; an operation whereby a government takes advantage of a prevailing low interest rate to repay stocks at the earliest date possible, replacing them by new issues bearing a lower rate of interest; repayment of bank borrowing by a company out of the proceeds of an issue of debentures.

Funds. Money, finances, pecuniary resources; money lent to a government and constituting a national debt; the stock of a national debt regarded as an investment; Consols and other government securities are referred to as "the Funds". **Advisory Funds.** Funds left with a bank by a customer for investment on his behalf, after consultation. Such funds are held in large amounts by Swiss banks, and their use for investment in Eurobonds assists the ability of the bank to place new issues. Also known as *Discretionary* or *In-House* funds.

Fusion. (*Fr.*) *See* Amalgamation; Merger.

Future Goods. Goods to be manufactured or acquired by the seller after the making of the contract of sale.

Futures. Goods for delivery at some future time. Contracts of purchase or sale are made in the produce markets at prices fixed at the contract dates, but for future receipt or delivery of the commodities dealt in, and therefore at prices appropriate to the agreed delivery dates.

G

Gage. (*Eng.*) *Gage* (*Fr.*) Security deposited against a loan.

Gain Comptable. In the case of the sale or revaluation of assets, the gain arising from the difference between book and market values, a difference formerly constituting a hidden reserve.

Garantie de Cours. *See* Hedging.

Garnishee. One who has received notice not to pay any money which he owes to a third person, who is indebted to the person giving the notice.

Garnishee Order. A remedy open to a judgment creditor. The order *nisi* attaches money belonging to the judgment debtor (the customer) in the hands of the third party (the banker). The order restrains the garnishee from parting with any money due or accruing due to the judgment debtor. The order is effective from the moment it is served. It attaches money in all accounts in the debtor's name, including deposits, but excepting savings account balances. A debit balance on one account must be set off against a credit balance on another (there is no set-off with a loan account) so as to arrive at the attachable sum. If the account is an overdrawn one, or there is a net overdrawn position, there is nothing to attach, and the judgment creditor's solicitor should be informed of this, so that he may arrange for the order to be withdrawn. Where a balance is attached the account must be stopped. The garnishee must appear in court (in the case of a bank, through the bank's solicitor) a few days after the service of the order to show cause why the money he holds should not be taken in satisfaction of the debt due to the judgment creditor. If the judgment debtor wishes to enter a defence he attends also. Failing such cause shown, or defence, the order is made absolute and thereupon the garnishee must pay over to the creditor the amount of the debt plus costs, or the balance of the account if this is less. Because of the inconvenience caused by attaching a large sum for a small debt the limited order has been devised. This is issued for the amount of the judgment debt plus an estimate for costs, so that this sum may be transferred by the garnishee banker to a suspense account, leaving the main account of the customer capable of continued normal operation.

Garnishee Summons. The operation of a garnishee summons is the same as that of a garnishee order, except that the summons is issued by a county court, where it is returnable, and service is made by an officer of the court. The banker may settle the matter as far as he is concerned by paying the amount due, or the amount of the balance, if less, to the county court registrar within eight days of the service of the summons. A garnishee summons is invariably limited in its nature.

G.A.T.T. *See* General Agreement on Tariffs and Trade.

Gavelkind. An old custom prevalent in Kent and Wales whereby the lands of a person dying intestate descend to all the sons in equal shares or, in default of sons, to all the daughters equally. The custom was abolished in 1925.

Gazette. An official publication issued twice weekly giving details of petitions, bankruptcies, liquidations, statutory declarations, dissolutions of partnerships, etc. It is issued in London, Edinburgh and Belfast. *See also* Stubbs' Weekly *Gazette.*

Gearing. A relationship between the various classes of capital in a company. If some of the capital comes from loans, then gearing is the relationship between the loan capital and the total capital. The higher the loan capital, the higher the proportion of trading income allotted to meet the loan interest charge. But however much this may be, it is a fixed sum, and therefore any increase in trading income has a more than proportionate effect on the surplus available for net profit. If the gearing is between preference shares and ordinary shares, then a relatively small increase in profits over the level required to pay the fixed preference dividend will result in a more than proportionate sum becoming available for the payment of the ordinary dividend.

Gebundener Zahlungsverkehr. State-approved trade payments overseas.

Gedeckt. Secured, covered, guaranteed.

Gedeckterkredit. Secured borrowing.

Gehältskonto. A bank account of an employee, kept at a privileged rate, and fed by wages or salary payments by the employer. Drawing facilities are as for a current account.

Gekreuzter Check. *See* Crossed Cheque.

Geld. (*Ger.*) Generally recognised means of payment in the form of paper or coins of pure or alloyed metal, each similar in appearance, size and weight with the other; money; bank and Giro deposits, the amount which will be offered on a purchase of securities or goods.

Geldmarkt. The sale and purchase of short-term money.

Geldmenge. The amount of cash and bank deposits existing in a domestic economy.

Genehmigteskapital. Authorised capital.

General. Pertaining to a whole class or order; not precise, particular, or detailed; usual, ordinary or prevalent.

General Acceptance. One which assents without qualification to the order of the drawer.

General Agent. An agent employed to conduct a particular trade or business, having implied or ostensible authority to do whatever is incidental to that trade or business.

General Agreement on Tariffs and Trade (G.A.T.T.). An agreement made in 1947 to which the U.K. was a signatory, designed to maximise the growth of world trade by the progressive reduction of tariffs, quota restrictions and import controls between the signing nations. On a number of occasions the countries concerned have reduced tariffs by a set percentage, the "Kennedy Round" being a conspicuously successful example. G.A.T.T. also seeks to put an end to "most favoured nation" clauses and any kind of discrimination amongst the member countries. There are certain escape clauses for countries getting into acute difficulties which might, for example, lead to a devaluation. The liberalisation of world trade which was G.A.T.T.'s primary aim is taking longer to achieve than was hoped. In the nature of things free trade benefits most the strongest and most advanced countries in technology and industrialisation. The poorer countries are the ones who most need help, and they have not in many cases yet been able to see their way to forego the advantages which restrictions on imports confer on their domestic industries. The organisation has no real power and economic blocs such as the E.E.C. are contrary to its aims.

General Average. A loss incurred by intentional measures taken at sea to preserve the safety of the ship or the cargo generally, *e.g.* by cutting away part of the ship, or jettisoning a part of the cargo. This loss is apportioned amongst the shipowner and the owners of the cargo, the proportions being calculated by an average adjuster.

General Clearing. *See* Clearing House.

General Crossing. *See* Crossed Cheque.

Generaldirektor. Managing Director.

General Equitable Charge. An equitable mortgage of unregistered land not protected by deposit of the title deeds with the lender. It should be registered at the Land Charges Department as a land charge, class C(iii). *See* Land Charges Register.

General Index of Retail Prices. Since 1947 the index has measured the monthly change in the average level of prices of goods (other than luxuries) and services purchased by households in the United Kingdom. The figure is published monthly by the Department of Employment on the basis of a revision in January 1974 which now serves as a base point of 100. The goods and services making up the index are usually called the "basket", and this is divided into eleven broad groups, as follows—

	Weighting
Food	232
Alcoholic drinks	82
Tobacco	46
Housing	108
Fuel and light	53
Durable household goods	70
Clothing & footwear	89
Transport & vehicles	149
Miscellaneous goods	71

(includes books, newspapers, medicine, travel & sports goods, photographic and optical goods, toys, and many others)

Services	52
Meals bought and consumed outside the home	48
Total	1,000

These groupings are, of course, split even further into sections, e.g. clothing and footwear extends to twelve sections, food to thirty-two sections. The weighting figures indicate the relative importance as a consumer item in the survey of household expenditure carried out during a one-year period to 31 March 1974. Prices must be compared for the same goods and services each month, as the Retail Price Index measures price changes only. The "basket" and weights are revised each January. 150,000 separate price quotations on 350 goods and services are collected from 200 towns spread over the country.

General Issue. An issue of certain articles on a large scale; a legal issue which denies the whole declarations or charge, equivalent to a plea of "not guilty", in contradistinction to a special issue (*q.v.*).

General Lien. The right to retain goods in the possession of a dealer, warehouse-keeper, etc., which extends not only over the particular goods which gave rise to the debt, but over all the goods of that owner in his possession.

General Meetings. *See* Annual General Meeting.

General Partner. *See* Active Partner.

General Policy. Where an exporter is continually dispatching goods which he wishes to insure, it would be tedious and time-consuming to arrange for a separate insurance policy on each occasion. Under a general policy he may declare the value of each shipment to the insurance company as and when he makes it, up to a total figure previously agreed with the company. Certificates under the general policy, often prepared by the insured himself, are issued as evidence of the cover.

Genus. A stock, a species, a kind.

Genussaktie. A participating share.

Genusschein. *See* Bon de Jouissance.

Geschäft. Business.

Geschäftsleitung. Management.

Geschlossener Fonds. Closed end fund.

Gesellschaft. Company.

Gesellschaft mit Beschränkter Haftung (GmbH). Limited company.

Gesetzlich. Legal.

Gesichert. Guaranteed, secured.

Gespaltener Devisenmarkt. A division of foreign rates into foreign bill rates for commercial transactions, and those for financial transactions.

Gestion. Management.

Gewerkschaft. Trade union.

Gewinn. Profit.

Gewinnmitnahme. Profit taking.

Gewinn und Verlustrechnung. Profit and loss account.

Gift *Inter Vivos*. A gift which takes effect in the lifetime of the donor, a gift between living persons. Such a gift might attract estate duty before 1975, but in that year the Finance Act provided that gifts *inter vivos* are, in the U.K., subject to capital transfer tax. A gift *inter vivos* is now described as "a chargeable transfer of value which reduces the estate of the transferor and is intended to benefit someone else".

Gilt-Edged. Securities of the highest class (*e.g.* government stock) which are readily realisable.

Giralgeld. Bank deposits, giro balances.

Giro. *See* Bank Giro; National Giro.

Giro Bancaire. *See* Bank Giro.

Glatt Stellen. To smooth out a position by further purchases, *e.g.* of foreign exchange, securities or goods.

Glaubiger. Creditor.

Global Zession. A particular kind of credit against the assignment of debts, in which the bank takes as security from its customer not a single assignment, but the whole of his book debts. This has certain risks attached and is therefore seldom found in practice.

Godown. An eastern warehouse for the storage of goods.

Go-Go Fund. A unit trust which aims at a greater-than-average appreciation in values; this implies an aggressive and risk-taking investment policy, as well as frequent changes in the composition of the portfolio in order to make important gains quickly.

Going Concern. A business which is in full working order. The only type of business to which a banker will willingly give accommodation. *See also* Gone Concern.

Going Naked. In connection with an options trading market, when operators take option money on stock which they do not own and cannot deliver in the hope that it can be bought back at a lower level.

Gold. The precious metal which has always been relied upon as the foundation for national economies—the reserves of countries are held in gold and foreign exchange. While there is distrust of paper money, gold, which has persisted through the ages as a store of value, will continue to maintain its worth because the desire to hoard it means that it is the only currency with a steady real value, measured in terms of goods. Attempts have been made by the major trading nations to get away from reliance on gold (*e.g.* special drawing rights, "baskets" of currencies) because they realise that while gold retains its dominant position world trade must be limited by the supply of new gold coming from the two major sources of South Africa and Russia, but it seems that no other medium of exchange commands such widespread general confidence.

Gold Bullion. Gold in the form of metal bars each weighing 400 oz (11·3 kg), held by central banks and dealers in a gold market.

Gold Bullion Standard. A monetary system under which the export and import of gold is freely permitted for the settlement of international obligations, but where the internal currency consists of token paper. The gold bullion standard is therefore a modified form of the gold standard. When it was in use in the U.K. between 1925 and 1931, convertibility of paper into gold was secured by the availability of gold bars of 400 oz (11·3 kg) for exchange with notes to the value of the gold. In this way important economies were made in gold, while the currency was still kept convertible. Gold bullion is quoted in U.S. dollars per fine ounce. The morning and afternoon fixing prices are also given in sterling.

Gold Clause. A clause in an offer to lenders to the effect that repayment will be made at the rate of the gold equivalent of the loan currency at the time the loan was floated. This offers protection against a devaluation of the currency.

Golden Handshake. Compensation paid by a company or firm to a highly-placed executive for loss of office.

Gold Exchange Standard. A form of gold standard where a country using it has neither a gold currency in circulation nor reserves held in gold for external purposes, but instead keep its reserves mostly in the currency and securities of another country which is on the gold standard. In this way both sterling and dollars have been reserve currencies.

Gold Fixing. Setting the price of gold on the Gold Market in London or Zürich.

Goldgerändert. Gilt-edged.

Goldklausel. See Gold Clause.

Gold Market. See London Gold Market.

Goldparität. A parity based on the proportions of fixed content of fine gold.

Gold Points. See Specie Points.

Gold Premium. Where any commodity can be exchanged into gold, and it also has an intrinsic or face value of its own, it may happen that it will be more profitable to exchange the commodity for the gold equivalent and then sell the gold than it is to simply sell the commodity for cash. When this happens, gold is said to be "at a premium" and the difference is the "gold premium".

Goldpunkt. See Specie Points.

Gold Reserves. The reserves of gold coin and bullion held by any central bank for its government; these are the gold reserves of the country. In the U.K. the gold reserves of the nation are held on the Exchange Equalisation Account by the Bank of England.

Goldsmiths' Notes. Receipts given by goldsmiths in the seventeenth century, which acknowledged the deposit of money put with them for safe keeping, and incorporated a promise to return it on demand. These receipts circulated for value among merchants, and came to be described as goldsmiths' notes. The original function as a receipt came to be superseded by the importance of the function as a promissory note. These were the forerunners of our modern banknotes.

Gold Standard. A system of note-issue banked by gold, used in the U.K. from 1821–1914. The system has the advantage that it gives an automatic check on inflation, and the disadvantage that the total of world trade must always be limited by the total output of gold in the world. Three conditions must be satisfied for a gold standard to work: (1) there must be free mintage of gold into the standard legal coins; (2) gold must be free to be imported into or exported from the country without restraint; (3) the legal paper money of the country must be convertible by the central bank into gold on request.

Goldwährung. Currency of which the unit worth is equivalent to a fixed and definite quantity of gold.

Gone Concern. A departure from the normal assumption that a business will continue to operate indefinitely (*see* Going Concern), the "gone concern" concept attempts to measure what a business is currently worth at a break-up value in the hands of a liquidator. Where it seems to a banker asked for accommodation that a company customer may be in danger of liquidation, he will assess the company's resources as a gone concern. Each asset has to be valued on a forced-sale basis; the estimated proceeds may then be notionally apportioned among the various classes of creditors and a very rough rate of dividend calculated.

Good. Right, proper, safe, adequate, honest; commodity.

Good and Marketable Title. A desirable form of words which solicitors acting for the banks are often asked to use when reporting on the title of freehold or leasehold property passing to the bank by way of security for a loan.

Good Consideration. Consideration which is enough to support a simple contract, *i.e.* good in a court of law.

Good Delivery. On the Stock Exchange, good delivery is made when a security which has been sold is handed over, perfectly in order. If anything is not in order, *e.g.* where bearer bonds are delivered with one or more coupons missing, it is not good delivery.

Good Faith. A thing is done in good faith when it is in fact done honestly, whether it is done negligently or not. To take a bill in good faith is to take it without any notice or even suspicion of any flaw or defect in the title of the negotiator.

Good For. Able to pay, as in a banker's enquiry "whether good for £200 in one amount".

Good Leasehold Title. A title granted by the Land Registrar for leases with twenty-one years or more to run, if they are in order. A good leasehold title gives the proprietor the same rights as an absolute title except that it says nothing about the lessor's right to grant the lease. A good leasehold title may be converted into an absolute title after ten years if the proprietor, or successive proprietors, have been continuously in possession.

Good Marking Names. *See* Marking Names.

Good Merchantable Condition. Goods up to standard, and having no defect which will in any way affect their sale.

Good Root of Title. A document which will act as the starting point for checking a land title. The document chosen must be at least fifteen years old. It must cover all the essential facts about the land, describing it in terms sufficient to identify it clearly, stating who then had the legal interest in it, saying whether there were any equitable interests, and if so who had them, and generally leaving no doubts or ambiguities about the authenticity of the title at that time. Examples are an assent, a deed of conveyance or a deed of mortgage.

Goods. Property; wares, commodities, merchandise, freight; all chattels personal other than things in action and money, and in Scotland all corporeal moveables except money. The term includes emblements, industrial growing crops, and things attached to or forming part of the land which are agreed to be severed before sale or under the contract of sale. *See also* Future Goods; Warrant for Goods.

Goods and Chattels. Goods, possessions and property, belongings.

Goods Shed. A shed for the storage of goods at a railway station or docks.

Goodwill. The established popularity of a business, sold with the business itself; the expectation that the customer will return to the same place for further purchases.

Government Broker. The broker acting on the stock exchange on behalf of the government, buying and selling government stocks to influence the prices at which they are quoted.

Government Securities. Funded stocks and Treasury Bills.

Government Stock. *See* National Debt.

Grant. To transfer the title to; to confer or bestow (a privilege, charter, etc.); the act of granting, the thing granted, a gift, an assignment, a conveyance in writing, the thing conveyed.

Grantee. The person to whom property, etc., is transferred.

Grant-in-Aid. A grant made by central government to a local authority to reduce pressure on the local rates; a sum granted towards the maintenance of a school or other institution.

Grantor. The person who transfers property.

Gratisaktie. Bonus share.

Gratuity. A gift, present or tip given voluntarily in respect of some service; an amount payable under a pension scheme at the time of commencement of the pension payments.

Green Clause. A clause appearing in anticipatory or pre-shipment types of documentary credits authorising the seller of goods to obtain an advance payment before shipping the goods, enabling him to pay for the goods and all expenses including storage costs prior to shipment on board an ocean vessel. *See also* Pre-Finance Credit; Red Clause.

Green Paper. The report of a committee appointed by the Government, to be circulated for discussion and comment, possibly as a guide to later legislation. *See* Exposure Draft; White Paper.

Green Pound. The accounting unit in which farm import and export prices are calculated in the E.E.C. for transactions between the U.K. and the E.E.C. It is a special rate of exchange which does not necessarily move in line with the normal exchange rate.

Grenze. Margin.

Grenzwert. Marginal value.

Gresham's Law. When coins have been debased, coins of the proper weight and value will circulate side by side with the "light" coins. When this happens people will tend to hoard the good coins and pass on the bad ones. This tendency for debased coins to drive good coins out of circulation is called Gresham's Law, after Sir Thomas Gresham, Queen Elizabeth I's financial adviser, who was the first official to note the working of this tendency.

Gross. Unrefined; total, not net; general, not specific; twelve dozen. *In Gross.* In bulk, wholesale.

Gross Cash Flow. The sum of a company's net profit after tax and directors' remuneration, and provision for depreciation as shown in the accounts.

Gross Domestic Product. The value in money at market prices of all goods and services produced within a country, but excluding net income from abroad, for a given period, usually one year.

Grossed-up Redemption Yield. The net yield adjusted by adding back income tax and, where applicable, capital gains tax and any other tax to which the recipient is subject. *See also* Gross Yield.

Grosshandelspreis. Wholesale price.

Gross Income. A person's total income from all sources before deduction of tax.

Grossing Up. A term used in connection with income which is paid free of basic tax (*e.g.* building society interest received). The grossed-up amount is the measurement of such income for tax purposes, and is calculated by adding notional tax, of a percentage of the interest according to the taxing rates currently in force. The inflated interest is then known as the "gross equivalent". In the example given, that of building societies, investors receive their interest with income tax at the basic rate already paid. The societies therefore quote a net interest figure. Investors, however, must know the grossed-up equivalent figure—first, to enable them to make accurate comparisons with similar investments which quote gross rates, and second, so that higher-rate tax payers can work out the additional tax to be paid on the interest. Liability is calculated on the grossed-up figure by the tax authorities. Building society interest is the usual example quoted, but of course grossing-up applies to any interest received net of tax at standard rate—*e.g.* debenture interest and interest on government stocks.

Gross Interest. Interest received on an investment before payment of tax.

Gross National Product (G.N.P.). The total output of an economy—the domestic product of the nation plus net income from abroad—for a given period, usually one year. No depreciation is deducted from the figure, the calculation for which is usually at market prices. If indirect taxes are deducted and any subsidies added the result is at factor cost. The majority of items are included at price (cost to buy), but a figure is estimated for the product of the self-employed, for which no statistics are available, and the public services are included at cost.

Gross Profit. Total profit before deduction of expenses and tax.

Gross Receipts. Total receipts before deduction for expenses.

Gross Rental. The rent of a property before outgoings such as rates, taxes and repairs are deducted.

Gross Value. The annual rental of a property to be expected on the basis that the landlord pays maintenance, repairs and insurance, and the tenant pays rates and taxes.

Gross Weight. The weight of the goods together with the package, case or container in which they are packed.

Gross Yield. A yield which takes no account of the taxes which will have to be paid on the yield by the recipient. *See also* Grossed-up Redemption Yield.

Ground Rent. A yearly rent payable to the freehold owner of land by a lessee in return for the lease of the land to him for a number of years. Such a lease is often so that the lessee may build upon the land, thereafter selling the houses off to individual buyers. As the value of each plot has been enhanced by the building of a house upon it, the builder is able to charge a higher ground rent. The difference between this and the ground rent which he is paying to the freeholder is termed the *Improved Ground Rent.*

Ground Rent Receipt. Ground rents are reserved to the owner of a freehold estate and are payable by the person to whom he has leased the land. A ground rent is a yearly rent, payable usually by four quarterly instalments on the quarter days, and if the bank is lending against leasehold property security the borrowing customer must exhibit the receipts for the payment of ground rent to the banker as he gets them. The reason for this is that if the rent is not paid the landlord may after notice re-enter upon the property and bring the lease to an end. This would mean that the bank's security would disappear.

Group Accounts. A system of linking companies engaged in similar business, or a holding company acting as parent to a number of subsidiary companies, is found where taxation advantages are to be expected, where the problems of control and management are more easily handled, or where it is desired to gain the advantages of large-scale production and distribution. The banker asked to lend, whether to a holding or subsidiary company, is confronted by specialised balance sheets. He may well find, on examining the balance sheet of a subsidiary company, that it includes in its assets money owing by another subsidiary, or money lent to the holding company; the balance sheet of the holding company will show shares in the various subsidiaries and perhaps loans to them. It is therefore primarily a question of disentangling various interlinked items, which will cancel each other out, if properly married up, so as to arrive at the true position. The banker must settle down to a study of the group balance sheets and must satisfy himself that he has identified and discounted the debts, investments and contra-entries within the group itself. What he is left with should be the true assets and liabilities of the group. *See also* Consolidated Balance Sheet.

Groupage Documents. Container documents covering more than one consignee's goods.

Groupage Shipment. Shipments from different exporters handled in one or more containers by one forwarding agent to save freight charges and handling costs. The goods have a common destination.

Group de Dix. *See* Group of Ten.

Groupement d'Actions. A re-organisation in the division of share capital, by merging a certain number of shares with some of another class which have a higher nominal value; a reduction in the share capital of a company by a reduction in the nominal value of old shares to form a new share issue.

Group Insurance. Insurance or life assurance obtained by a person as a member of a group, such as a professional organisation, rather than as an individual, because in this way better terms can often be obtained. This is because there is an administrative saving for the company, and sometimes also because a particular group has a better life expectancy than people in general.

Group of Ten. As a step towards ensuring that the International Monetary Fund should have an adequate supply of the currencies most useful in its lending operations, arrangements were made in 1962 (known as general arrangements to borrow) for the Fund to get, direct from member countries, additional supplies of the main currencies. The countries participating were the United Kingdom, the United States, France, Italy, Japan, West Germany, Canada, Belgium, Sweden and the Netherlands. The countries became known as the "Group of Ten". The original agreement, valid for four years only, has been extended indefinitely. The group was responsible for the new currency parities agreed in 1971.

Group Trading. A method adopted by wholesalers and independent retailers in an effort to compete on more equal terms with supermarkets, multiple shops and big stores. The retailers associated with a wholesaler agree to make bulk purchases of various commodities from time to time, at lower prices. The retailer can then reduce his prices slightly to the consumer. Farmers also form groups for buying their farming requirements in bulk, and therefore at cheaper rates, and selling the produce to the market in bulk. Certain credit facilities are available to members of a cooperative.

Growth Share. A company share which offers a long-term appreciation in value because of expansion of the company's production, goods market, and initiative, shrewdness and good management on the part of the executives of the company.

Growth Stock. A stock or share which can be expected to appreciate in capital value. A growth stock is associated with a rather higher purchase price on the Stock Exchange and with a rather low current rate of yield. It is a good proposition for long-term investment. *See also* Growth Share.

Grund. Ground, base, basis.

Gründeranteilschein. A founder's share.

Grundkapital. Share or business capital.

Grundmaterial, Grundstoff. Commodity, raw materials.

Grundpfandverschreibung. The registration in the register of landed property of a charge on a piece of property as security for an outstanding or possible future indebtedness.

Grunt. A computer term, a measure of computer power; the total resources of a computer complex are measured in terms of "grunt".

Guarantee. An undertaking to be collaterally responsible for the debt, default or miscarriage of another. In a banking context it is an undertaking given by the guarantor to the banker accepting responsibility for the debt of the principal debtor, the customer, should he default. The guarantor may or may not be a customer. A guarantee must be in writing if it is to be enforceable at law. A bank guarantee should really be called an indemnity, for it invariably contains an indemnity clause which puts a direct responsibility on the guarantor in place of a collateral one. A direct responsibility leaves the guarantor liable whatever may happen: collateral responsibility leaves him with the same degree of responsibility as has the principal debtor. If, therefore, the principal debtor is excused for any reason, then the guarantor must be excused also. *See also* Cross Guarantees.

Guaranteed Minimum Pension (G.M.P.). Under U.K. pensions legislation a State scheme provides a pension in two parts, the basic pension and an additional earnings-related pension. Employers with their own pension schemes can arrange with the Occupational Pensions Board to contract out of the additional State pension. Contracting-out is subject to a number of conditions, of which one is that the individual employee's pension must be at least as much as he would have got from the additional State pension, had the scheme not been contracted out. This guaranteed pension is called the guaranteed minimum pension.

Guaranteed Stock. Stock upon which the interest is guaranteed (sometimes the interest and the principal) by the company issuing the stock, by another company, or by a government.

Guarantee Fund. A fund built up with a society or other organisation to replace any defalcations of an employee.

Guarantor. One who undertakes that the promises of another will be fulfilled, a surety, a warrantor. The guarantor has certain rights which must be carefully observed if the contract is to remain binding. Before he signs the guarantee he should ask any relevant questions about the principal debtor's account and financial position which he thinks necessary, and the bank manager must answer them truthfully. This may include disclosing the amount of the principal debtor's overdrawn position. If the guarantor is also a customer of the same bank even greater care should be employed. In particular, emphasis must be placed on what will or might happen in the event that the guarantor is called upon. After the guarantee is signed the guarantor may enquire how much he is contingently liable for and he must be told if the amount is below the amount of the guarantee. Otherwise he should be told that the guarantee is fully relied upon. A guarantor who pays off the principal debtor's borrowing in full is entitled to claim from the banker any securities which have been deposited against the debt, not only by the principal debtor, but also by any other person or body. If the bank is obliged to sue the guarantor for payment of the debt guaranteed, the guarantor is entitled to the benefit of any counterclaim or set-off which the principal debtor may have against the bank. As against the principal debtor the guarantor usually acquires an immediate right of action as soon as he makes any payment under his guarantee. Before any payment is made, however, the guarantor may call upon the principal debtor to pay the debt and relieve him of his obligation, should he think this step worth taking.

Guardian. One who has the charge, care or custody of any person or thing; a protector—one who has the charge, custody and supervision of a person not legally capable of managing his own affairs.

Guichet Drive-in. *See* Drive-in Bank.

Guichetkommission. Commission paid on the occasion of a new issue, by those banks handling the new issue, to other banks and authorised agents (notaries, property managers, trust companies, etc.) as remuneration for their services in placing the issue.

Guild. A society or corporation belonging to the same class, trade or pursuit, combined for mutual aid and protection of interests.

Guinea. A gold coin formerly current in the U.K., whose value was fixed at 21s (now 105p) in 1717; a sum of money equivalent to a guinea. It was applicable to professional fees and subscriptions.

Gült. Registered or bearer securities giving title to a plot of land, a building site, or a residential property. The security gives recourse against the land only; the debtor therefore has no personal liability for the debt.

Gute Lieferung. Good delivery: the condition of documents resulting from buying or selling contracts. Such documents should transfer a good title and should conform with agreed and customary rules of business.

H

Haftpflich. Liability.
Half a Bar. A transaction for half a million pounds.
Half Commission Man. A member of the Stock Exchange who is attached to a member firm of brokers and receives half the firm's commission on any deal which he has introduced, plus a retaining fee.
Hallmark. The mark used to indicate the standard of tested gold and silver; to stamp with this mark.
Hammered. The fate of a member of the Stock Exchange who is unable to meet his liabilities. Three blows with a mallet are struck on the rostrum of the "House" by a waiter to attract the attention of the members, after which the name of the defaulter is announced, and his name is posted on a board showing those who are expelled from the House. Any loss to that member's clients is then met from the compensation fund, which is guaranteed by all members.
Hamstern. Hoarding.
Handel. Trade, business.
Handelsbilanz. A country's balance of trade.
Handelspreis. Trade price.
Handler. Dealer, trader, retailer.
Harbour Dues. Charges for mooring or accommodating a vessel in a harbour.
Hard Arbitrage. Borrowing from a bank under an existing overdraft limit and re-lending the money at a profit on the inter-bank market or on some other secondary market.
Hard Currency. The currency of any foreign country for which there is a greater demand than there is for the currency of one's own country.
Harte Wahrung. Hard currency.
Haulage. The act of pulling; the charge for hauling a boat; the carrying of goods, material, etc., by road; the charge for this.
Hauptgeschaftsführer. General manager.
Haushalt. Budget.
Hausse. Boom.
Hausser. To rise, as of a share quotation on the *Bourse*.

Haussespekulant. Bear.
Haussier. A "bull".
Havarie. Damage to ship or cargo.
Head Lease. The original document executed by a freeholder in favour of the leaseholder on the occasion of the first granting of the lease.
Head Mortgage. Where a mortgagee of property offers the mortgage to a lender as security for a loan, a sub-mortgage is created. The original mortgage is then known as the head mortgage and the newly-created mortgage is a sub-mortgage.
Health Certificate. *See* Zoological Certificate.
Hedge against Inflation, *Hedgegeschäft.* An investment in land or shares which is expected to appreciate in value at a time of inflation, thus protecting the investor against loss due to the fall in money values.
Hedging. The use of market machinery by a trader to protect himself against loss through fluctuation in the price of the commodity in which he is dealing; laying off a risk.
Heir. One who by law succeeds or is entitled to succeed another in the possession of property or rank; one who succeeds to any gift, quality, etc. Originally the person entitled by law to the real property of a person deceased intestate. The heir was then the eldest son and his descendants, followed by any other sons in order, and their descendants. If there were no sons, but daughters only, they succeeded as coparceners, *i.e.* equally. The doctrine of heirship was abolished in 1925.
Heir Apparent. The manifest heir, the one who will succeed on the death of the present possessor, in contra-distinction to the heir presumptive.
Heir Presumptive. An heir whose actual succession may be prevented by the birth of one nearer akin to the present holder of the title, estate, etc.
Hereditament. A right capable of passing by way of descent to heirs; any real property which might upon an intestacy

before 1926 have passed to an heir. *See also* Corporeal Hereditaments; Incorporeal Hereditaments.

Heritable. Capable of being inherited, passing by inheritance, especially of lands and appurtenances, attached to the property or house as distinct from movable property.

Heritable Bond. In Scotland, a bond given by a debtor as security for the repayment of a loan, the security consisting of a conveyance of land in favour of the creditor, which can be implemented upon failure in repayment of capital or interest.

Herstellung. Manufacturing.

Hidden Reserve. A secret reserve not apparent from a scrutiny of the balance sheet, *e.g.* premises shown at less than their real value.

High Coupon. Yielding a high rate of interest.

Hire. The price paid for labour or services or the use of things; the engagement of a person or thing for such a price; to procure at a certain price for temporary use; to employ a person for a stipulated payment; to grant the use or service of for a stipulated price.

Hire Purchase. A system by which a hired article becomes the property of the hirer after a stipulated number of payments.

Hire-Purchase Agreement. An agreement, other than a conditional sale agreement, under which (1) goods are bailed (or in Scotland hired) in return for periodical payments by the person to whom they are bailed or hired, and (2) the property in the goods will pass to that person if the terms of the agreement are complied with and one or more of the following occurs; (i) the exercise of an option to purchase by that person, (ii) the doing of any other specified act by any party to the agreement, or (iii) the happening of any other specified event.

Hire Purchase Companies. Finance houses engaged in the business of hire purchase, credit sale and leasing. They obtain their funds by way of discount, by advertising to the public, and by borrowing from banks and accepting houses. Periodical governmental directives control the amount of the deposit and the length of the repayment time, making hire purchase easier or more difficult according to the economic climate. About thirty of the larger and better known finance houses are members of the Finance Houses Association. Together they represent about 85% of all hire purchase business.

Hirer. The individual to whom goods are bailed (or in Scotland hired) under a consumer hire agreement, or the person to whom his rights and duties under the agreement have passed by assignment or operation of law. In relation to a prospective consumer hire agreement this includes the prospective hirer.

Hochkonjunktur. Boom.

Holder. The payee or indorsee of a bill or note who is in possession of it, or the bearer thereof.

Holder for Value. A holder of a bill of exchange who has given value for it, or who is in possession of a bill for which value has at any time been given, is deemed to be a holder for value as regards the acceptor and all parties to the bill who became parties prior to such time. If the holder of the bill has a lien on it, whether the lien arises from a contract or by implication of law, he is deemed to be a holder for value to the extent of the sum for which he has a lien.

Holder in Due Course. A holder of a bill of exchange who has taken it, complete and regular on the face of it, under the following conditions, namely (1) that he became the holder of it before it was overdue, and without notice that it had previously been dishonoured, if such was the fact; (2) that he took the bill in good faith and for value, and that at the time the bill was negotiated to him he had no notice of any defect in the title of the person who negotiated it.

Holding. That which is held, especially land, property, stocks or shares.

Holding Company. A company which is a member of another company and either controls the composition of the board of directors of that other company, or holds more than half in nominal value of its equity share capital.

Holding Deed. The deed which transferred the ownership of land to the person now holding it.

Holding Gain. *See* Inflation Accounting.

Holdinggesellschaft. Holding company.

Holding Out. Maintaining or representing oneself to be in a position in which one is not; by words or conduct encouraging an impression that a special relationship exists, *i.e.* that of an agent or a partner. Persons who are not partners may be treated as though they were when it is a question of being responsible for the debts of a firm, if they have held themselves out to be partners, so influencing another party to enter into a contract with the firm. In such cases the doctrine of estoppel may be applied.

Holding Over. Postponing until the next occasion, deferring consideration until a subsequent hearing, as at a board meeting or in a court of law; in relation to land, remaining in possession of land without the consent of the landlord after a term has come to an end; on the Stock Exchange, deferring payment until the next settlement day.

Holograph. Wholly in the handwriting of the author or signatory; a document, letter, etc., so written.

Home Safe. A container for the saving of small sums issued by some banks. When the home safe is full it can be opened at the bank and the contents credited to a home safe deposit account, carrying interest (sometimes now called a savings account). An adaptation of the Victorian idea of a piggy bank.

Homme d'Affaires. A business man, an agent.

Honorarium. A fee or payment voluntarily made to a professional man for his services.

Honour. To pay on presentation, to meet a claim when due.

Horizontal Combination. An amalgamation or merger of two or more companies at a particular point or stage of manufacture in their common industry.

Horten, Hortung. Hoarding.

Hotchpot. Bringing into account sums already received by a beneficiary under a will during the lifetime of the testator, so that his share of the total sum available shall not exceed that of other beneficiaries of equal title under the same will. Especially used in relation to a class of beneficiaries such as children of the testator.

Hôtel de la Monnaie. See Mint.

Hot Money. Speculative money which crosses frontiers rapidly to take advantage of changes in interest rates. As repatriation of such funds is not normally covered forward, any sign of falling rates of interest or exchange will cause it to flow out just as rapidly.

Hot Treasury Bills. Treasury Bills allocated on the last day of the tender.

House. A noble family; a school boarding house; the audience at a place of entertainment; a general term in commerce to refer to a large or old-established firm or company, *e.g.* a discount house; the House of Commons or House of Lords; the Stock Exchange; the Bankers' Clearing House.

House Bill. A bill drawn by a company or firm upon itself. *See also* Pig on Pork.

House Bill of Lading. A bill of lading issued by forwarding agents.

Householder's Protest. A document in the form of a certificate given by any householder or man of some substance, attesting the dishonour of a bill of exchange. Such a certificate requires the signature of two witnesses and can only be issued in the case where a notary cannot be contacted at the place of dishonour. In such circumstances the householder's protest is equivalent in its effect to a formal protest.

Human Relations. A general term covering the relationship between workers, who should be regarded as individuals rather than units of production, and management, together with such factors as affect the environment in which workers work, the facilities afforded to them (*e.g.* free medical attention during working hours), and conditions of remuneration and pension rights. The emergence of staff and personnel departments has paid witness to the increasing recognition of the importance of this subject, which should be based on the recognition of human dignity rather than on the mere expectancy of increased output. The relationship should work both ways: workers and staff who are well treated should feel that they wish to do a good day's work, and ought to feel a part of the organisation which employs them.

Hypothec. A security in favour of a creditor over the property of his debtor, while the property continues in the debtor's possession.

Hypothecation. A type of security where neither ownership nor possession passes to the lender. In maritime law, the term refers to the charging of a ship's cargo, or the ship herself, in certain circumstances: in banking, it means an agreement to give a charge over goods, or over the documents of title to goods, in circumstances which make it impossible to give the banker possession. If this were possible the banker would take a pledge. In recognition of this fact the agreement usually undertakes to give a pledge when the goods or documents become available.

Hypothek, Hypothèque. A mortgage of real property, protected by registration at the Land Registry.

Hypothekarkredit. Credit extended against the security of a charge on land. *Direktem Hypothekargeschäft* is where the bank takes over the title to the land in its own name. *See* Legal Mortgage. *Indirektem Hypothekargeschäft* is where the bank holds the title to land but does not enter into its ownership. *See* Equitable Mortgage.

I

Ibidem (Ibid.). "In the same place".
Idem. "The same".
Id Est (i.e.). "That is".
Ignorantia Juris Haud Excusat. Ignorance of the law excuses no one.
Immaterialwerte. Intangible assets.
Immediate Annuity. One which takes effect at once.
Immediate Parties. Those parties to a bill of exchange who are in a close relationship to each other, such as drawer/acceptor, drawer/payee, indorser/second indorser.
Immobiliarkredit. A loan against the security of real property.
Immobilienfonds. Money invested in real property.
Immobilisations. *See* Fixed Assets.
Impersonal Accounts. Accounts in book-keeping which deal with things rather than persons, *e.g.* interest, stamps in hand, premises.
Impersonal Payee. Drafts payable to "Cash or order", "Wages or order", etc. Such drafts are not cheques, not being payable to a specified person. They are usually paid to the drawer or his known agent only, against an indorsement.
Implied Trust. A trust arising either from the presumed intention of the donor, or by the operation of the rules of law or equity.
Import. To bring in goods or produce from abroad; the act of importing.
Import Agent. An agent who arranges a contract between his principal, an importer of goods or services, and a foreign seller.
Importation. *See* Import.
Import Deposit. A restriction on imports by obliging importers to make a cash deposit to a central authority before permission to import can be given.
Import Duties. Taxes imposed on goods entering a country.
Importer. One who has goods originating in another country consigned to him.
Import Licence. Where it is a feature of exchange control that certain types of goods imported have to be approved by the monetary authorities, a system of licensing may be instituted to restrict imports to those who have applied for permission to import certain goods and have received approval.
Import Quota. A means of restricting imports by the issue of licences to supplying countries, assigning to each a quota, after determination of the amount of any commodity which is to be imported during a period. The device works against free trade and the maximisation of international trade generally, but may be forced upon the government of a country by internal pressures from traders and workers suffering from competition which they cannot match.
Import Restrictions. A country with an adverse trade balance may desire to control the volume of goods coming into the country from other countries, and for that purpose may impose tariffs or import quotas, restrict the amount of foreign currency available to imports, institute import deposits, impose import surcharges or prohibit various categories of imports.
Import Specie Point. *See* Specie Points.
Import Surcharge. A tax on imports, either general or particular, with a view to improving a balance of payments deficit.
Impost. That which is imposed or levied as a tax, a tribute, a duty (especially on imported goods).
Impôt. Tax, duty.
Impôt à la Source. Tax at source.
Impressed Stamps. Stamp duty on certain documents (such as a policy of life assurance) must be paid by impressing the right amount of duty on the document. This is done by a stamping office after the duty has been paid.
Imprest. In book-keeping, the fixed sum of money available for petty expenses; a loan, an advance, especially for carrying on any of the public services.
Imprest Bill, Bill of Imprest. An order entitling the bearer to have money paid in advance.
Improved Ground Rent. *See* Ground Rent.
Improvement Loan. *See* Lands Improvements Company.

In. Within, on behalf of, by, through, because of.

In Arrears. Unpaid, unsatisfied, behind with instalments of repayment.

In Bond. Goods on which customs duty has not yet been paid, pending which event they are kept in a Customs bonded warehouse.

In Camera. In secret.

In Case of Need. *See* Case of Need.

Incentive Shares. Shares issued by a company to its staff at preferential rates, sometimes convertible to ordinary shares at a later date, to encourage them to work hard and stay with the company.

Inchoate Instrument. An instrument incomplete in some respect, *e.g.* a cheque issued with no payee stated.

In Clearing. *See* Clearing House.

Income. The amount of money (usually annual) accruing as payment, profit, interest, etc., from labour, business, professions or property. *See also* Real Income.

Income Bond. A bond for a fixed period obtained in return for a single lump sum payment, where an element of life assurance cover is obtained together with the right to make regular withdrawals.

Income Debenture. A debenture which states that interest will be payable only out of the company profits.

Income Tax. A tax payable, subject however to various reliefs, by an individual who is permanently resident in a country, on all sources of income, whether arising in that country or in another.

Income Yield. The interest paid to a holder of any stock over a period; of dated stocks, the proceeds received by way of interest as opposed to the capital redemption yield.

Incoming Partner. A new partner joining the firm. He has no liability for any of the partnership debts contracted before the date of his joining. If the firm's banking account is overdrawn it should be ruled off and a fresh one started, unless the incoming partner is prepared to sign a statement accepting liability for the overdraft. If there is any security he should add his signature to any completed forms of charge held by the bank.

Inconvertible. Incapable of being exchanged for something else.

Inconvertible Paper Currency. Paper money which cannot be exchanged for metal at the central bank on demand.

Inconvertible Stocks or Securities. (1) Securities which cannot readily be turned into cash. (2) Securities having no right of transfer from one form of holding to another.

Incorporated Company. A company which has been registered in accordance with the requirements of the Companies Acts, and has received a certificate of incorporation.

Incorporeal. Immaterial, intangible.

Incorporeal Hereditaments. Non-tangible interests attached to land, such as rentcharges or rights of way.

Incumbrance. A burden, a hindrance to freedom of action or motion, a liability upon an estate, such as a mortgage.

In Curia. In open court.

In Demand. Much sought after.

Indemnifier. One who guarantees to a lender that if any loss occurs, no matter how created, he will make it good. Thus the liability of an indemnifier is absolute, and does not depend on the position of a principal debtor.

Indemnity. An agreement to render a person immune from a contingent liability; compensation for property annexed by the State or local authority in the public interest; an undertaking issued by a banker at the request of a customer in respect of missing bills of lading, lost share certificates, etc. *See also* Counterindemnity; Guarantee.

Indent. To set in farther from the margin than the rest of the paragraph; to make an indent or order upon, as where a branch bank indents upon its stationery office for a supply of stationery; an order, placed through an agent, from an overseas buyer. *See also* Closed Indent.

Indenture. An agreement or contract under seal, especially one binding an apprentice to a master, so called because the two documents had thin edges cut or indented exactly alike so as to correspond with each other; a written agreement between two or more persons, each party originally receiving a copy of the deed, all copies being notched or indented so as to establish the authenticity of any copy of the document. Since 1925 a deed has the effect of an indenture although not requiring to be indented.

Index. An alphabetical list; a directing sign; that which points out.

Indexanleihe. *See* Index-linking.

Indexation. This is the adjustment of long-term contracts, such as insurance contracts, to take account of inflation; this means that debts would be expressed in real terms, wage settlements would incorporate cost-of-living clauses, and income tax thresholds would be automatically adjusted as prices rise. Indexation removes some of the distortions and injustices caused by continuing inflation. The arguments against include the view that the implied recognition that a permanent state of inflation exists tends to diminish the struggle to contain it, and that the link perpetuates a classic inflationary spiral. If one accepts the cost-push theory of inflation, then to build automatic adjustments into the system would tend to encourage the further progress of inflation.

Index-Linking. Index-linking of wages was introduced in Belgium for miners in 1920, and has been generally applied to both public and private sectors since shortly after the Second World War. The system was introduced in France in 1937 and in Italy and Denmark in 1945. In Britain some S.A.Y.E. contracts and savings certificates (the latter for pensioners only) were linked to the index in 1975. Index-linked house insurance and the first index-linked permanent life assurance contract appeared in the same year. The arguments in favour of linking wages with an index are that indexation contributes to monetary and labour stability, and obliges public authorities and companies to watch price rises very closely.

Index Number. A percentage figure, used in statistics, to show fluctuations over a period as compared with a fixed standard.

Index of Retail Prices. *See* General Index of Retail Prices.

Indice. Index number, a number used for statistical comparisons of all kinds. A representative period is chosen as a base, then all other figures are related to and compared with it. *See also* General Index of Retail Prices.

Indice de Charge. Loading Charge.

Indice des Actions. A method of calculation by which an observer can follow the progress on a stock exchange of shares generally, or of certain groups of shares; a share index.

Indice Dow Jones. New York Stock Exchange index figure based on the mean prices of a selection of stocks and shares. It is calculated separately on industrial shares, railway shares and public utility shares. It serves in particular to indicate the tendencies of the market according to the theories of Dow. (Dow, Jones & Co. were owners of the *Wall Street Journal*.)

Indifferente Geschäfte. Banking business which is not subject to any depreciation in the balance sheet, *e.g.* deposits.

Indirect. Oblique, circuitous, nor resulting directly or immediately from a cause.

Indirect Arbitrage. *See* Compound Arbitrage.

Indirect Evidence. Evidence deduced from collateral circumstances.

Indirect Exchange. Exchange operations between two countries carried out through the medium of a third.

Indirect Tax. A tax on a commodity which is collected from the manufacturer or supplier, but is ultimately paid by the consumer.

Indirektem Hypothekargeschäft. *See* Hypothekarkredit.

Indorse. To write one's name, or a note of some kind, on the back of a document; to assign by indorsement; to ratify, confirm or approve. In the case of a bill of lading or a bill of exchange, to sign one's name on the back. **To Indorse Over.** To transfer one's rights (in a bill, etc.) to another person.

Indorsation. *See* Indorsement.

Indorsee. The person to whom a bill of exchange, a bill of lading, a delivery order, or any such document of title is transferred by indorsement, thus enabling him to deal with the instrument in his own right.

Indorsement, *Indorsation*. A writing on the back of a document. In the case of a bill of exchange, the writing on the back by which the value of the instrument is transferred from one person to another. Indorsements may be blank, restrictive or special. The writing must be completed by the signature of the indorser. The simple signature of the indorser is sufficient to transfer the value (bearer instruments need no indorsement). Indorsement means indorsement completed by delivery. *See also* Conditional Indorsement; Qualified Indorsement; Restrictive Indorsement; Special Indorsement.

Indorsement in Blank, Blank Indorsement. An indorsement which consists of the name only of the payee or indorsee of a bill of exchange, written on the back of the bill. Such an indorsement specifies no indorsee, and the bill becomes payable to bearer.

Indorser. The person who signs his name on the back of a document of title in order to negotiate it to another person. In the case of a bill of exchange the payee wishing to negotiate the bill becomes the (first) indorser when he so signs, and when and if the bill is later negotiated to other persons each person may indorse it in turn and so become an indorser (second indorser, third indorser, etc.). Each indorser of a bill of exchange is liable upon it. By indorsing it he (1) engages that on due presentment it shall be accepted and paid according to its tenor, and that if it be dishonoured he will compensate the holder, or a subsequent indorser who is compelled to pay it, provided that the requisite proceedings on dishonour are duly taken; (2) cannot deny to a holder in due course the genuineness and regularity in all respects of the drawer's signature and all previous indorsements; (3) cannot deny to his immediate or a subsequent indorsee that the bill was, at the time of his indorsement, a valid and subsisting bill, and that he had a good title thereto.

Indossament. Indorsement.

Industrial and Commercial Finance Corporation (I.C.F.C.). A corporation formed to provide long-term capital for British based small- and medium-sized companies which were capable of using additional resources profitably. It also provided a wide range of financial and specialist services, and had a number of subsidiary companies financing new technical development, assisting with mergers and flotations, providing renting and purchasing services, and financing British ships. The corporation was merged with Finance Corporation for Industry in 1973 to form Finance for Industry, but continues in its former role as a provider of funds for smaller companies. Loans are in the range of £5,000–£1m, administered through eighteen branches around the country, which to some extent liaise with the regional offices of the clearing banks.

Industrial and Provident Societies. A variety of institutions registered under the Industrial and Provident Societies Acts and other legislation which confer upon them a number of privileges, such as limited liability, and subject them to various obligations and limitations. They include wholesale and retail co-operative societies, building societies and trade unions. *See also* Friendly Society.

Industrial Bank. A finance house engaged in financing hire purchase transactions, obtaining its funds through advertisement to the public and offering a high rate of interest on deposits. When the Banking Act 1979 comes into force these bodies will no longer be able to call themselves "banks".

Industrial Life Policy. A policy of a life assurance where small premiums are collected weekly by door-to-door salesmen. The amount involved is small, and there is usually a prohibition against assignment, which will almost always, however, be removed on request by the banker.

Ineligible Bill. A bill payable in London and accepted by an agency bank or other bank, but which does not qualify for re-discount at the Bank of England. Ineligible bills may also be trade bills bearing a bank indorsement.

Inertia Selling. The delivery of goods which have not been ordered on the terms that they may be considered on approval for a specified term, on the expiry of which it is assumed that the receiver has decided to purchase them. An example of this was seen on the introduction of one of the major credit card companies in the U.K.

In Esse. In being, actual.

In Extenso. In full, at length.

Infant. *See* Minor.

Infeft. To invest with heritable property, to place a person in possession of a fee simple.

Inflation. A steady and progressive fall in the value of money, shown by price rises. The causes and effects of inflation are subjects of argument as much among economists as laymen. Suggested theories are those of demand-pull, where demand exceeds supply, thus causing buyers to bid up prices; cost-push, where rises in manufacturing costs, particularly wage costs, lead to price rises; and the excessive issue of paper money. It is clear that there is no one single cause of inflation. Also to be considered are external factors such as the world prices of raw materials affecting the balance of payments and the stability of the country's unit of currency. The sufferers in terms of inflation are those on fixed incomes and those with little negotiating power.

Inflation Accounting. Accounting which tries to evaluate and compensate for the falling value of money—a method of adjusting every figure in a balance sheet, based on movement of the retail price index. This, it is argued, should give an indication of relative value because the index measures the current purchasing power (C.P.P.) of the pound. An alternative suggestion has been that physical assets should be valued at replacement cost (R.C.). C.P.P. is described as an independent adjustment which depicts price, but not value, while R.C. is criticised for being no more than a subjective estimate which leaves shareholders in the dark as to the value of their stake in the company. Some insurance companies covering houses and contents have accepted the R.C. system, indemnifying the householder for what he regards as his true loss, the replacement cost figure. Profit is normally measured as the increase in value of a business undertaking measured from one year to the next. In a time of inflation this profit figure will include an element due to rising costs which is not strictly profit at all, but merely money needed to keep the business going. Inflation accounting therefore seeks to describe as "profit" only those sums which are left over after meeting working needs. As this system will reduce tax payable, it is not favoured by the Treasury. Also, some companies who like to declare big profit figures either for prestige reasons or to inflate their stock or share quotation on the Stock Exchange, or those who object to the reduction in dividend cover, are not in favour. The Sandilands Committee, reporting in the autumn of 1975, proposed a system called *Current Cost Accounting* (C.C.A.), designed to separate gains or losses arising out of the operations of the business from "holding gains". A holding gain is the difference between the measured value to a company of an asset at any point of time and its original cost. Holding gains are shown on a separate account and are not included in the computation of profit. The "value to the business" of assets used or owned by a company is not based on what they originally cost (the *"Historic cost"*). In most cases the value will be the R.C., less an allowance for depreciation, calculated on the adjusted value of the asset. But if this figure is higher than the second-hand value (the net realisable value) or the economic value of the assets to the firm, then whichever of these two values is the higher is the figure to be placed on the assets in the balance-sheet. The *"Economic value"* is the current value of the expected future earnings on the asset.

Informatique. See Data Processing.

Ingot. A mass of cast metal, especially copper, steel, gold or silver; a bar of gold or silver for assaying.

In Gross. In bulk, wholesale.

Inhaber. Holder, bearer.

Inhaberaktie. Bearer share.

Inhaberpapier. Documents of title payable to bearer, bearer bonds.

Inhaberschuldbrief. A document of title payable to bearer, possession of which is without further evidence *prima facie* proof of the title of the holder.

Inherent Vice. A particular quality of some product or element which renders it especially liable to cause damage or loss to itself or other goods, particularly during transport. In general, therefore, insurance companies exempt loss so caused from cover.

Inherit. To receive by descent, or by will or intestacy, to fall heir to.

Inheritance. That which is inherited—property, mental or moral quality, tradition, etc.

Inhibition. A writ to prevent a person from burdening his heritable property to the prejudice of a creditor; in the law of registered land, a notification to the Land Registrar to protect a minor interest, such as a receiving order where land is affected.

In-House. Within an organisation. Thus if it is said that the credit provided is wholly in-house, it means that the bank has itself found all the funds necessary, without calling upon any other bank or banks to assist.

In-House Funds. *See* Advisory Funds.

Injunction. An order or command, an exhortation, a precept; an equitable remedy which takes the form of an order of the court commanding something to be done (a *"mandatory" injunction*) or forbidding something (a *"prohibitory" injunction*). An *interlocutory injunction* is one granted provisionally before the hearing of an action to prevent the defendant doing something before the case is tried. A *perpetual injunction* is one granted after the issue between the parties has been tried. All injunctions are at the discretion of the court.

Inland. Carried on within a country, interior, domestic.

Inland Bill. A bill both drawn and payable in the United Kingdom.

Inland Money Orders. Money orders obtainable at post offices for sending money from one part of the country to another.

Inland Revenue. National income derived from taxation, stamp duties, licences of various kinds, and duties levied on home trade, excluding *excise*. The collection of these taxes is supervised by the Commissioners of Inland Revenue, Somerset House, Strand, London W.C.2.

In Loco Parentis. In the position of a parent.

Innerer Wert. The worth of a share calculated by reference to the company profits, usually reflected in the Stock Exchange quotation.

Innocent Misrepresentation. One made without intent to deceive. In the case of a contract so secured the injured party has a right to damages and/or recission, the other party having the defence of proving, if he can, that he believed the representation was true.

In Perpetuity, *In Perpetuum.* For ever.

In Personam. An action *"in personam"* is one against an individual, a person, who may have to pay damages or make restitution in some way.

In Re. In the matter of.

In Rem. An action *"in rem"* is one against property, usually land.

Inscribe. To write, carve or engrave (in or upon a paper, stone, or other surface), to mark, to address, to enter in a book, list, etc., especially to register the name of a stockholder in the stock register of a company or corporation; to issue (loans) with the names of holders so registered.

Inscribed Stock. Stock where the name of a stockholder was inscribed in the books of the registering authority and a stock receipt issued. A stock receipt is no evidence of title, because it was never necessary to produce it on sale of the stock. It was a simple receipt, never withdrawn once issued. The system was discontinued for all British government securities in 1943, and most inscribed stock is now converted into registered stock.

In Situ. In its original position.

Insolvable. Insolvent.

Insolvency. The state of being unable to pay one's debts as they arise.

Inspect. To view narrowly and critically, to examine officially.

Inspection. Careful survey, official examination; the examination of a branch bank by a party of inspectors appointed by the bank for that purpose, to confirm that the proper amount of cash is held and that the business of the branch is generally run in accordance with the bank's regulations. *See also* Committee of Inspection.

Inspection Certificate. *See* Certificate of Inspection.

Inspection of Company's Register. A company's register of members must be open to inspection by members free, and by other people on payment of a small charge, during business hours.

Inspectorate. A body of inspectors generally; the inspection department of a large bank.

Instalment. A part of a debt or sum due paid at successive periods; a part of anything supplied at different times.

Instalment Allotment. An allotment of stock, etc., where the purchase price is to be paid in a number of instalments.

Instalment Credit. Hire purchase finance.

Instandhaltung. Maintenance.

Instanter. At once.

Institute. To establish, to found, to appoint, to originate; a society or organisation established for the purpose of promoting some public object; the building in which such a society meets; the person who first takes estate or interest by deed of settlement of land on several people in succession.

Institute of Bankers, The, 10 Lombard St., London EC3V 9AS. The Institute of Bankers, founded in 1879, is one of the oldest professional bodies and certainly one of the biggest, with more than 100,000 members engaged in banking all over the world. The aims of the Institute are two-fold: to provide the educational foundation on which any man or woman can build a banking career; and to keep its members in touch with the latest developments in banking and business generally. Like other professional bodies, the Institute maintains educational standards through qualifications which are awarded to those who are successful in the examinations. The Institute's members are men and women engaged in banking at all levels. They range from trainees who have just left school or university to chief executives and directors. Membership is individual. Banks as banks are not members. The whole emphasis is on personal development. Associates of the Institute of Bankers (A.I.B.) are elected exclusively from those who have passed their Associateship examinations and they find the qualification accepted by some 2,000 banks and financial institutions in over 100 countries around the world. Fellows of the Institute of Bankers (F.I.B.) are elected by the Council from Associates who have achieved senior professional status. Their function is to give a lead in Institute affairs at both national and local level. Most of the leading figures in British banking are Fellows of the Institute. Policy is decided by an elected Council, and the central administration is in London. However, the membership is so large and so widespread that many of the activities are organised by a network of local centres. These local centres—over 100 of them in England, Wales and overseas—are organised voluntarily by the local members, who run seminars, debates, group discussions, lectures and industrial visits, all of which make their contribution to a banker's professional education. All members, whether or not they have completed the examinations, can attend local centre meetings. The centres also help bankers to play their role in their local communities by bringing them into social and professional contact with other organisations in the area. The Institute produces its own professional magazine, the *Journal of the Institute of Bankers*, which is distributed free to all members; and also publishes text books, study guides and other books on banking. The Institute's library in London contains an outstanding collection of financial and commercial books and periodicals, and also provides information service facilities for the use of Institute members. At national level, the Institute runs seminars, management courses and study tours. Internationally, the annual International Banking Summer School attracts senior bankers from more than fifty countries to discuss topics of professional importance. It was started by the Institute in 1948 and is now held all over the world, returning periodically to the United Kingdom. Further information about the Institute and details of the Institute's examinations are obtainable from its London headquarters.

Institute of Bankers in Ireland, The, Nassau House, Nassau Street, Dublin 2, Eire. The Institute is an association of those connected with the various branches of banking. Its objects are (1) to enable the members to acquire a knowledge of the theory and practice of banking and to promote the consideration and discussion of matters of interest to the profession; (2) to provide for the reading and discussion of approved papers, and for the delivery of lectures on banking and other professional subjects; (3) to maintain a library, consisting of works on banking, commerce, finance, political economy, etc.; (4) to afford facilities for the cultivation of social relations amongst its members.

Institute of Bankers in Scotland, The, 20 Rutland Square, Edinburgh EH1 2BB. The Institute was founded in 1875 "to improve the qualifications of those engaged in banking and to raise their status and influence". This is done mainly through an educational scheme for young bankers and the conduct of examinations to assess candidates' performance. In addition short courses are run on specific topics, lectures and meetings are arranged through local centres and wider information is disseminated through *The Scottish Bankers Magazine*, published quarterly. Qualifications: F.I.B.(Scot.), A.I.B.(Scot.), Dip.I.B. (Scot.).

Institutes. A book of precepts, principles or rules, a textbook on legal principles, *e.g. Justinian's Institutes.*

Institution. The act of instituting or establishing; an established law, custom or public occasion; the formal designation by one person of another to be his heir; an organised pattern of group behaviour established and generally accepted as a fundamental part of a culture.

Institutional. Instituted by authority; educational; in advertising, having as an objective long-term goodwill and reputation, rather than quick sales.

Institutional Investors. Banks, pension funds, investment trusts, unit trusts and insurance companies.

Institutionelle Anleger. Institutions which have as business aims the investment of large capital sums, *e.g.* insurance companies, pension fund managers, investment fund managers; institutional investors.

Instrument. A formal or written document such as a promissory note, bill, cheque, contract, grant, deed, etc.; a term sometimes used to describe a written order which is drawn on a banker, but does not satisfy the definition of a bill of exchange. Its meaning is not confined to this, however (*e.g.*, a negotiable instrument includes a bill of exchange).

Instrumentarium. The means at the disposal of a central note-issuing bank to ensure the fulfilment of its economic policy, *e.g.* manipulation of the discount rate, open market operations, etc.

Insurable Interest. As a matter of public policy, the assured or insured person must have a pecuniary interest in the person or thing to be covered, to distinguish the transaction from one of a gambling nature. Insurable interests exist in these cases: (1) a man or woman may assure his or her own life; (2) a man may assure the life of his wife, or *vice versa*; (3) a creditor may assure the life of his debtor; (4) a litigant may assure the life of his judge; (5) a company may assure the life of its director; (6) an employer may assure the life of his employee, or *vice versa*; (7) a trustee may insure in respect of the interest of which he is a trustee. An assignee need not have an insurable interest. The insurable interest need only exist at the time the policy is taken out.

Insurance. A contract between two parties whereby the insurer agrees to indemnify the insured upon the happening of a stipulated contingency, in consideration of the payment of an agreed sum, whether periodical or fixed (the premium). Insurance falls into the main groups of life; property; marine, aviation and transport; motor vehicle; third-party liability; and personal accident and sickness. The term "assurance" is generally limited to the first of these, because the event in respect of which the policy is taken out—namely the death of the person—is assured, or certain. Only the time of the death is uncertain. *See also* Credit Insurance; Fire Insurance; Group Insurance; Life Assurance; Marine Insurance; Mutual Insurance.

Insurance Agent. An agent who arranges a contract of insurance between his principal, an insurance company, and a beneficiary who will receive the sum covered when and if the risk insured against actually happens.

Insurance Bond. *See* Income Bond.

Insurance Broker. An agent arranging insurance on ships, cargo, etc.

Insurance Certificate. A document issued to the insured certifying that insurance has been effected and that a policy has been issued. It is not transferable by indorsement and is therefore not usually acceptable under a documentary credit which stipulates for the insurance of goods. Such a certificate is not valid in a court of law without a policy, and is primarily used when goods are insured under the terms of a floating policy. It is widely used to save time and labour and is often prepared by the insured person himself.

Insurance Policy. A document which is legal evidence of the agreement to insure, which may be issued at the time when the contract is made, or at a later date.

Insurance Premium. The payment of an agreed sum, whether in one amount or by instalments, to an insurance company by the person insured in return for the company's undertaking to indemnify the insured upon the happening of a stipulated con..ngency. *See also* Policy Underwriter.

Intangible Assets. Patents, trademarks or goodwill, which have a real value, sometimes a considerable one.

Inter. Between, among.

Inter-Bank Market "Bid" Rate (I.B.B.R.). The rate of interest which first-class banks are prepared to pay for deposits for a specified period. Such "bids" may be limited in amount.

Inter-Bank Market "Offered" Rate (I.B.O.R.). The rate of interest at which funds are offered on loan for a specified period in the inter-bank market to first class banks. Offers are subject to availability within dealing limits, and may be limited in amount. The London interbank offer rate (L.I.B.O.R.) is a possible alternative to a bank's base rate from which the bank relates its interest charges on lending. L.I.B.O.R. is always a true reflection of the cost of funds to the bank, and it is logical to use it as a true base rate, particularly in the case of medium-term lending where the interbank market is the only assured source of term funds.

Interbankrate. Rate of interest for loans between banks on the Euromarket.

Inter-Bank Research Organisation, The, Moor House, London Wall, London EC2Y 5ET. The Inter-Bank Research Organisation (I.B.R.O.) is a multidisciplinary organisation set up in 1968 by the London and Scottish clearing banks to consider matters of common interest to the banking industry. Initially, I.B.R.O. was chiefly engaged in long-term research on the money transmission activities of the clearing banks. While this still represents an important part of its work, I.B.R.O. also serves the banks in several quite different ways and covers a much wider variety of subjects than hitherto. In fact relatively little of I.B.R.O.'s work is now "research" in the normal sense of the term; rather it involves providing advice and assistance in various ways on topical matters requiring collective decisions and actions by the clearing banks. As such, the work often has more in common with the activities of a trade association than those of a research organisation. Most of I.B.R.O.'s work is undertaken in direct support of the specialist sub-committees and working parties of the Committee of London Clearing Bankers. In addition, I.B.R.O.'s assistance is also made available on certain issues to different groupings of banks, notably the British Bankers' Association. However, I.B.R.O. does not normally undertake assignments for individual banks or for any other sponsors. I.B.R.O. has a highly qualified professional staff of about thirty, with backgrounds in such fields as accountancy, economics, law, operational research, systems analysis and market research. Over the years they have been involved to a greater or lesser extent in almost every type of issue reckoned to be of joint concern to the banking industry. I.B.R.O.'s main areas of interest can be divided into two groups: the banks' money transmission systems and services, and changes in the banks' legislative and regulatory environment. Prominent in the former category have been studies by I.B.R.O. into the economics of money transmission, the markets for the banks' services, the rationalisation of existing systems and the development of new, automated systems. In addition, the Inter-Bank Standards Unit exists within I.B.R.O. to further the standardisation of bank systems. Prominent in the latter category have been investigations into bank licensing and regulation, monetary policy, exchange control, taxation, accountancy and a wide range of political and legislative developments of relevance to banking, including those initiated in the E.E.C. Most of I.B.R.O.'s output takes the form of working papers, reports and other documents confidential to the sponsoring banks. A certain amount, however, is either published directly or incorporated in material published by the sponsoring banks. Overall control of I.B.R.O. is the responsibility of a managing committee of senior clearing bankers, while I.B.R.O.'s detailed work programme is overseen by two specialised steering committees.

Inter-Bank Sterling Market. A market which has arisen to satisfy the placing and taking of sterling deposits between London banks. It acts as a way in which the banks can balance their books, or obtain the funds they need when lending would otherwise be limited by the amount of money deposited by the customers of the banks. (The terms "wholesale" and "retail" banking have been used to describe these two sources of funds.) All transactions on the market are unsecured, but each bank has its own limits on how much it will deposit with any one other bank. All agreements are arranged by telephone, usually through brokers.

Inter-Company Loans Market. Loans for fixed sums made between larger commercial and industrial companies when bank accommodation is not forthcoming. The market originated in 1969 as a result of the qualitative and quantitative controls at that time exercised by the Bank of England over the lending banks.

Interesse Wahrend. A qualification of a "best rate obtainable" order given in connection with stock exchange transactions, whereby the bank acting is authorised, when carrying out a purchase order on a rising rate, or a sale order on a falling rate, to amalgamate or stagger transactions in what they judge to be in the best interest of the customer giving the order.

Interest. The profit per cent derived from money lent; payment for the use of borrowed money or on a debt; an advantage, an asset, a holding, a share in something. *See also* Accrued Interest; Compound Interest; Contingent Interest; Gross Interest; Simple Interest; Vested Interest.

Interest Clause Bill. A bill more commonly met in Eastern or Australian trading, which is drawn for a fixed amount plus interest at a stated rate per annum from the date of the bill or from the time of negotiation until the proceeds of the bill are received.

Interest in Suspense. Interest calculated and passed to a suspense account because the borrowing customer is insolvent.

Interest on Deposit. The interest paid by banks to deposit account holders and by building societies to those depositing money with them.

Interest on Overdraft. *See* Charges.

Interest Warrant. An order or warrant issued by a government or a company and drawn on its bankers, authorising them to pay the interest specified thereon to the stockholder.

Intérêt. Interest.
Intérêts Courus. Interest not yet due, interest accruing.
Intérêts Intérimaires. Interest payable on account of an interim period.
Intérêts Moratoires. Where there is delay in settling a debt, interest thereon stipulated by law or by agreement, and calculated from the date of default to the date of settlement: overdue interest.
Intérêts Pro Rata Temporis. See Intérêts Courus.

Interim Budget. An additional budget, introduced part-way through the financial year, usually to increase taxation.

Interim Dividend. A dividend paid by a company during the course of the company's year, leaving a final dividend to be paid at the end of the year when the company's financial position at that time has become known.

Interimsschein. Provisional certificates of title issued pending the issue of definitive documents.

Interlocking Directorate. The situation where a number of directors act on the boards of several companies, so that the policies of the companies may be unobtrusively harmonised or made complementary one to another.

Interlocutory Injunction. *See* Injunction.

Intermediary. One who acts as a go-between or a mediator; a middleman, an agent, a broker.

Internal Debt. That part of a country's National Debt owed by a state to its own nationals.

Internal Loan. A public loan made within a country where the principal and interest are payable only in the same country.

International. Pertaining to, subsisting or carried on between, or mutually affecting, different nations.

International Bank for Reconstruction and Development (the World Bank). Established, together with the International Monetary Fund, after the Bretton Woods Conference, 1944. Its purpose was to help countries to reconstruct their economies after the damage inflicted by the war. It is prepared to assist member countries by lending to governmental agencies or by guaranteeing private loans. Loans are usually for fifteen to twenty years and finance agricultural modernisation, hydro-electric schemes, port improvements, and in general programmes of economic reconstruction. The funds come from the developed countries and the bank acts as a medium-term loan agency in channelling them to the less-developed countries.

International Credit Clubs. Organisations devised to arrange medium-term credit for exporters, consisting of a number of European finance companies who have combined to facilitate instalment credit business as between one country and another.

International Date Line. The line on either side of which the date differs, running meridianally across the world from the poles and theoretically at 180° from Greenwich. When travelling westwards it is necessary to put one's watch back: this has the effect of lengthening the day or night for the westbound traveller. When travelling eastwards it is necessary to advance one's watch: this has the effect of shortening the day or night for the eastbound traveller.

International Finance Corporation. A corporation founded in 1956 to promote loans to under-developed countries where private enterprise has been unable to raise funds locally. The corporation is affiliated with the World Bank and is able to mobilise funds from other international banks as well as providing them its own resources.

International Law. An accepted system of laws or jurisprudence regulating intercourse between nations.

International Monetary Fund (I.M.F.). The fund was set up in 1946 as one result of the international monetary conference held two years earlier at Bretton Woods, U.S.A. The intentions were to develop some method of economising in the use of gold and currency reserves, to establish free convertibility between the currencies of the participating nations, and to set up a scheme for giving temporary assistance to member countries in short- or medium-term balance of payments difficulties. The I.M.F. is therefore in effect a bank to smooth out the fluctuations of the world trade cycle. The member countries have contributed gold and currencies to the fund on the basis of quotas allocated to them. When a country runs into difficulties it can apply to the Fund for a loan to finance its deficit. At that time it must show that it is taking appropriate action to correct its deficit and to restore and maintain the external value of its currency. Any such loan is related strictly to the member country's economic size and repayment is expected to be made in three to five years, for it is no part of the Fund's purpose to give semi-permanent support to a country with fundamental weaknesses which it cannot or will not put right. The Fund has had some successes in restoring confidence in currencies affected by short-term capital movements, and it has enabled some countries to expand their economies and their foreign trade. But it has not been able to prevent devaluations, nor to ensure exchange stability. Its effectiveness is currently limited by its composition, for about one-third of its assets is in the non-convertible currencies of minor countries, and some is in gold whose valuation is out of line with market rates. However, good progress was made at a meeting in Kingston, Jamaica, in January 1976 where increases in credit were authorised—a measure which should help the developing countries; an agreement concluded with the Organisation of Petroleum Exporting Countries whereby they will allow their currencies to be used for I.M.F. lending operations; and a proposal adopted to sell off one-sixth of I.M.F.'s gold holdings to finance a trust fund to help the developing countries.

International Money Order. A means of transferring comparatively small sums from one country to another through the agency of the Post Office.

International Securities. Securities which can be bought or sold on an international market, *i.e.* in several different countries, at more or less the same prices.

Interplead. To take legal proceedings in order to discuss and determine an incidental issue.

Interpleader. A suit by which the claims of two parties to money or property are determined, in order that a third party (such as a banker), on whom the claim is made, may know to which party payment or delivery is due.

Inter Se. Amongst themselves.

Intervention Rate. The rate at which the central authority will intervene on the foreign exchanges to buy its currency (if it is falling) or sell its currency (if it is rising). Since convertibility was established in 1958, central banks have normally had intervention points only in U.S. dollars and have solely used that currency as a means of intervention.

Interventionskurs. A stock exchange price which has risen as the result of buying orders.

Interventionspunkte. See Intervention Rate.

Interview. A meeting between two persons face to face; a discussion between a manager and one of his staff, or between a banker and his customer. An interview with a customer may be arranged by appointment or, less satisfactorily, requested by the customer when he is in the branch. As far as possible the manager should prepare for the interview by glancing at the customer's correspondence file, ledger balance, safe custodies and securities held, etc. At the interview he should ascertain as quickly and thoroughly as possible what the customer wants, and decide how far he can go to satisfy him. He must be sure to elicit all the essential information and he must remember that he is engaged on a public relations exercise on behalf of the bank. However, the interview may be at the request of the manager and may relate to the unsatisfactory conduct of the account, when the customer must be told the bank's views politely but firmly. A staff interview is at the branch with the manager, or at an area, regional, or head office with a staff or personnel manager. It may be at the request of the staff member, or by the direction of the staff manager. It may be an annual progress review, or it may be for the giving of advice of a disciplinary nature, or it may be a preliminary to promotion.

Inter Vivos. Among the living.

Intestate. Not having made a valid will, not disposed of by will. In a case of intestacy an administrator will be appointed on the death to wind up the affairs of the deceased.

Intimation. The notice given to a debtor by the assignor of a debt or obligation. Such notice is not necessary in the case of negotiable instruments or securities.

In Toto. Wholly.

In Transitu. In the course of being transported from one place to another. *See also* Stoppage *in Transitu.*

Intra Vires. Within the powers (usually of a company).

Intrinsic Value. Genuine or real value. When used of coin, it means that the metal in the coin is worth the face value of the coin.

Introduction. The act of introducing or bringing into notice, the act of making persons formally acquainted with one another; a method by which a company can obtain a Stock Exchange quotation when it has reached such a size in terms of capitalisation and spread of shareholders as to meet the requirements of the Stock Exchange, or where its securities are already listed on another stock exchange. *See also* Offer for Sale; Placing.

Introduction à la Bourse. The granting of a quotation on a stock exchange.

Inventar. Inventory, stock.

Inventory. A detailed list or catalogue of goods and chattels, the articles enumerated on such a list. A list of the effects of a house, required for probate or insurance purposes.

Investissement Étranger. Investment overseas.

Investissements. The placing of capital at long term in industry in the form of machines, equipment for work-shops, fixtures, etc.; by extension, capital investment in general.

Investitionen. Long-term investment by industrial and manufacturing concerns in buildings, machines, etc.; capital investment generally.

Investitionrisikogarantie. Similar to the State guarantee against export risks, but in respect of investment abroad. In principle limited to investment in the developing countries, the State investment guarantee is obtainable in part cover and subject to conditions.

Investitionsgüter. Capital goods.

Investitionskredit. Long-term investment in property, buildings, machinery, equipment, etc.

Investment. The act of laying out money; the capital invested or lent to produce interest or profit; using money to buy something which it is hoped will bring in some return and will not lose its value. *See also* Trade Investments.

Investment Bank. A bank which provides long-term fixed capital for industry, in return taking over shares in the borrowing companies, so that some measure of influence or control can be exercised. Additionally it may exercise many merchant bank functions such as merger making, commodity trading, advising on investments, counselling in corporate finance, broking, etc.

Investment Currency. Foreign funds in this country, in respect of which permission has been given by the Bank of England for U.K. residents to purchase foreign-quoted securities. Investment currency is quoted in U.S. dollars and is normally at a premium. This is based on U.S. $2.60 per £1.

Investment Income Surcharge. An additional amount of tax over and above the basic rate, levied on the excess of investment income above a certain figure. At present people under sixty-five pay another 10% on investment income between £1,701–£2,250, and thereafter 15%. Those aged sixty-five and over pay 10% between £2,501–£3,000, but this is their only advantage. Investment income is derived principally from interest and dividends. Certain deductions are allowed from investment income (interest paid out, maintenance payments up to £1,000) which have the effect of diminishing the surcharge.

Investment Portfolio. See Portfolio.

Investmentsparen. A savings scheme, an investment plan.

Investment Trust. A public corporate body registered under the Companies Acts and formed for the purpose of holding investments, obtaining its capital from public issues. Investors in the trust can obtain holdings only by buying shares from existing holders. The investment trust enables the small investor with limited capital resources to spread his risks over a wide range of securities under full-time specialist management.

Invisible Exports. The various services performed in one country for persons in another, for which payment has to be made, interest, profits and dividends on investments abroad, air transport receipts, profits on plays abroad and royalties, all cause a flow of currency into a country. In the case of Great Britain, whose banking, insurance and shipping facilities regularly earn large sums of foreign money, it is often the case that her invisible exports go far to offset or even reverse a deficit on the balance of visible imports and exports. After the proceeds of investment abroad and the services performed by the City, the money earned by tourism is the next most important factor. See also Visible Exports.

Invoice. A list of goods dispatched, with particulars of quantity and price, sent to a consignee. See also Consular Invoice.

Invoice Discounting. A less comprehensive factoring service than Recourse Factoring where a company may sell its sales invoices at a discount in return for immediate payment. It provides no sales ledger accounting service or credit cover. Other names for this are Invoice Factoring, Confidential Invoice Factoring, and Receivables Financing, which is the provision of loans against money due—receivables—without any of the service elements of factoring. See also Factoring.

Invoice Factoring. See Invoice Discounting.

I.O.U. A written acknowledgment of a debt of a specified sum bearing these letters, addressed to the creditor, dated, and signed by the borrower. It is not evidence that money has been lent and it is not a negotiable instrument.

Irish Bank Federation. Nassau House, Nassau Street, Dublin 2, Eire. The Federation was formed in 1973 with the objects (1) of providing facilities for the discussion of matters of common interest to Irish licensed banks, of protecting those interests, and, where appropriate, of making representations on their behalf; (2) of advising and assisting the authorities on all matters of material concern to Irish banking; (3) of representing Irish banking in matters relating to the European Economic Community. Membership is restricted to banks which are licensed under the Central Bank Act 1971.

Irredeemable Debenture. A debenture with no date for repayment, intended to be a permanent debt.

Irredeemable Stocks. Government stocks which have no date of redemption.

Irrevocable Credit. Once this type of credit has been arranged, its terms cannot be varied or changed without the concurrence of all the parties to it. An exporter who is in a sufficiently strong bargaining position to do so should therefore always insist on payment by irrevocable credit. All credits are revocable unless it is specifically stated that they are irrevocable.

Irrevocable Power of Attorney. *See* Power of Attorney.

Issue. The act of sending out, the whole number sent out at one time to be put into circulation, as notes; a topic of discussion or controversy; publication, that which is published at a particular time; progeny, offspring; the specific point in an issue between two parties requiring to be determined; to come to a point in fact or law, on which the parties join, and rest the decision of the cause. *See also* General Issue; New Issue; Public Issue; Rights Issue; Special Issue.

Issued Capital. That part of the authorised capital which is issued to shareholders and paid for by them, not necessarily fully paid up.

Issue of Bill. The first delivery of a bill, note or cheque, complete in form, to the person who takes it as a holder. Thereafter the instrument is said to be "negotiated"; only a drawer can "issue" a bill, etc.

Issue Price. The price at which stock or shares are issued to the public; not necessarily the nominal price.

Issuing Bank. *See* Bank of Issue.

Issuing House. A group of accepting houses, merchant banks and other institutions who act as intermediaries between those seeking capital and those who are able to supply it, sponsoring capital issues if they are satisfied that the amount required can be raised on conditions which are acceptable to investors. They make themselves responsible for taking up any of the issue which has not been taken up by others, although they may arrange for others to share the risk. (*See* Underwriter.) The issuing house agrees the timing of the issue with the Bank of England, and where a quotation is to be granted it handles the negotiations with the Quotations Committee of the Stock Exchange. Issuing houses also give advice over a wide range of company problems.

Issuing Houses Association. An association formed in 1945 to represent the interests of the merchant banks and other institutions acting as issuing houses, to act as a consultant and advisory body and to be the spokesman for the views of its members on matters affecting their activities.

J

J Curve. A description of the state of the balance of trade of a country, graphically displayed, after a devaluation. This has the effect of making the country's exports cheaper, so they will increase, and the imports dearer, so they will fall. The initial effect, however, will be the other way, because many exports are made of imported raw materials. The immediate impact, therefore, is an increase in the cost of imports. The expansion in the volume and value of exports follows, but after an inevitable time lag. There is a short down turn, following the devaluation, followed by a long up turn. A graph of this would look like a letter J leaning backwards slightly. The effect can also apply to other types of remedial action, *e.g.* the delayed effect on unemployment of an increase in the level of production, because this first absorbs the surplus capacity and higher productivity sufficient to meet the requirements of the early stage.

Job. A piece of work, especially one done for a stated price; habitual employment or profession; to act as a broker; to hire out for a specified time.

Job Analysis. The examination of industrial output with a view to eliminating waste of time or energy.

Jobber. A middleman, a dealer on the Stock Exchange who carries on business with stockbrokers; a dealer in the professional inter-bank foreign exchange market when local factors influencing rates in one centre tend to give rise to jobbing opportunities.

Jobber's Turn. The difference between the two prices quoted by a jobber for a stock or share—the higher being his selling price, the lower his buying price.

Job Card. A card to record time spent on any particular job; a card containing details of any particular task to be undertaken.

Job Evaluation. The calculation of the content of any particular job in an organisation, the qualifications required for it, and possibly the subsequent grading of staff accordingly.

Joint Account. A banking account maintained by two or more people. All must sign on any relevant documents unless the mandate provides otherwise. All are jointly liable for any overdraft unless the mandate establishes joint and several liability. On the death of one party to a joint account, any credit balance on the banking account normally becomes the property of the survivor(s). In some cases, however, particularly where a husband-and-wife joint account is in question, the appropriation of the balance of the survivor on the death of one may depend upon the intention of the party who opened the account in the first place. The banker should guard against any embarrassment arising from a claim on the bank by the personal representative of the deceased party by including in the mandate a specific clause authorising him to pay the balance to the survivor. *See also* Dispensing Notice.

Joint and Several Liability. A banker dealing with joint account holders should be careful to establish joint and several liability by a suitable clause in the mandate. Then the account holders will be individually as well as jointly liable for the repayment of any accommodation taken, and the bank will have as many rights of action as there are account holders. With joint account holders of an overdrawn account the debt is not pursued into the estate of one of them if he dies, but with joint and several liability the debt remains as a charge on the estate. In the bankruptcy of a partnership the bank gains a right of double proof: against the firm on an equal footing with the firm's creditors, and against each partner on an equal footing with that partner's private creditors. Any security held can be allocated to whichever estate will show the banker an optimum return.

Joint and Several Liability of Directors. It is a common practice of bankers to supplement security offered by a company by the joint and several guarantees of the directors. The guarantees themselves may or may not be worth much, but the intention is to bring it home to the directors that they are personally responsible. This will make them more careful in their actions, and more prudent in the use they make of the accommodation granted. As they are asking the bank to express its confidence in the future of the company (by lending it money), they can hardly refuse to show a similar confidence themselves.

Joint and Several Promissory Note. *See* Promissory Note.

Joint Annuity. An annuity payable throughout the lifetime of two people (often husband and wife) and continuing until the death of the survivor.

Joint Consultation. Dialogue between management and workers on matters affecting them both; discussion between government and representatives of capital and labour.

Joint Heir. One who shares an inheritance with another.

Joint Liability. Joint holders are regarded by the law as together making up the "owner". A claim against joint defendants should be made against them jointly, and not against one or other of them. If a case is brought against one, and it fails, the claimant cannot then sue the other, for there is only one right of action against joint owners.

Joint Lives Policy. A life assurance policy which is payable on the death of the first of joint policy owners.

Joint Promissory Note. *See* Promissory Note.

Joint Stock Bank. A bank which has issued shares to shareholders who hold them jointly, as opposed to a partnership. The term was originally meant to distinguish banks which were public limited companies from private partnership banks, but it is not so much used nowadays, when all the big banks are joint stock banks.

Joint Stock Company. A mercantile, banking or operative association with capital made up of transferable shares.

Joint Tenancy. A tenure of land, property, etc., by more than one person. On the death of one joint tenant the property passes to the survivor to the exclusion of the personal representative of the deceased joint tenant.

Jointure. Property settled on a woman at marriage, to be hers on the death of her husband.

Jouissance. The date from which newly issued securities will begin to pay interest; the expectation of interest or dividend on new share issue.

Journal. The ledger containing details of the daily transactions of a business; a diary, a daily newspaper, a periodical publication.

Judge. A civil officer invested with power to hear and determine causes in a court of justice; one authorised to decide a dispute or contest; to hear and try (a case), to decide (a question), to sentence.

Judge-Made. Based on legal interpretations of the law as made by judges.

Judg(e)ment. The act of judging; a legal decision arrived at by a judge in a court of law; an order or decree made by any court.

Judg(e)ment by Default. A decision given in favour of the plaintiff when the defendant fails to appear.

Judg(e)ment Creditor. A creditor who has obtained judgment against a debtor for the payment of a debt. He may enforce this in a number of ways, such as by a writ of *fieri facias*, by a garnishee order, by the issuance of a bankruptcy notice, by a charging order, etc.

Judg(e)ment Debt. A debt secured by a judge's order, under which an execution can be levied at any time.

Judg(e)ment Seat. A judge's bench, a tribunal, a court.

Judg(e)ment Summons. A legal summons for failure to settle a judg(e)ment debt.

Juge de Paix. A Justice of the Peace.

Juge d'Instruction. An examining magistrate.

Jugendsparheft. A savings book in the name of a young person evidencing an account on which interest is allowed at a somewhat higher rate than usual in order to encourage thrift.

Jurisdiction. The legal power or right of administering justice, making and enforcing laws, or exercising other authority; the district or extent within which such power may be exercised.

Jus Canonicum. Canon law.

Jus Civile. Civil law.

K

Kaffirs. South African mining shares.
Kapital. Capital. *See also Dotationskapital*; *Eigenkapital*; *Genehmigteskapital*.
Kapital Autorisiertes. Authorised capital.
Kapitalertragsteuer. *See* Withholding Tax.
Kapitalexport. The outflow of capital from a country in various different forms, as for expenditure overseas, purchase of foreign bonds and shares, the granting of loans to foreign debtors, the financing of overseas subsidiaries, etc.
Kapitalisierung. The calculation of capital worth by measurement of the performance of invested funds over a period; profits capitalised at a given interest rate; valuation of an undertaking on the stock exchange by multiplying the share quotation by the number of outstanding shares.
Kapitalmarkt. The sale and purchase of medium- and long-term funds.
Kapitalverkehrsbilanz. The balance of short- and long-term capital imports and exports of a country.
Kapitalzuwachsteuer. Capital gains tax.
Kassa. Spot. *Per Kassa.* A transaction for cash.
Kautionskredit. An undertaking from the bank to a third party for the due repayment of a debt or obligation, due from the beneficiary under the credit. *See also Aval*; Cautionary Obligation.
Kautionswechsel. A bill or promissory note held as security.
Keeping House. A term for the action of a debtor who makes it difficult for his creditors to see him. A writ has to be served personally, so if a debtor will not answer his door, and never goes out, it is a difficult matter to effect service. Keeping house is an act of bankruptcy.
Kennedy Round. An agreement made in 1967, and subsequently carried out, by which the signatory countries to the General Agreement on Tariffs and Trade made a general reduction of tariffs. The conference was the result of a suggestion by President Kennedy of the U.S.A., and the "round" of tariff reductions was accordingly designated with his name.

Kerb Market. The carrying on of business in the street after the Stock Exchange has closed.
King. *See* Sovereign.
Kite. An accommodation bill; a representation of fictitious credit.
Kite-Flying. Raising money by the use of accommodation bills; a procedure to discover how the public at large will react to some proposal, seeing "how the wind blows".
Kleinkredit. Credit of a relatively modest amount, repayable by instalments, often for small traders, to give them temporary help, or for private needs such as durable consumer goods, repayment being from earnings or profits.
Konjunkturzyklus. Trade cycle.
Konkurs. Bankruptcy, insolvency.
Konkursverwalter. Receiver in bankruptcy.
Konossement. *See* Bill of Lading.
Konsolidierte Bilanz. Consolidated balance sheet (*q.v.*).
Konsortialgeschäft. Business undertaken by consortium banks.
Konsumgüter. Consumer goods.
Konsumkredit. Loans to finance the acquisition of consumer goods.
Konto, Kontokorrent. A running account, especially one with a bank.
Kontokorrentkredit. Accommodation up to a fixed figure made available for the short-term needs of the borrower on a running or current account, mostly unsecured.
Kontoüberziehung. Overdraft.
Konvention. An agreement on the uniform handling of certain transactions.
Konversion, Konvertierung. *See* Conversion (*second meaning*).
Konvertibilität. *See* Convertibility.
Konvertierbare Währung. Convertible currency.
Konzern. *See* Combine.
Konzernbilanz. Consolidated balance sheet.
Kopfsteuer. *See* Poll Tax.
Körpershaftsteuer. Corporation tax.
Kosten, Versicherung, Fracht. Cost, insurance, freight (C.I.F.).

Kotierung. Quotations.
Kotierungsgebühr. The yearly fee charged by a stock exchange for giving quotations for any particular stock.
Kraftloserklärung. The legally prescribed procedure to be followed upon the loss of a valuable document of title.
Kredit. Credit, accommodation, lending. See also: *Akzeptkredit*; *Baukredit*; *Betriebskredit*; *Blankokredit*; *Bürgschaftkredit*; *Gedeckterkredit*; *Hypothekarkredit*; *Immobiliarkredit*; *Investitionskredit*; *Kautionskredit*; *Kleinkredit*; *Kontokorrentkredit*; *Mobiliarkredit*; *Personalkredit*; *Postlaufkredit*; *Rahmenkredit*; *Realkredit*; *Saisonkredit*; *Schiffshypothekarkredit*; *Titelkredit*; *Unternehmerkredit*; *Verpflichiungskredit*; *Warenkredit*; *Zessionskredit*.
Kreditbrief. An arrangement for bank customers to draw money at other banks while away on short trips; a credit advice, a circular credit.
Kreditcarte. Credit card.

Kreditlimit. The highest figure to which a borrowing customer may draw.
Krugerrand. A South African gold coin, popular with the private investor because it contains exactly one ounce of pure gold. Two prices are quoted on the London market as a result of U.K. Exchange Control regulations—resident and non-resident.
Kumulative Vorzugsaktie. The redemption of a loan by equal amounts, the capital repayment element becoming cumulatively greater as interest on earlier instalments is saved.
Kurs. Stock exchange or market quotation for stock, shares, foreign securities, etc.
Kurzfristig. Short term.
Kux. A registered share in a mining company. The holders of *"Kuxen"*, unlike ordinary shareholders, carry a responsibility for the debts of the company, and are obliged, in cases of loss, to make payment to the company's creditors.

L

Labour. Toil, work demanding patience and endurance; manual workers, collectively or politically; one of the factors of production. In economics the term includes all forms of labour whether manual or clerical, excepting management. As a factor of production it is similar to the other factors, land and capital, as being one of a number of productive resources to be utilised by entrepreneurs.

Laches. Negligence, neglect to do something. The equitable doctrine of laches may prevent a suitor who has been remiss or idle in pursuing his claim from obtaining a judgment from the court.

Ladefaktor. Loading factor.

Ladeschein. Bill of lading.

Lageschein. Warehouse warrant.

Laissez Faire. The principle of non-interference, especially by government in industrial and commercial affairs.

Land. Land has been defined in terms which include anything on the land (whether natural, *e.g.* a tree, or artificial, *e.g.* a house), anything in the air over the land, and anything in the ground underneath, right down to the centre of the earth. It is an old definition, but then land is a very old type of security, probably the oldest. The law was active on the rights of landowners long before the concept of a law of contract had taken form. For lenders, land has a great attraction as a security because it is always there. You cannot pick it up and carry it away. There is no risk of losing control over the security; all that is necessary is to make certain that the borrower has a good title to offer. A statutory definition is "Land includes land of any tenure, and mines and minerals, whether or not held apart from the surface, buildings or parts of buildings (whether the division is horizontal, vertical, or made in any other way), and other corporeal hereditaments; also a manor, an advowson, and a rent or other incorporeal hereditament, and an easement, right, or privilege, or benefit in, over, or derived from land". Land includes an interest in land and, in relation to Scotland, includes heritable subjects of whatever description.

Land Agent. A person employed by an estate owner to collect rents, let farms, etc.

Land Bank. A bank whose function is to lend to farmers for the purchase of land or for its development.

Land Certificate. A document issued under the seal of the Land Registry to the registered owner of freehold or leasehold land. The certificate is a copy of the entry at the Land Registry in respect of the particular piece of land. The entry is in three parts; (1) the Property Register gives the index letters and title number accorded to the land, a short description of the property, whether freehold or leasehold, and a reference to the Land Registry General Map for purposes of identification; (2) the Proprietorship Register gives the name, address and description of the proprietor, the date of the registration, and the type of freehold or leasehold title and (if the registered proprietor has made a specific request) the consideration paid; (3) the Charges Register gives details of charges affecting the land, such as restrictive covenants or mortgages. The registered land certificate is *prima facie* evidence of ownership, in the same way as the deeds are in the case of unregistered land.

Land Charges. Charges against unregistered land which must be registered at the Land Charges Department by the holder of the charge to give notice of it to anyone else who is, or may become, interested in the land. There are five main registers at the department, dealing with pending actions, annuities, writs and orders, deeds of arrangement and land charges. *See also* Land Charges Register; Local Land Charges.

Land Charges Register. A register dealing with unregistered land, maintained at the Land Charges Department. Under the Land Charges Act 1925, five main registers, dealing with pending actions, annuities, writs and orders, deeds of arrangement, and land charges, are kept. The land charges register is sub-divided into six classes, letters A–F. Class A consists of charges on land as the result of an application by some person under the provisions of some statute. Class B consists of similar charges on land imposed by a statute, without the need for any application. Class C is sub-divided into (i) puisne mortgages, (ii) limited owners charges, (iii) general equitable charges, and (iv) estate contracts. Class D is sub-divided into (i) Inland Revenue charges for capital transfer tax. (ii) restrictive covenants, and (iii) equitable easements. Class E is for annuities charged upon land created before 1926, but not registered until after 1925. Class F is for charges on land registered by spouses under the Matrimonial Homes Act 1967.

Landeswährung. A national currency.

Landing Account. A document issued by a warehouse, giving details of goods and charges incurred.

Landlord. One who has tenants holding land under him, the lord of the manor; the master of an inn or of a lodging house.

Land Register. The records at the Land Registry dealing with the registration of land. The Land Register is in three parts: (1) the Property Register; (2) the Proprietorship Register; (3) the Charges Register. *See also* Land Certificate. The Land Register can be inspected only by permission of the registered proprietor: the customer's written authority must therefore be taken in appropriate cases. The registered land certificate is a copy of those entries in the Land Register which affect the land in question, with the addition of a copy of a Land Registry General Ordnance Map, with the property marked thereon, for purposes of identification.

Land Registration. A system of registration of title to land, based on the system of registration of title and transfer of stock and shares, arising out of the disadvantages of the system of deeds as evidence of title. A comprehensive system of land registration was set up in 1925, since when the two systems have been running side by side. It is intended that compulsory registration should be extended to the whole of the country, and this process is now nearly complete. A registered land certificate is issued to the title holder, and the Land Register is kept up to date with changes as and when they occur. The accuracy of the certificates is guaranteed by the State. *See also* Land Register.

Lands Improvements Company. A State-sponsored institution formed more than a century ago and still in operation. It makes medium-term loans and package deal finance to farmers for improvements to their land such as drainage and irrigation, water supply, fencing, installation of electricity, etc. After application has been made to the corporation the Ministry of Agriculture makes two surveys over the land. If the loan is granted it is secured by a rentcharge over the property. These loans are called *Improvement Loans*.

Langfristig. Long term.

Langlebige Verbrauchsgüter. Consumer durables.

Lapse. To slip or fall; to pass from one proprietor to another because of negligence; to pass slowly by degrees; an error of omission; failure to do one's duty; the termination of legal possession through negligence; the failure of a gift under a will because the donee dies before the testator.

Lapsed Policy. A policy of insurance which has become worthless to the insured because of failure to maintain payments of the premium.

Larceny. Theft, the unlawful taking away of the personal goods of another with intent to convert them for one's own use, that is, to permanently deprive that other of them. Since 1969 the Larceny Act of 1916 has been abolished, the Theft Act 1968 coming into force in that year. Instead of larceny, a person becomes guilty of theft if he dishonestly appropriates property belonging to another, with the intention of permanently depriving that other of it.

Lateral Combination. An integration of companies engaged in like stages of industrial production, whether in the same industry or in another.

Laufende Zahlungen. Profit balance.

Laufender Zins. Interest accruing due.

Laufzeit. Time to run to maturity date.

Law. Rules of conduct imposed by authority or accepted by the community in general as binding; a system of such rules regulating the intercourse of mankind, of individuals within a state, or of states with one another; a condition of order and stability; legal knowledge. *See also* Canon Law; Case Law; Maritime Law; Roman Law; Statute Law; Unwritten Law.

Law List. A list of barristers, solicitors and other legal practitioners, giving names and addresses and dates of qualification, issued annually by the Law Society.

Law Merchant. The usages and customs of merchants, adopted by the common law and comprising a body of mercantile regulations for the conduct of commerce.

Law Society. A professional association of solicitors, established in 1825.

Lay Days. Days allowed for the loading and unloading of a ship's cargo, during which the charterer is not liable to pay for demurrage.

Lead Manager. The principal house in a syndicate handling a new issue, which co-ordinates and directs the efforts of the syndicate.

Leads and Lags. The hastening or delaying of payment, by or to residents respectively, of international payments, at a time when the rate of exchange of a country's currency is rising or falling. *Leads* refers to the payment for goods by importers. When, for example, the value of the pound sterling is falling on the exchanges, importers pay as quickly as they can. *Lags* refers to the payment for goods to exporters. In similar circumstances exporters allow their customers longer periods of time than usual to pay for goods. Such actions can have a serious effect in the short-run on the country's balance of payments. Of course, both leads and lags apply only where goods are invoiced in currency.

Lease. To grant or to take or hold land on lease; a letting of land or tenements, usually for a fixed rent, for a specified period; the written contract for or the term of such letting.

Leasehold Estate. A right to enjoy the possession of land for a term of years as stated in the lease granting the right. To be a legal estate a lease must either be created by deed or be one which takes effect in possession for a term not exceeding three years at the best rent obtainable. Any kind of informal lease other than the latter gives rise to an equitable interest only.

Leasing. Renting houses, lands, etc., for a specified period of time; the hiring of an asset for the duration of its economic life. The asset is initially purchased by a finance company and then leased to the user who has no option to purchase. The system is suitable for large and costly assets such as computers, aircraft, containers and container ships, and specialised plant and equipment. Leasing is an alternative to purchase of an asset by instalment credit or through the aid of a mortgage or term loan. It has the advantage that it involves no capital outlay, requires no down payment, and may have tax benefits for the user. It does not count as borrowing for the purpose of a company's memorandum and articles of association. *See also* Big Ticket Leasing; Cross Border Leasing; Finance Lease.

Lebensfähig. See Viable.

Lebenshaltungskosten. Cost of living.

Lebensversicherungspolice. Life assurance policy.

Ledger. A book in which a business firm enters all debit and credit items in summary form; a cash book; a book in which is kept a list of customer's accounts and balance.

Leerverkauf. Sale by a speculator of stock which he does not possess, in the hope of buying it back later at a cheaper rate; a "bear" operation.

Legacy. A bequest, personal property bequeathed by will. *See also* Statutory Legacy.

Legal. Of, pertaining to, or according to law; lawful, legitimate.

Legal Assignment. *See* Equitable Assignment.

Legal Estate. In the case of land, a fee simple absolute in possession, or a term of years absolute. In the case of other property, the right to hold the legal title and to sell the property if desired. The holder of a legal estate may be a lender who has taken security by way of legal mortgage from a borrower, whose only remaining right is the equity of redemption; or he may be a trustee holding the property for the benefit of the holder of the equitable estate.

Legal Fiction. The assumption that something is a fact, in order to avoid technical difficulties.

Legal Interest. A right, based in law, to some claim against the property of another person. In relation to land, where the term is commonly found, a legal interest has been defined as an easement, right or privilege in or over land for an interest equivalent to a freehold or leasehold estate; a rent charge in possession charged on or issuing out of freehold or leasehold land; a charge by way of legal mortgage; certain rights of entry upon land. A claim against another person's land, as described above, must correspond in duration to one of the two legal estates, freehold or leasehold.

Legalisation. An official stamp of approval put on a document.

Legal Mortgage. The conveyance of a legal estate in real or personal property as security for a debt or for the discharge of an obligation. A legal mortgage of freehold land is accomplished by a charge by deed expressed to be by way of legal mortgage, or by the demise of a term of years absolute.

Legal Tender. Any means of payment that a creditor is obliged by law to accept in settlement of a debt. Thus while a debt can be settled by cheque, or by a postal order, this is at the option of the creditor, for neither is legal tender. He can, however, be compelled in the U.K. to accept Bank of England £1 notes, for these are legal tender to any amount. As to coinage, 50p pieces are legal tender up to £10, other cupro-nickel coins up to £5, and bronze coins up to 20p. A debtor must tender the exact amount owing, that is, he cannot demand change.

Legatee. One to whom a legacy is bequeathed. *See also* Residuary Legatee.

Leichter. A mild downwards tendency in stock exchange quotations.

Leihgeld. Money borrowed by banks on the money market.

Leistungsbilanz. Balance of trade.

Lender of Last Resort. A lender to whom borrowers may go when all other sources have failed, who will be sure to lend, albeit at a higher rate of interest than other possible lenders. Thus, the Bank of England acts as lender of last resort for the London discount houses, and the Public Works Loan Board acts as lender of last resort for local authorities.

Lending Ceilings. During a period of quantitative restrictions, banks and other lending institutions are restricted as to the total amount which they may lend. This figure of maximum permitted advances is the lending ceiling.

Lending Ratio. The ratio found by a comparison of money lent with money lodged.

Lessee. The person to whom a lease is granted.

Lessor. The grantor of a lease.

Letter. A written or printed communication; to print in special lettering; to stamp a title on a book cover. *See also* Facility Letter.

Letter of Advice. A letter notifying dispatch of goods, drawing of a bill of exchange or draft, receipt of an item for credit of a customer's account, etc.

Letter of Allotment. *See* Allotment Letter.

Letter of Application. An application for an allotment of a number of shares out of an issue announced and advertised to the public or to existing shareholders. The letter will state the number of shares required and enclose a cheque for the amount required to be paid on application.

Letter of Credit. An arrangement made by a bank for a customer proposing to stay abroad for a period who wishes always to be sure of being able to obtain money wherever he may be. The bank agrees a total sum with the customer, debits his account in advance, and writes to a correspondent bank or agent authorising him to cash on demand any cheques or drafts drawn by the beneficiary, charging the sums to the debit of the issuing bank. A specimen of the customer's signature is sent to the agent bank. The letter of credit is given to the customer who must present it to the agent bank each time he needs to draw money, so that a note of the amount he has had may be written on the back. Where only one agent is used the letter of credit is sometimes called a *Direct Letter of Credit*. If the customer is travelling about it will not be possible to send individual letters to all the agents he may wish to use. A *Circular* or *World-wide Letter of Credit* is then issued to the customer which will be available at the offices of any agent of the issuing bank in any country in the world. The customer is supplied with a *Letter of Indication* having a specimen of his signature. He should keep this letter separately from the letter of credit. He will use the letter of indication, which can be printed in several languages, to identify himself when he wishes to draw any money.

Letter of Deposit. *See* Memorandum of Deposit.

Letter of Hypothecation. A trust release, or a trust letter, signed by a customer who has already given a pledge over goods to a lending banker, and who now wishes to obtain the documents of title for the purpose of obtaining the goods, selling them, and repaying his debt out of the proceeds. *See also* Trust Letter.

Letter of Indication. *See* Letter of Credit.

Letter of Introduction. A letter addressed by banks, business houses or mercantile concerns to their agents or correspondents abroad, formally presenting the bearer of the letter for their favourable consideration. A customer of a bank travelling abroad or emigrating will find such a letter a considerable help and may through its agency obtain assistance with the purpose of his visit (such as identifying markets or learning local conditions).

Letter of Licence. A letter embodying an agreement by the creditors of a defaulting and insolvent debtor that they will for a certain time permit him to continue his business without taking legal steps against him.

Letter of Lien. *See* Lien Letter.

Letter of Regret. A letter sent, by a company which has made an issue of shares, to an unsuccessful applicant for an allotment.

Letter of Renunciation. A letter by which the allottee of shares gives up his entitlement of shares in favour of some other person. Such a form of renunciation is often printed on the back of an allotment letter.

Letter of Rights. *See* Rights Letter.

Letter of Set-Off. *See* Lien Letter.

Letter of Trust. *See* Letter of Hypothecation.

Letters of Administration. The document issued by a probate registry to a person who will act in administering the estate of a deceased person who has died intestate. The Letters of Administration are the official authority for the administrator to proceed. An administrator will also be appointed if the deceased left a will but named no executor therein, or where he left a will naming an executor but the person named died before the testator, or refused to act, or was unfit to undertake the duty. If a will exists, the estate will be administered in accordance with its terms.

Letters Patent. A grant from the Crown, under the seal of the State, granting some property privilege or authority, or conferring the exclusive right to use a design or an invention.

Letters Requisitory, Letters Rogatory. A document requesting the court of another country to procure evidence on behalf of the country issuing the request.

Lettre d'Attribution. *See* Allotment Letter.

Lettre de Change. Bill of exchange.

Lettre de Crédit. *See* Letter of Credit.

Lettre de Crédit Circulaire. *See* Letter of Credit.

Lettre de Rente. A security incorporated in a registered or bearer share or bond title, representing a land charge on real property, whether a rural site, a residence, or a building site. The *Lettre de rente* is exclusive of all personal debts.

Lettre de Voiture. Railway receipt or consignment note. *See* Consignment Note.

Lettres de Cachet. Warrants ordering the arbitrary arrest and imprisonment of a person without trial.

Leverage Fund. An investment or unit trust of a particularly speculative nature. For its investments it uses not only its own money but also other capital such as bank overdrafts or loans. As these last, and the interest charges which they attract, are fixed, losses and gains rebound with increased effect on the fortunes of the trust.

Levy of Execution. An execution against a debtor by seizure of his goods under process in an action in any court. A judgment creditor may obtain a writ of *fieri facias* under which the debtor's stock or property may be forcibly seized and auctioned off to raise money to pay the debt. The sheriff is the officer of the court responsible for the proper execution of this remedy. If the goods are sold, or have been held by the sheriff for twenty-one days, the levy of execution is an act of bankruptcy.

Lex Loci. The law of the place.

Lex non scripta. The unwritten law, common law.

Lex Scripta. The written law.

Liabilities. The debts of a person, an estate of a company; the total of the liabilities side of a balance sheet. *See also* Current Liabilities; Long-Term Liabilities.

Liability. The state of being liable; that for which one is liable; a debt, a pecuniary liability. *See also* Limited Liability.

Libel. A defamatory statement published in a permanent form, usually writing or printing, but including also a recording, inclusion in the sound track of a film, or radio or television broadcasts. *See* Defamation.

Libération. The payment for bonds or fully-paid shares. In the case of registered shares a part-payment is sometimes called for.

Liberierung. Payment of the subscription on the occasion of a new issue. In the case of registered shares part only of the amount may occasionally be called for; in this case the shareholder remains liable for the remaining amount.

Licence. Authority, leave, permission, consent granted by a constituted authority for the carrying out of some act or trade. Where imports are controlled by a system of quotas, exporters are issued with licences which specify the amounts allotted to them. In the U.K. all institutions concerned with consumer credit services, including banks and finance houses, require a licence issued by the Director-General of Fair Trading. Such a licence will normally be renewed every three years, but can be varied or cancelled altogether if the licensee does not comply with its conditions.

Licence d'Importation. Import licence.

Licence to Assign. A landlord may be content to lease his land to a lessee but he may not be ready to allow the lessee to underlease or sub-let the property, thus bringing on to the lessor's land someone of whom he may not approve. A lease therefore commonly includes a clause that the lessee may not assign, demise, sub-let or otherwise deal with the property without the permission or licence of the lessor. However, it is provided that a licence to sub-demise by way of mortgage shall not be unreasonably refused.

Liebrente. Annuity, life annuity.

Lieferschein. A receipt or docket; a temporary certificate of title pending issue of the definitive certificate.

Lieferung. Delivery, cargo.

Lieferungsgeschaft. Business transactions where delivery of documents and payment for them are postponed until a later settlement day; carrying-over.

Lien. The right to retain property belonging to another until a debt due from the owner of the property to the possessor of the property is paid. The ownership of the property is left undisturbed—that is, the borrower continues as owner, but the lender has possession. In general the lender has no right to sell the property. *See also* Banker's Lien; General Lien; Maritime Lien; Particular Lien; Possessory Lien; Unpaid Seller's Lien; Warehousekeeper's Lien.

Lien Letter. Where a customer's credit balance is held as security for his advance on another account, the customer should sign an agreement to this effect, which is called a lien letter or a *Letter of Set-Off*. The letter agrees that the credit balance shall not be reduced below a certain figure (that of the debt) and that the banker may combine the accounts without notice.

Lieu de Paiement. Usually a bank, nominated by those responsible for a new issue. The bank's task is to execute all the transactions resulting from the issue and the circulation of the security.

Life. Animate existence, the period of such existence, any specified portion of a person's existence; the average period which a person of a given age may expect to live; a person considered as object of a policy of insurance.

Life Annuity. A sum of money paid yearly during the portion of a person's life from a specified age to death.

Life Assurance. A contract by which the insurer/assurer undertakes to pay the person for whose benefit the cover is effected, or to his personal representatives, a certain sum of money on the happening of a given event, or on the death of the person whose life is assured.

Life-Belt. Security for a debt.

Lifeboat Committee (Support Group). A rescue operation organised by the Bank of England in 1974, when many of the so-called "secondary" banks were faced with liquidation. The crisis of confidence was so bad that it was thought that it might spread to the clearing banks, accepting houses and discount houses. Accordingly the sum required to support the ailing banks—£1,200 million—was duly advanced and is thought to have been found by the lifeboat banks in these proportions:

Barclays	£300m
National Westminster	£300m
Midland	£225m
Lloyds	£150m
Bank of England	£120m
William & Glyn's, Coutts and the Scottish banks	£105m
	£1,200m

The lifeboat operation was expected to last for six months, but in the event the support has been required for much longer than that, and may indeed be needed for some years. The bulk of the security is in the depressed property market, which has been slow to recover. It has therefore been necessary to divide the secondary banks into those who have some chance of recovery, so meriting continued support, those who might be taken over, and the others who may be abandoned to liquidation. At the time of writing there are still some fifteen companies in the lifeboat. The total owed by this group amounts to just under £900m. The Lifeboat Committee is technically known as the "Support Group".

Life Certificate. *See* Certificate of Existence.

Life Insurance. *See* Life Assurance.

Life Interest. Interest in an estate or business which continues during one's life, or sometimes during the life of another, but which cannot be bequeathed by will.

Life Policy. A document containing the particulars and conditions of the contract by which the assurance company, in return for a premium, undertakes to pay to the assured or his personal representatives or his assigns a certain sum of money on the happening of a specified event or upon the death of the life assured. *See also* Policy.

Life Rent. A rent which one is legally entitled to receive during one's lifetime.

Life Table. A table of statistics, used by assurance companies, which estimate the expectation of life of persons at different ages.

Life Tenant. One who has a life interest in an estate.

Limit. (1) The figure to which a customer may overdraw. (2) In the inter-bank market, the figure which limits the amount of deposits which can be left with any one bank at any time. Such limits are roughly based on the figure of capital and reserves of the borrowing bank. (3) On the Stock Exchange, a fixed price quoted to the broker by his client above which he is not to buy, or below which he is not to sell.

Limitation. The act of restricting, the state of being limited or confined, qualification; a definite statutory time-limit within which an action must be brought; in land law, a form of words creating an estate and denoting its extent by specifying the event upon which it is to commence and the time for which it is to endure.

Limitation of Actions. To encourage litigants to bring their actions promptly, it is provided that actions founded upon a simple contract must be brought within six years after the accrual of the cause of action; actions founded upon a special contract must be brought within twelve years after the accrual of the cause of action. Any acknowledgment in writing of the debt, or any part payment, will operate to restart the running of the statutory period, but the mere debiting of quarterly or half-yearly interest by the banker will not be sufficient to have this effect. Although an action may become statute-barred it still exists and recourse can still be had against any security held (except in the case of land).

Limite. Extreme price or rate specified by the client on a purchase or sale of stock, a limit order; in the granting of credit, the maximum amount authorised.

Limited and Reduced. A suffix to the name of a company indicating that the capital has been reduced from that originally held or issued. Such a reduction requires the sanction of the court.

Limited by Guarantee. The liability of company members for the debts of a company is limited to the amount they guarantee to pay in the event of the company's being wound up.

Limited by Shares. The liability of company shareholders for the debts of a company is limited to the amount of their shareholding (provided that the shares are fully paid). If the value of a shareholding drops to nothing, this is the maximum loss which the shareholders can suffer.

Limited Company. A form of business organisation legally recognised as having an existence separate and apart from its shareholders or directors. The liability of the shareholders for the debts contracted by the company is limited, either to the amount which they have guaranteed, or to the nominal amount of their shareholding. In order to protect creditors, all limited liability companies must carry the title "Limited" (or "Ltd.") after their names, and must publish a balance sheet and profit and loss account each year. (If the company has its registered office in Wales, it may use the title *Cyfyngedig* instead of Limited.)

Limited Garnishee Order. *See* Garnishee Order.

Limited Liability. The limitation of the liability of the shareholders of a company for the debts of the company to the nominal amount of the shares they hold or to the amount they have guaranteed.

Limited Owner. A tenant for life who pays capital transfer tax in respect of the estate out of which his life estate is carved.

Limited Owner's Charge. *See* Land Charges Register.

Limited Partner. A partner whose liability is limited to the amount of capital he contributes and who does not take part in the management of the firm. He cannot draw cheques on the firm's banking account, and he cannot bind the firm by his actions. His rights are to inspect the books (but not the firm's bank statement without the consent of the other partners) and to give advice to the general partners.

Limited Partnership. A partnership consisting of one or more limited partners, whose liability is limited to the amount of capital invested in the firm, and one or more general partners, who are fully liable for the firm's debts.

Limite Maximale d'Avance. The ceiling of a loan calculated as a percentage value of the monetary valuation of the security.

Limite Pour Cautionnements Bancaires. An undertaking for a certain amount by a bank which guarantees to a third party that the obligations of its customer will be promptly and properly fulfilled. *See also Aval*; Performance Bond.

Line of Credit. A sum of money available for a debtor to draw upon as long as he uses it to obtain goods or services from his creditor; bank accommodation available to a customer as long as it is used for agreed purposes and as long as he maintains his account with the lending bank. In the international trading sense, a line of credit may be arranged where a buyer wishes to place a number of contracts which may not all be related to a single project and cannot therefore be practically concluded at the outset. In such cases a line of credit covers multiple contracts, is operated on a buyer credit basis, and covers contracts placed over a twelve-month period.

Liner Bill of Lading. A bill of lading issued by a shipping line operating liners following a predetermined route which has reserved berths, as opposed to a tramp steamer which picks up cargoes wherever it can.

Liquid. Readily convertible into cash.

Liquid Assets. Cash and assets easily convertible intc cash; *e.g.* in a manufacturing company—stock, sundry debtors; in a bank—balances with other banks, money at call and short notice with a maximum maturity of seven days, Treasury Bills, certificates of deposit and bills discounted.

Liquidated Damages. A sum of money agreed as payable in the case of a breach of contract and written into it as a term.

Liquidation. The process of clearing up financial affairs; to have a company's assets and liabilities wound up; payment of a debt.

Liquidation of a Company. *See* Compulsory Liquidation or Winding-up; Voluntary Liquidation.

Liquidationswert. Break-up value.

Liquidator. A person appointed by the court (in a compulsory liquidation), or by the creditors of a company (in a creditors' voluntary winding-up), or by the members of a company (in a members' voluntary winding-up), to get in what is owed to the company, to take charge of the assets and turn them into money, to pay the company's debts, and then, if there is anything left, to distribute it amongst the members in proportion to their shareholdings. A banker asked to open an account for the liquidator in a compulsory liquidation should ask to see the court order appointing him, together with the evidence of the sanction of the Department of Trade for him to maintain a banking account at a bank other than the Bank of England. In the other two cases a liquidator may bank wherever he pleases. The banker should see, as evidence of the appointment, the creditors' resolution in the first case, or a certified copy of it, and the members' resolution in the second.

Liquid Capital. Capital in the form of money.

Liquid Deficiency. The excess of current liabilities over current assets.

Liquidity. An immediate capacity to meet one's financial commitments. The degree of liquidity depends upon the relationship between a company's cash assets plus those assets which can be quickly turned into cash, and the liabilities awaiting payment; an ability to turn certain assets into the form of cash.

Liquidity Ratio. The relationship between those assets of the bank which are in money, or can very quickly be turned into money, and the total balances which the customers of the bank have on their banking accounts (*e.g.* liquid assets to deposits). Before September 1971, banks maintained a liquidity ratio of 28% as a minimum, but thereafter the place of this ratio was taken by a reserve asset ratio which is fixed at a minimum of 12½% of total eligible liabilities.

Listed Bank. A bank within the United Kingdom sector which makes returns to the Bank of England. Loans to such banks may be deducted from a bank's total eligible liabilities before calculation of the reserve asset requirement.

Listed Stocks. Stocks and shares dealt with on the Stock Exchange.

Listing. Quotation on a stock exchange.

Livraison. Delivery, part, instalment. À

Livraison. On delivery.

Livraison Contre Remboursement. Cash on delivery.

Livret de Dépôt. Deposit passbook.

Lizenz. Licence, patent.

Lloyd's. An association of London underwriters, first engaged in the marine insurance business at the end of the seventeenth century, and now an international market for almost any type of insurance. The word is also used to refer to a society, incorporated under Act of Parliament in 1871, and known as the Corporation of Lloyd's, which provides the premises, shipping information services, administrative staff and other facilities by which the market is able to carry on its business.

Lloyd's List. A daily newspaper published by Lloyd's containing shipping, insurance, air and general commercial news, together with reports of the latest shipping movements received and casualty reports—ships and cargoes damaged or sunk.

Lloyd's Policy. A policy of marine insurance written by Lloyd's underwriters and sealed by the Corporation.

Lloyd's Register of Shipping. An annual alphabetical list of all merchant ships of any nationality of 100 tons and over, published by a society for the purpose of surveying and classifying ships in order to give an independent opinion as to a ship's seaworthiness and reliability for employment or insurance purposes. The Committee of the society grants certificates after periodical examinations of vessels. Those vessels with the highest standard of efficiency are classed A.1. A publication—*Lloyd's Register of British & Foreign Shipping*—containing particulars of all vessels afloat of 100 tons upwards, is revised and reissued annually.

Loading. An element in the premium of an assurance policy to cover the expenses of management; an increase in the charges passed to the debit of a customer's banking account to reflect some exceptional service given or some exceptional difficulty encountered in the maintenance or supervision of the account.

Loan. The act of lending (money); a banking account where upon approval a loan account is opened in the customer's name, the sum being made available by transfer from the loan account to the customer's current account, whence he may draw sums out. The loan is to be reduced at agreed intervals by an instalment taken from the current account.

Loan interest is charged quarterly or half-yearly on the amount of the loan outstanding and debited to the current account. *See also* Back-to-Back Loan; Business Development Loan; Farm Development Loan; Lands Improvements Company; Long-Term Loan; Personal Loan; Short-Term Loan.

Loan Capital. That part of the capital of a company which has been derived from outside loans and is so described in the balance sheet.

Loans Bureau of the Chartered Institute of Public Finance & Accountancy. *See under* Local Authority Bonds.

Loan Stock. An acknowledgment of long-term borrowing on which interest is paid—it may be redeemed or issued for a specified period; an alternative name for debentures. Loan stock is (1) unsecured; (2) secured by a floating charge on the company's assets; or (3) secured by a fixed charge on certain assets (usually property). The interest rate is fixed to final maturity and the stock usually has a term of at least fifteen years. It is set up by a trust deed under which the rights of the stockholders are protected, and which specifies certain restrictions to which the company has agreed to conform. A trustee is appointed to look after the holder's interests.

Local. Of or pertaining to a place; peculiar to a particular place; an inhabitant of a particular place; a professional man practising there.

Local Acceptance. *See* Qualified Acceptance.

Local Authority. A general name for county councils, boards, municipalities or elected representatives, responsible for administration by local government; a decentralisation from central government. The Local Government Act 1972, which took effect on 1 April 1974, divided Great Britain (excluding Greater London) into metropolitan counties or districts, or non-metropolitan counties or districts, represented by local authorities in England, Wales and Scotland. Parish and community councils are also covered by the Act and are regarded as local authorities. Bank accounts of county councils must be in the name of the council, or in the name of the treasurer. In the latter case the name of the treasurer must be qualified by the description "Treasurer of the ———— County Council". A resolution of the council must be obtained to the effect that the treasurer is authorised to maintain the account(s) at the particular branch, together with the instructions as to the way in which cheques are to be signed. Bank accounts of district councils are to be maintained in the name of the council. Parish and community council accounts are similarly to be maintained in the name of the council, cheques being signed by two council members. In each case signing instructions must be covered by a resolution of the appropriate council. Local authorities may keep as many separate accounts as they wish.

Borrowing powers. A county or district council has authority under the Act to borrow in order to on-lend to any authority, such as water or harbour authorities. A local authority has authority (provided that the sanction of the Secretary of State is procured) to borrow for any purpose. No sanction other than that of the Act is required for temporary borrowing by loan or overdraft, where the purpose of the advance is to defray expenses pending the receipt of revenue due in the same period as that in which the expenses have to be met, or to defray expenses to be met out of a loan to be raised to meet those expenses. Long-term borrowings may be secured by a mortgage of the rates, but short-term advances are often made unsecured. In all cases an appropriate borrowing resolution should be obtained from the council, or from the finance committee, and, where the sanction of the appropriate government department is necessary, this must also be obtained. The borrowing of a county council will be taken on the County Fund account. If any accommodation is required on subsidiary accounts the necessary resolution should be formally passed by the finance committee. The Act provides that a person lending money to a local authority shall not be bound to enquire whether the borrowing of the money is or was legal or regular, or whether the money raised was properly applied, and shall not be prejudiced by an illegality or irregularity in the matters aforesaid, or by the misapplication or non-application of any such money. This should afford protection to the lending banker unless it can be shown that, prior to the lending of the money, he had notice that the purpose of the proposed borrowing was illegal. A general account of a local authority is available for all purposes, and a credit balance may therefore be set off against a debit balance on any other account. Revenue accounts may also be set off against each other, but a credit balance on a capital account is earmarked for some particular purpose and cannot be set off. Items for safe custody should be lodged in the name of the authority and the bank should be supplied with a sealed copy of the resolution authorising withdrawals by the treasurer or other named individuals.

Local Authority Bonds, Local Authority Loans. All local authorities constantly need to borrow money and for this purpose make various offers and issue various bonds or loans (*see below*). This is a very active market, and various authorities will offer different rates, on various amounts each week. Up-to-date information is therefore very important to the would-be investor. A free list of what is on offer is published each week and is obtainable from the Loans Bureau of the Chartered Institute of Public Finance and Accountancy, 232 Vauxhall Bridge Road, London SW1V 1AU, on receipt of a stamped, addressed, foolscap-size envelope.

Local Authority Escalator Loans. These are loans for fixed periods of one year or longer where the rate of interest applied changes from time to time during the life of the loan, *e.g.* on a five-year loan the rate would normally change (either upwards or downwards) on the anniversary date.

Local Authority Lenders' Option Loans. Such loans are similar to Mutual Option Loans (below) except that only the lender of funds may give notice for repayment.

Local Authority Mutual Loans. Loans to a local authority for a period of one year or more with a normal maximum of five years. Such loans will include a clause whereby either the lender or the borrower has the option to give one month's notice of repayment at any time after a specified date, usually eleven months from the commencement of the loan. Mutual loans are secured by a mortgage on the rates and revenues of the authority.

Local Authority Yearling Bonds. Introduced in 1964, these Bonds are issued by local authorities in Great Britain and Northern Ireland, and by various water boards and drainage authorities. They are normally issued for periods of one year ("yearlings") and, occasionally, for up to five years. The issue of Bonds is placed weekly on Tuesdays for settlement the following day. Some Bonds are placed directly with discount houses and other financial Institutions. Other issues are handled by stockbrokers and will be quoted on the London Stock Exchange. Bonds are registered securities and delivery is effected by normal form of transfer. Dealings are in multiples of £1,000, plus or minus accrued interest.

Local Clearing. An exchange of cheques between banks locally once daily to avoid the necessity of sending cheques to a central clearing organisation. As computerised accounting and sorting takes over the work of clearing, local centres tend to disappear.

Local Land Charges. Commitments to which land may be subject as a result of town and country planning legislation. Under planning law, local authorities have decided upon development plans for their areas, and the details of these plans are to be found in the registers of district, borough and county councils. Here will be found such information as road charges, town planning schemes, demolition orders, and building preservation orders. *See also* Local Land Charges Register.

Local Land Charges Register. Under the Town and Country Planning Acts 1947–1970, local planning authorities have decided upon development plans for their areas, and the details of these plans are to be found in the registers of district, borough and county councils. Here will be found such information as road charges, town planning schemes, demolition orders and building-preservation orders. Where land is mortgaged as security a search on the local land charges registers is made, against the address of the property. Usually it is necessary to send two search forms in respect of each property, one to the county council office and one to the borough council, urban district council, or rural district council, whichever is applicable.

Local Searches. *See* Local Land Charges Register.

Lockartikel. *See* Loss Leader.

Loco. In that place (the name of the place being next mentioned).

Locus Sigilli. The place for the seal. A printed circle with the letters "L.S." inside often to be found on a form of charge or transfer, to show where the seal or label is to be placed.

Lombardgeschäft. Credit granted against the security of easily realisable property.

Lombardsatz. The rate of interest applicable to a Lombard credit.

Lombard Street. A term almost synonymous in London with the money market. It is the centre of the banks' head offices and discount houses. The name comes from the Lombards, a group of Italian merchants and bankers who came to this country from Lombardy in the Middle Ages, bringing their trade of money exchange with them.

London Association for the Protection of Trade. A credit-assessment organisation for the protection of those considering lending money. A country-wide register is maintained giving a list of unsatisfactory customers of hire-purchase companies. Banks who are members of the association can search against the name of any person to whom they are thinking of lending, particularly by way of personal loan.

London Bankers' Clearing House. *See* Clearing House.

London Chamber of Commerce. An association representing the interests of its members in all branches of commerce, particularly domestic and overseas trade, banking, insurance and transport. There are a number of such chambers, the London chamber being the largest. It is an examining body for students in a wide range of commercial subjects, and in conjunction with the Royal Society of Arts organises examinations in similar subjects and in ordinary national certificate and diploma studies for overseas students in foreign centres.

London Commodity Exchange. A market in tea, coffee, cocoa, spices and rubber, centred in Mincing Lane, London.

London Discount Market. *See* Bill Broker; Discount Market.

London Foreign Exchange Market. A market for fixing the rates at which foreign money will be bought and sold, consisting of banks authorised by the Bank of England to deal in foreign currencies, and some firms of foreign exchange brokers who act as intermediaries. The market is conducted over the telephone and by telex and cable; good communication facilities and therefore vital. Contracts in spot and forward currency deals are made by word of mouth and confirmed by written contract notes.

London Gazette. *See* Gazette.

London Gold Market. A market for fixing the price of gold in London. It consists of five firms dealing in gold bullion. The members meet twice on each working day for trading, the results of which fix the price at the end of the day. The price is expressed in U.S. dollars per fine ounce troy. The daily meetings of the members are known as "fixings".

London Inter-Bank Offer Rate (L.I.B.O.R.). *See* Inter-Bank Sterling Market.

London Money Market. The market in London for very short-term loans. The market members are the clearing and other commercial banks, the discount and accepting houses, the London branches of some foreign banks, and the Bank of England as a lender of last resort. The discount houses borrow at call or short notice from the commercial banks, but if they are unable to satisfy their wants in this way can always rely on assistance from the Bank of England at minimum lending rate. The system represents a method of regulation by the Bank of England of the money supply, in that the commercial banks, if they need their cash supplies replenishing, will call in their loans to the discount houses, thereby ensuring that the latter must resort to the lender of last resort. *See also* Bill Broker; Discount Market.

London Stock Exchange. *See* Stock Exchange.

Long. Of great extent in time, far-reaching; in the foreign exchange market, the position of a dealer when his purchases of a particular currency exceed his sales in that currency.

Long Bill. A bill having a usance of three months or more.

Long Dozen. Thirteen, a baker's dozen.

Long End of the Market. That part of the money market which deals in long dated government stocks. See Long-Term Loan.

Long Exchange. On the foreign exchanges, bills with a currency of sixty or ninety days, or more.

Long Firm. A company of swindlers who obtain goods on credit, sell them, and disappear without paying for them.

Long Hundred. One hundred and twenty.

Longitude. Angular distance east or west of a given meridian.

Long Rate. A term used to indicate the price in one country at which a long bill, drawn payable in another country, can be bought.

Long Tap. Tap (q.v.) having, say, fifteen years or more to maturity.

Long-Term Liabilities. Liabilities which are not to be repaid for some years, *e.g.* mortgages, debentures, a company's loan capital. See also Joint Account; Joint and Several Liability.

Long-Term Loan. A loan for ten years or more; Government stocks issued for a similar period, or for redemption in a certain stated year "or after", or in perpetuity; irredeemable stock.

Loro **Accounts.** Third-party accounts in domestic or foreign currency.

Loro Konto. See *Conto Suo.*

Losanleihe. A bond paying little or no interest, repayable by lot, on which occurrence a premium is paid.

Loss Leader. The practice of offering goods or a service at under cost price in order to bring in customers, who may then make other purchases so that in total the seller will show a profit; a device for stimulating consumer interest in a wider range.

Lost Cheque. The person who loses a cheque should at once notify the drawer so that the latter may request his bank to stop payment. The holder of a bill lost before it becomes overdue may apply to the drawer to give him a duplicate bill, but must, if required, give the drawer an indemnity to protect him if the bill should be found again and come into the hands of a third person.

Lost Deed. An attested copy of a lost deed may be accepted by a purchaser of land, but if no such copy is available a declaration by a person having knowledge of the purport and effect of the deed may be offered.

Lost Share Certificate. A shareholder who has lost a share certificate belonging to him may apply to the company to issue him with a duplicate. The company will send him a form of application, for completion by him, which has on it an indemnity to be completed by his banker.

Lot. A distinct portion, collection, or parcel of things offered for sale, especially at auction; a parcel of land; choice or decision by chance drawings, as in the redemption of some stocks, debentures or bearer bonds over a period of years.

Lot. (*Fr.*) The minimum amount of capital admitted for a quotation on the *Bourse,* similarly the minimum number of share titles.

Lot Money. The auctioneer's fee on each lot of goods sold by him at a public auction.

Lump Sum. A total sum, as in a single payment of an insurance, instead of instalments spread over several years; a sum of money paid on retirement as an alternative to instalments of pension or in reduction of such instalments.

Lustlos. Quiet, showing little activity (of stock exchange business).

M

M1, M3. *See* Money Supply.

Macro-Economics. The branch of economics dealing with large totals on a world- or nation-wide scale, *e.g.* gross national product, total unemployment figure, savings and investment aggregate, the government's annual spending figures, etc., and the relationships between them.

Made Bill. A bill drawn, negotiated and indorsed in this country, but payable abroad.

Magnetic Ink Character Recognition (M.I.C.R.). The coding of information on vouchers before they are fed into a computer, so that magnetic characters embodying the information are evaluated by a reading head. This evaluation determines the appropriate action taken within the computer. In the U.K., characters are at the bottom of a cheque, are recognisable by a computer, and signify the national number of the branch bank, the number of the cheque, and the number of the customer's account. As soon as the cheque is paid back into the banking system, the collecting bank will add a further set of magnetic characters indicating the amount of the cheque. The computer can then debit the right amount to the account of the right customer at the right branch.

Mail Transfer. *See* Telegraphic Transfer.

Maintenance. Means of support; keeping equipment in working order; helping a party in a law suit illegally.

Majoration. An application for a new issue of shares, an intentional over-application when there is reason to suspect that the issue will be over-subscribed and allocations therefore will be made only in part.

Majorisierung. See Majoration.

Maker of Promissory Note. The person who writes out a promissory note is called the "maker". By making it he engages that he will pay it according to its tenor, and is precluded from denying to a holder in due course the existence of the payee and his then capacity to endorse.

Making-Up Day. On the Stock Exchange, the first day of the bi-monthly settlement. Also called Contango Day.

Making-Up Price. On the Stock Exchange, the price at which stocks and shares are closed off for the settlement.

Makler. Broker, jobber.

Maklergebühr. Brokerage.

Maklersgeschäft. Commission, turn.

Mala Fide. In bad faith.

Managed Bonds. An investment spread over fixed interest securities, equities and property shares, the management having the power to vary the proportions of holdings from time to time as they see fit.

Managed Currency. A currency where the country's government intervenes from time to time, whether to buy or sell, in order to maintain a desired exchange value.

Management. The act of directing, controlling and carrying out the functions of an organiser, promoter or contractor; the conduct and control of a branch bank or department by its manager.

Management Shares. Shares apportioned to the managers of a company with the intention of giving them a personal stake in the company and thus ensuring their energy, interest and enthusiasm in the business.

Management Trust. An investment or unit trust where complete discretion as to the investments to be made is given to the managers of the trust.

Manager. One in charge of a business, especially a branch of a bank, a department, a theatre or a cinema; one appointed by the Court of Chancery to manage affairs on behalf of creditors; the bank arranging a syndicate for the purpose of lending large sums, which acts as paying agent for interest and capital repayments and supervises the service of the loan by the borrower. *See also* Co-Manager; Lead Manager.

Managers' Discretionary Limits (M.D.L.s). The limits to which a branch manager may commit the bank to lend without reference to higher authority.

There may be two figures, one for secured lending and a lower one for unsecured lending. M.D.L.s are personal to managers and do not attach to the branches which they manage.

Managing Director. A director of a limited company who has the responsibility of controlling the day-to-day activities of the company.

Managing Trustee. In a trust, the trustee who buys and sells the property comprising the trust to the best advantage of the beneficiaries.

Mandamus. An order of the Crown requiring a person, corporation or inferior court to perform a particular duty.

Mandate. An official order, command or charge; a judicial command to an officer or a subordinate court; a contract of bailment by which the mandatory undertakes to perform gratuitously a duty regarding property entrusted to him; a direction from electors to a representative to undertake certain legislation; an authority in writing, signed by a bank customer, authorising another to sign cheques or conduct banking business on his behalf; the instructions from a customer to his bank as to the method of signing on the account. *See also* Principal's Mandate.

Mandatory Injunction. *See* Injunction.

Manifest. A detailed list of a ship's cargo for the scrutiny of Customs officers.

Manko, Manque. Shortage, loss, deficit.

Manteau. A bond with neither coupons nor talon attached; a list of shares; the share capital of a company which is practically in liquidation.

Mantel. Bearer bond sheet without talon or coupons; total share capital of a company which is practically in liquidation.

Manufacturing Account. This account shows the direct cost of the production of goods, starting with the cost of the raw materials used and their transport into the factory, and then listing the three items of expense—fuel, power and labour—which are essential in the manufacture. Where there is a considerable amount of work which has passed from the raw materials stage but has not, by the date of the account, reached the status of finished stock, a further entry, work-in-progress, will be seen. A trading concern which buys goods for re-sale does not, of course, manufacture them, and will not, therefore, keep a manufacturing account.

Marché. A market, a deal, a bargain, a contract. *See also* Bon Marché; Prix de Marché.

Marché à Terme. Forward market.

Marché au Comptant. Spot market.

Marché de l'Argent. The demand and supply of funds at short term. *See also* Money Market.

Marché des Capitaux. The demand and supply of medium- or long-term funds.

Marché Hors Cote. The market in unquoted shares or stock; business done outside the *Bourse*.

Marché Monétaire. The money market; more generally, a market where short-term money is exchanged for long-term money.

Marché Noir. Black market.

Marché Ouvert. *See* Open Market Operations.

Marché Parallèle. *See* Parallel Market.

Marchzins. Interest rates.

Marge. *See* Margin.

Marge Benéficiare. Profit margin.

Marge d'Intérêt. The difference between the average rate charged on money lent and the average rate allowed on money borrowed. For an institution dealing in credit this results in a margin of gross interest. To ascertain the net interest a proportionate deduction for expenses must be made.

Margin. The difference between the selling price and the buying price of a commodity; a deposit of money to safeguard a broker against loss; an allowance made for contingencies; the difference between a bank overdraft or loan and the security deposited by the customer; the difference between the spot price and the forward price of a currency expressed as a premium or a discount; the difference between the rate charged by a bank for overdrafts and the rate allowed for deposit.

Marginal. Only just worth doing.

Marginal Cost. The extra cost of increasing output by one more unit.

Marginal Relief. Tax relief for a taxpayer who exceeds only slightly a figure which would entitle him to a greater relief of duty.

Marginal Risk. The loss that may possibly arise on foreign exchange operations if, through the failure of a contracting party, the bank has to "undo" a transaction, or series of transactions, by buying in or selling out the foreign currency, and the rate has meantime moved against them. This risk is represented by the difference between the total of "boughts" and the total of "solds" in each currency and that difference, or the total of several such differences if more than one currency is involved, is termed the "straddle". This risk only becomes of serious consequence if the rates tend to fluctuate sharply.

Marine Insurance. A contract by which underwriters engage to indemnify the owner of a ship, cargo or freight against losses from certain perils or sea risks to which their ship or cargo may be exposed. A marine insurance policy is subject to the provisions of the Marine Insurance Act 1906.

Marine Insurance Broker. An agent between a shipper wishing to obtain cover on his ship or cargo and the Lloyd's underwriter.

Maritime Law. The law pertaining to ships and the sea. Originally based upon international customs, the law is now administered in the U.K. by the Admiralty Court, which has instance jurisdiction, dealing with collisions at sea, and prize jurisdiction, which originated with the seizure of enemy ships in time of war and dealt with the questions of international law in this respect and the allocation of prize money. This jurisdiction, of course, can only occur in wartime. The court rarely sits, for insurers in shipping cases may settle claims without dispute, or, where there is dispute, the parties usually go to arbitration, as being quicker and cheaper.

Maritime Lien. A right which attaches to a ship and/or its cargo in respect of a liability connected with a voyage of the ship. It is independent of possession and attaches to the ship whether in port or at sea. It may be enforced by the arrest and sale of the ship after legal process in the Admiralty Court.

Mark. A visible sign, a character made by one who cannot write, a cross. A person signing cheques in this way, or signing a receipt, should put a cross in the presence of two witnesses to the act of marking, one of whom should add the name of the marksman and the fact that it is his mark. *See also* Trade Mark.

Mark Down. To reduce prices or a valuation of securities held.

Marked Abstract. An abstract of title mentions some documents which are necessary to show a clear chain of title, but which are not usually handed to a purchaser, such as probate, marriage certificates and death certificates. Such documents will not be with the deeds, but the abstract will be "marked" in the margin to show that they were, at the time, examined and found to be correct. Thereafter every subsequent solicitor checking the title is content to rely on the marking, which has been made by the solicitor making the examination, or his clerk. *See also* Abstract of Title.

Marked Cheque. At one time it was customary for a banker to "mark" a cheque to indicate that its payment when presented was guaranteed. The practice is disliked by bankers who would prefer to issue a banker's draft for an equivalent amount. The modern use of a cheque card has a similar effect to marking up to any amount covered by the card.

Marked Transfer. *See* Certified Transfer.

Market. A public meeting place for the purchase and sale of commodities, a trading-centre; demand; a country or geographical area regarded as a buyer of goods; price or value at a stated time.

Market Maker. A bank undertaking to make a secondary market for Eurobonds, either by taking any bonds offered on to its own books or by finding takers for them among or through other banks active in the secondary market.

Market Overt. A public market where goods are on open offer. By custom, shops in the City of London form a market overt for articles which are sold in the normal business of such shops; elsewhere the term applies to markets established by grant or prescription. Stolen goods which find their way on to market overt become the property of the buyer in such a market, save only if the original thief is prosecuted to conviction, in which case the title reverts to the original owner.

Market Partnership. A partnership on the Stock Exchange where two or more members notify the secretary that although they deal and settle bargains in their own names, they have agreed between themselves to be jointly responsible to the Stock Exchange for any transactions carried out by either or any of them.

Market Report. An account describing the conditions of a market and listing the prices; a communication from a broker to banks and others who have money to invest, whether on their own behalf or on behalf of customers; a description of the previous day's trading on the Stock Exchange in the financial pages of a newspaper; a summary by a marketing manager of the results of market research carried out.

Market Research. An investigation into what the consumer wants, so that a firm may know what to supply, whether in goods or services, and how to package it. *See also* Certificate of Deposit; Parallel Market.

Marketable Securities. Securities dealt with on the Stock Exchange, or otherwise readily turned into cash.

Marketing. The distribution of a product from the place where it was made, or from the port of import, to the people who are going to use or consume it; the identification and satisfaction of the needs of the consumer or producer; the management process which controls this sequence, from the identification of the market to the profitable satisfaction of the consumer's demand.

Marking. A Stock Exchange term to describe the prices recorded for business done in any security during the day.

Marking Names. In the case of an American-type certificate the registered holder commonly signs the form of transfer printed on the back of the certificate and this allows the certificate to pass from hand to hand like a bearer bond, delivery transferring title. Unlike a bearer bond, however, there are no coupons, and the dividend is sent to the registered holder, from whom the owner must claim it. At one time dividends were "marked" on the back of the certificate when they were paid, and this has given rise to the description of the registered holder as a "marked name". A list of firms recognised by the Stock Exchange as good for the purpose of receiving and transmitting dividends has been made: they consist mostly of bankers or members of the Stock Exchange. These are known as "good marking names", and the more active shares registered in such marking names are quoted in the Stock Exchange Daily Official List as separate entries from the shares of the same companies registered in "other names". Shares registered in good marking names command an appreciably better price than those in other marking names, because it is known that there will be no trouble in obtaining the dividend each time it is due.

Markt. Market, business.
Marktanteil. Market share.
Marktbewertung. Market valuation.

Mark Up. To increase prices or a valuation of securities held; the gross profit on an article.

Marqué. Ticked as correct—used of a bank statement which has been verified by the customer on receipt.

Marque de Fabrique. See Trade Mark.
Marque Déposée. Registered trade mark.
Marque d'Origine. Mark of origin.

Marry Up. To link together; to identify the original query when the answer becomes available (as with a status report); to link a credit item with a debit, or *vice versa*; to sort an item under an appropriate head.

Marshal. To dispose in order, to arrange.

Marshalling. The act of arranging in a certain order: the application of the principle that a prescribed order will always be observed whatever the method of distribution.

Marshalling of Assets. An equitable doctrine governing the rights of beneficiaries under a will amongst themselves vis-à-vis the creditors of the estate. Where the estate is solvent but there is not enough left over after all the debts have been paid to satisfy all the beneficiaries, some beneficiaries must lose their rights so that creditors are paid in full. The order in which they lose their rights is set out in the Administration of Estates Act 1925, s. 34(3), and Part Two of the First Schedule to that Act. A beneficiary who loses property through the application of this order may claim to be indemnified out of undisposed property to which another beneficiary in a better position in the order is entitled.

Marshalling of Securities. An equitable doctrine regulating the position of creditors amongst themselves vis-à-vis the debtor. Thus where X mortages properties A and B to Y, and later grants a second mortgage on B to Z, Z may demand that the claim of Y shall be satisfied as far as possible from property A.

Masse Monétaire. The total of the means of payment in an economy, including the bank notes and coin in circulation together with all bank deposits.

Material Alteration. On a bill of exchange material alterations are alterations to the date, the sum payable, the time or place of payment, any alteration of the crossing on a cheque and, where a bill has been accepted generally, the addition of a place of payment without the acceptor's assent. If a bill or acceptance is materially altered without the assent of all parties liable on the bill, the bill is avoided except as against a party who has himself made, authorised or assented to the alteration, and subsequent indorsers. It is furthermore provided that, where an alteration is not apparent, a holder in due course, in whose hands the bill is, may avail himself of the bill as if it had not been altered, and may enforce payment of it according to its original tenor.

Mate's Receipt. A receipt for goods received on board by a ship's mate. A mate's receipt is not a document of title and is purely temporary. It is later exchanged for a bill of lading.

Matières Brutes. *See* Raw Materials.

Matrimonial Home. The house in which a husband and wife live. In spite of the modern view of the equality of the sexes, it is still the duty of the husband to support his wife, and she has a personal right against her husband to live in the matrimonial home. To gain precedence over purchasers and mortgagees this right must be registered as a Class F land charge, at the Land Charges Department. A husband has a similar right of registration. *See also* Land Charges.

Matrix. The place where anything is generated or developed; the centre of an organisational structure.

Matrix Organisation. A design to keep human or material resources fully employed by deployment in different places or in different ways. Thus, members of a working party or a project team may be temporarily assigned from branches or departments to work under a project manager, who has need of their specialist abilities, but who cannot employ them full-time. Such a project manager could determine the schedules and demands of the project's activities and, in conjunction with the branch of department managers, would determine how and when the members of the team would work with him, and when with their own managers or departmental heads. Also an organisation in which managers report to different superiors functionally, and act as line managers simultaneously.

Maturity. The date on which a bill of exchange or a promissory note falls due or becomes legally payable. A bill is due and payable in all cases on the last day of the time of payment fixed by the bill or, if that is a non-business day, on the succeeding business day. Non-business days in the U.K., for the purposes of the Bills of Exchange Act 1882, are (1) Saturday, Sunday, Good Friday, Christmas Day; (2) a bank holiday under the Banking & Financial Dealings Act 1971; (3) a day appointed by Royal Proclamation as a public fast or thanksgiving day; (4) a day declared by an order under section 2 of the Banking and Financial Dealings Act 1971 to be a non-business day.

Maturity Factoring. *See* Factoring.

Maundy Money. Money distributed annually by the Queen's Almoner to poor people on Maundy Thursday, the day before Good Friday. These silver coins of 1p, 2p, 3p and 4p become collectors' pieces, worth at the present time about £60 per set.

Maximum Load Line. *See* Plimsoll Mark; Dead Weight.

Mean Price. The middle point between the buying and selling price of stocks and shares.

Media. Television, radio and the press; any means of mass communication.

Mediation. Interposition between two parties in order to reconcile them; a method of settling industrial disputes; the achievement of a compromise settlement. A mediator must be approved by both parties to the dispute. *See also* Arbitration.

Medio. The middle day of the month.

Medium. An agency, anything serving as an intermediary, instrumentality. *See also* Circulating Medium.

Medium of Exchange. *See* Money.

Medium-Term Credit. Loans for from three to ten years.

Meeting of Creditors. A meeting called by an insolvent person, perhaps with the intention of suggesting a composition; a meeting following the making of a receiving order by the court, to consider whether any arrangement can be considered, or whether the debtor shall be made bankrupt. This must take place within fourteen days after the making of the receiving order. In cases of company liquidation, the meeting summoned by the Official Receiver to determine on the appointment of a liquidator; the meeting summoned by the liquidator to ascertain the wishes of the creditors in regard to the liquidation.

Meetings, Company. *See* Annual General Meeting; Extraordinary General Meeting; Statutory Meeting.

Mehrheitsbeteiligung. Possession of more than 50% of the share capital of a company; controlling interest.

Members' Voluntary Winding-Up. *See* Voluntary Liquidation.

Memorandum. A note or reminder, a brief record; a summary, outline or draft of an agreement.

Memorandum of Association. The memorandum of a company is a document drawn up by the founder members of the company. It has six parts: (1) the name of the company, with "Limited" as the last word in the case of a company limited by shares, or by guarantee (a company may now declare a Welsh registered office and use "Cyfyngedig" in its title); (2) whether the registered office of the company is to be situated in England or in Wales or in Scotland; (3) the objects of the company; (4) whether the liability of the members is limited; (5) details of the capital structure of the company—that is, the amount of the share capital and the way in which it is divided into shares; (6) the association clause. To ensure a personal stake in the company, it is provided that every subscriber to the memorandum shall take at least one share, writing opposite to his name the number of shares he takes. The memorandum regulates the affairs of the company as against the outside world. The objects clause sets out the purposes for which the company was formed and the ways in which it is intended to do business. For an activity stated specifically therein, the company has legal power. Anything else has in the past been *"ultra vires"* the company (beyond its powers). The European law on this subject, however (to which we must now subscribe) is that a contract entered into in good faith by a person dealing with a company should not be set on one side on the ground that it is beyond the powers of the company. The memorandum may be altered if the alteration is for the better carrying on of the company's business, for the sale of part or all of its undertakings, or for amalgamation with some other concern. A special resolution of the company is required to make this change, which does not have retrospective effect.

Memorandum of Deposit. A form of bank charge over securities, usually stock exchange securities. It contains a number of provisions which may or may not be required in any particular charging of security. The form is normally executed under hand, and should describe the security and state that it is deposited as security. The bank is to have the right to sell the security at any time after failure to repay on demand made by the bank. The security is to be a continuing security and the customer agrees to accept on re-transfer stocks and shares of the same class and denomination as those charged. He undertakes to do anything or sign any document which the bank may request him to do or sign in order to allow the bank to perfect their security or assist them in selling it. He undertakes to maintain a specified margin of cover if so requested. The form can represent an equitable or legal mortgage as required. Not the least of its purposes is to act as evidence of intention, *e.g.* when bearer bonds are offered as security, or when title deeds or a registered land certificate is deposited on an equitable basis.

Memorandum of Interview. A note completed by a manager after an interview with a customer, recording brief details of the business discussed. Such a memorandum may be circulated around senior staff for information and should also be filed with the customer's papers, where it may later prove useful in showing what the intention of the parties was, e.g. for demonstrating that the bank was exercising pressure on the customer to repay. A memorandum may also be completed by a staff controller after interviewing a member of the staff, to be filed with his record.

Memorandum of Satisfaction. A notice addressed to the Registrar of Companies and filed with him, to the effect that a mortgage or charge has been wholly (or partly) satisfied. The notice is originated by the creditor.

Mental Illness of Customer. The difficulty for a banker is to decide when his customer's mental health is so disturbed that he does not know what he is doing. This may be presumed when the customer is compulsorily admitted to a hospital on the certificate of two medical practitioners, or when the customer is placed under the guardianship of a local authority or of a person authorised by a local authority. In either of these cases the customer can be regarded by the banker as mentally incapable, and the banker should stop the account and regard all authorities and mandates as cancelled. But a further possibility is that a customer may voluntarily enter a hospital for mental treatment. The mere entry into hospital is not of itself therefore sufficient justification to stop the account.

Mercantile. Pertaining to commerce, relating to buying and selling.

Mercantile Agent. One having in the customary course of his business as an agent authority to sell goods, to buy goods, to consign goods for sale, or to raise money on the security of goods. *See also* Factor.

Mercantile Law. That part of the common law which deals with the customs and practices of business and commerce (also known as the *Law Merchant*).

Merchandise. Commodities bought and sold in home or foreign markets.

Merchandise Advances. The banker will make merchandise advances only to customers of undoubted integrity with experience in the trade. He will usually be willing to make such advances against goods imported on consignment, goods being built up by the customer in anticipation of seasonal requirements, or goods pre-sold to reputable buyers. A margin of cover should be obtained, depending on the type and marketability of the goods, and the banker's valuation of the security should take into account the length of time the goods can be held without deterioration, and the condition and quality of the goods. Advances should be by way of loan, one separate loan for each consignment of goods. In this way the margin to be maintained can be more effectively controlled. The security is obtained when the documents of title come into the bank's possession, or when goods are warehoused in the bank's name (including the case where the warehousekeeper attorns to the bank). *See also* Attornment; Delivery Order; Trust Letter; Warehousekeeper's Certificate; Warehousekeeper's Warrant.

Merchandise Marks. Marks on the outside of cases, packets, bales, etc., containing goods, especially those being imported or exported. The marks are used for identification purposes and are specified on the bill of lading and insurance policy.

Merchant Banks. Banks which have developed from the activities of immigrants to Britain during the eighteenth century. These men were originally merchants trading in particular commodities such as wool or cotton, during the course of which they acquired a comprehensive knowledge of the world markets relevant to their trading. They became well known and were asked to accept bills of exchange, so as to make them more readily saleable. As London developed and became the financial centre of the world it attracted representatives of foreign merchanting and financial houses: they brought with them a detailed knowledge of the trading resources and customs of their native countries, together with initiative and shrewd abilities to develop new financial methods to meet growing demands. In particular, they took the lead in raising long-term loans for foreign governments and for companies engaged in major enterprises. The present-day activities of the merchant banks include acceptance, deposit banking, raising of capital, participation in consortia, underwriting, management of clients' funds, advice to companies, management of mergers and take-over bids, dealings in foreign exchange, the issue and placing of shares and debentures, and marine and other insurance business.

Merger. The absorption of a smaller estate in a larger one; the combination of industrial or commercial firms. *See* Amalgamation.

Messuage. A dwelling-house with the adjacent buildings and ground for the use of the household.

Metageschaft. See Affaire à Demi.

Metric System. A decimal system of weights and measurements based on the French metre, at present in use in most countries of the world. There are seven base units: length (metre); mass (kilogram); time (second); electric current (ampere); temperature (kelvin); luminous intensity (candele); amount or substance (mole). The system is being gradually introduced into the U.K. at the present time, and the changeover to metrication is expected to be completed by 1981.

M.I.C.R. *See* Magnetic Ink Character Recognition.

Micro-Economics. The branch of economics dealing with unit productions, *e.g.* single firms, their raw materials, costs and output; or the wages or salaries of one man; or the fashioning and sale of one product, etc.

Middle Price. *See* Mean Price.

Milker. One variety of thief specialising in travel cheques. He takes a book of travel cheques from a wallet, handbag, or hotel room, and tears out half-a-dozen cheques from the middle of the book before replacing it. The victim will probably not find out for a little while that any are missing, so the loss will not be reported quickly.

Milling. The indenting on ridging transversely of the edge of a coin, to defeat the practice of clipping or shaving a little metal from the edge of the coin, a practice profitable only when the coin was of intrinsic value. The temptation does not exist in the case of cupro-nickel coins; nevertheless the milled edge, which was introduced into the London Mint in the second half of the seventeenth century, continues to be used, because it is customary.

Minderheitsbeteilung, Minderheitsinteresse. Minority interest.

Mindestpreis. See Reserve Price.

Mindestreserve. The minimum figure which a country's banks have to keep with the central note-issuing bank; the position resulting after a need to safeguard liquidity has been met, or after a market movement politically inspired under a credit policy with the object of combating inflation.

Minimum Lending Rate. Previously known as Bank Rate. The minimum rate at which the Bank of England, acting as lender of last resort, normally lends to members of the discount market against security of Treasury bills, other approved bills, or government stocks with five years or less to maturity. From 13 October 1972, the rate is automatically set $\frac{1}{2}\%$ higher than the average rate of discount for Treasury bills established at the weekly tender, rounded to the nearest $\frac{1}{4}\%$ above. The rate normally becomes effective, for lending by the Bank, from the following working day. Special changes in the rate are not excluded under this system, in which event the operation of the formula is temporarily suspended until market rates have adjusted themselves to the new rate.

Minor. A person under the age of eighteen, formerly described legally as an infant. The term, in relation to Scotland, includes pupil. Money lent to a minor cannot be recovered, even if he gives security. All contracts entered into by a minor for the repayment of money lent shall be absolutely void.

Minor Interests Index. An index in the Land Registry for the registration of a third class of interest, not in land but in equitable interests therein, additional to (1) those which can be registered on the Land Registry, and (2) overriding interests—namely, minor interests. These interests may in some cases be binding on a purchaser if registered, or are equitable interests created under a trust for sale, which will be overreached on a sale. Minor interests are protected by notices, restrictions, cautions, or inhibitions. A deed of arrangement affecting the land would be protected by lodging a notice. Land held upon trust for sale should have a restriction to make sure that sale moneys are paid to two trustees, or to a trust corporation. A pending action affecting the land would be the subject of a caution; a receiving order, of an inhibition. Any of these except a notice will appear in the charges section of the Land Certificate.

Minority Shareholder. A shareholder in a company who is one of those who does not support a resolution of the company which is passed by the majority. Where the resolution concerns the voluntary winding-up of the company so that the whole or part of its property may be transferred or sold to another company, a minority shareholder may express his dissent in writing, addressed to the liquidator, and leave it at the registered office of the company within seven days of the passing of the resolution. The liquidator will then be obliged either to abstain from carrying the resolution into effect, or to purchase the interest of the minority shareholder at a price to be determined by agreement or by arbitration.

Mint. The place where money is coined under governmental supervision; to make by stamping, as of coins; fresh, unused, new. *See also* Royal Mint.

Mintage. A charge made by a mint for turning bullion into coins; the process of minting coins.

Mint Par of Exchange. A par of exchange between the coins of two countries both using the same metal, *e.g.* silver. The weight and fineness of one, compared with that of the other, will give the mint par of exchange by reference to the amount of pure metal in each coin.

Mint Price. The value of the quantity of coins into which a bar of metal can be made.

Mint Ratio. Where a bimetallic currency is in circulation, the ratio between the values of the two metals.

Minute Book. A book for recording the business carried through at company meetings.

Minutes. The official record of business transacted at a meeting. Minutes of all company meetings are to be entered in books kept for that purpose. They are signed by the chairman of the meeting. They list the date and place of the meeting, name those present, and record all resolutions proposed. They are read over as the first item of business at the next meeting to check their accuracy.

Mise à Prix. Reserve price.

Misrepresentation. A false or incorrect representation; facts reported inaccurately. *See also* Fraudulent Misrepresentation; Innocent Misrepresentation.

Mitarbeiteraktien. Company shares issued to staff either generally or on the basis of merit.

Miteigentumszertifikate. Deeds or documents evidencing a title in a property estate.

Mittel. Mean, average; remedy; expedient.

Mittelfristig. Medium-term.

Mittelman. Intermediary, middleman.

Mixed Economy. An economic system planned and directed partly by the State, and partly by private enterprise.

Mixed Policy. A marine policy combining voyage and time insurance, in that a ship is insured from one certain place to another over a certain period of time.

Mobile Bank. A motorised caravan fitted out as a small bank, which can tour outlying districts on one or more days per week, or go to fairs or agricultural shows.

Mobiliarkredit. Accommodation against the security of negotiable securities or moveable property generally.

Mobilisation. A measure allowing a simple realisation of an asset—for example, a bank draws on a drawee beneficiary under a credit, and can by re-discount turn this bill into cash.

Modifying Agreement. A regulated agreement which varies or supplements an earlier agreement. A modifying agreement revokes the earlier agreement, but its provisions reproduce the combined effect of the two agreements.

Modus Operandi. The way of proceeding or of setting to work; a plan of working.

Moiety. A half part or share.

Monetarism. The view that inflation is caused principally by excessive supply of money by the government. Monetarists believe that this extra money results in a rise in prices as the value of money falls because there is more of it about.

Monetary. Concerning money or the coinage.

Monetary Economy. An economic system in which exchange is effected by means of money, as opposed to barter.

Monetary Policy. The regulation by the government of a country of the supply and control of money so as to promote the achievement of national ends, such as the maintenance of full employment, a progressive rate of national economic growth, the restraint of inflation, and the stability of the national currency on the foreign exchanges.

Monetary Reform. The introduction of a new currency after a period of hyperinflation, or the introduction of a new decimal currency unit.

Monetary System. The internal and external provisions of a government for managing the media of exchange. Internally it refers to such things as whether notes are convertible, what is legal tender, whether coins are of intrinsic or conventional value. Externally it refers to the type of exchange adopted, such as the floating pound, a managed currency, exchange rates free to fluctuate within certain limits, whether these are discriminatory rates for specialised use such as property or investment currency, etc.

Monetary Union. An agreement between countries to maintain a fixed exchange rate between their currencies.

Monetary Unit. The standard unit of a country's currency.

Money. Coin or other material used as a medium of exchange; banknotes, bills, promissory notes and other documents representing coin; wealth, property regarded as convertible into coin; coins of a particular country or denomination; receipts or payments. *See also* Near (or Quasi-) Money; Paper Money; Ready Money.

Money at Call and Short Notice. Bank advances to stockbrokers, jobbers and bill brokers, repayable on demand ("at call") or at up to seven or fourteen days ("at short notice"). This item represents the bank's most liquid item, after cash.

Money Broker. Certain stockbroking firms authorised to borrow from City of London banks and institutions, and to on-lend to jobbers.

Moneylender. A person whose business it is to lend money at interest; a person whose business was governed by the Moneylenders Acts.

Money Lent and Lodged. A comparison between the total advances made by a bank, whether by way of overdrafts, loans, discounts, etc., and the total of money deposited with it, whether by way of current, deposit, or savings accounts, or by borrowing from the inter-bank market. This comparison gives the bank's lending ratio.

Money Market. A market consisting of financial institutions and dealers in money and credit who either have money to lend, or want to borrow money. In the U.K. the London Money Market is composed of the Bank of England, the deposit banks, the discount houses and the accepting houses.

Money of Account. A denomination (*e.g.* the guinea) not actually coined, but used for convenience in keeping accounts.

Money Order. Any order for money granted at one post office and payable at another.

Money Shops. Quasi-banks operated by finance companies and some American banks in offices in the High Streets of many towns, in London and the provinces. They are designed to be comfortable, informal and to appeal to the private individual. The accent is on lending, and home improvement and mortgage loans, life and general insurance facilities and investment advice are provided. Money shops are open from 9–5 or 5.30, six days a week.

Money Supply. The total value of banknotes, coin and bank deposits. According to one view, inflation is a direct, though delayed, consequence of increasing the money supply of a country too quickly (*See* Monetarism): for this and other reasons it is desirable to have a formula for deciding just how much money is circulating in the economy at any one time. M.1 includes notes and coins in circulation with the public plus the sterling current accounts, minus 60% of items in transit. M.3 is M.1 plus other term deposits, which include deposits at discount houses, deposit accounts at banks, and public sector deposits. Normally M.1 and M.3 move in parallel but, when high interest rates in the open money market have temporarily exceeded overdraft rates, arbitrage operations by big companies and local authorities have been large enough to cause divergencies.

Monnaie. See Money.

Monnaie Faible. Money not convertible or with poor reserve backing, money in little demand, currency falling on the foreign exchanges.

Monnaie Forte. Freely convertible money backed by adequate reserves, currency in demand on the foreign exchanges.

Monnaie Scripturale. Bank deposits.
Monometallism. A monetary system based on a single metal.
Monopole. *See* Monopoly.
Monopoly. An exclusive right secured to one person, group or company to make, supply or sell a certain commodity. A monopoly supplier is therefore one with no competitors, who is able to charge whatever price he likes unless restrained by legislation. The Fair Trading Act 1973, section 6 (1) defined a "monopolist" as one having a quarter or more of the market; such a company may be examined by the Monopolies and Mergers Commission. In Britain most monopolies are nationalised industries with legislation preventing competition, *e.g.* postal services, gas and electricity, transport.
Montanaktie. Mining stock.
Moratoire, Moratorium. An act authorising the suspension of payments or reparations by a bank or debtor state for a certain period of time; the period of suspension of payments; the agreement by creditors with an insolvent debtor that they will not enforce payment for a certain time.
Mortgage. The conveyance of a legal or equitable interest in real or personal property as security for a debt or for the discharge of an obligation. In relation to Scotland, the term includes any heritable security. *See also* Equitable Mortgage; First Mortgage; Legal Mortgage; Puisne Mortgage; Second Mortgage; Sub-Mortgage.
Mortgage Annuity Scheme. An arrangement whereby a mortgage is taken out against the uncharged capital value of a property. The sum raised in this way is used to buy an annuity which will be paid to the owners of the property, usually a married couple over sixty-five years of age. Both transactions attract tax relief. If the mortgage is taken out on an interest-only repayment basis, no capital is repaid during the joint lifetimes. The amount borrowed has to be repaid in full on the death of the surviving partner and it may well be necessary to sell the property in order to effect this repayment.
Mortgage Bond. A bond backed by mortgage of real property.
Mortgage Caution. *See Caution.*
Mortgage Debenture. A debenture accompanied by a charge on the assets of the borrowing company.
Mortgagee. The person to whom property is mortgaged by a borrower.
Mortgage of Company Assets. *See* Registration of Charges.
Mortgage of Equitable Interest. Where property is left by will or deed to trustees for the benefit of others, those beneficiaries have an equitable interest on which they can borrow. Such a beneficiary may be a joint tenant, a beneficiary under a trust for sale, or a remainderman. The property in the trust is eventually intended to be sold but the sale is postponed so that the income from the trust property is paid by the trustees to the life tenant. As a security the interest leaves something to be desired. There is no legal estate to be obtained, for that is held by the trustees, so the ownership of the trust property cannot be transferred to the bank. All the banker can do is to take a legal assignment by way of mortgage of an equitable interest. If there is land included in the trust property, the deeds cannot be obtained, for the trustees hold them. The mortgage cannot be protected by registration in the Land Charges Department, for it is a mortgage, not on land, but on the proceeds of sale of the land. (However, if the land is registered land, a mortgage of the equitable interest can be protected by registration on the Minor Interest Index; and stocks and shares can be protected by notices in lieu of distringas to the various registrars). A mortgage will be drawn up by the bank's solicitors, and notice of the charge given to the trustees concerned. Their acknowledgment must be obtained and they must confirm that no notice of any prior charge has been received. If the borrower's interest is contingent only, the security must be supported by a life policy to repay the loan if the borrower should die before his interest becomes vested in him.
Mortgage of Ship. Registers of British ships are maintained at most ports in Britain, and in some British possessions abroad. A ship is divided into sixty-four parts or shares, and any person may be registered as owner of any number of shares. A ship is a specialised form of security and has the disadvantages that it is difficult to value, difficult to realise,

and suffers from a high rate of depreciation. A legal mortgage must be as prescribed in the Merchant Shipping Act 1894. On production of this instrument the registrar of the ship's port of registry shall record it in the register book. Mortgages are recorded for priority by hour and date of the day. The statutory mortgage is usually supplemented by a supplementary form of mortgage, which will contain many clauses for the banker's protection not available in the statutory form. Before lending, the banker should make a search on the register to see if there is any prior registration outstanding. He should ensure that proper insurance cover has been obtained by way of marine and war risks and club or mutual insurance. The statutory mortgage, if given by a limited company, should also be registered at Companies House. It is desirable that any mortgage should be of thirty-three shares or more, so that the operation of the ship can be controlled.

Mortgage Term. The period for which land is vested in the mortgagee by the mortgagor.

Mortgagor. The person who mortgages his property in favour of the lender.

Mortmain. Formerly possession or tenure of lands or tenements by a corporation, especially an ecclesiastical corporation or monastery which could not alienate the land. Thus it was said to be held by a "dead hand". A corporation may now hold land in practically the same way as an individual.

Motion. A proposal put before a company meeting for discussion and possible adoption as a resolution; a proposal made in an assembly; an application to a court for a ruling on some particular point in the course of proceedings.

Mot Juste. Exactly the right word.

Moveables. A term embracing all property other than land.

Moyenne. See Pound Cost Averaging.

Moyens d'Action. The methods of monetary policy which may be used by a central bank to influence the position of the economy, principally by regulation of the discount or bank rate, by open market operations, and by the fixing of minimum reserves to be maintained by banks and financial institutions, etc.

Moyen Terme. A medium-term transaction; according to the nature of the business this will be from one month to three or five years.

Multilateral. Having several participants.

Multilateral Trade. A state of complete freedom of trade between countries unhampered by tariffs, quotas, or any other restrictions.

Multinational Companies. Very large trading concerns with interests and organisations in several countries.

Multiple Agreement. In the Consumer Credit Act 1974, an agreement whose terms are such as (1) to place a part of it within one category of agreement mentioned in the Act, and another part of it within a different category of agreement so mentioned, or within a category of agreement not so mentioned; or (2) to place it, or a part of it, within two or more categories of agreement so mentioned.

Multiple Exchange Rates. Where a restrictive system of exchange control is in operation it is possible for different exchange rates to be available according to the purpose for which the money is required, *e.g.* tourist rate, investment rate, property rate. These may be at a premium or a discount according to whether it is desired to encourage or to restrict the particular activity.

Mundelsichere. Gilt-edged.

Municipal. Pertaining to a corporation or city, or to local self-government in general.

Municipal Bank. Although an Act of 1916 authorised the formation of banks under the control of a local corporation, the Birmingham Municipal Bank was the only one to be opened. It was primarily a savings bank and was merged in 1976 with the Trustee Savings Bank movement.

Municipal Corporation. *See* Local Authority.

Muniment. A title-deed, charter or record kept as evidence or defence of a title.

Münzprägeanstalt. Mint.

Mutatis Mutandis. After making the necessary changes.

Mutilated Bank of England Notes. Such notes must be presented to the Bank of England for replacement. This will not be unhesitatingly done unless the fragment is of more than half a note, contains the whole of the sentence beginning "I promise to pay", etc, has some portion of the signature, one complete print of the series index and serial number, and some part of the other series index and serial number.

Mutilated Cheque or Bill. A cheque or bill may be partly or wholly torn and repaired with adhesive tape. If it is apparent that the instrument has not been wholly torn through it may be treated as any other by a paying banker, but if it has been torn right through the paying banker will expect to see indorsed on the instrument an explanation, confirmed by the collecting banker, of the circumstances of the mutilation. If such an explanation is not present the paying banker should return the draft unpaid with the answer "Mutilated cheque". If there is an explanation there, but it lacks the confirmation of the collecting banker, the answer should be "Mutilation requires confirmation".

Mutual Fund. *See* Open-Ended Trust, under Open Ended.

Mutual Insurance. Insurance provided by shipowners throughout the world who have clubbed together in various mutual protection and indemnity associations to cover hazards which are not covered by marine policies, which have standard clauses leaving a number of contingencies unprovided for, or only partially provided for. The liabilities of the mutual insurance company are periodically divided amongst the subscribers in proportion to the tonnage they have entered with the company. Also known as *Club Insurance*.

N

Nachdeckungspflicht. An obligation to give further supplementary guarantees to re-establish a margin of security which has diminished by reason of a fall in stock exchange valuations.

Nachfrage. Inquiry, demand. *See also* Angebot und Nachfrage.

Nachgangshypothek. A second or subsequent mortgage.

Nachrucküngsrecht. The right of a subsequent mortgager, on the failure of a mortgage interest ranking before him, to be brought forward in the order for claiming.

Nachzugaktie. Deferred share.

Naked Debenture. An acknowledgement of indebtedness, not accompanied by any security.

Naked Trustee. One who holds property for the absolute benefit of beneficiaries of full age, and who has himself no beneficial interest in the property and no duty except to transfer it to its owners.

Name Day. The second day of the Stock Exchange semi-monthly settlement. Also called Ticket Day, it is the day when the names of buyers are transmitted to the sellers of securities.

Named Policy. A marine policy in which the name of the ship carrying the insured goods is particularised.

Namenaktie. Registered share.

Namenpapier. Valuable documents showing title to be with a particular specified person or company.

Nantissement. Negotiable security charged in support of a loan.

Narrow Market. When there is only a small supply of any particular security available on the Stock Exchange.

National Agricultural Advisory Service (N.A.A.S.). *See* Agricultural Development and Advisory Service.

National Capital. The financial value of the total real capital of a country at any particular time.

National Debt. Money owed by the State; the debt of a nation in its corporate capacity.

National Development Bonds. *See* British Savings Bonds.

National Economic Development Council (N.E.D.C.). An attempt to plan on a national scale by meetings between the government, industrialists, and trade union leaders, set up in 1962. The N.E.D. Council ("Neddy") brought together senior ministers, economists, leading industrialists and trade union leaders. From 1964, a number of smaller committees ("little Neddies") were hived off to deal with specific industries. These consisted of senior managers and trade union leaders, had independent chairmen, and were serviced by the N.E.D. Office. The "little Neddies" try to improve standards in the industries with which they are concerned by educational means, and they publish a wide range of booklets on matters of concern to the industries and on the future prospects for them.

Nationaleinkommen. *See* Gross National Product (G.N.P.).

National Giro. A giro banking system opened in 1968, and run by the Post Office. Factors reinforcing the setting up of the National Giro were the need to modernise the remittance services of the Post Office and the substantial increase in recent years of the sort of transactions for which a giro system is particularly appropriate; the payment of rates and bills by instalments, hire purchase and mail order remittances, and payments for the renting of consumer durables. All accounts are kept at the Centre in Bootle. The "branches" are the post offices of the country. Debts between account holders are settled by transfers from one account to another, or in the case of non-account holders by giro cheques. Withdrawals, up to £50 at a time, may be made from either of two post offices nominated by the account holder. Standing orders and automatic debit transfers are available; personal loans and overdrafts are also granted. *See also* Bank Giro.

National Income. The value in a country's money of the total production of goods and services in that country for one year.

National Institute for Economic and Social Research (N.I.E.S.R.). A non-profit making research centre set up in 1938, which works closely with the Treasury in making quarterly projections of the economic trends in the country, using a computer-based model of the British economy.

Nationalisation. The acquisition and management of industrial and distributing organisations by the State.

National Mark. A grading mark placed on foodstuffs and other products, authenticating their British origin.

National Savings Bank. Established in 1861, under the name of the Post Office Savings Bank, the National Savings Bank offers simple banking facilities for people who have no need for cheques. Anyone over the age of six can open an account at any Savings Bank post office with a minimum deposit of 25p. A bank book is issued in which all transactions are recorded. Ordinary accounts are subject to a condition that no more than £10,000 may be kept on balance. Interest is paid on these accounts at a rate varying from time to time with general money rate levels. The first £70 of interest is exempt from income tax. Withdrawals on demand are limited to £30, but larger sums may be withdrawn at a few days' notice. Ordinary account holders are offered a cumbersome cheque-type facility through crossed warrants, which can be obtained only by sending a completed withdrawal application form, together with the bank book, to Savings Bank headquarters. The Bank also offers investment accounts, paying a better rate of interest, but requiring one months' notice of withdrawal. A limit of £50,000 is placed on these. All interest on these is subject to tax. These accounts are available to any investor, whether or not he has an ordinary account.

National Savings Certificates. Certificates obtainable at banks and post offices designed to encourage savings. The first issue was offered in 1916, under the name of "War Savings Certificates", the name being changed in 1920. Since then there have been many fresh issues from time to time offering various rates of interest, always free of tax. Interest is by way of accruals to the capital value and is paid out only when the Savings Certificates are cashed. An index-linked Savings Certificate was introduced in 1975. The link with the cost-of-living index figure should ensure that the holder's capital is protected against inflation. (This index-linking is limited to pensioners and regular savers who would be eligible for "Save As You Earn"). The pensioners' certificate is available, in minimum units of £10 each up to a maximum of £700, to men aged sixty-five or over and women aged sixty or over. A bonus of 4% of the purchase price is added if the certificate is left untouched for five years.

"Natural" Deposit. A deposit obtained from an industrial or commercial company, or from a private individual, as opposed to those obtained through the interbank sterling market as a result of bidding, in order to finance a particular asset.

Natural Rights of Property. Those rights which supplement the direct rights, for example the right of ownership, by imposing duties on other persons. Examples are the right of a landowner to such support from his neighbour's land as will maintain his own land at its natural level; the right of a riparian owner that other similar owners shall not divert the course of the stream. Such a right is distinguished from an easement in that it is not initially created by a grant.

Near (or Quasi-) Money. A term sometimes applied to bills, cheques, promissory notes, postal and money orders, or anything which is not banknotes, coin or bank deposits.

Nederlandse Bankiersvereniging, Herengracht 136, Amsterdam C. An association representing the banks in the Netherlands and acting as an intermediary between them and the central bank (*De Nederlandsche Bank*). The banks in the Association are bound by its rules, which consist in the main of agreements in respect of minimum charges which the banks make for their services. There are no agreements on interest rates. Any commercial bank registered as a credit institution is eligible for membership of the Association.

Negative. Containing, declaring or implying negation; denying, contradicting, prohibiting, refusing.

Negative Certificate of Origin. A certificate frequently requested by an Arab company, to the effect that no element in any product was imported from or produced by an Israeli firm or associate. These are certified before a notary public and then counter-signed by the Foreign Office.

Negative Dealing. Eurocurrency market operations not always viewed with approval by the authorities, *e.g.* U.S. dollars are borrowed for one year fixed, swapped into sterling on a three-month swap (fully covered), and the sterling proceeds lent out for three months, at the end of which period (depending on rate movements) a further three-month swap can take place as before, or the dollars can be lent out for nine months.

Negative Income Tax. Payments from the State to people with incomes below subsistence level.

Negative Interest. When a country has a strong currency everyone wants to buy its currency. As a result this country finds itself with large foreign deposits on which it would normally pay interest. If, however, there are no profitable outlets for the use of this money, such deposits must be discouraged. Negative interest is a charge for keeping deposits. *See also* Clause Négative.

Negative Pledge. A clause in an agreement whereby a borrowing company customer undertakes not to pledge its assets elsewhere without the bank's consent.

Negativklausel. See Clause Négative.

Negligence. Breach of a duty to take care. As a tort in its own right, there must exist for proof of negligence: (1) a duty of care owed to the plaintiff; (2) breach of that duty by the defendant; (3) consequent loss or damage to the plaintiff. The plaintiff must show all three. The duty may be independent of any contract. In banking, however, negligence is more likely to appear in connection with the banking contract with the customer. If a banker is careless in dealing with the affairs of his customer, he will be liable, because being negligent is a breach of his contractual duty to take care of his customer's interest (when sending back a cheque unpaid, for example, he must mark it with that answer which, while correct, will harm the customer's reputation least). The majority of actions against a banker alleging negligence, however, are to be found where the banker has collected a cheque for the account of someone not entitled to the proceeds. In this context negligence may be defined as the failure to make inquiry in cases when a reasonably competent banker would make an inquiry; or, when such an inquiry has been duly made, the failure to appreciate that the answer obtained is an unsatisfactory one. Negotiated cheques require special care, especially when they are for large amounts. The conduct of the account for which the cheque is being collected is a relevant factor; where the account has been giving trouble the banker is expected to look more carefully at the transaction. The contributory negligence of the plaintiff has, since 1971, been recognised as a possibility in such cases. *See also* Contributory Negligence of Plaintiff.

Negotiable Instrument. Any instrument which satisfies the three tests of negotiability. These are (1) the property in the instrument passes by mere delivery or by indorsement and delivery; (2) a transferee taking the instrument in good faith and for value with no notice of any defect in the title of the transferor obtains an indefeasible title against all the world, and may sue on the instrument in his own name; (3) no notice of the transfer need be given to the person liable on the instrument. Negotiable instruments are banknotes, bearer bonds, Treasury bills, certificates of deposit, bills of exchange, promissory notes, cheques, share warrants and share certificates to bearer, and debentures payable to bearer. Where a bill is negotiable in its origin it continues to be negotiable until it becomes overdue or has been (1) restrictively endorsed; (2) discharged by payment or otherwise; or (3) (if a cheque) crossed "Not Negotiable".

Negotiation. The transfer of a bill or note for value received. A bill is negotiated when it is transferred from one person to another in such a manner as to constitute the transferee the holder of the bill. A bill payable to bearer is negotiated by delivery. A bill payable to order is negotiated by the indorsement of the holder completed by delivery.

Negotiation Credit. One where an importer opens a credit in favour of the exporter, not in the exporter's country, but in a third country. However, the exporter's bills on the bank which opened the credit are negotiated in his country. Thus a French buyer from Singapore might pay by means of an irrevocable credit in sterling opened with a London bank. The exporter's bills drawn on the London bank are purchased with recourse by a bank in Singapore.

Negotiation Fee. The fee charged by anyone for arranging a loan or a service —particularly by the bank arranging a syndicate of lending institutions.

Negotiator. For the purposes of the Consumer Credit Act 1974, the person by whom negotiations are conducted with the debtor or hirer.

Negoziierung. The business of selling, particularly documents and bills, chiefly those drawn under a letter of credit; negotiation.

Nemine Contra Dicente (Nem. Con.). Without opposition.

Nennwert, Nominalwert. Nominal value, par.

Net, Nett. Left after all deductions.

Net Cash Flow. Retained profits for the year plus depreciation as charged (*i.e.* gross cash flow less dividends paid).

Net Income. The annual amount received after payment of tax; the annual income from a business after the expenses of running it have been deducted.

Net Investment. The amount of investment made in a given period after having made allowance for the depreciation of capital in that time.

Net Price. Cash price without discount.

Net Profit. Gross profit less expenses listed on the debit side of a Profit and Loss account.

Net Rate of Tax. Where interest payments are taxed at source, the amount which can be reclaimed from the Inland Revenue by a taxpayer who does not pay the full rate of income tax.

Net Rental. The rent of a property after payment of all sums for repairs, taxes and expenses.

Net Saving. Total savings less adjustments for depreciation and stock appreciation.

Nett. Left after all deductions.

Netto. Net.

Netto Aktiva. Net assets.

Nettogeschäft. Sale or purchase of bills through a bank without addition or deduction for commission, this being already included in the rate.

Net Weight. The weight of goods without their packaging.

Net Worth. The net worth of a business is calculated by subtracting the current liabilities from the total assets, after deducting fictitious assets. The surplus will vary with the nature of the business, but it should be adequate for the company's trading requirements.

Net Yield. A yield which is assessed after deduction of tax.

Neuausgabe, Neuemission. New issue.

Neue Rechnung. A new accounting period.

New Issue. An issue of stocks, etc., to the public by a company in need of capital. Such capital issues are sponsored by an issuing house which makes itself responsible for taking up any of the issue which has not been taken up by others. New issues may be for public companies already having a quotation on the Stock Exchange, or they may be for private companies "going public". Securities may be made available to the public either by means of an offer for sale by the issuing house, or by an issue by the company. In the case of an offer for sale the issuing house buys the whole of the issue for cash from the company and itself offers it to the public. In the case of an issue by the company the issuing house undertakes to find subscribers in full for the whole issue. New issues may also be "placed", that is, sold privately to a limited number of investors, usually the big institutions, but in these cases a proportion of the securities is allocated to the market to be available for the general public. Still another alternative is for the new issues to be made available by the company to existing shareholders only, by rights issue or by open offer. *See also* Issue.

Next Friend. One who acts on behalf of another who is unable, from infirmity or legal incapacity, to act for himself.

Next-of-Kin. Nearest blood relative.

Niederlage. See Entrepôt.

Night Safe. A bank safe connected by a chute with an aperture in the outer wall of the bank. Customers wishing to pay in cash or cheques after hours may obtain a wallet from the bank, put their money in it, and drop it down the chute.

The entrance to the chute has a locked cover to which the customer is given a key. In the morning the bank staff clear all the wallets out of the safe and list them in the night safe record book. Wallets are of two kinds, one to be opened by the bank staff and the proceeds credited to the customer's account; the other to be handed back to the customer, or his agent, during banking hours, because he prefers to open his wallet and then pay in himself.

Nisi Prius (**Unless Before**). A name given to trials by jury in civil cases, the words *nisi prius* being the first in the old Latin form of the writ commanding the parties to appear at Westminster "unless before" this the case had been dealt with on circuit.

Nochgeschäft. A term operation including an option. The buyer has the right to demand double or several times the same number of shares, etc., at the fixed same price.

Nominal. Existing only in name, formal, ostensible.

Nominal Capital. An alternative name for Authorised Capital (*q.v.*).

Nominal Consideration. A consideration which is less than a real consideration, but which is inserted in a contract so that its validity may be maintained. Consideration to support a contract need not be adequate, but it must be real, that is, it must consist of some measure of value. Where shares are transferred for other than a monetary consideration a nominal consideration is entered in the instrument of transfer, so as to attract a reduced rate of stamp duty.

Nominal Damages. Damages awarded when the plaintiff has proved that his legal rights have been infringed, but has been unable to prove that any actual damage was done.

Nominal Partner. A person with no financial interest in a firm, but who allows his name to be used in the firm's title for the sake of preserving goodwill. *See also* Quasi-Partner.

Nominal Price. The face price of stocks and shares, as opposed to the price for which they can be bought or sold on the Stock Exchange.

Nominal Rate. A rate founded on an estimation, but one at which no transactions have taken place.

Nominal Value. The face value on a certificate or bond, as compared with the market value.

Nominal Wages. Wages in money terms, as distinct from the true value of wages in terms of what they will buy in goods and services.

Nominalwert. Nominal value.

Nominee. One named or proposed for office; a person on whose life an annuity or lease depends.

Nominee Company. A company formed by a bank to hold the legal titles of stocks and shares transferred to the bank as security by borrowing customers, or for the convenience of customers who may be living abroad, in which the execution of transfers, etc., is facilitated.

Nominell. Descriptive of a rate depending upon a valuation, but not one at which any transactions have taken place.

Non-. A prefix in the formation of compound terms signifying absence or omission.

Non à Ordre. A "Not negotiable" crossing on a cheque.

Non-assented Bonds. Bonds for which a plan of financial re-organisation has not been approved by the bondholder.

Non Assumpsit. A general legal plea by which a defendant refutes entirely the allegations of his opponent.

Non-Business Day. A day which is not counted as one on which normal business is transacted. For the purposes of the Bills of Exchange Act 1882, "non-business days" are (1) Saturday, Sunday, Good Friday, Christmas Day; (2) a bank holiday under the Banking and Financial Dealings Act 1971; (3) a day appointed by Royal Proclamation as a public fast or thanksgiving day; (4) a day declared by an order under section 2 of the Banking and Financial Dealings Act 1971 to be a non-business day. Any other day is a business day. Where, by the Bills of Exchange Act 1882, the time limited for doing any act or thing is less than three days, in reckoning time non-business days are excluded. Where a bill is due and payable on a non-business day it is payable on the succeeding business day. *See also* Maturity.

Non-Claim. A failure or omission to make a claim within the prescribed limits of time.

Non-Commercial Agreement. A consumer credit agreement or a consumer hire agreement not made by the creditor or owner in the course of a business carried on by him.

Non Compos Mentis. Not of sound mind.

Non-Contributory Pension. A pension awarded on the grounds of age and not on contributions paid during a working life; an old-age pension.

Non-Cumulative Preference Shares. Those shares where interest lost one year is lost for ever.

Non-Essentials. In foreign trade, a designation for goods which are not judged to be of primary importance for the economy of the country.

Non Est Factum. "I did not make it". A plea which can be put forward by a person seeking to avoid a legal obligation, originally applicable to cases where the defendant sought to avoid liability on the grounds that a signature on a document was not his. Later the plea referred to cases where the signature was genuine, but has been obtained through a mistake, often as the result of a misrepresentation. It was granted sparingly, but blind or illiterate signatories were often favoured. In modern times the doctrine has been more narrowly circumscribed and a high standard of care is required from signatories, however handicapped they may be. As the plea is in direct conflict with the cardinal principle that a person is bound by his or her signature, it is only in exceptional cases that the plea is successful, but it remains a possible threat to the banker who is relying upon a guarantor's signature.

Non-Feasance. Failure to perform an act that is legally incumbent upon one.

Non-Intervention. Not intervening or interfering in the affairs or policies of another, especially in international affairs.

Non-Joinder. Failure to join with another as party in a suit.

Non Licet. It is not permitted.

Non-Marketable Securities. Securities which are not dealt with on the Stock Exchange.

Non-Participating Policy. A "without-profits" policy where a fixed sum is to be paid, irrespective of whether the company does well or badly in the currency of the policy.

Non Possumus. A declaration that it is impossible to comply with a request.

Non-Residents. For exchange control purposes, persons, firms, or companies who are resident outside the United Kingdom (including the Channel Isles, Gibraltar and the Isle of Man) and Eire; for tax purposes, people who are not residing in the U.K. and are therefore entitled to U.K. tax exemption on income from foreign and colonial investments and from some British Government stocks. In the latter case visits to this country amounting to no more than an annual average of three months are permitted, but if this figure is exceeded a review of the non-resident status will be made.

Non Sequitur. "It does not follow": an illogical inference, an irrelevant conclusion.

Non-Suit. The withdrawal of a law suit, whether by mutual agreement or by the judgment of the court.

Non-Trading Partnership. A partnership such as that of doctors or solicitors, which does not depend on the buying and selling of goods, but is concerned with the provision of services of a professional nature. In such a case a partner's authority is limited to the drawing of cheques. This distinction will not affect the banker as long as he has taken his usual mandate, by the terms of which any partner makes the firm liable for anything he does in the ordinary course of the firm's business.

Non-User. Neglect to use a right, by which it may become void.

Non-Valeur. A negotiable instrument or a share having little or no value.

Non Versé. Uncalled capital.

Non-Voting Shares. Usually called "A" Ordinary shares, these securities stand on an equal footing with Ordinary shares as far as dividend and capital return rights are concerned, but give to their owners no right to vote at the annual company meeting. Non-voting shares were originally invented to allow the founder of a family concern to be able to bring in outside capital without losing control of the company. In modern times they are not favourably regarded and the Stock Exchange will allow only companies already possessing them to create more. The companies themselves are gradually converting them into Ordinary shares, often on the death of the founder.

No Par Value. Shares issued with no stated nominal value, but valued according to the current stock exchange assessment.

Norske Bankforening, Den, Haakon VII's Gate 6, Oslo. The Norwegian Bankers' Association was founded in 1915. The Association represents the banks in their dealings with the Norwegian Government and other organisations, deals with questions of economic policy, undertakes investigations and publishes information. Its objects are: (1) to promote a sound development of the banking system in Norway, so as to enable the banks to fulfil their social functions; (2) to encourage efficient co-operation between the banks and to safeguard their common interests; (3) to participate in co-operation with the public authorities and other organisations with a view to promoting the general interests of the banking system.

Nostro Account. Accounts maintained by home banks with banks abroad.

Nostro Konto. See Nostro Account.

Notarial Act of Honour. If, after a bill of exchange has been protested, a third party intervenes to pay the bill for the honour of the party on whom it is drawn, such a payment must be attested by a notary public and is known as a notarial act of honour.

Notary Public. A person, usually a solicitor, authorised to record statements, to certify deeds, to take affidavits, etc., on oath, especially for use in legal proceedings abroad. When a dishonoured bill is "noted" it is presented again by a notary public and "noted" for non-acceptance or non-payment. If necessary, the noting can be extended into a protest.

Note Issue. The total amount of bank notes in circulation in the country at any particular moment. In England and Wales the Bank of England has a monopoly of the issue of notes, but certain Irish and Scottish banks still issue their own notes. The 'note issue" of one of these banks means the total amount of its own notes which it is legally authorised to issue.

Notendeckung. The reserves held at the central bank to cover the note issue.

Notenmonopol. A monopoly of note-issuing exercised by the State through a central institution.

Note of Hand. A promissory note, a written promise to pay a certain sum by a stipulated time.

Note Reserve. The difference between the amount of banknotes in circulation and the highest permitted legal limit.

Notice. Information, warning, a written or printed paper giving information or directions, a formal intimation, a communication indicating pending loss of employment; in the law of registered land, a notification to the Land Registrar to protect a minor interest, such as a deed of arrangement affecting land. For the purposes of the Consumer Credit Act 1974, notice means notice in writing. *See also* Default Notice; Despensing Notice.

Notice Deposit. A deposit repayable only after the specified period of notice has been given (*e.g.* seven days' notice), which may be given by either the borrower or lender. If repayment is requested and made at less than the prescribed notice, interest is deducted in respect of the days of short notice. The interest rate applicable may also be varied, subject to the appropriate period of notice.

Notice in Lieu of *Distringas*. See *Distringas*.

Notice Loan. A loan repayable only after the specified period of notice has been given (*i.e.* seven days' notice), which may be given either by the borrower or the lender. The interest rate applicable may also be varied, subject to the appropriate period of notice.

Notice of Assignment. *See* Assignment of Debts; Assignment of Life Policy.

Notice of Cancellation. For the purposes of the Consumer Credit Act 1974, a notice served within a specified period by the debtor or hirer under a cancellable agreement on (1) the creditor or owner; or (2) the person specified in the notice; or (3) a person who is the agent of the creditor or owner. If the notice, however expressed, indicates the intention of the debtor or hirer to withdraw from the agreement, it shall operate to cancel the agreement and any linked transaction, and to withdraw any offer by the debtor or hirer, or his relative, to enter into a linked transaction.

Notice of Deposit. A Land Registry form which is completed by a banker who has received from his borrowing customer the land certificate which is to serve as security by way of an equitable mortgage. The notice of deposit is addressed to the Land Registrar and informs him that the land certificate has been deposited with the bank as security. The registrar enters the mortgage on the charges register, thus giving notice to any possible purchaser or mortgagee. Also, if the proprietor attempts to sell the land or to deal with it in any way other than by legal mortgage the registrar would notify the banker.

Notice of Dishonour. Where a bill has been dishonoured by non-acceptance or non-payment, notice of dishonour must be given to the drawer and each indorser, and any drawer or indorser to whom notice is not given is discharged. The notice must be given by or on behalf of the holder, or by or on behalf of an indorser who, at the time of giving it, is himself liable on the bill. The notice may be given in writing or by personal communication, and may be given in any terms which sufficiently identify the bill, and intimate that the bill has been dishonoured by non-acceptance or non-payment. The return of a dishonoured bill to the drawer or an indorser is deemed a sufficient notice of dishonour.

Notice of Second Charge. A banker, being the first lender against deed security, who receives notice of a second charge on the deeds, must rule off his customer's overdrawn account to avoid the operation of the Rule in Clayton's Case to his detriment, and must thereafter hold the deeds in trust for the second mortgagee. If the land is registered land, the procedure is the same except that, although notice will almost certainly come direct from the second mortgagee in any case if the second mortgagee makes application to register his charge and the bank's prior charge is a registered charge, the Registrar will advise the bank. If the bank's interest is equitable, and protected by notice of deposit, the second mortgagee will be unable to have his mortgage registered until the bank's interest is re-registered as a legal interest. In the case of a company, registration of the second charge at Companies House will constitute notice and must be watched for in *Stubbs Gazette*.

If the bank *takes* a second charge it must give notice to the first lender. *See also* Second Mortgage.

Notice to Suspend Payment. An advice from a debtor to his creditors that he is unable to pay his debts. Such a notice is an act of bankruptcy. The notice must be a definite statement that payment is suspended. There must be some statement by the debtor from which any reasonable person would infer that it was his intention to suspend payment. Anything short of this is not notice and therefore not an act of bankruptcy. A meeting of creditors is not of itself an act of bankruptcy, but in the course of the meeting some such statement as above may be made.

Notierung. A firm holding of rate or prices on the stock exchange.

Noting a Bill. *See* Notary Public.

Notional Income. Where an investment is assumed to bring in a yield to the owner of property, on which he may be taxed, although in reality he receives only a non-financial benefit.

Notleidend. Unpaid, as of loans of which capital repayment or on which interest payments are in arrears.

Not Negotiable. Where a person takes a crossed cheque which bears on it the words "Not negotiable", he shall not have and shall not be capable of giving a better title to the cheque than that which the person from whom he took it had.

Not Transferable. A crossing placed on a cheque to ensure that the cheque is paid to the named payee only. An alternative would be to make the cheque out to the payee and then to add the word "only". To make the drawer's intention quite clear, the words "order" or "bearer" should be struck out and the alteration initialled by the drawer.

Nouvelle Émission. New issue.

Novation. The substitution of a new obligation or debt for an old one, by mutual agreement. The word may refer to a new arrangement between the same parties, or to the substitution of a new debtor for the old one.

Nudum Pactum. An agreement not in writing.

Nulla Bona. Having no goods or assets (against which recourse may be had).

Nulli Secundus. Second to none.

Nursery Finance. Equity participation

lending as carried out by merchant and investment banks in the U.K. The lending bank takes a large (but minority) stake in a company and usually puts a director on the company's board. This "locks-in" the bank on a commitment to provide further capital when and if required, and ensures that the company receives the best available advice.

O

Obiit (Ob.). He/she died.

Obiter Dictum. A casual remark, a remark by the way; a statement by a judge on a point of law which is not essential for the judgment (plural: *obiter dicta*, words by the way). Such an opinion is not binding on other judges, but is "persuasive". The higher the standing of the judge, the more persuasive his *obiter dicta*.

Objects Clause. The clause in the memorandum of association of a company which lists the business objectives which the company will pursue. *See* Memorandum of Association.

Obligation. A debt, most often at a fixed interest, represented by a bond or certificate.

Obligations Convertibles. Holdings which, on the demand of their owners and subject to certain conditions, can be converted into ordinary shares of the company which has issued them.

Obligations de Caisse. Bonds at medium term carrying coupons, issued for round amounts by banks according to their needs.

Octroi. A customs duty levied on certain goods, especially foodstuffs, entering French towns; the seat of administration or place of levy; an internal tariff system between different regions of a country.

Offene Position. Open position.

Offenmarktpolitik. *See* Open Market Operations.

Offer. To put forward, to tender for acceptance or refusal; to bid (as a price); to show for sale; a price or sum bid. *See also* Open Offer.

Offered Price. A price quoted by a jobber on the Stock Exchange at which he will sell stocks or shares enquired for. *See also* Bid Price.

Offer for Sale. An invitation to the public to buy the shares of a new issue from an Issuing House which has bought the issue from the company concerned. *See also* Introduction; Placing.

Offer Price. A price quoted by the management company of a unit trust at which they will sell sub-units of the trust. *See also* Bid Price.

Official. Pertaining to an office; vouched for by one holding office, authorised; one who holds a public office.

Official List. The list of prices ruling on the Stock Exchange, published daily.

Official Quotations. The prices quoted in the Stock Exchange Daily List.

Official Rate. The rate at which the authorities of a country are prepared to deal in the foreign exchanges or, between 1968 and 1973, in the gold market. There may be "two-tier" rates, as for example in currency between the official rate on the one hand and a tourist, property or investment rate on the other.

Official Receiver. A public official charged with certain duties in the winding-up of companies and the bankruptcy of individuals.

Official Referee. A judicial officer of the High Court to whom is remitted for trial cases which involve prolonged examination of documents or accounts.

Offizieller Diskontsatz. The official rate of discount, minimum lending rate, Bank Rate.

Offizieller Kurs. Official rate of exchange.

Offre. Bid, offer.

Offre et Demand. Supply and demand.

Offre Publique d'Achat. *See* Offer for Sale.

Offshore Funds. Unitised investment funds operating in countries with comparatively low taxes. Many of the original funds were set up in the Bahamas or in Bermuda. They were designed to appeal to investors resident in different parts of the world: the assets of a fund are also invested to a very large degree outside its nominal place of residence. There is a clear difference between an offshore fund and the unit funds which attract money in the country where they are located. The tax havens in which most offshore funds are located normally allow them greater freedom of action, and some abuses have occurred. Offshore funds are not now able to offer any great advantage to private persons resident in the U.K. The situation is different for those living elsewhere and most of the funds have been set up accordingly. Offshore funds include all Eurocurrency transactions.

Ohne Kosten. A clause on a bill of exchange to indicate that, in the event of the dishonour of the bill by non-acceptance or non-payment, the bill is not to be protested.

Oil Deficit. The foreign exchange cost of importing oil to any country. The term is also used, however, to mean the money owed by the oil-importing countries to the oil-exporting countries which has not been offset by spending by the exporting countries on imports of goods and services provided by the oil-importing countries.

Old-Age Pension. The weekly allowance paid by a government to persons who have attained a certain age and fulfil certain conditions, usually known as the *Retirement Pension*.

Oligopoly. The system where in any industry there are few sellers, where a small number of companies command most of the sales—such as, in Britain, sugar, newsprint, detergents, banking services, petrol.

Omnibus Resolution. *See* Resolution to Borrow.

Omnium. On the Stock Exchange, the value of the aggregate stocks in a funded loan.

On Consignment. Goods sent to an agent who will sell them at the best terms he can obtain.

Oncost. Overhead costs, the total charges borne by any commercial or industrial concern, exclusive of salaries and wages.

On Demand. At call whenever required; of a bill of exchange, payable on presentation.

One-Man Company. One in which practically all the shares are held by one person, the remainder being allotted merely to make up the statutory number of persons required to form a company.

One Off. The production of a specialised article or service to suit the needs of one particular customer; a single print from a script; an achievement that can never be repeated.

Onerous. Burdensome, oppressive.

Onerous Covenants. Promises and obligations concerning land which will be expensive for the estate owner to fulfil, as where a leasehold in its last stages requires the repair of the property before it is handed back to the freeholder. A trustee in bankruptcy may, with the leave of the court, refuse to accept any land possessed by the bankrupt if, because of onerous covenants, it is likely to prove a liability rather than an asset.

On Line. A computer term indicating that a distant outlet (such as a branch bank) can communicate directly with the computer, can feed information or queries in, and can receive data and records out. A branch not "on line" must send its work to a local centre for transmission to the computer, or directly, by post, to the computer centre.

0.0. (ohne Obligo). Without responsibility.

O.P.E.C. Funds. *See* Petrodollars.

Open. Without restrictions; to establish or set going.

Open Account. 1. In foreign trade, the sending by the seller of the documents of title to goods to the buyer without making any condition that the documents are to be given up only against payment or acceptance of a bill of exchange; a method of business whereby the seller allows the buyer, whom he trusts, to have control over the goods. 2. An account which is still running or one on which final clearance on or agreement to all entries has not yet been secured as between the parties; an account on which the final balance is yet to be paid.

Open Cheque. A cheque not bearing a crossing and therefore payable across the counter of a bank.

Open Contract. A simple agreement to sell real property, signed by the vendor identifying the property and naming the price, and by the purchaser as evidence of his agreement to purchase.

Open Ended. A description applied to an agreement by a banker to lend against security although what the security is has not been decided; an agreement to lend a certain sum with an understanding that further sums will later be required; any trust where the trustees have discretion to vary the investments constituting the trust.

Opening a Crossing. Where the drawer cancels the crossing on a crossed cheque by writing across it "Pay Cash" and adding his signature. Initials should not be accepted by the banker as they are more easily forged than a full signature.

Opening an Account. A current account may be opened provided that all necessary formalities are duly completed. The new customer usually pays something in to open the account, and gives the bank a specimen of his signature and the name of either one or two referees according to the practice of the bank. When these referees have replied satisfactorily, and in their turn have been favourably reported on by their bankers, a cheque book may be issued to the new customer. In the case of a joint account or a partnership account the appropriate mandate must be signed indicating how cheques and correspondence are to be signed, and establishing joint and several liability. In the case of a limited company the bank must see a certified copy of the Memorandum and Articles of Association, the certificate of incorporation and, in the case of a public company, the trading certificate. A resolution should be provided giving the names of the officials who will act for the company, the way in which cheques and authorities will be signed, and appropriate specimen signatures.

Open Market. A market where prices are decided solely by supply and demand.

Open Market Operations. The purchase or sale of securities on the Stock Exchange or money market by the central bank for the purpose of expanding or contracting the volume of credit.

Open Offer. An offer to a shareholder by a company to take up any amount which he already holds. *See also* Rights Issue.

Open Policy. A type of marine policy covering goods, the value of which is not stated, but has to be proved in the event of a loss occurring.

Open Position. The position of a dealer in foreign exchange at any time when an exchange risk is run.

Operating Lease. *See* Finance lease.

Operation. The act or process of operating; working, action, mode of working; activity, performance of function; effect.

Operational. In production, working, effective.

Operational Research. The consideration in business of all possible ways of doing something, the evaluation of different methods possible, the estimated cost of each, etc., in order to arrive at the best, most effective and cheapest solution. *See also* Systems Analysis.

Opération à Prime. On the *Bourse*, a transaction at a term in which one of the parties reserves to himself certain rights of option, for example, to withdraw from the bargain on payment of a forfeiture sum called a premium.

Opération à Terme. A share or stock transaction in which delivery and payment for the securities sold do not take place at the conclusion of the contract, but at some later date fixed by the parties.

Opération de Couverture. On the *Bourse* an undertaking to complete engagements incurred—for example, to purchase shares in order to be able to deliver holdings sold earlier at a term.

Opération de Mise en Pension. Credit granted by a bank against the security of bills of exchange. Contrary to the procedure under a discount, the bills of exchange remain in the possession of the borrower.

Opération Descompte. Discounting.

Opérations Actives. Transactions entered into by the bank which show up on the assets side of the balance sheet, particularly advances to customers and others.

Opérations Neutres. Banking transactions which are not reflected in the balance sheet—for example, safe deposit services or stock exchange operations effected for the customer.

Opérations Passives. Entries showing on the liabilities side of a bank's balance sheet which reflect the interests of third parties, to whom the bank stands in the position of debtor.

Operative Clause. The words in a deed of conveyance which actually have the effect of transferring the property from one party to another.

Opportunity Cost. The theory that the real cost of a product is the amount of profit on other goods which could have been produced if the factors of production had been used otherwise.

Option. The right of choosing, a choice. On the Stock Exchange a method of speculation by which a purchaser obtains, for an agreed sum, the right to buy or sell a certain number of shares or amount of stock at a fixed rate on a specified date, usually within three months. A *"Put" Option* is taken out on shares which are thought to be likely to fall, a *"Call"* Option on shares thought likely to rise. If the shares do not perform as expected, the option is allowed to lapse. A *"Put and Call"* is a double option to buy or sell: a double option is not worthwhile unless there is a very big swing in the share price. *"Call of More"* is the right to call at a certain date for an amount of stock equal to that already bought; the option to double a purchase. *"Put of More"* the sale of a certain stock with the option to sell a similar amount on a specified date at a certain price: the option to double a sale. In the foreign exchange market the option is not whether to buy or sell currency on the forward date, but as to the precise date within a given period on which the transaction will be effected. For tax purposes an option is a chargeable asset for capital gains tax purposes. Where there is an option to sell, the cost of the option is added to the proceeds of sale. In the case of an option to buy the cost of the option is deducted from the cost of the purchase. *See also* Share Option Scheme.

Option Forward Rate. The rate at which foreign currency can be bought or sold for delivery between two future dates at the option of the buyer or seller. The option is as to the precise day of completion.

Option Mortgage Scheme. A system in the U.K. having a number of features not found in conventional mortgage loans. Mortgage interest on one's own house is usually allowed as an off-set against personal taxation, but this is no advantage to people who do not pay tax. It is for these people that the Option Mortgage Scheme is intended. A borrower who "opts" agrees to forgo tax relief in return for a lower mortgage rate. For tax payers who are paying more than the basic rate, the tax relief system is the more attractive; that is, it is wiser to have a tax relief mortgage if one's taxable income is in excess of a full year's mortgage interest, at the full rate. For borrowers paying tax at the current basic rate there is not much in it, but the scheme is likely to be of interest to those starting out on home ownership with lower incomes. An option mortgage is subject to the condition that the home being bought is intended as a main residence. The loan must not be in excess of £25,000. The difference between the option rate and the mortgage rate of interest is paid by the Government.

Optionsschein. Mostly in connection with a new issue, the right conferred shareholders to subscribe at a pre-determined price for the new shares within a certain period. The options can be bought or sold on the Stock Exchange independently of the shares.

Options Trading. Consideration has been given to the setting up of an options trading market in London. In theory there seems no reason why partly expired options should not be traded on the London Stock Exchange, but in practice it never happens. In a market on the American pattern, options to buy or sell certain shares would have a life of nine months, the cost of the options varying with their life. The value of an option to buy increases if the price of the shares concerned rises in the early months of the option, and an active market can develop, not so much in the shares themselves, as in the options to buy the shares. Conversely, the value of an option to sell increases if the price of the shares concerned falls in the early months of the option. There is no limit to the number of options that dealers in an option can write. Not all company shares are considered suitable—a list of blue chip companies fulfilling the suggested requirements, two of which concern the total market value of shares held by the public and turnover in the stock market itself, would be decided upon as "optionable". For some time a committee set up by the Stock Exchange Council has been co-operating with backers of the venture in setting up the procedure, but the starting date has been steadily put back as the system proved difficult to implement. Operations are now expected to start in mid-1978. Trading at first is likely to be confined to five or six market leaders. Plans are, however, well advanced for a European Options Market in Amsterdam, which is expected to start trading on 4 April 1978. Countries interested are the U.K., France, West Germany, Belgium, Luxembourg, Austria, Switzerland, Spain and Italy.

Order. Rank, class, group; regular arrangement; command or direction. *See also* Receiving Order; Standing Order; Standing Orders.

Order Bill. A bill payable to a specified person or to his order.

Order Cheque. A cheque payable to a named person or to his order.

Order for Foreclosure. *See* Foreclosure Order.

Order in Council. An order issued by a British Sovereign with the advice of the Privy Council.

Orderklausel. The words "or to order" after the name of the beneficiary endorsed on a bill of exchange, bill of lading, etc.

Order of Payment of Debts in Bankruptcy. When a bankrupt's trustee has converted the estate into cash, as far as he can, by the sale of the bankrupt's assets, he has the task of paying the creditors whose proofs he has passed for payment. He is obliged to pay creditors in a certain order of priority, set out in the Bankruptcy Act 1914, as amended, which is as follows: (1) local rates due from the bankrupt at the date of the receiving order, having become due and payable within the twelve months next before that time, and income tax, land tax, or property tax not exceeding in the whole one year's assessment; (2) wages or salaries of clerks, servants, workmen or labourers, in respect of work done for the bankrupt during the four months before the date of the receiving order, not exceeding £800 per man; (3) all amounts due in respect of compensation under social legislation of various kinds, liability for which accrued before the date of the receiving order, not exceeding in any individual case £100; (4) all contributions payable under the National Insurance Act 1911 by the bankrupt in respect of employed contributors in an insured trade during the four months before the date of the receiving order. These are preferential debts, to be paid in priority to all other debts. They rank equally amongst themselves and abate in equal proportions if the property of the bankrupt is insufficient to pay even these preferential debts. The trustee is to retain such sums as may be necessary for the costs of administration and must then discharge these preferential debts as soon as possible. This is the bankruptcy order of payment of debts, and it has also been taken into the Companies Act 1948. In that Act there is provision for a lender of money for the purpose of paying wages to stand in the shoes of the clerks, servants, workmen, or labourers who otherwise, being unpaid, would have a preferential claim. There is no such provision to assist a lending banker in the Bankruptcy Act 1914, which has the practical effect that a lending banker is usually prepared to give more assistance to a limited company than to a sole trader or partnership. These preferential creditors are all unsecured creditors; secured creditors rely on their security. Unsecured creditors therefore fall into two main groups, preferential and ordinary. In addition, a married woman claiming against the estate of her bankrupt husband is postponed to all other creditors, while any money or property of hers lent or entrusted to the husband for the purpose of his trade or business shall be treated as assets of his estate. The same considerations apply where it is a married woman who is bankrupt and the husband who is making a claim against her estate. The order of payment is therefore: (1) money retained by the trustee to cover the costs of administration: this includes the cost of the petition, legal and court charges, and the remuneration of the trustee; (2) preferential creditors; (3) ordinary creditors; (4) deferred creditors (husbands or wives). In addition to the above, the Employment Protection Act 1975 provides for certain moneys to be paid by the Secretary of State from a redundancy fund, such payments being deemed to count as wages and salaries for the purpose of section 319 of the Companies Act 1948, and section 333 of the Bankruptcy Act 1914, thus being preferential. They include remuneration payable as a result of suspension of employees on medical grounds and payment for time off for carrying out trade union duties, or when under notice of dismissal by reason of redundancy. A bank claiming to be a preferential creditor in respect of sums advanced for wages and salaries may therefore find itself in competition with the Secretary of State.

Orderpapier. Bills or notes payable to the payee or to his order.

Ordinary Partner. *See* Active Partner.

Ordinary Resolution. One which may be passed by a simple majority.

Ordinary Shares. The usual type of shares issued by a company, which carry the main risk of the business and are rewarded accordingly. Ordinary shares rank for dividend after preference shares, and are paid only if profits permit. In bad years ordinary shareholders may receive nothing in dividend, but in good years there is theoretically no limit to the amount they may receive. (There may be a limit imposed by the government for political or financial reasons.)

Ordinateur. Computer.

Ordre du Jour. The agenda for a meeting or conference.

Ordre Ouvert. Standing order.

Organisation Development. A plan to implement ways of developing and changing an organisation as a whole in order that it can meet its objectives more effectively, both at the present time and in the future.

Organisation for Economic Co-operation and Development (O.E.C.D.). An organisation set up under a convention signed in Paris in December 1960 by the United States and Canada together with the member countries of the Organisation for European Economic Co-operation. This convention provided that the O.E.C.D. should promote policies designed (1) to achieve the highest sustainable economic growth and employment and a rising standard of living in member countries, while maintaining financial stability, and thus contribute to the development of the world economy; (2) to contribute to sound economic expansion in member as well as non-member countries in the process of economic development; (3) to contribute to the expansion of world trade on a multilateral, non-discriminatory basis in accordance with international obligations. The organisation examines and co-ordinates statistics provided by member countries and publishes economic studies and booklets on a wide range of subjects. The member countries are Australia, Austria, Belgium, Canada, Denmark, Finland, France, West Germany, Greece, Iceland, Ireland, Italy, Japan, Luxembourg, Netherlands, New Zealand, Norway, Portugal, Spain, Sweden, Switzerland, Turkey, the United Kingdom and the United States.

Organisation of Petroleum Exporting Countries (O.P.E.C.). *See* Petrodollars.

Original Bill. A bill drawn and discounted before it has attracted any indorsement.

Or-Papier. *See* Special Drawing Rights.

Ostensible Authority. An implied authority of an agent in a particular trade or business.

Other Names. *See* Marking Names.

O.u.O. (Ohne unser Obligo). Without our responsibility, without claim on us.

Out. Not in, from, among, not at home, on strike, in error, wrong.

Out Clearing. *See* Clearing.

Outgoing Partner. A partner who is leaving the firm, whether for retirement or for a change of occupation. He is responsible for the firm's debts as at the date of his leaving the firm, and should then give notice of his retirement to all those with whom the firm deals. This may be done by individual letter or, in the case of a large firm, by advertisement in the *London Gazette* and in a local newspaper. If this is not done he will continue to be liable for the firm's debts contracted after his retirement. An overdrawn partnership banking account should be ruled off if reliance is placed on the retiring partner.

Out-of-Date Cheque. *See* Antedated Cheque.

Output. Production, the amount of goods produced in a given time, the produce of a factory, mine, etc.

Outside Broker. A broker not belonging to the Stock Exchange.

Over. Above, upon, more than, in excess of, in excess, finished.

Overcapitalised. Said of a company whose assets are worth less than its issued capital, or when its earning capacity is insufficient to pay interest on the capital.

Overdraft. Borrowing from a bank on current account, up to a maximum agreed with the bank, interest being calculated on a daily basis. The customer pays only for what he uses.

Overdue Bill. A bill of exchange is overdue the day after it is due for payment. A bill payable on demand is deemed to be overdue when it appears on the face of it to have been in circulation for an unreasonable length of time. What is an unreasonable length of time is a question of fact. For purposes of negotiation this appears to be ten to twelve days, for purposes of payment six months. *See also* Antedated Cheque.

Overhead Costs. The cost of services, material and labour which are incurred whether or not any production is achieved, thus the costs of indirect labour, material and expenses.

Overnight Loan. Lending by bankers at call to the discount market against the security of bills of exchange from one day to another. Although the loan is initially repayable on the following day, it may be renewed.

Overriding Interest. Certain interests may affect registered land without being disclosed in the certificate. The two most important are short leases (not more than twenty-one years) and easements, such as rights of way, light, drainage, etc. A purchaser of registered land should, if he wishes to satisfy himself upon these points, visit the property and inspect it for rights of way or light, etc., and he should enquire of the occupier the terms on which he holds the land, A note to this effect will be found on the back page of the registered land certificate. Overriding interests can also exist in respect of unregistered land and may be revealed by search of the Land Charges Register (class D(iii)) or Local Land Charges Register.

Overseas Trading Corporation. A British trading company which does all its trading with overseas countries and none with the home market. To encourage this (for the trend is in favour of the country's balance of trade) tax concessions are given to such a company.

Oversubscribed. Where in a new issue the number of applications for shares is in excess of the number of shares available, the issue is said to be "oversubscribed".

Over the Counter. *See Marché Hors Cote.*

Overtrading. A situation which arises when a company engages in too-rapid expansion so that its financial resources become progressively less able to support the increased scale of operations. The only cure is the provision of further capital from one source or another. The signs of overtrading in the bank account are the rising of an existing overdraft until it is checked by the return of cheques unpaid. The account ceases to swing and develops a hard core of debt. Cheques to suppliers may be in round amounts—something on account to keep creditors quiet for the time being. There is a chronic shortage of cash, and difficulty over finding cover for the weekly wages cheque.

Owner. A lawful proprietor, a rightful possessor. For the purposes of the Consumer Credit Act 1974, an owner is a person who bails or (in Scotland) hires out goods under a consumer hire agreement, or the person to whom his rights and duties under the agreement have passed by assignment or operation of law. In relation to a prospective consumer hire agreement this includes the prospective bailor or person from whom the goods are to be hired.

Ownership. The legal title to property vested in a person, as opposed to the possession of it which may very well not amount to ownership (as where something has been borrowed). The owner has the right to do anything he wants with his property (subject to social laws and the public health) including the right to destroy it if he so wishes.

P

Packing List. A list, often requested by Customs, showing what each parcel or packet contains.

Pacta Conventa. Conditions agreed upon.

Pactum. An agreement, a condition.

Paid Cheques. Once a cheque is cancelled at the paying bank its purpose as a medium of transmission of money is concluded; indeed, it can no longer be described as a cheque since it no longer satisfies the definition of a bill of exchange (it is no longer "payable on demand"). A paid cheque is the property of the drawer, although the banker is entitled to keep it as a voucher until the account becomes a settled account. However, the custom was to send the paid cheques with the statement, so that the customer might verify the entries. Increasing postal charges caused some re-thinking on this point, and most banks now retain paid cheques for six years and then destroy them, and never send them to their customers. An unindorsed cheque which appears to have been paid by the banker on whom it is drawn is evidence of the receipt by the payee of the sum payable by the cheque. If therefore the paid cheque is required as evidence in a court of law, the banker must supply it.

Paid-Up Capital. Money received from shareholders in exchange for issued shares.

Paid-Up Policy. A life assurance policy in respect of which no further premiums are payable.

Paid-Up Shares. *See* Fully-Paid Shares; Partly-Paid Shares.

Paiement Par Compensation. The settling of mutual debts by a book entry for the balance due, as in the bank giro system.

Pair. See Par.

Pair Réciproque. The exchanges are at reciprocal par when the exchange rate of the currency of country A in country B, and the exchange rate of country B's currency in country A, are the same.

Panel on Take-overs and Mergers. A panel set up in the late 1960s, as a result of the City's anxiety about the way in which certain take-overs had been conducted. There is a full-time professional executive which deals with day-to-day problems and enquiries and a panel consisting of leading City representatives who meet to consider any matter of particular interest and to adjudicate upon any cases where a decision of the executive has been disputed by a company. The rules formulated by the panel are published in a City Code.

Paper. A newspaper, a document, bills of exchange, promissory notes, a set of examination questions.

Paper Bid. An offer of its own shares by a company making a take-over bid.

Paper Currency. Banknotes representing money made legal tender by government, which circulate as an accepted medium of exchange.

Paper Gold. *See* Special Drawing Rights.

Paper Money. Documents representing money, such as banknotes, promissory notes, bills of exchange, or postal orders.

Paper Profit. An increase in the value of an investment which has been retained and not, as yet, sold to realise the profit.

Papier. Paper, document; valuable paper such as banknotes, cheques, bills of exchange, stock or share certificates, deeds, life assurance policies, etc.

Papier à l'Ordre. Valuable paper transmissible by indorsement and delivery, either by its character of negotiability (for example, the bill of exchange or cheque) or because a specific order clause has been inserted into the wording. An indorsement in blank has the effect of making an order document of value, such as a cheque or bill of lading, payable to the holder.

Papier au Porteur. An instrument payable to bearer, the title being presumed to vest in the holder.

Papier Gold. See Special Drawing Rights.

Papier Lourd. A share with a high quotation, not as a percentage of the nominal value, but in relation to its monetary cost.

Papier Nominatif. A document of title in the name of a person specified.

Papier Valeur. A document incorporating a right which one cannot assert or transfer without it; a document of title.

Par. Equality of value; the nominal amount of securities. **Above Par.** At a price above the face value, at a premium. **Below Par.** At a discount. **On a Par With.** Of equal value, degree, etc.

Parallel. Precisely corresponding, similar; a thing exactly like another, a counterpart, a comparison.

Parallel Market. Side by side with the traditional short-term money markets in which the discount houses are prominent, secondary or parallel money markets have developed in short-term funds. These markets are mainly in the foreign currency deposits of non-residents, the sterling deposits of non-residents, or the surplus sterling funds held by domestic banks. They comprise the Eurocurrency market, the sterling and dollar certificate of deposit markets, the inter-bank sterling market, and the local authority market. The merchant banks, the discount houses, and the British overseas and foreign banks are prominent in each of these markets.

Parallel Rate of Exchange. Where two tier rates of exchange are in operation, the unofficial rate.

Parallels of Latitude. Imaginary circles whose planes are parallel to that of the equator, the latitude of every point upon each circle being the same.

Paraph. The flourish beneath a signature, originally intended as a precaution against forgery; to initial or sign.

Parcel. A bundle or package; a number of things forming a group or lot; a piece of land; a number of bills of exchange assembled by a bank which have the same due date, or a similar parcel providing a series of bills which fall due for approximately the same amount each day for a period of days, or each month for a period of months.

Parcener. A joint heir. *See* Co-Parceners.

Parent Company. A holding or operational company controlling a number of subsidiaries.

Pari. Par.

Parikurs. Rates at par.

Pari Passu. At the same rate or pace, with equal step, in the same degree or proportion, likewise, enjoying the same rights.

Parität. Parity.

Parité. See Parities.

Parité-Or. The definition of the external value of a currency by reference to its legal proportion of fine gold.

Parities. Rates of exchange—the value of one currency in terms of another. Parities are fixed by supply and demand and therefore reflect confidence in a country's general economic situation. *See also* Multiple Exchange Rates; Purchasing Power Parity.

Parol. Word of mouth. All interests in land created by parol and not put in writing and signed by the persons so creating the same have, notwithstanding any consideration having been given for the same, the force and effect of interests at will only.

Parquet. Originally the official brokers on the Paris Exchange, where only they were admitted; now the unified market.

Par Rate of Exchange. Par values for currencies related to the gold content of coinage.

Part de Fondateur. An interest in a company reserved to the founders of the business, for services rendered without pay or financial recognition.

Partial. Affecting a part only, incomplete, not total, biased in favour of one party, unfair, having a preference for.

Partial Acceptance. *See* Qualified Acceptance.

Partial Intestacy. The case where a testator has left instructions in his will for the disposition of some, but not all, of his assets.

Partial Loss. The damage, short of total loss, suffered by a ship or her cargo from any risks against which insurance has been taken out.

Participating Policy. *See* "With Profits" Policy.

Participating Preference Shares. Those entitling the holders to a preferential payment of a fixed dividend before other classes of shareholders and in addition to a share in any surplus profits of the company provided that the ordinary shareholders have received a specified maximum rate of dividend.

Participation aux Benefices. Profit sharing.

Participation en Nom. The participation of a banking group in a new issue with a mention of their name(s) in the prospectus.

Particular. Pertaining to a single person or thing, special, peculiar, characteristic, single, separate, individual, private, minute; precise, exact; remarkable, noteworthy; specially attentive; an item, detail, an instance.

Particular Average. An accidental loss involving part of the cargo on a ship, such as damage by fire or sea water, or even by being washed overboard, in circumstances where the safety of the ship itself is not endangered. Such a loss is borne wholly by the owners of the cargo concerned.

Particular Lien. The right of a dealer, warehousekeeper, etc., to retain goods in his possession until the debt in respect of those particular goods is paid.

Partizipationsschein. The right to take a share in a company on a non-voting rights basis, expressed in a certificate giving title to the current holder. As a rule it has a fixed, though small, nominal value. The share of the company's net profit, or in any appreciation of capital, and the rights in the event of a liquidation, are set out in the Articles.

Partly-Paid Shares. Are those on which there is a percentage of uncalled capital. They are comparatively rare, and are not popular with shareholders because of the liability to further calls. Although the value of the shares may increase as the calls are paid, and in the long-term the shareholder should suffer no loss, nevertheless in the short-term he has to find the money at a time which may not be convenient for him.

Partner. A partaker, a sharer, an associate in business, a member of a partnership. *See also* Active Partner; Bankrupt Partner; Deceased Partner; Dormant Partner; Incoming Partner; Limited Partner; Nominal Partner; Ordinary Partner; Outgoing Partner; Quasi-Partner; Salaried Partner; Surviving Partner.

Partner by Estoppel. *See* Quasi-Partner.

Partnership. The relation which subsists between persons carrying on a business in common with a view of profit. No written agreement or deed between the partners is legally necessary, though it often exists. All that is necessary is a written, verbal or implied agreement between the partners. A partnership can consist of from two to twenty people; qualified persons practising as solicitors or accountants, and persons carrying on business as members of a recognised stock exchange, may number more. *See also* Deed of Partnership.

Part Payment. A payment of less than the full amount owing, a payment on account. If an acceptor of an inland bill makes part payment only on the due date it may be accepted, but the other parties to the bill should be notified to retain their liability for the balance, and the bill should be noted for the unpaid balance. A record should be endorsed on the bill, which is retained by the holder, that the sum paid has been received in part payment without prejudice to the rights of other parties. In the case of a foreign bill, it must be protested. In England a cheque is either paid in full or not at all, but in Scotland if a cheque is presented and there are funds on the account, but insufficient to meet the bill, they are attached. *See also* Cheque as an Assignment of Funds.

Part Sociale. In general, the share of a partner, particularly the share of a partner in the capital of a society or partnership with limited liability; the document representing a stated portion of the capital of a co-operative society—it is not a document of title, but a means of proof; and a share of no nominal value giving a right to a determined share of the net profit of a limited company.

Par Value. Nominal value.

Pasigraphy. A universal system of writing, by means of signs representing ideas, not words. Although this is a very old and primitive system, modern advertising has come back to it by way of illustration and to supplement figures; viz., in the presentation of balance sheets or the asset and liability position of a bank.

Passbook. A book in which debit and credit entries on a banking or deposit account are entered. Formerly common on bank current accounts, the passbook has been superseded by the computerised statement which also shows a balance, and passbooks for deposit and savings accounts are also being replaced. The passbook is still found,

however, in savings banks and building societies.
Passif. Liabilities.
Passifs Transitoires. Accounting entries used to make adjustments between one financial year and another; receipts already taken into the old accounting period, but which concern the following period; or expenses which will be paid during the current period, but which relate to the past period.
Passing the Dividend. Making no dividend payment at the end of the year's trading because insufficient profits, or no profits, have been earned.
Passiven. Liabilities.
Passivgeschäfte. That part of the business of a bank which is represented by entries on the Liabilities side of its balance sheet.
Pawn. Something deposited as security for money borrowed, a pledge.
Pawnbroker. One who lends money on something deposited with him. The borrower may redeem his pledged property within six months, in default of which it can be sold.
Pawnee. One who accepts goods as security for a loan. For the purposes of the Consumer Credit Act 1974, the term includes any person to whom the rights and duties of the original pawnee have passed by assignment or operation of law.
Pawner, Pawnor. He who pledges goods. For the purposes of the Consumer Credit Act 1974, the term includes any person to whom the rights and duties of the original pawner have passed by assignment or operation of law.
Pawn-Receipt. A term used in the Consumer Credit Act 1974 to describe a receipt in a prescribed form given by a person who takes any article in pawn under a regulated agreement to the person from whom he receives it at the time he receives it. A person who takes any article in pawn from an individual whom he knows to be, or who appears to be and is, a minor, commits an offence. The above has no application to a pledge of documents of title or a non-commercial agreement (s. 114 of the Act). *See also* Non-Commercial Agreement; Regulated Agreement.
Pay. To discharge one's obligations; to give money for goods received or service rendered, to compensate, to discharge a debt: reward, wages, salary, compensation.
Pay As You Earn (P.A.Y.E.). A system of tax collection whereby the tax owing is deducted from weekly or monthly wage or salary earners by employers who are made responsible for the collection of the tax. Each employee is given a code number dependent upon his personal allowances. The employer uses coding tables which tell him how much to deduct each month or week.
Pay Day. The last day of the settlement on the Stock Exchange. Also called Account Day or Settling Day.
Payee. The person named on a bill to whom, or to whose order, payment is to be made. Where a bill is not payable to bearer, the payee must be named or otherwise indicated therein with reasonable certainty. *See also* Fictitious Payee; Impersonal Payee.
Paying Banker. Without a customer's authority the banker has no right to pay away his money. The authority is the customer's signature. The first duty of the cancelling clerk is therefore to assure himself that he is dealing with a signature which corresponds with the specimen signature supplied. A banker paying a cheque with a forged signature has no defence unless he can plead estoppel. He will also check the following points: (1) the cheque must not be "stale" or postdated; (2) words and figures must agree; (3) the cheque must not be stopped; (4) the cheque must be drawn on the branch; (5) there must be an acceptable payee's name specified; (6) if the cheque is marked to show that a receipt is required, the receipt must have been duly completed; (7) if the cheque bears evidence of transfer to an external account, exchange control sanction must be available; (8) the cheque must not be crossed by two bankers (unless one is acting as agent for the other); (9) a final practical point is to check that the customer has got the money. Statutory protection is available to the banker paying an open cheque bearing a forged indorsement if he pays in good faith and in the ordinary course of business; to one paying a crossed cheque if he pays in good faith and without negligence; and to one paying a cheque, whether crossed or open, which is not indorsed or is irregularly in-

dorsed. No protection is available to the banker who pays a bill of exchange (other than a cheque) bearing a forged indorsement. Indorsements are found only where a bill or cheque has been negotiated; in such cases the paying banker must see that the indorsement(s) purport(s) to be correct. Across the counter cheques payable to "wages" or "cash" should be paid only to the drawer or his known agent. In the case of order cheques paid across the counter it is the practice to require the signature of the payee by way of indorsement. In the case of bearer cheques the cashier should refer to the manager before paying such cheques for an amount in excess, usually, of £100.

Paying-In Slip. *See* Credit Slip.

Paymaster General. The officer appointed to make payments on behalf of the various Departments of the British Government.

Payment. Settlement, discharge of a debt or obligation. For the purpose of the Consumer Credit Act 1974, "payment" includes "tender".

Payment for Honour *supra* **Protest.** *See* Notarial Act of Honour.

Payment in Due Course. Payment made at or after the maturity of a bill to the holder thereof in good faith and without notice that his title to the bill is defective if such be the case.

Payroll Credit. A list of weekly or monthly wage or salary payments prepared by a customer for his workforce and passed, together with a single debit, through the banking system so that individual credits will reach the accounts of individual employees on a given day, a single total being debited to the account of the employer. Customers who have their own computer may prepare payroll tapes which are passed through the Bankers' Automated Clearing Service. Banks operating a payroll service will prepare periodic payments from information supplied by the employer and continue to pass entries until advised of any change.

Payroll Tax. A tax on a business according to the number in the workforce employed.

Peg. To fix or mark with a peg; on the Stock Exchange, to keep the price of shares steady at a given price by buying (or selling); on the foreign exchanges, to maintain a country's currency at a fixed rate of exchange by the intervention of the central authority; of prices generally, to control by governmental decree. *See also* Crawling Peg.

Penalty. A punishment for an offence, a sum to be forfeited for breach of a rule or contract. *See also* Stamping under Penalty.

Penalty Clause. A clause in a contract fixing a sum of money to be paid by the party in default of any of the contractual conditions.

Pence Rates. Rates of exchange quoted in pence per foreign unit.

Pendente Lite. While a law-suit is pending.

Pending Action. Any law-suit which is to be heard at a future time, but which may well affect the title to property, whether real or personal, in the present. Thus an action pending as to the ownership of land must, in the case of unregistered land, be registered on the Pending Actions Register at the Land Charges Department; or, in the case of registered land, be protected by a caution on the Land Register. In both cases the object is to warn intending purchasers of the fact that the title is less than perfect. An action pending as to the validity of a will may lead to the appointment of an administrator *pendente lite*.

Penny. The bronze penny was introduced in 1860, superseding the earlier copper coin of the same value. The present penny, originally called a new penny, was introduced in 1971. It was worth 2·4 old pence. There is a silver penny in the Maundy Money set.

Penny Bank. A savings bank of the late nineteenth century, so called because it would accept a sum as small as one penny on deposit.

Penny Stocks. Speculative shares, most often of new mining societies, of which the price never rises above a few pence or cents.

Pension. A periodical allowance for past services paid by a government or an employer; an annuity paid to retired officers, soldiers, etc. *See also* Contributory Pension; Non-Contributory Pension; Old-Age Pension.

Pension Funds. Investments maintained by companies and other employers to pay the annual sum required under the business organisation's pension scheme.

Large pension funds operate quite heavily on the Stock Exchange and in the capital markets. Insurance companies managing private pension schemes also buy and sell stocks, shares, etc., as they endeavour to obtain the highest returns. Many pension funds have power to make wide investments; loans on long-term mortgages are sometimes made available and some pension funds have even taken equity stakes in unquoted companies.

Pensiongeschäft. Credit guarantees of a bank through support of bills of exchange by indorsing them.

Peppercorn Rent. A nominal rent.

Per. Through, by means of, by, for each.

Per Annum. By the year, yearly.

Per Capita. Individually, each, per head.

Per Cent, Per Centum. By the hundred.

Per Contante. For cash.

Per Contra. On the other side (of the account), to balance it, on the other hand.

Per Diem. By the day, daily.

Perfect Entry. *See* Bill of Entry.

Performance Bond. A bond for due performance issued by a bank at the request of its customer who is tendering for a contract in the building or construction industries. The bank must be satisfied that its customer is technically capable of handling the work and financially strong enough to see it through. The bank takes a counter-indemnity to cover its own position.

Performance Fund. An investment or unit trust where the investment policy is intended to yield higher than the average.

Per Kassa. A transaction for cash.

Permanent Building Society. *See* Building Society.

Per Mensem. By the month, monthly.

Permissive Waste. Allowing the buildings on an estate to fall into a state of decay, thus a wrong of omission.

Perpetual. Unending, eternal, persistent, continual, constant.

Perpetual Annual Rent Charge. *See* Fee Farm Rent, *under* Fee.

Perpetual Annuity. An annuity payable for ever.

Perpetual Debenture. A debenture with no date for repayment, intended to be a permanent debt.

Perpetual Injunction. *See* Injunction.

Perpetuity. The number of years purchase to be given for an annuity; a perpetual annuity. **In Perpetuity.** For ever.

Per Plures. By a majority.

Per Procurationem (Per Pro.). By the agency of, by proxy. A form of words used by an agent when signing for his principal, *i.e.* "*per pro* John Jones, S. Smith", where Jones is the principal and Smith the agent. "*Per Pro*" is sometimes shortened still further to "*p.p.*".

Per Se. By itself, of itself.

Personal. Peculiar to a person as a private individual; directed against a person; of possessions, belonging to a person.

Personal Cheque. A service for bank customers who wish to issue cheques from time to time but do not wish to have, or to pay for, a full banking service. The personal cheque service is therefore made available to them on a basis of so much per cheque.

Personal Credit Agreement. An agreement between a debtor and a creditor by which the creditor provides the debtor with credit of any amount.

Personal Estate. Any property other than freehold land is personal estate.

Personalisation of Cheques. The printing on each cheque of the name of the customer, to assist in the recognition of signatures and in sorting.

Personalkredit. Credit granted without specific security, but based on the quality and character of the borrower.

Personal Loan. A bank loan where the interest is added to the amount borrowed and the total is then repaid by regular monthly repayments over an agreed period, usually six months to three years or, in some cases, longer. Each repayment consists partly of capital and partly of interest. If any instalment is not paid on time, the whole of the debt becomes repayable immediately. This gives the bank a right to bring an action for the money. Unlike a hire purchase contract (to which the personal loan is intended to be a cheaper alternative) the bank has no rights over the object purchased with the money lent. Personal loans range from £50 to £1,500 or more.

Personal Property. Moveable property, goods, money, etc., leasehold estates.

Personal Representative. An executor or an administrator, whose duty is to stand in the place of the deceased for the purpose of winding up his estate, paying his debts and legacies and distributing any residue according to the will or to the rules for succession on intestacy. The personal representatives for the time being of a deceased person are deemed in law his heirs and assigns within the meaning of all trusts and powers.

Personal Security. Security for an advance which consists of a guarantee by a third person.

Personal Tax. A tax on an individual, such as income tax, in contradistinction to general taxes such as customs duty and value added tax.

Personalty. Personal effects, moveable property, e.g. furniture, jewels, as distinguished from realty.

Per Stirpes. A term in succession law where children share amongst them the benefit under a will which their deceased parent would have taken, had he or she lived.

Perte. Loss.

Perte Comptable. A loss originating from a sale or a valuation below asset value. This represents the difference between book and market values.

Petit Crédit. A loan by a bank of a relatively small amount, repayable in equal instalments. It is designed to finance the purchase of durable consumer goods and is a form, therefore, of consumer credit; a personal loan.

Petite Bourse. The evening market of the *Bourse*.

Petition. An earnest request or prayer, especially one presented to a sovereign or to Parliament; a written supplication, an entreaty; a formal written application to a court, as by an unpaid creditor that his debtor be made bankrupt, or that a company be put into liquidation. See also Bankruptcy; Compulsory Liquidation.

Petrodollars. Surplus cash gained by the oil exporters (the Arab countries, Nigeria, Venezuela, Indonesia) which they have not spent on imports, but have invested at interest in other countries in varying proportions, mostly on short call. As the oil was at one time mainly invoiced and quoted in dollars, the term "petrodollars" was invented. These sums were so vast that considerable uneasiness was felt at one stage as to whether the world's existing financial systems could cope with them. It was also thought that so much cash taken out of world trade was one cause of the world recession experienced in 1974. Most of this money was invested in New York and in London; it is sometimes called "O.P.E.C. funds". As things turned out, the oil producers' spare revenues declined considerably, so that in the U.K. the anxiety became that there would not be enough for London to attract the funds necessary for the U.K. to finance its vastly increased fuel bills, support sterling, live with inflation, and stave off the onset of serious unemployment.

Petty Cash. Small items of expenditure, especially in an office.

Pfandbrief. See Mortgage Bond.

Pflichtaktie, Pflichtstück. See Dépôt d'Actions d'Administrateur.

Pflichtreserve. See Mindestreserve.

Phillips Curve. Professor Phillips posited the theory that workers get larger pay rises when the unemployment figure is low than when it is high. When labour is scarce employers bid higher for what labour there is; when labour is plentiful wage increases get smaller. The Phillips curve is a graphed line which shows these tendencies, and leads to the supposition that at a certain height of unemployment wage rises would theoretically cease altogether, while beyond that point wages would begin to fall. If this theory is correct then the way to deal with inflation caused by excessive wage demands is to allow unemployment to increase.

Piece Goods. Textile fabrics, e.g. shirtings, long cloths, etc., sold by recognised lengths of the material.

Piece Rates. Payment by results. The worker's wages depend upon the volume of production he attains.

Piggy Bank. A china model pig with a slot for money; a symbol of Victorian thrift—the forerunner of the home safe.

Pig on Pork. Bills drawn by one branch of a firm or company on another, or by one person or firm on another intimately connected, the implication being that the bills are not truly two-name bills.

Pilgrim's Receipts. Receipts issued in Saudi Arabia in exchange for cash to foreigners arriving for the annual Muslim "*Haj*" pilgrimage to Mecca and Medina. Before 1961, when banknotes were introduced by the Saudi Arabian Monetary Agency, the receipts formed, with silver riyals and gold coins, the only currency.

Placement. *See* Investment.

Placing. A private sale of a new issue to a limited number of investors, usually the big institutions, a proportion of the issue being allocated to the market to be available to the general public. *See also* Introduction; Offer for Sale.

Placing Broker. An insurance broker who places various percentages of a risk he is employed by a client to cover with various syndicates at Lloyd's.

Plaint. An accusation, a charge, a statement in writing of the complaint, etc.

Plaintiff. The one who sues in a court of law.

Plan d'Investissement. The systematic acquisition over a given period of unit or investment trust holdings by means of regular purchases up to a given amount. The investor remains free to cancel the plan at any time.

Planning Permission. *See* Change of User.

Plant. Fixed machinery, tools, etc., used in an industrial undertaking.

Plead. To allege in proof or vindication, to offer as an excuse, to argue at the bar, to carry on a law suit, to present any answer to the declarations of the plaintiff.

Pleader. One who pleads, especially a lawyer who makes a plea in a court of justice, an advocate.

Pleading. The art of conducting a case, as an advocate. *See also* Special Pleading.

Pleadings. Written statements of plaintiff and defendant in support of their claims.

Pledge. A delivery of goods, or the documents of title to goods, by a debtor to his creditors as security for a debt, or for any other obligation. It is understood that the subject of the pledge will be returned to the pledgor when the debt has been paid or the obligation fulfilled. For the purposes of the Consumer Credit Act 1974, "pledge" means the pawnee's rights over an article taken in pawn. *See also* Negative Pledge.

Pleno Jure. With full authority.

Plimsoll Mark. A line required to be placed on every British ship, marking the level to which the authorised weight of cargo sinks her.

Plus Value. Appreciation in price.

Poinding. Distraint, the impounding or the seizing and selling of a debtor's goods.

Point. An unit of measure of a rate or an index number; thus if a rate goes from 60 to 80, (whether per cent or in monetary terms), the increase in the rate is 20 points.

Points d'Intervention. See Intervention Rate.

Points d'Or. See Specie Points.

Policy. A document issued by an insurance company containing the terms and conditions of an insurance contract and which is legal evidence of the agreement to insure. *See also* Comprehensive Policy; E.C.G.D. Policy; Endowment Policy; Family Protection Policy; Floating Policy; General Policy; Industrial Policy; Joint Lives Policy; Life Policy; Lloyd's Policy; Mixed Policy; Named Policy; Non-Participating Policy; Open Policy; Paid-Up Policy; Short-Term Policy; Single Premium Policy; Survivorship Policy; Time Policy; Tontine Policy; Unit-Linked Policy; Valued Policy; Voyage Policy; Whole Life Policy; "With Profits" Policy.

Policy Holder. The person who has a policy in his possession or under his control, usually the insured.

Policy Underwriter. One who writes his name under a policy of marine insurance, thus undertaking to indemnify the insured against the risks specified in the policy; a member of an underwriting syndicate at Lloyd's.

Politique du Taux d'Escompte. The policy of the central bank in lowering or raising the official discount rate, thus influencing indirectly the other rates of interest in the money market and through them regulating the volume of credit in the economy.

Poll Tax. A capitation tax or one levied on each person.

Port Bill of Lading. A bill of lading bearing an authorised signature indicating that the goods covered have been received by the signatory at the port of shipment.

Portefeuille. See Portfolio.

Portfolio. The securities held by, or on behalf of, an investor; the list of such securities; the holdings of bills of exchange by banks or discount houses.

Portfolio Management Service. The management by a bank or financial institution of the quoted securities of a customer. This includes the safe-keeping of securities, dealing with scrip and rights issues, the collection of dividends and the preparation of valuations.

Portion. A part, a share, an allotment, a dowry, the part of an estate descending to an heir.

Port Register. *See* Register of Ships.

Position. State, situation; the balance on a running account, etc.

Possession. The act or state of possessing, holding or occupying as owner; the exercise of such control as attaches to ownership, actual detention or occupancy; property, goods, wealth. Contrasted with ownership (having the legal right to) in cases where an equitable title is taken by way of security for a loan, the lender taking possession of the document of title to the security, while the owner retains its ownership. *See also* Writ of Possession. **In Possession.** In actual occupancy, holding. **To Give Possession.** To put another in possession. **To Take Possession.** To enter on, to seize.

Possessory Lien. The right to keep possession of the property of another until a debt due from the latter is paid. There is at common law no right of sale, thus the lien has nuisance value only. In some cases, however, a right of sale is given by some statute.

Possessory Title. The title acquired by a person who has been in the undisputed possession of real property for a period of twelve or more years, not having paid any rent in that time nor acknowledged the right or claim of any other to that land. In registered land, the title granted by the Registrar in cases where the deeds when examined showed no more than that the applicant was in possession of the land. A purchaser or a mortgagee must therefore investigate the title prior to registration as thoroughly as if it were an unregistered title, for the State guarantee only refers to the period after issue of the certificate and not before. The Registrar has power to convert a possessory freehold title into an absolute freehold title after fifteen years, and to convert a possessory leasehold title into a good leasehold title after ten years.

Post. To advertise, to make known, to pass entries to an account; a postal letter-box, a dispatch of mails; a duty; a place of employment.

Postal Giro. A system of transferring money through the post offices of a country as an alternative to other systems of money transmission provided by either post offices or banks. Many European countries operate a postal giro. The British system was introduced in 1968. *See* National Giro.

Postal Order. An order for a sum of money, specified on the face of the instrument, issued to a customer at one post office for payment at another. This is not a negotiable instrument. It may be paid into the credit of a customer's account at a bank. At the end of the day the bank will list all the postal orders received, total them, and claim the amount from a local post office.

Postdate. To date after the day of issue. On cheques postdating may be the intention of the drawer in isolated cases, but if it happens frequently it is a sign of financial weakness on the customer's part. Banks are bound to respect the drawer's instruction not to pay a postdated cheque until the due date, but they strongly discourage the practice of postdating because it holds many risks for the banker. If the banker pays the cheque without noticing the postdating, he runs the following risks; the customer may stop payment before the due date, or notice of his death or mental illness may be received. There are a number of possibilities connected with bankruptcy. Notice of an act of bankruptcy committed by the customer would restrict the banker to paying cheques only to the customer himself; notice of a petition or receiving order against the customer would stop all payments. If the customer is a limited company the corresponding notice would be notice of a resolution to wind up, or a winding-up order. There may be notice that the customer is an undischarged bankrupt, when again the account would have to be stopped. There may be service of a garnishee order or summons. But most of these, though real risks, are unlikely ones: in practice the most likely danger is that of a stop being received, the next most likely, that payment of a postdated cheque may result in another cheque which ought to have been paid being returned for lack of funds, resulting in a possible action by the customer against the bank for breach of contract, or libel, or both.

Legally, however, a bill is not invalid by reason only that it is postdated.

Postes Correctifs. Correcting entries.

Postlaufkredit. Credit granted on very short terms such as one to two days, *i.e.* the time necessary for a customer to effect repayment by return of post.

Postnumerando. Coming after, following.

Post Obit. Bond. A bond in which a person agrees to pay a certain sum of money after the death of another.

Post Office Register. *See* Director of Savings.

Pound. The British money of account consisting of one hundred pence, a sovereign, written £.

Poundage. Commission, allowance or charge of so much in the pound.

Pound Cost Averaging. Where stock or shares are bought in instalments over a period at varying prices, an average cost price will be established (as with unit-trust linked life assurance policies). The lower this average price, the higher the ultimate profit is likely to be when the securities are sold.

Pound Sterling. The British standard pound of one hundred pence as a gold coin or a paper note.

Poursuite pour Effets de Change. The aggravating effect upon the position of a debtor in danger of being made bankrupt of an unpaid bill of exchange or cheque appearing against his name in the *Registre du Commerce.*

Power of Attorney. A legal document empowering one person to act for another, either generally or for some specific transaction. The power is usually under seal, and must describe precisely the extent of the authority of the agent. It may be for a fixed period of time. A trustee may by power of attorney delegate for a period not exceeding twelve months the execution or exercise of all or any of the trusts, powers and discretions vested in him either alone or jointly with another or others. Such delegation may not be made to his only other co-trustee (unless a trust corporation). The instrument of delegation must be witnessed. The donor of the power is liable for the acts or defaults of the donee. An Irrevocable Power of Attorney is one so expressed to be, and which is given to secure a proprietary interest of the donee of the power, or the performance of an obligation owed to the donee. So long as the donee has that interest, or the obligation remains undischarged, the power cannot be revoked by the donor without the consent of the donee; nor by the death, incapacity or bankruptcy of the donor nor, if the donor is a body corporate, by its winding-up or dissolution.

Power of Attorney Clause. A clause in an equitable mortgage of land by means of which the lending banker can obtain a legal title as a preliminary to sale of the security, in cases where the customer has failed to repay and has also failed to keep his promise to sign any documents which the bank may require him to sign (where such a clause has also been incorporated in the form of mortgage). The power of attorney clause may run as follows: "I hereby irrevocably appoint any one of the Controllers of the Bank to be my attorney, and in my name and on my behalf to sign, seal, or otherwise perfect any deed for conveying the freehold estate in the mortgage property to any purchaser thereof". A suitable conveyance to the bank as mortgagee (a term included in "purchaser") by the attorney will pass the title to the bank, after which the property can be sold and the indebtedness repaid. Because land must be conveyed under seal, any attorney expected to convey land must be appointed under seal. The Deed of Appointment in this case is the bank's form of equitable mortgage, which must therefore be under seal for this reason.

Power of Sale. A bank, if it is to realise its security should the necessity arise, must be able to sell it. Where the legal interest has been transferred into the name of the bank's nominee company, no difficulty exists, for the bank is the owner, and an owner can sell. Where an equitable mortgage only has been taken the customer retains the ownership. Because of this the equitable mortgage form contains a clause by which the customer is obliged to promise to sign any papers as desired by the bank in order to realise the security. If the customer will not keep his promise the remedy must be sought in the courts. The bank will usually ask for an order to sell or an order for transfer and foreclosure and if this is granted the bank will be able to deal with the security. An alternative to the recourse to the court is to take a blank undated signed form of transfer before the money is lent. This can be filled in later, if required, and does not need the co-operation of the customer. However, because the date of a deed is the day on which it was delivered this method cannot be used where the transfer has to be executed under seal. In the case of land the legal mortgagee has a statutory or express power of sale on default. If the mortgage is equitable only, application to the court for an order for sale is again necessary.

Powers of Mortgagee. The legal mortgagee may on default by the borrower enter into possession of the property, apply to the court for an order of foreclosure, sell the property, appoint a receiver of rents, or sue the debtor on his personal covenant to repay. (The last of these remedies is appropriate where the lender is only partly secured and wishes to obtain judgment so as to issue a bankruptcy order or levy execution.) The banker seeking to exercise his rights will in practice either sell the property or appoint a receiver. An equitable mortgagee has only the right to sue on the covenant to repay, or to apply to the court for an order of foreclosure.

Prämienanleihe. See *Losanleihe*.

Prämiengeschäft. Speculative business on the stock exchange in which an operator pays an agreed sum to acquire the right to withdraw from a bargain, if he so later decides.

Prämiensparen. Bank savings accounts on which, through the observance of certain conditions, an additional premium is paid over and above the interest due.

Pränumerando. Prior to, before.

Präsentationsfrist. A customary period of time for the payment of valuable paper; in the case of bills of exchange, up to acceptance and payment.

Precatory Trust. A trust which arises from a construction of words of supplication or entreaty, which are interpreted to show that the donor intended to impose a trust.

Precept. A command, an injunction respecting conduct, a mandate, a writ or warrant, an order directing a payment to be made.

Pre-Emption. A right to buy, or the act of buying, before others; the right of a vendor in certain cases to buy back land which he has had to sell under the terms of some statute, *e.g.* where the land has been forcibly purchased in the national interest, and is subsequently found not to be required.

Pre-Emptive Bid. A very high bid, as for the shares of another company in an attempted take-over bid, to shut out opposition; or similarly at a public auction.

Preference. The act of favouring one person or thing before another or others. See also Fraudulent Preference.

Preference Shares. Those shares carrying a fixed rate of interest, provided for in the company's Articles of Association. Such shares are to receive their interest before any other payments out are made. If, therefore, in any one year the profits made are only just enough to pay the preference shareholders, no other class of shareholder will receive anything.

Preferential Creditor. One who in a winding-up, or in a bankruptcy, is entitled to settlement of his debts before ordinary creditors receive anything. See Order of Payment of Debts in Bankruptcy.

Preferential Wages Account. See Wages and Salaries Account.

Pre-Finance Bill. A bill drawn under a pre-finance credit. See Documentary Credit.

Pre-Finance Credit. A credit which provides for finance to be made available on certain conditions to the exporter before the goods are actually shipped. Such a credit may also be known as an Anticipatory Credit or a Pre-Shipment Credit. It is used in the case of some primary commodities from certain countries. See also Red Seause; Green Seause.

Preis. Price. See also *Einzelhandelspreis*; *Grosshandelspreis*; *Handelspreis*; *Mindestpreis*.

Preisbindung der Zweiten Hand. See Resale Price Maintenance.

Preisnotierung. Quotation.

Preisverdienst-Relation. Price–earnings ratio.

Premium. A recompense, a prize, a bounty; a fee paid to learn a profession or trade; the amount exceeding the par value of shares or stock; the periodical instalment paid for insurance. **At a Premium.** Above par, in great demand. **To Put a Premium on.** To act as an incentive to.

Premium Bond. An acknowledgment by a foreign state of a debt on which interest may not be paid, but which offers a chance to the investor to get a large prize by maintaining regular drawings.

Premium Bonus. A term applied to any system whereby a worker is paid according to his output in a given time, but receives an additional payment if his output exceeds a certain standard.

Premium Savings Bonds. Bonds issued in £1 units in the U.K. which offer no interest but carry the chance for the investor of winning a large prize. The maximum holding for any one individual is £3,000: they are sold in multiples of 5 × £1 units. A bond must be held for three months before it qualifies for the draw. Draws are held weekly and monthly.

Premium Stripping. Making an illegal profit by breaking the exchange control regulations relating to the payment of the dollar premium on the remittance from abroad of the proceeds from the sale of assets such as shares or property. The dollar premium is the extra money one must pay for currency to buy shares or property abroad. (Whatever the actual currency required may be, the premium is payable in dollars. It is a deterrent to discourage buyers.) If and when these assets are resold, only 75% of the premium is repaid, the authorities keeping the other 25%. If stock, etc., is bought abroad without "going through the premium" and is then sold, the money coming into this country being converted at the current rate of exchange would not attract the return of the 75% premium. If, however, the stock were wrongly represented as having been purchased with investment currency (*i.e.* as being "premium stock") such a return would be made. "Premium stripping", therefore, is representing foreign currency securities as eligible for the investment currency premium when in fact they do not so qualify.

Preneur. A beneficiary.

Prepay. To pay in advance, as by affixing a postage stamp to a telegraph form, to be sent to someone for completion and speedy reply (as in some special clearances).

Prerogative. An exclusive right or privilege vested in a particular person or body of persons, especially a sovereign, by virtue of his position or relationship; any peculiar right, option, privilege, natural advantage, etc.

Prerogative Orders. Orders, formerly writs based upon the principles of natural justice, devised to protect the rights of the subject against abuse of excess of power by public authorities, government departments, tribunals, courts or individuals. All are discretionary. *See also Certiorari*; *Mandamus*; Prohibition.

Prescription. (*Fr.*) The delay in time after which a right cannot be enforced by legal action. *See* Limitation of Actions. More generally, a modification of a right caused by the effluxion of time.

Present. Here or at hand; writings or documents; the offer of a bill for acceptance or payment.

Presentment. The act or state of presenting, representation, delineation, the laying of a formal statement before a court or an authority; notice taken by a grand jury of an offence from their own knowledge or observation.

Presentment for Acceptance. It is usual to leave a bill with the drawee for twenty-four hours for his acceptance, which should be obtained as soon after the drawing of the bill as possible. If the bill is payable after sight, presentment for acceptance is necessary in order to fix the date of payment. If the bill stipulates it be presented for acceptance, or where a bill is drawn payable elsewhere than at the residence or place of business of the drawee, it must be presented for acceptance before it can be presented for payment. The presentment must be made by or on behalf of the holder to the drawee or someone authorised to accept or refuse payment on his behalf at a reasonable hour on a business day and before the bill is overdue.

Presentment for Payment. If a bill is not duly presented for payment on the date it falls due, the drawer and indorsers are relieved from their responsibilities on the bill. A bill if on demand is "duly presented" if presented within a reasonable time after its issue (to keep the drawer liable) and, if it has been indorsed, within a reasonable time after its indorsement (to keep the indorser liable). Presentment must be made by the holder or by some person authorised to receive payment on his behalf at a reasonable hour on a business day, at the proper place, to some person authorised to deal with it. If a place of payment is specified in the bill, that is the "proper place"; if not, but if the address of the drawee or acceptor is given in the bill, then that address is the proper place; if neither, then the bill should be presented at the drawee's or acceptor's place of business, if known, or otherwise at his ordinary address. A cheque must be presented for payment within a reasonable time. *See also* Antedated Cheque; Overdue Bill. A promissory note, where payable on demand and indorsed, must be presented within a reasonable time of the indorsement (to keep the indorser liable). Where the note is in the body of it made payable at a particular place, it must be presented for payment at that place in order to render the maker liable. In any other case presentment for payment is not necessary to render the maker liable, but it is necessary to render the indorser liable.

Present Value. (1) The sum which will be paid now by a discounting bank for a bill of exchange at a term. This is found by deducting discount rate for the term from the face value of the bill. (2) One method of finding the value now of a series of payments, such as annuity or pension payments, due to be made at regular intervals. (3) The calculation of the value now of a deferred payment taking compound interest on the sum to be paid.

Pre-Shipment Credit. *See* Pre-Finance Credit.

Président. Chairman.

Président Directeur Générale. Chairman and Managing Director.

Presumption. The act of, or grounds for, taking something for granted; a strong probability.

Presumption of Fact. An inference as to a fact from facts already known.

Presumption of Law. Assumption of the truth of a proposition until the contrary is proved; an inference established by law as universally applicable to particular circumstances.

Presumption of Survivorship. In the law of succession where two people die in circumstances which make it impossible to say who died first, the presumption that the elder died first.

Presumption of Value. Every party whose signature appears on a bill of exchange is *prima facie* deemed to have become a party thereto for value.

Presumptive Evidence. Evidence derived from circumstances which necessarily or usually attend a fact.

Prêt. A loan; an advance of a certain amount for a certain time.

Prévision. Forecast.

Price. The amount at which a thing is valued, bought or sold; value, cost.

Price Consumption Curve. A graph showing the changes in the consumption of a commodity with price changes, assuming that consumer income remains constant.

Price Control (Price Fixing). A limit, usually an upper limit, set on prices by government or a price ring. Price control by government is usually a prominent political factor where trade unions are in negotiation with government, the latter desiring to restrain wage increases, the former demanding price control. A maximum price fixed by the state is to protect consumers against high prices and must be fixed below a "free" price level, or equilibrium. This may entail rationing, as in the case of goods and food in war-time or, more recently, petrol. A minimum price fixed by the state is to protect producers, *e.g.* farmers.

Price Discrimination. The charging of different prices to different groups of customers for the same product or service, *i.e.*, where a bank charges companies full rate on the conduct of their current accounts, but charges nominal rates only to a staff group of a very large customer, this is price discrimination. In the past this has been described as "charging what the traffic will bear"; a similar but more recent pronouncement has been that charges are "subject to negotiation". Other examples are railway cheap day fares, electricity off-peak rates, summer coal prices, etc.

Price/Earnings Ratio. A method of arriving at the relative price of shares offered for sale to the public. Net earnings per share are found by dividing the profit after taxation by the number of issued shares. This figure is then divided into the current market price of the shares (usually the middle price) and gives the price/earnings ratio.

Price Fixing. *See* Price Control.

Prima Facie. On the first view, on the first impression, at first sight.

Prima Facie **Check of Deeds.** (1) Check the deeds and documents against the schedule that accompanies them, to make sure that they are all there; (2) check that there is a good root of title, at least fifteen years old; (3) check that there is a good chain of title from the good root to the holding deed; (4) check that the holding deed is in the name of the borrowing customer.

Primage. A percentage on the freight, originally paid to the master of the ship, now retained by the ship owners, for care in looking after goods and in loading and unloading them.

Primary Period. *See under* Finance Lease.

Primary Risks. In some E.E.C. countries banking risks are graded into *Primary* (high risk lending or investment), *Secondary* (average risk) and *Tertiary* (low risk).

Prime. Original, foremost, first in degree or importance.

Prime. (*Fr.*) *See* Premium.

Prime Bank Bill. *See* Fine Bank Bill.

Prime Costs. Those direct items of cost which enter into and form part of the product; those costs which are primarily and directly connected with it, *e.g.* materials, wages, expenses, and long-term administrative costs. Also known as Direct Costs, or First Costs.

Prime Credit. *See* Countervailing Credit.

Prime Entry. An entry made from particulars given on another document, such as a bill of lading or invoice; a first entry made from a source of information.

Prime Rate. The American term for Bank Rate; the discount rate for prime bills.

Primo. In the first place.

Primogeniture. Seniority by birth amongst children of the same parents; the right, system or rule by which the eldest son succeeds to the real estate of his father or mother where there was no will. Heirship was abolished in 1925.

Primus inter Pares. The first among equals.

Principal. Chief, leading, main; constituting the capital sum invested, as distinguished from income; the chief actor in a crime; a chief debtor; a person for whom another is an agent.

Principal's Mandate. The document embodying the duties of an agent. Each power delegated must be clearly described. A third party should for his own protection ascertain the extent of the agent's powers by studying the mandate carefully: the principal will not be bound where the agent has exceeded his powers. *See also* Application Form for Delegation of Authority; Undisclosed Principal.

Prior. Previous, former, earlier, preceding in time.

Prior Charges. Any claims against a security which will prejudice the rights of the present lender. Thus before advancing against the security of a life policy the banker must enquire of the assurance company whether there are any prior charges. Such charges are regulated by the date order of receipt by the company. Priority of mortgages, whether legal or equitable, not protected by deposit of the title deeds is determined by the date of registration in the Land Charges Department. With registered land, charges rank for priority according to the order in which they are entered on the register. Mortgages other than registered charges made under seal may be protected by a caution in the register, and rank for priority according to the order in which the caution is entered in the register. A mortgage on a ship takes priority from the hour and the day on which the statutory form of mortgage is registered at the port of registry.

Prioritätsaktie. Preference share.

Priority Notice. A puisne mortgage or a general equitable charge, neither being supported by the deeds, require therefore protection by registration in the Land Charges Department. Such a mortgage or charge was, by section 13 of the Land Charges Act 1925, to be void against a purchaser of the land, unless it was registered before the completion of the purchase. "The completion" means the signing and delivery of the deed and until this is done the banker will not lend. If his search certificate, giving a clear title, was dated *before* the date of the mortgage deed, there was therefore a danger that after he had searched the Register another mortgage of the same land might have been registered in favour of someone else, the effect of which would have been to render his mortgage at the moment of its completion void against that other person. When this was appreciated corrective legislation in 1926 (Law of Property Amendment Act 1926, section 4, again amended by the Land Charge Rules 1940) removed the difficulty by providing that any person intending to apply for the registration of any contemplated charge might register notice of his intention at the Land Charges Department. This notice is called a priority notice. It must be given at least fourteen days before the registration is to take effect. When the contemplated charge is actually created and later registered, then, as long as it is lodged within fourteen days and registered within twenty-eight days after the priority notice, it takes effect as if registration had been contemporaneous with its creation. If the land is registered land the priority notice is sent to the Land Registry together with the relevant land certificate, and if the charge is sent for registration within the next fourteen days it will have priority over any other instrument which may have been received at the Land Registry in the meanwhile. In addition to the registers already mentioned, local registers are maintained by the various district and borough councils and county councils in which local land charges may be registered. On these registers also a priority notice may be registered where a local land charge is contemplated. Similar time limits are applicable.

Prise de Contrôle. Takeover.

Private. Not public, belonging to or concerning an individual, secret, not publicly known; not holding public office, confidential.

Private Act, Private Bill. One affecting a private person or persons and not the general public.

Private Bank. A banking firm in which the number of partners must not exceed twenty. Until 1967 the number was ten, but in that year the Companies Act 1967 allowed an increase to twenty persons if each is for the time being authorised by the Department of Trade to be such a partner. The liability of each partner for the debts of the partnership is unlimited.

Private Bill. *See* Private Act.

Private Company. One that does not invite the public to subscribe, limits the number of its members to fifty, and restricts their rights to transfer shares.

Private Company Shares. The shares of private companies are not good banking security and are taken for what they may be worth only when there is nothing else to be had. There is no public quotation and so it is difficult to ascertain their value. This can be worked out approximately from the balance sheets of the past three or four years and the dividends that have been paid, or the secretary of the company can be asked to certify the value. If any shares have changed hands recently, or if any have recently been valued for probate, the price given will be a guide. Again, private company shares may be virtually unsaleable. The articles of the company may restrict their transfer to existing directors or members of a family (so that control of the company cannot pass to an outsider).

Private Enterprise. A system of economics whereby private individuals can own property, run businesses and seek to make profits. Such productive enterprises are, however, subject to State control by way of laws of general application, and business profits of private enterprise are subject to tax.

Private Placing. *See* New Issue; Placing.

Private Treaty. A method of sale whereby the price of the thing to be sold is decided by bargaining between seller and buyer, as in the case of house property.

Private Trust. A trust which is enforced at the instance of beneficiaries, as opposed to a "public" or charitable trust which is generally enforced at the suit of the Attorney General acting on behalf of the Crown.

Privatplazierung. See Placing.

Privatsatz. The discount rate for first-class bills.

Privity of Contract. The relationship between parties to a contract. Only such people who are "privy" to a contract can normally be affected by it. Such a contract can bind only the parties to it, it cannot impose obligations on other people, nor confer rights upon them. In the law of leaseholds, privity of contract refers to that relationship which exists between lessor and lessee by virtue of the covenants contained in the lease. This relationship, springing from the contract itself, continues to exist despite any assignment of the respective interests. *"Privity of Estate"* refers to the relationship between the two parties who respectively hold the same estates as those created by the lease, as where one holds the original reversion and the other the residue of the original term. In banking there is privity of contract between the banker and his customer, but not, *e.g.*, between the banker and the person who sends him a status enquiry (unless that person also happens to be a customer). There is no duty of care as with the banking contract although there is a duty to reply carefully, truly and faithfully where such an enquiry is made in reliance on the banker's special knowledge of his customer. Liability may be disclaimed by a suitable clause in the reply.

Privity of Estate. The relationship between two parties who respectively hold the same estates as those created by a lease, *e.g.* lessor and lessee, lessor and assignee from the lessee, lessee and assignee of the reversion of the freehold estate. *See also* Privity of Contract.

Prix. Price.

Prix au Détail. Retail price.

Prix de Gros. Wholesale price.

Prix de Marché. Market price.

Prix Marchand. Trade price.

Prix Plafond. Reserve price.

Pro. For, before, in front of, on behalf of.

Probate. The process by which a last will and testament is legally authenticated after the testator's death; an official copy of a will.

Probation. The act of proving, proof; a trial or test of a person's character, conduct, ability, etc.; the testing of a candidate before admission to full membership of a body, etc.

Proceeds. The sum realised by a sale; produce, yield; the credit resulting from a foreign collection or negotiation.

Procès. A law suit, proceedings.

Process Costing. A method of costing applied to manufacturers according to the characteristics of the manufacturing process, *i.e.* that different though related products are produced simultaneously.

Procès-Verbal. A written statement of particulars relating to a charge; an official record of proceedings, minutes.

Procuration. Management of another's affairs; the instrument empowering a person to transact the affairs of another. *See also* Per Procurationem.

Procuration Écrite. See Power of Attorney.

Procuration Fee. The money paid for an agent who negotiates a loan.

Procuration Signature. *See* Per Procurationem.

Procurator. One who acts for another, especially in legal affairs, an agent.

Produce Advances. *See* Merchandise Advances.

Produce Broker. An agent engaged in buying or selling on a produce exchange.

Production. The manufacture of commodities and the provision of services; the changing of raw material into finished goods together with the distributory services or the training of staff to give good service to customers.

Produit National Brut (P.N.B.). Gross national product (G. N. P.).

Produktionsgütter. Goods which themselves assist in the production of further goods, *e.g.* machines, industrial equipment, etc.

Produktiver Kredit. See Betriebskredit.

Pro et Con. For and against.

Profit. That portion of the gains of an industry received by the capitalist or the investors; the excess of returns over expenditure; pecuniary gain in any transaction or occupation; emolument.

Profit and Loss. Gains credited and losses debited to an account so as to show the net profit or loss for the period concerned.

Profit and Loss Account. This account shows the gross profit made by a business together with unusual items of gain from sources other than normal trading—for example, a profit on the sale of land. On the debit side will occur the overhead and administrative charges incurred during the year. The balance on the account is the net profit, on which tax is charged. The profit and loss account is concerned with the distribution of goods.

Profit and Loss Appropriation Account. An account disclosing the allocation of the balance of the profit and loss account among dividends, transfers to reserves, etc.

Profit à Prendre. A right to take something off another's land, *e.g.* to pasture cattle on another's land, to take fish from another's river, or to take turf from another's estate.

Profit Sharing. A system of remuneration by which the workers in an industrial concern are apportioned a percentage of the profits in order to give them an interest in the business.

Pro-Forma. As a matter of form.

Pro-Forma Invoice. In foreign trade, both exporters and importers may use a sample specimen invoice of the goods to be consigned, the seller estimating a price from current rates and adding charges, commission and freight, thus informing himself of the total cost; the buyer using it to find out the current market price of the goods, cost of packing, discount, etc., thus arriving at the approximate cost of the proposed order.

Progressif, Progressiv. On an upward course, rising, going forward.

Progressive Tax. A system of taxation which follows the principle that the rate of taxation shall increase as income increases.

Prohibition. The act of forbidding, interdict; a prerogative order to prevent excess of jurisdiction by an inferior court, or by any public body or person exercising a public duty or exercising judicial or quasi-judicial powers. It will lie against the Crown, but not against domestic or private tribunals.

Prohibitory Injunction. *See* Injunction.

Project Finance. The arrangement from a variety of sources of the finance which will be required to appraise, set up, and begin to operate a large capital project. Such loans would normally be made by a syndicate of lending banks. The financial security for the loans made to the borrowing concern is often considered to be represented by future assured cash flows and is independent of third party guarantees.

Project Planning. A process whereby management, confronted by a number of possible solutions to a specific problem, considers each in turn before arriving at a decision.

Project Team. A team formed by temporary attachment from a variety of departments or specialisations, linked together by the need to meet a new statutory requirement (*e.g.* decimalisation) or to sell a new product or service. Such a team or working party may be required to make recommendations as to the best way in which to achieve the desired end, or may be given the authority and resources to carry the work through in all its stages.

Prolongation. (*Fr.*) An extension of time for a bill of exchange or a credit; on the *Bourse*, an extension of a contract until the next settlement.

Promesse. A written undertaking to deliver; a temporary share certificate; an I.O.U.

Promissory Note. An unconditional promise in writing made by one person to another, signed by the maker, engaging to pay, on demand or at a fixed or determinable future time, a sum certain in money to, or to the order of, a specified person or to bearer. A note payable to the maker's order must be indorsed by the maker. The note is inchoate and incomplete until completed by delivery to the payee or bearer. It is often used in the finance of foreign trade. A promissory note may be made by two or more makers, and they may be liable thereon jointly and severally, according to its tenor.

Promoter. One who, or that which, promotes, a supporter, an initiator, one who organises a new business venture, one who undertakes to form a new company and who does the necessary preliminary work to form or float it.

Promotion. Advancement, preferment, a higher rank; the advancement of a business interest by advertisement or exhortation.

Promotion Money. Money paid to the first board of directors of a new limited company for their efforts in floating the company. The money is found from the subscriptions of shareholders, and the sum involved must be disclosed in the prospectus.

Proof. A test or trial; any process to ascertain correctness, truth or facts; demonstration; a trial impression of a printed work; trial before a judge alone instead of a jury; designating a certain standard or quality; the balancing of a day's work. In bankruptcy, affidavits by creditors of the claims they are making against the bankrupt's estate. (The Insolvency Act 1976 has done away with the need for affidavits unless the Official Receiver or the Trustee insists.)

Proofing Machine. A machine which lists and details all debits and credits in a day's work in a branch bank and at the same time provides detailed lists of the cheques to be remitted for payment under the headings of the other banks and branches concerned, thus saving a separate machining of these items at the end of the day's work.

Proof of Death. Production of a death or burial certificate, or of probate or letters of administration.

Property. Peculiar or inherent character, nature, that which is owned; a possession, an estate, ownership; anything yielding an income to the owner. *See also* Personal Property; Real Property.

Property Premium. The excess payment required over the market rate for currency used in purchasing property abroad. Such transactions must be authorised by the Bank of England and paid for in investment currency.

Property Register. *See* Land Certificate.

Proportion. Relative size, number or degree; comparison, relation, equal or just share; in the Bank of England Return, the relationship of notes and coins to the total assets of the Banking Department.

Proposal. An approach to a life assurance company by a person who wishes to take out life assurance cover, an offer which may be accepted or rejected by the company on the basis of the information set out on the proposal form.

Proprietary. Belonging or pertaining to an owner; made and sold by a firm or individual having the exclusive rights of manufacture and sale.

Proprietary Company. A parent company owning a quantity of land suitable for mining, etc., which it lets out to other interested companies on a joint proprietorship basis, all profits to be equally divided.

Proprietor. One who is the owner of property; the owner of registered land.

Proprietorship Register. *See* Land Certificate.

Proprietor's Stake. The fixed capital of a business, including the paid-up capital, the reserves, and the balance of the profit and loss account. The total of all these sums is the proprietor's stake in the business. All this money must be lost before the sums due to creditors become endangered. A comparison between the proprietor's stake and the remaining liabilities should therefore disclose a reasonable position which will ensure a kind of "buffer" for the creditors.

Pro Rata. In proportion.

Pro Rata Temporis (p.r.t.). In proportion to time elapsed.

Pro-Ratazins. See Ratazins.

Prorogation. (Fr.) In the case of an option contract for a term, the waiting period for the holders of the option to decide whether to close the contract, or retire from it on payment of the premium due; the postponement of payment of a credit.

Prospectus. A circular or pamphlet outlining the main features of a proposed commercial undertaking, especially a new company. In the U.K. the prospectus for a new limited company is regulated closely by the Companies Act 1948, which details the information to be included in a prospectus which offers shares in the company to the public. The prospectus must also comply with the requirements of the Stock Exchange.

Prospekt. See Prospectus.

Prospekthaftung. The liability of all taking part in the flotation of a new issue for loss or damage caused as a result of incorrect statements in the prospectus, or of any failure to comply with legal requirements.

Pro Tanto. For so much, to that extent.

Protection. (Fr.) An undertaking given by a managing bank during the selling period of a new issue to one or more banks in the selling group that they will receive specified allotments in full.

Protection of Depositors. An Act of 1963 under this name was designed principally to control advertising for deposits. A financial institution calling itself a "bank" and advertising for deposits was required to comply with certain regulations laid down by the Department of Trade before being allowed to advertise, the advertisement itself had to be acceptable to the Department, and up-to-date accounts had to be provided for both the Department and for depositors. Fresh regulations came into force on 1 February 1977, as a result of the comments of the Department of Trade inspectors inquirying into the London and County Securities crash. These call for more detailed information, especially on loans to directors and their associates, loans to associated companies, deposits and other loans to the company and instalment credit agreements made by the company. The regulations do not apply to trustee savings banks, building societies, friendly societies, industrial and provident societies, nor to the banking or discount companies recognised as such for the purposes of the Protection of Depositors Act 1963. A White Paper, published in August 1976, provided for a deposit protection scheme to be instituted and administered by the Bank of England. This will take the form of deposit insurance. (Deposit insurance involves banks paying a form of premium to a central fund whose resources would be used to repay depositors if they were in danger of losing their money on the failure of a bank.) The only detail arranged so far is that the scheme, when it is finalised, shall relate to sterling deposits up to £10,000 (or to the first £10,000 of larger deposits) with all licensed deposit-takers and recognised banks. Contributions to the fund will be obligatory on both types of licensed deposit-taking institutions. *See also* Supervision of Banks.

Protective Trust. A provision in a trust instrument that the beneficiary shall no longer receive the income if, for any reason, he would be deprived of the right to receive it. In a settlement on marriage, for example, where the wife has provided the trust property, the wife may be indicated as the first beneficiary during her life, after which the income may pass to the husband for his life, if he survives her. To guard against his possible extravagance or misfortune, a protective trust may be attached by which the husband is given, not a life interest, but an interest which would cease if he became bankrupt. In such a case the income would be held by the trustees for others, probably the children of the marriage, if any. Without such a protective trust the income would pass to the creditors of the husband. A similar clause may operate if he attempts to alienate or charge the income.

Pro Tempore (Pro Tem.). For the time being.

Protest. To make a solemn affirmation; to make a formal declaration against some act or proposition; to make a formal declaration, usually by a notary public, that acceptance or payment of a bill of exchange has been demanded and refused (*see* Certificate of Protest); a written declaration by the master of a ship, usually before a magistrate, assessor or consul, stating the circumstances attending an injury or loss of a ship or its cargo. *See also* Formal Protest; Householder's Protest.

Protest. *See* Protest.

Prôtet Faute d'Acceptation. Protest for non-acceptance.

Prôtet Faute de Paiement. Protest for non-payment.

Provision. A measure taken beforehand; an amount retained to provide for depreciation; a sum retained to offset against a bad or doubtful debt; a sum of money set on one side to meet a known payment which has to be made, *e.g.* payment of pensions to retired staff.

Provision. (*Fr.*) A bank deposit on which the bank allows the account holder to draw cheques; an amount carried to the liabilities side of the balance sheet by a debit to profit and loss account to provide for a future acquisition or probable loss.

Provision. (*Ger.*) *See* Commission.

Provisional Certificate. A certificate issued for new shares to evidence ownership until the definitive certificate is ready; a scrip certificate issued to a bond purchaser during the payment of instalments of purchase money.

Provisions. The articles of an instrument or statute.

Proviso. A condition or stipulation in a deed or contract; a special enactment in a statute; a clause in a covenant or other document rendering its operation conditional, *e.g.* a proviso in a lease for re-entry and forfeiture in case of a breach of a covenant, or a proviso for forfeiture in case of bankruptcy.

Proximate Damage. Damage which arises naturally from a breach of contract, or damage of an extraordinary nature where it is shown that the parties did in fact contemplate its possibility. In either case compensation may be awarded.

Proxy. The agency of a substitute for a principal; one deputed to act for another, especially in voting; a document authorising one person to act or vote for another; a vote given under this authority.

Prudential Ratios. The ratios by which the banks ensure that their business is conducted cautiously and judiciously: in particular, the ratio between a bank's capital resources and its total deposit liabilities (the *solvency ratio*); the various ratios of capital adequacy and liquidity. The onset of inflation, by increasing the figure of deposits, has lowered the solvency ratio. This can be restored by raising new equity capital through a rights issue, which has to be carefully timed, or by borrowing on the Euromarket, or by increasing charges and widening the difference between their lending and deposit interest rates. (This last device does not have any direct effect but it has the effect of increasing profits and, therefore, the amount that can be retained in the business.)

Public. Pertaining to the people as a whole, open to general use; the community or its members.

Public Act, Public Bill. One involving the interests of the community.

Public Company. A company that offers its shares to the public for subscription.

Public Enterprise. Economic activity undertaken by the central government, *e.g.* nationalised industries, or by local authorities, *e.g.* provision of a water supply.

Public Funds. Debts owing by the government; government stock and public securities; the National Debt.

Public Issue. An issue of shares publicly offered to investors.

Public Law. International Law.

Public Relations. The relations of an organisation or authority with the general public.

Public Relations officer. One who is employed in the distribution of information to the public, whose duty is to represent the aims, policies and achievements of the organisation by whom he is employed in the most favourable light possible.

Public Trust. *See* Charitable Trust.

Public Trustee. A trust corporation set up by the Public Trustee Act 1906, with the object of providing for members of the public stability, continuity and responsibility. Since that date many big banks and insurance companies also established trust corporations, so that the Public Trustee no longer enjoys a monopoly of such services. The Public Trustee may act as an executor or administrator of estates, as a trustee, and as an administrator of small estates of negligible value: the Public Trustee is obliged to take on the unprofitable estates which no one else wants to handle. *See also* Custodian Trustee; Trust Corporation.

Public Utilities. Enterprises ensuring certain public services such as gas, water, electricity, telephone, telegraph; on the Stock Exchange, the shares of such concerns.

Public Works Loan Board. A governmental body set up for the purpose of making loans to local authorities, particularly the smaller authorities which might experience difficulties in raising the money required on the capital market. The lender of last resort for local authorities.

Puisne Mortgage. A legal mortgage not protected by deposit of the title deeds. It should be registered at the Land Charges Department as a land charge, Class C (i). *See also* Land Charges Registration.

Punitive Damages. *See* Exemplary Damages.

Punkt. Point, unit of a quotation.

Pupil. In Scotland, a child up to the age of fourteen, (in the case of males) or twelve (in the case of females).

Pur Autre Vie. *See* Estate for Life.

Purchase. To buy, to obtain by any outlay of labour, time, sacrifice, etc., to obtain by any means other than inheritance; value or worth.

Purchaser. The one who buys. In land law, a purchaser of real or leasehold property in good faith and for valuable consideration. The term includes a lessee, mortgagee or other person who for valuable consideration acquires an interest in property, such as a lending banker.

Purchase Tax. A percentage tax added to the retail price of certain articles.

Purchasing Power Parity. The theory

that when exchange rates are free to fluctuate they will be determined by the relative purchasing power of the currencies in their home markets.

Pursuer. Scots law term for *Plaintiff.*
Put Option. *See* Option.
Put and Call Option. *See* Option.
Put of More Option. *See* Option.

Q

Qua. As, in the capacity of.

Qualified. Invested with the requisite qualities; modified, limited.

Qualified Acceptance. One which in express terms varies the effect of the bill as drawn. A qualified acceptance is one which is conditional, partial, local, qualified as to time or is the acceptance of some one or more of drawees, but not of all. A *Conditional Acceptance* makes payment by the acceptor dependent on the fulfilment of a condition therein stated. A *Partial Acceptance* is one to pay part only of the amount for which the bill is drawn. A *Local Acceptance* is one to pay only at a particular specified place. It must expressly state that the bill is to be paid there and there only.

Qualified Indorsement. An indorsement where an indorser has added after his signature an express stipulation (1) negativing or limiting his own liability to the holder (*e.g.* "*Sans recours*"); (2) waiving as regards himself some or all of the holder's duties.

Qualified Title. A type of title met with in registered land, given by the Land Registrar in cases where title can be established only for a limited period, or subject to certain reservations. It is very rare.

Qualitative Directives. Directives from the Bank of England to the lending banks and financial institutions as to classes of customers who may be allowed to borrow. *See also* Competition and Credit Control.

Quality Certificate. A certificate that goods are of a required standard, issued by a third party after an inspection.

Quality Control. Periodic checks at various intervals to ensure that the quality of a product is maintained, as where bank inspectors visit branches at regular intervals to check that the branch is properly run and that the customers are getting proper service.

Quantitative Directives. Directives from the Bank of England to the lending banks and financial institutions as to the total amount of money which they may lend. *See also* Competition and Credit Control.

Quantity Rebate. A discount or reduction of price on the purchase of a large number or quantity of a product.

Quantity Theory of Money. Basically, the economic theory that the more money printed, the less its value in terms of goods and services (*i.e.* prices go up). This basic theory is modified by taking into consideration the factors of velocity of circulation and the volume of production. The theory is expressed as $MV = PT$, where M is the quantity of money, V is the velocity of its circulation, P the general level of prices, and T the total of all transactions financed by money.

Quantum Meruit. An amount earned. The name of an action brought under the terms of a contract which has been broken. The aggrieved party may sue upon a *quantum meruit* for the amount earned by the services he has performed, as an alternative to claiming damages. It is also a way of recovering a reasonable return where one party has performed his duties, or some of them, under a contract for which no specific remuneration has been agreed.

Quantum Valeat. So much as it may be worth.

Quartalsdividende. *See* Abschlagsdividende.

Quarter Days. *In England*; Lady Day, March 25th; Midsummer Day, June 24th; Michaelmas, September 29th; Christmas Day, December 25th.

In Scotland; Candlemas, February 2nd; Whitsunday, May 15th; Lammas, August 1st; Martinmas, November 11th.

Quarterly Bulletin. A publication of the Bank of England available in March, June, September and December of each year, which gives economic commentaries, financial reviews, information about credit control, savings, foreign exchange markets, policy decisions, and various tables of statistics.

Quasi-. Apparent, seeming, not real.

Quasi-Money. *See* Near Money.

Quasi-Negotiable Instrument. A document which contains some but not all of the characteristics of a negotiable instrument. Thus a bill of lading can transfer title by indorsement and delivery, the transferee acquiring the right to one in his own name. But it cannot transcend any lack or defect of title in the transferor, so that in such a case the transferee, although for value and in good faith, does not obtain a good and indefeasible title.

Quasi-Partner. One who is not a partner, but has acted in such as way as to make people think he is. Under the doctrine of "holding out" he may be estopped by his conduct from denying that he is a partner, and may consequently be held responsible for some or all of the firm's debts.

Quasi-Rent. A term used for the rent of any property other than land, *e.g.* as in the case of the leasing of a capital asset to a manufacturing company by a finance company.

Quayage. A charge for the use of a berth alongside a quay.

Queen. *See* Sovereign.

Quellensteuer. Tax at source.

Quick Assets. Assets which can be converted into cash quickly and easily. *See* Liquid Assets.

Quid pro quo. Something for something, a mutual consideration, an equivalent.

Quit Rent. A rent formerly paid to the lord of the manor in lieu of service. It was abolished in 1925.

Quittance. Discharge from a debt or obligation, acquittance, receipt, requital, repayment.

Quitting. A written receipt.

Quod Vide (q.v.). Which see.

Quorum. The number of persons who must be present at a meeting before any official business can be done. Thus in the case of a company its Articles of Association may state that in a meeting of directors the quorum is three. A certain number of members must also attend a company general meeting.

Quota. A proportionate share or part: an allowance which must not be exceeded. In an economic context, used to refer to a restriction on imports. A quota is imposed to protect a particular home industry or, if imposed generally, to protect scarce supplies of foreign currency and to influence the balance of trade in favour of the importing country. If every country imposed protective quotas world trade would be damaged severely. Quotas are not, therefore, generally approved.

Quotation. A stated price at which a person is prepared to do some work or provide a service; a price of shares on the London Stock Exchange as reported in the financial press. For the purposes of the Consumer Credit Act 1974, any document issued by a person who carries on a consumer credit business or a consumer hire business, which gives prospective customers information about the terms on which he is prepared to do business.

Quotations Committee. The committee appointed by the Stock Exchange to decide the conditions on which an official price quotation can be granted to a company, and to consider such applications and to decide upon them.

Quote. (*Ger.*) *See* Quota.

Quoted Company. A company whose shares are quoted on the Stock Exchange.

Quotenaktie. Share of no par value.

Quotes. Prices, being selling and buying rates of exchange, or bid and offered rates of interest given by brokers or dealers, to customers or other enquiring parties in the market.

Quotidian, *Quotidien.* Daily.

R

Rabais. A reduction in price, usually expressed as a percentage of the purchase price.
Rabatt. Discount, rebate.
Rachet. Redemption.
Rack Rent. A rent, once considered exorbitant, which is equal to the full annual value of the property; a rent which has been stretched until it is the most that is obtainable.
Radiation System. A method by which a bank can circulate an urgent message quickly among its branches. The message is first telephoned to a number of key branches, each of which has lists of other branches to whom the message must be passed on. In this way the message "radiates" through the entire branch network of the bank.
Rahmenkredit. An agreement for credit up to a given maximum amount for the financing of many types of export business, normally handled by a bank consortium of the exporting country in conjunction with the government or the central bank of the importing country. Because of favourable conditions relating to the credit and repayment terms it is suitable for the supply of long-term capital, investment goods and equipment to the developing countries.
Railway Consignment Note. *See* Consignment Note.
Rally. To recover, a recovery, as in the price of a commodity, or of stocks and shares on the market.
Rapport. Yield, profit, ratio.
Rapport Cours/Bénéfices. *See* Price/Earnings Ratio.
Ratazins. A general term indicating interim interest or interim rates.
Rate. Degree, standard, proportion, value, price; to estimate, to assess, to calculate, to appraise. *See also* Cheque Rate; Intervention Rate; Long Rate; Short Rate.
Rateable Value. Assessment of local rates is on property-owners. Each house, shop, etc., is assessed for its value in relation to the rent which it can command, the rating figure being fixed at so many pence in the pound, that some proportion of the rateable value being payable in two six-monthly instalments.
Ratenkauf. *See* Abzahlungskauf.
Rate of Exchange. *See* Parities.
Rate of Interest. Payment for the use of borrowed money, the rate charged varying with the degree of risk run by the lender. Interest rates in large British banks are fixed by reference to a base rate, which varies as the bank thinks fit. Interest is allowed on the deposit accounts, savings accounts and by some banks on current accounts. Interest at a notional rate is allowed on credit balances against charges on current account. Building societies allow interest on deposits made with them and charge interest on mortgages granted by them, the difference between the rates giving a "turn" in favour of the institution.
Rate of Return. A means of calculation of the profit expected from an item of capital investment, based on the relationship of its likely profit figure with its original cost.
Rate of Turnover. The number of times the value of an average stock figure is sold in a given trading period.
Ratification. Confirmation, making valid; official approval of an action taken unofficially, as when a branch manager in an emergency grants a loan in excess of his discretionary limits, and later has it approved or ratified by higher authority. In agency, an agent who has concluded a contract with a third party, acting in excess of his powers in so doing, may have the contract ratified by his principal, who thereupon becomes liable upon it. The ratification dates back to the contract.
Ratio. Relation between.
Ratio Decidendi. The main legal principle which forms the core of a case.
Rationalisation. The unification of control in business, industry and commerce for buying, producing, and distributing goods or services, to secure greater efficiency and profits.
Ratios. *See* Balance Sheet Ratios; Prudential Ratios.
Raw Materials. Primary products form-

ing the basis of industrial manufacture *e.g.* cotton, timber, etc., which are made into clothes and furniture.

Ready Money. Cash; money paid, or ready to be paid, for a purchase, etc.

Real. True, genuine; consisting of fixed and permanent things, *e.g.* lands or houses, as opposed to personal things.

Real Cost. As factors of production are limited, they can only be employed in one direction at one time. The real cost of production, therefore, is whatever these factors of production could have produced had they been employed in another direction.

Real Estate. Immovable property covering freehold land and buildings and proprietary rights in or over lands, *e.g.* mineral rights.

Real Income. Money income in terms of the goods and services which it will buy.

Real Investment. Sinking money into a capital asset, *e.g.* plant, rather than investing it in the purchase of stocks and shares.

Realisation Account. An account maintained when a business is being wound up or sold, or on the dissolution of a partnership.

Realised Profit. An investment which has appreciated since it was bought is showing a paper profit until such time as it is actually sold, when the paper profit becomes a realised profit.

Réaliser. Realise.

Realkredit. Credit secured by a charge on real or personal property.

Re-Allowance. *See* Selling Group.

Real Personal Disposable Income (R.P.D.I.). The total income available to private individuals after tax, National Insurance and other contributions and adjusted for the rise in prices. It describes income in terms of what it will buy.

Real Property. Freehold land and buildings, as opposed to personal property. Real property can itself be recovered if the owner is dispossessed; the remedy is not an award of damages, but the restoration of the land itself, the real remedy.

Real Time. A computer term indicating that an account in the computer is up-dated instantaneously with information fed in at a terminal, as opposed to a system whereby all such information is stored on tape until a daily computer up-dating is undertaken.

Real Wages. *See* Real Income.

Rebate. A deduction, a drawback, a discount; in the case of a bill paid before maturity, the allowance of interest at an agreed rate for the days still to run, deducted from the amount of the bill; an adjustment of discount so that only interest relating to the period covered by accounts is treated as earnings.

Receipt. An acknowledgment in writing that money or other property has been received. An unindorsed cheque which appears to have been paid by the banker on whom it is drawn is evidence of the receipt by the payee of the sum payable by the cheque (Cheques Act 1957, s. 3). Some cheques have a form of receipt on the back which has been incorporated into the printing of the cheque because the drawer, not relying on section 3, (*above*) wishes to obtain the signature of the payee by way of receipt. To draw the attention of the payee to this requirement, a large letter "R" is printed on the face of the cheque. This also serves to alert the cancelling clerk that it is necessary to turn the cheque over to confirm that the form of receipt has been duly completed. Cheques are not now found expressing the need to sign the receipt as a condition of payment and such a cheque is therefore a true cheque and not a conditional document: the banker, who will send the cheque back unpaid with the answer "Receipt required" if the form of recipt is not completed (thus demonstrating that the cheque is conditional in practice although not in law), takes this action merely as a service to the customer.

Receivables Financing. *See* Factoring.

Receiver. An officer appointed by the court to collect debts or rents from property which is in dispute in a suit in that court; an officer appointed by the Bankruptcy Court to receive the profits or takings of any business or undertaking which is being wound up by that court; a person appointed by the court to receive and administer the assets of a person who has been certified as mentally incapable, under the Court of Protection. The order of the court, which is the authority of the receiver, should be inspected by the banker; unless such an order authorises the receiver to borrow money he has no such power.

Receiver for Debenture Holders. A debenture deed will specify the acts or omissions of the company (such as failure to repay capital or interest within a specified period) which will entitle the creditor(s) to appoint a receiver. On his appointment, any floating charge contained in the debenture will crystallise and fix upon the assets available on the day of the receiver's appointment. The receiver will take charge of the company and administer its assets so as to apply them towards the repayment of the debenture holder's advance. The debenture deed may have appointed the receiver as agent of the company so as to make it responsible for his acts and for his remuneration.

Receiver for Partnership. The Partnership Act 1890 contains provision for application to the court for dissolution of a partnership, and where this happens the court will appoint a receiver to wind up the firm. His duty is to complete existing commitments of the firm, realise the assets, pay the debts, and pay any surplus to the partners in the proportions in which they shared the profits. On the appointment of the receiver the partners no longer have power to bind the firm and their signatures should not be accepted.

Receiver of Rents. One of the remedies open to a mortgagee, upon default by the mortgagor, is to appoint a receiver to collect the rents and manage the estate; this is particularly appropriate for property which is let, *e.g.* a block of flats. On the appointment the receiver takes possession of the property and therefore collects rents and profits, applying them in reduction of the mortgagor's debt. The receiver is regarded as agent of the mortgagor, who is therefore responsible for his defaults. *See also* Official Receiver.

Receiving Order. A stage in the bankruptcy procedure. The petition to the court that the debtor should be made bankrupt is based on the commission by the debtor of an act of bankruptcy. The petition for the receiving order may be made by a creditor or by the debtor himself. On receipt of the petition the court will make a receiving order, which is a temporary measure to protect the estate of the debtor by putting it under the control of an official of the court, the receiver, while the necessary inquiries are made. The making of a receiving order must be gazetted and advertised in a local paper. The receiving order is deemed to operate from the first moment of the day on which it is made. On notice of the making of a receiving order the banker must stop the debtor's account.

Recession. A falling off in the economic progress of a country, which if it persists will lead to a depression and then to a slump. A recession may be only a temporary check and will not necessarily impair confidence sufficiently to reduce or stop the longer-term investments.

Recherche Opérationelle. *See* Operational Research.

Rechnung. Account, invoice.

Rechnungsprüfer. Accountant.

Reciprocal Business. Banks engaged in international trade use correspondent banks abroad to represent them in various transactions and usually have a choice of several such correspondent banks with whom to place their business. The selection of the actual bank to be used may well depend upon how much business is placed in the reverse direction by the correspondent bank with the home bank. Most banks keep records of such reciprocal business and are influenced by them.

Reciprocity. Tariff concessions in international trade made by one country to another in return for similar concessions; in banking, business put in the way of a correspondent bank abroad in return for similar favours.

Réclamation. Claim.

Réclamation pour Défauts de la Chose. A formal protest following the delivery of documents of title presenting formal defects. When the protest is in respect of goods it is usually because the generality of the goods does not conform to a sample.

Recognised Marking Names. *See* Marking Names.

Reconciliation Statement. A check between a firm's cash book and its bank statement, by which the two are brought into agreement by allowances for cheques issued but not yet presented, and credits received but not yet paid in.

Reconnaissance de Dette. A document acknowledging a debt. It is not a document of title.

Reconstruction of a Company. The reorganisation of a company structure in order to obtain new capital, or following an arrangement with creditors of the company, or to give effect to an agreement to merge with another company. Where a compromise or arrangement is proposed between a company and its creditors, the court may order a meeting of creditors. The arrangement, if approved by a majority in number representing three-fourths in value of the creditors shall, if sanctioned by the court, be binding on all the creditors and on the company. In the case of a merger or amalgamation with another company, the approval of the shareholders to the extent of nine-tenths in value of share holdings is required within four months of the making of the offer. *See also* Minority Shareholders.

Reconvention. A counter-action in a suit brought by the defendant against the plaintiff.

Reconveyance. Transfer of a title to lands back to their original owner. Since 1925, the legal estate in mortgaged property remains with the mortgagor, consequently no reconveyance is necessary, a statutory receipt being enough. A reconveyance is, however, still necessary in cases where part only of the mortgaged land is being released from the charge, because the statutory receipt is not applicable to such a case.

Recorded Delivery. A Post Office service providing for the sender proof that the packet, etc., has been received by the addressee. The sender fills in a recorded delivery form giving the name and address of the addressee, pays a small charge and gets a receipt. The delivery postman obtains the signature of the recipient. Recorded Delivery letters must not contain coin, banknotes, or certain other forms of money, nor jewellery.

Recours. An action for specific performance or to sue for damages which one has against another person; an appeal.

Recourse. A source of help, that which is resorted to. If a bill of exchange is dishonoured at maturity the holder has the right of recourse against any of the other parties to the bill, unless any such party has expressly negatived this recourse. **With Recourse.** Where a bank discounts or negotiates a bill of exchange for a customer it does so "with recourse", that is, if the bill is dishonoured at maturity the bank is able to claim the amount of the bill from the customer. **Without Recourse.** A party to a bill of exchange may negative his liability on the bill by adding these words (or the words *Sans Recours*) after his signature on the bill. Such a clause will make the bill less easily negotiable.

Recourse Factoring. This is similar to Maturity Factoring with the exception that there is no credit protection extended to the supplier; the factor has full recourse against him in the event of the insolvency of a customer. Recourse factoring can be either disclosed or undisclosed. *See also* Factoring.

Rectification. The act of rectifying or setting right; an equitable remedy applicable where it is sought to correct or rectify a document purporting to contain the terms of a contract, which does not properly reproduce the agreement between the parties.

Reçu. Receipt.

Recycling. When the oil exporting countries were able to make very large profits on their oil exports, they had so much money in hand that it seemed impossible to spend it all, even though they imported many goods and services which their economies and military policies needed. The task of mobilising and redistributing these vast sums caused considerable concern. The name given to the methods of investing them was "recycling". The amount in question was approximately $60 billion in 1974. Something up to one-third of this sum was invested through London, the lenders insisting on extremely liquid investments (*see* Hot Money). Most of this went into the Eurodollar market.

Red Clause. A clause in a documentary letter of credit designed to enable the beneficiary to draw up to 100% of the credit amount before shipping documents are presented and even before shipment. The clause is so called because it is typed in red in the letter of credit. It is used principally in the Australian wool trade, where the beneficiaries, reputable wool shippers, require the pre-shipment finance to be able to pay the up-country shearing station from which the wool originates, and to finance its despatch to the port where it is made ready for loading on board an ocean vessel. See also Green Clause; Pre-Finance Credit.

Redeemable. That which may be regained; money which is capable of repayment; a mortgage of property which may be discharged by the payment of the principal, interest and costs of the mortgage.

Redeemable Bonds or Stock. Government securities which are repayable at par on a certain date, or at any time between two given dates, or after a certain date.

Redeemable Debenture. A debenture where the issuing company agrees to repay the money lent at a stipulated time or after a certain period of notice, or by drawings and/or purchase. A company may redeem all or some of its debentures and may either cancel, hold or re-issue its redeemed debentures. Re-issued debentures give the new holder all the priorities which attached to the original issue. The lending banker should therefore insist that any such redeemed debentures should be cancelled, re-issued to the bank, or placed on safe custody with the bank (so that they cannot be re-issued to anyone else).

Redeemable Preference Shares. Preference shares which the company has stated are liable to be redeemed. Redemption must be out of profits or from the proceeds of a fresh issue of shares made for the purpose; the shares must be fully paid; any premium payable on redemption must be found from company profits before the shares are redeemed.

Redemption Dates. The dates between which government stock is repayable at par.

Redemption Period. For the purposes of the Consumer Credit Act 1974, a pawn is redeemable at any time within six months after it was taken. Subject to this, the period within which a pawn is redeemable shall be the same as the period fixed by the parties for the duration of the credit secured by the pledge, or such longer period as they may agree.

Redemption Yield. A return calculated on the total profit obtainable on a fixed interest stock redeemable at a predetermined price. It is composed of (1) the flat yield, and (2) the present value of the future capital profit which will be obtained on redemption. Where redemption is to be at a point in a range of years, it is usual to base the calculation on the latest possible redemption date. Although redemption yield is worked out by reference to a term of years it is expressed in annual terms for comparison purposes.

Redevance. The cost of a licence for the exploitation of a patent and the proceeds of manufacture; the cost of a concession for the exploitation of mineral rights.

Re-Discount. The act of a person who has discounted a bill of exchange in subsequently selling to another person; for example, a bank discounts a bill for a customer and then has it re-discounted by the central bank.

Rediskontierung. Re-discount.

Reducing Balance Method of Depreciation. See Depreciation.

Reduction of Share Capital. A company may wish to reduce its share capital either because the share value has risen far above the nominal value, with an accompanying difficulty in trading in the shares, or because the share value has fallen so far below the nominal value that it is apparent that the capital has been irretrievably lost. In such cases the company may be special resolution reduce its share caital and alter its memorandum accordingly. It may then apply by way of petition to the court for an order confirming the reduction. The court must be satisfied that creditors of the company have consented or have been secured and will then issue a confirming order, which may direct that the words *"and Reduced"* shall be added after the word *"Limited"* in the name of the company.

Re-Entry. The resumption of possession of land; in leasehold land, the re-entry of the lessor into possession of land as a consequence of the failure of the lessee to observe the covenants of the lease.

Ré-Escompte. Re-discount.

Réévaluation. See Revaluation.

Re-Exchange. In the case of a bill of exchange which has been dishonoured abroad, the holder may recover from the drawer or an indorser, and the drawer or an indorser who has been compelled to pay the bill may recover from any party liable to him, the amount of the re-exchange with interest thereon until the time of payment. The re-exchange is calculated to produce a sum equal to the amount of the dishonoured bill, plus costs of dishonour and incidental expenses, at the place where it was dishonoured. This is done by finding out how much would be required to purchase a sight bill at the existing rate of exchange drawn at the time and place of dishonour on the place of residence of the drawer or indorser.

Re-Export. A commodity re-exported; to export after having been imported. Re-export trade is carried on by a country which has a good location for redistributing goods to other countries and good air and shipping facilities to carry the goods. Also known as *Entrepôt Trade*.

Referee. One to whom a question is referred for settlement, an arbitrator; one whose name is given by a person desiring to open a current account with a banker; one who is named by a candidate for a post as willing to give testimony of good character. *See also* Official Referee.

Referee in Case of Need. *See* Case of Need.

Reference. A declaration as to a person's integrity. A banker opening a new current account must either obtain a personal introduction for the new customer, from someone already known to him, or take up either one or two references. The referee himself should be vouched for in this capacity by his own banker. Failure to complete this procedure will leave the banker at risk for negligence with regard to any cheques which he handles for his new customer, to which the customer has no title or a defective title.

Referential Settlement. *See* Settled Land.

Refinanceable Credit. Credit made available by banks to exporters and to home shipbuilders in respect of which refinance is carried out, for export by the Export Credits Guarantee Department, and for home shipbuilding by the Department of Trade. Finance for exports applies only where the transactions in question involve a period of credit (from the date of the contract) of two years or more, and all finance is provided in the first place by the banks, but a bank will be re-financed for advances beyond 18% of its non-interest bearing sight deposits (to be increased in monthly steps to 21%).

Re-finance Bill. A bill drawn under a re-finance credit (*q.v.*).

Re-Finance Credit. A credit with a clause to meet the case where the exporter wants to be paid immediately, but the importer needs, say, three months' credit. Under such an arrangement the bank granting and opening the credit will accept the importer's bill at three months as soon as the exporter's sight bill has been paid by the correspondent bank. The accepted bill is then discounted by the opening bank and the proceeds sent to the correspondent bank, who are thus reimbursed for the payment to the exporter.

Reflation. An attempt to inject a sluggish economy with a fresh supply of money with the object of increasing consumer demand. If this is successful, production should increase and if this is sustained manufacturers will be encouraged to increase their investment in capital equipment and to increase production yet more in the confidence that they can sell the goods they are producing. These measures decrease unemployment and lead to a healthy upswing of trade. Reflation may start by a series of government measures which show that money is easier, *e.g.* restrictions may be lifted from the banks in the matter of their lending (monetary methods) or income tax can be cut or the rate of V.A.T. reduced (fiscal methods). If reflation results in increasing demand so much that home manufacturers cannot satisfy the demand then prices will rise and imports will increase. Inflation and an adverse balance of payments will oblige the government to bring back the various methods of control. Reflation is thus a two-edged tool which must be used very carefully.

Regal. (*Ger.*) State monopoly.

Regeneration. The act of giving fresh life or vigour to; re-organisation; a word used to describe efforts to bring back companies and firms to London, which have de-centralised to other areas to such an extent that the process of inner city decay was considerably hastened in the capital.

Regional Trade. Trade between countries with common borders or situated in the same region, as the result of an agreement between them to pursue a common trade policy, *e.g.* the European Common Market.

Register. An official written record; a book, roll or other document in which such a record is kept; an official or authoritative list of names, facts, etc., as of shipping or charges against land; to enter in a register. For the purposes of the Consumer Credit Act 1974, the Director-General of Fair Trading shall establish and maintain a register giving particulars of (1) applications not yet determined for the issue, variation, or renewal of licences under the Act, or for ending the suspension of a licence; (2) licences which are in force, or have at any time been suspended or revoked, with details of any variation of the terms of a licence; (3) decisions given by him under the Act, and any appeal from those decisions; and (4) such other matters (if any) as he thinks fit. Any person shall be entitled on payment of the specified fee to inspect the register during ordinary office hours and take copies of any entry, or to obtain from the Director a copy, certified by the director to be correct, of any entry in the register. *See also* Land Certificate; Land Charges Register; Land Register; Lloyd's Register of Shipping; Local Land Charges Register.

Registered Capital. *See* Share Capital, *under* Share.

Registered Charge. A legal mortgage over registered land. The banker lending against this security should take the land certificate from his customer, get him to sign a form of legal mortgage, make a search on the Register, and prepare an office copy of the signed mortgage. He then sends to the Land Registrar the land certificate and both copies of the mortgage. The appropriate fee for registration of the charge must accompany the application. The Registrar will keep the land certificate and the copy mortgage. He will make the appropriate entry in the Register and then issue a charge certificate to the banker as evidence of his interest. This will have the original form of mortgage stitched inside it.

Registered Land Certificate. *See* Land Certificate.

Registered Office. The memorandum of every company must state whether the registered office of the company is to be situate in England, Wales or Scotland. The registered office is the official headquarters of the company to which communications are to be addressed, and at which various registers required by law, such as registers of directors, secretaries, members, charges and debentures given by the company, etc., are to be maintained.

Registered Post. A method of postal delivery by which letters are insured against loss or damage in transit.

Registered Provident Societies. A group of varied institutions registered under the Friendly Societies Acts and other legislation which give them certain privileges, such as limited liability, and impose upon them various limitations and obligations. Friendly societies are mutual insurance societies in which the members subscribe for provident benefits, in particular sickness, death, endowment and old age benefits, and provisions for widows and orphans. Although the National Health service now meets most of the needs for which the original friendly societies were set up, they still continue to operate and have diversified to include industrial insurance; industrial, provident and building societies; trade unions; certified loan societies; and some superannuation and pension schemes. All are closely controlled by various Acts.

Register of Charges. A record maintained by the Registrar of Companies of all changes made by limited companies and requiring registration under section 95 of the Companies Act 1948. The register may be inspected by any person on payment of a small fee. Additionally, each company is required to keep at its registered office a register of all property charged by the company including all floating charges on the undertaking of the company. The register is available for inspection by any member of the company without fee and by any other person on payment of a small fee. *See also* Land Charges Register.

Register of Companies. The list of approved limited companies in Great Britain which have complied with the formalities of registration and have been given a certificate of incorporation by the Registrar of Companies. Such a certificate issued by the Registrar is conclusive evidence that all the requirements in respect of the registration of the company have been complied with. A register of company mortgages is maintained by the Registrar, open to inspection by any person on payment of a small charge. If the Registrar gives a certificate of the registration of any mortgage or charge, this is conclusive evidence that the requirements of the Companies Act 1948 have been complied with.

Register of Debenture Holders. A register of holders of debentures issued by a company shall be kept at the registered office of the company and shall be open for at least two hours in each day to the inspection of the registered holder of any such debentures, or any shareholder in the company, without charge; and to the inspection of any other person at a small charge.

Register of Directors and Secretaries. Every company shall keep at its registered office a register of its directors and secretaries. With respect to each director, the register shall state his full name, address, nationality and business occupation together with particulars of any other directorships held by him, and, where the company is a public company, his date of birth. If the director is a corporation, its corporate name and registered office must be given. With respect to each secretary, the register shall state his full name and address. If the secretary is a corporation or a Scottish firm, its corporate or firm name and registered office must be given.

Register of Members. Every company shall keep a register of its members, entering therein the following particulars: (1) the names and addresses of the members, and in the case of a company having a share capital a statement of the shares held by each member, distinguishing each share by its number so long as the share has a number, and of the amount paid or agreed to be considered as paid on the shares of each member; (2) the date on which each person was entered in the register as a member; (3) the date at which any person ceased to be a member. The register of members shall be kept at the registered office of the company. It must be open for not less than two hours each day to the inspection of any member *gratis* and to the inspection of any other person for a small charge.

Register of Ships. Every British ship, unless not exceeding fifteen tons burthen and employed solely in navigation on the rivers or coasts of the U.K., shall be registered under the Merchant Shipping Act 1894. The chief officer of customs is the Registrar of British ships and is responsible for the maintenance of registers at any port in the U.K. approved by the Commissioner of Customs for the registry of ships. The Registrar issues a certificate of registry to the owner of the ship on registration. Mortgages of ships, or parts of a ship, are recorded on the register of the port in which the ship is registered, priority being calculated according to the hour and date of registration. *See* Mortgage of Ship. Most ships are also registered with Lloyd's Register of Shipping (*q.v.*).

Register of Transfers. On the application by the transferee of shares together with the completed Stock Transfer Form the company will make the transfer in its register of transfers of shares or debentures, recording the date of registration, the number of shares transferred with their descriptive numbers, the names and addresses of the transferor and transferee and the numbers of the old certificate returned and the new one issued. Any alterations to the Members' Register necessitated by the transfer will also be made. The record in the Register of Transfers may also be made at the request of the transferor of the shares. If the company refuses to register the transfer of any shares or debentures it shall send the transferee notice of the refusal within two months after the date on which the transfer was lodged with the company.

Registrar. An official whose duty it is to keep a register or record of transactions.

Registrar. (*Fr.*) The office of supervision of new issues emanating from the transfer agent.

Registrar-General. A public officer who superintends the registration of births, deaths and marriages.

Registrar of Companies. A public officer appointed by the Department of Trade to supervise the registration of companies and limited partnerships, to issue certificates of incorporation and registration of company mortgages, and to maintain facilities for the public inspection of company records.

Registration. Act of registering, entry or record, *e.g.* of births, etc.; a form of insurance on postal packages; the insertion of a company's name on the Register of Companies.

Registration Fee. The fee payable at a post office for the registration of a letter or packet; the charge made by a company for the registration of shares in the name of a new shareholder.

Registration of Business Names. Sole traders or partners may trade in their own names, or they may adopt a business name. Under the Registration of Business Names Act 1916, where a firm or individual carries on business under a business name which does not consist of the true surnames of the individual or partners without any addition other than the true Christian names or initials, then registration must be effected under the Act and a certificate issued. This certificate must be kept in a conspicuous position at the principal place of business of the firm or individual. Application for registration must be made within fourteen days of commencing business. Whenever a change occurs in any of the particulars registered in respect of any person or firm, a statement of the change must be sent to the registrar within fourteen days after such a change. The object of this Act, like any which provides for any system of registration, is the protection of the public. There must be some way in which innocent traders wishing to do business can find out with whom they are proposing to trade. The certificate formerly gave this information. In 1969, however, the Registrar issued the following notice:

"It has come to the Registrar's notice that certificates of the registration of a business name, which until very recently listed the names of the registered proprietors of the business in question, were being produced as evidence of its current ownership and that such evidence was being accepted in good faith. The Registrar has no means of verifying particulars submitted with applications for registration, and business names are not unique. Certificates are not returnable for cancellation or amendment on change of ownership or cessation of business. There are indications that certificates bearing the names of proprietors could, in certain circumstances, be used to mislead. The Registrar has decided that he should adhere strictly to the prescribed form of certificate, which makes no provision for the inclusion of the proprietors' names or the address of the principal place of business."

The issue of certificates in the new form commenced on 8 April 1969. Since this date, the banker wishing for full information must apply to the Registrar for a copy of the registered particulars. These are supplied on payment of the appropriate fees. Business names are likely to arise in two ways. A man may start trading with a name designed to show the public what he is dealing in—thus an account in a bank's book might read "Sports Cycle Spares Company: John William Bridger so trading". Here a certificate will be required. Or a firm may start out with the true surnames of the partners and trade for some years, building up a goodwill connected with the name. Suppose it is Jones, Rice, Freeman and Company, and they are well known as estate agents of good standing and repute. If then Jones, the senior partner, dies, and perhaps a new partner, Williams, is taken on, it may be decided that in spite of the changes the old firm name shall be kept for the sake of the goodwill attached to it. Then a certificate will be required, for the concern will be Jones, Rice, Freeman and Company, but the partners will actually be Rice, Freeman, and Williams.

The Act is not very well observed and would be even less well observed were it not for the bankers, who are constantly alert to obtain information in appropriate cases. This is done partly to protect the customer, who cannot bring an action in respect of any contract entered into in connection with the business name so long as it has not been registered, and who is liable to a penalty of £5 per day while a defaulter; but partly also to protect the banker, who might be faced with an accusation of negligence if he had not insisted on obtaining the relevant particulars. The requirements of the Registration of Business Names Act 1916 are extended in appropriate cases to limited companies by section 58 of the Companies Act 1948.

Registration of Charges. As to unregistered land, see Land Charges. As to registered land, in the case of a deposit of the land certificate with the lender, the latter will make a search on the Register by sending the registered land certificate back to the Registry to be written up to date. At the same time he will lodge Land Registry Form 85A, which operates to give the Registrar notice of his interest. The Registrar will enter this on the Charge Register, thus giving notice to any possible purchaser or mortgagee. Also, if the proprietor attempts to dispose of the land or deal with it in any way other than by legal mortgage the Registrar will notify the lender accordingly. The latter will then have fourteen days (or such other period as is indicated in the notification) in which to take action to protect his interest. In the case of a registered change, the borrower signs a form of legal mortgage and deposits his land certificate with the lender, who makes a search on the Register, using Land Register Form 94. The search form must be accompanied by the authorisation of the mortgagor or his solicitor. The duplicate of Form 94 is returned with the result of the search, and is then known as "the official certificate of search". If the certificate shows the title to be clear, the Land Registration (Official Searches) Rules 1969 give the lender priority for fifteen days after the date of the search, during which time he should complete and register his charge. The lender should take the form of mortgage, prepare an office copy of it, and send to the registrar the land certificate, the signed, sealed form of legal mortgage, and the copy mortgage. The Registrar will keep the land certificate and the copy mortgage. He will make an appropriate entry in the Register and will then issue to the lender, as evidence of his title, a document called a charge certificate. This will have the original form of mortgage stitched inside.

As to companies, any one of nine changes specified in section 95 of the Companies Act 1948 must be registered within twenty-one days of its creation and, if not so registered, becomes void against the liquidator and any creditors of the company. The charges specified are: (1) a charge for securing any issue of debentures; (2) a charge on uncalled share capital of the company; (3) a charge which in the case of an individual would need registration as a bill of sale; (4) a charge on land; (5) a charge on book debts of the company; (6) a floating charge on the undertaking of the property; (7) a charge on calls made but not paid; (8) a charge on a ship or a share of a ship; (9) a charge on goodwill, patent, licence, trademark or copyright. The company is primarily responsible for the registration of the charge but provision is made for registration to be effected by the lender. See also Agricultural Charges; Land Certificate; Register Of Ships.

Registration of Share Transfers. See Register of Transfers.

Registre des Actions. The share register of a company.

Règlements. Regulations.

Regress. (Ger.) Recourse.

Regressive Tax. A tax falling more heavily upon people with low incomes than on those with high incomes; thus as the income falls the proportion of tax increases.

Regressrecht. Right of recourse.

Regulated Agreement. A consumer credit agreement other than an exempt agreement.

Regulator. The name given to the power of the Chancellor of the Exchequer to vary the rates of indirect taxation to meet the economic and monetary needs of the time.

Reimbursement Credit. A credit created when a bank in the country of an importer requests a correspondent bank in the country of an exporter to authorise the exporter to draw bills on the correspondent bank, the opening bank undertaking to re-imburse the correspondent bank as and when such bills have to be honoured by the correspondent bank. Where the trade is between other countries but is to be financed through London (because the banks concerned hold sterling balances in London which can be utilised), the correspondent bank will be authorised to draw in sterling on a London bank in re-imbursement. The opening bank would then have to notify the London bank of any such re-imbursements which it had authorised.

Rein. Net.

Reingewinn. Net profit.

Re-Insurance. Where a risk is considerable an insurance company will insure the risk up to a certain amount themselves, and put the excess risk out to a re-insurance company, or to more than one, on the principle of diversifying the risk.

Reisecheck. Travel cheque (traveller's cheque).

Re-Issue. To issue again, to republish, to make again available; a reprint.

Re-Issue of Bill of Exchange. Where a bill is negotiated back to the drawer, or to a prior indorser or the acceptor, such party may re-issue and further negotiate the bill, but he may not enforce payment of the bill against any intervening party to whom he was previously liable.

Re-Issue of Debenture. *See* Redeemable Debenture.

Rektaklausel. The addition of the words "not to order" to a bill of exchange or cheque, by which a transfer by means of indorsement is excluded.

Relation Back. The sequence of events in bankruptcy shows that the trustee in bankruptcy is appointed quite late in the proceedings: long after the act of bankruptcy which started it all. In fact, by the time the trustee takes charge, it is possible that much of the debtor's property originally available will have been dissipated. The debtor may give his wife, relations, or friends things belonging to him, just to keep his creditors from getting them. So it is provided that the trustee's title to the assets of the debtor (including a credit balance on a banking account) shall "relate back" some way before the date of his appointment, and that he be given power to follow up any property given or transferred away by the debtor in dubious circumstances, and recover it. As the act of bankruptcy is the start of the bankruptcy sequence, the date of the act of bankruptcy is chosen as the date on which the assets of the bankrupt are deemed to pass to the trustee and become his property, to share amongst the creditors. This doctrine of relation back is set out in section 37(1) of the Bankruptcy Act 1914, as follows: "The bankruptcy of a debtor ... shall be deemed to have relation back to, and to commence at, the time of the act of bankruptcy being committed on which a receiving order is made against him. ..." Some debtors commit a number of acts of bankruptcy one after another. Some perhaps attract petitions, others not. The petition must be within three months of the act on which it is based. This is what is known as an "available" act of bankruptcy. One outside the three months is not available. So section 37(1) goes on to deal with debtors who have committed more than one act of bankruptcy: "... or if the bankrupt is proved to have committed more acts of bankruptcy than one, to have relation back to, and to commence at, the time of the first of the acts of bankruptcy proved to have been committed by the bankrupt within the three months preceding the date of the presentation of the bankruptcy petition." The assets of the bankrupt which pass to the trustee at this date are to comprise all property belonging to or vested in the bankrupt at the commencement of the bankruptcy and also any property which is acquired by him, or devolves on him, up to the day on which he secures his discharge from bankruptcy, including goods in his reputed ownership. *See also* Voluntary Conveyance.

Release. To set free from restraint or confinement, to loosen, to exempt from an obligation; to remit a claim; exemption, a discharge of a right.

Relevé de Compte. Statement of account.

Reliquat. Bills which have not been presented for payment on the due date.

Remainder. An interest in property under a will or settlement, whereby trustees hold the property for the benefit of the life tenant until his or her death, whereupon it passes to the remaindermen, *e.g.* a will may leave property in trust for a widow (the life tenant) subject to the stipulation that on her death the property is to pass absolutely to the children of the marriage, if of full age (the remaindermen).

Rembourskredit. Bank acceptance credit for produce lending against the security of the goods.

Remedies of Mortgages. *See* Powers of Mortgagee.

Remise. Putting back, remittance, delivery, rebate; a surrender, a release, as of a claim; to resign property by deed.

Remise. (*Fr.*) Discount, rebate.

Remisier. An introducing agent bringing business to a stockbroker in exchange for a share of the broker's commission.

Remission. The act of remitting an accused person or a case to another court.

Remittance. Act of transferring money or bills to a distant place; the money sent; a parcel of cheques or bills received at a branch or dispatched by it.

Remittance Basis. U.K. tax to be paid is worked out either on the income received during the year (earnings, U.K. pensions, etc), or received in the previous year (business profits, etc.). Money coming from abroad is liable to tax only on the amount which is actually remitted to the U.K. either during the previous year or within the actual year. This is known as the remittance basis. Previous year remittances are applicable to those resident in the U.K. but not domiciled there. The sources of income concerned are investment income from abroad, pensions from abroad, and income from trades controlled abroad. Actual year remittances apply in any case to U.K. residents not domiciled in this country in respect of capital gains from assets sold abroad. Where the taxpayer, apart from being resident there for the particular year, is also ordinarily resident in the U.K., actual year remittances also apply to emoluments from an employer not resident in the U.K. or Eire where the duties are performed wholly abroad. Finally, the remittances of the actual year also apply to those who are not ordinarily resident in the U.K. on emoluments from duties performed wholly abroad.

Remittent. *See* Wechselnehmer.

Remittitur. An order by a superior court sending back a case to an inferior court; the relinquishment by a successful litigant of part of his damages to save further proceedings.

Remote Damage. Damage which arises as a result of a breach of contract, but does not flow naturally from it. Where a loss is too remote from the breach, compensation will not be awarded.

Remote Parties. The parties to a bill of exchange who are not in immediate relationship with each other.

Rendement. Income expressed as a percentage of capital. Before deduction of tax at source income is gross; thereafter, net.

Rendite. Percentage return on a capital investment. On the payment document it is expressed as a gross yield before, or a net yield after, deduction of tax at source.

Renewal. Restoration, replacement; a reloan on a new note given in place of a former note; with the consent of all parties, the acceptance of a new bill of exchange for an old one, thus postponing the date when payment has to be made.

Renewal Bill. The name given to a bill which is drawn to be discounted so as to provide funds to meet another bill maturing; a method of extending borrowing at maturity on a short-term basis.

Rent. A periodical payment at an agreed rate for the use and enjoyment of something, such as land, houses, machines, films, etc.; rental hiring charge. In economics, a surplus accruing to a factor of production, the reward gained by any productive agency which is in short supply and cannot easily or quickly be increased. *See also* Chief Rent; Fee Farm Rent; Ground Rent; Quasi-Rent; Rack Rent.

Rentabilität, Rentabilité. Profitability.

Rental. A rent-roll, the annual amount of rent payable.

Rental Contract. *See* Finance Lease.

Rent Charge. Any rent expressly made payable out of land, other than rent payable by a tenant, to a reversioner; a charge on land payable to one who is no longer its owner.

Rente. Unearned income, pension, interest-bearing stock, annual income from stocks or an annuity, a French undated government stock.

Renten. The customary term in Germany for bonds.

Rentenanleihe. A state loan with no repayment date and carrying therefore no fixed repayment obligation, the state committing itself only to the payment of interest.

Rentenempfänger. Annuitant, pensioner.

Rente Viagère. *See* Annuity.

Rentier. A person whose whole income is derived from invested capital.

Rentrer dans ses Fonds. To get one's money back.

Rent-Roll. A schedule of rents, a list of those who pay rents.

Rent-Service. The annual payment by a tenant of land, whether by money, labour or provisions, in return for the right to live on the land. *See also* Fee Farm Rent.

Renunciation. The surrender of one's claim or interest, abandonment, disavowal, formal repudiation; the document expressing this; the giving up by a shareholder of new shares allocated to him by the completion of the form of renunciation on the back of the allotment letter. When the holder of a bill of exchange, at or after its maturity, absolutely and unconditionally renounces his rights against the acceptor, the bill is discharged. The renunciation must be in writing, unless the bill is delivered up to the acceptor.

Repartierung. Allotment of a fully or partly subscribed issue.

Repartition, *Répartition.* Distribution, sharing out, allotment.

Repatriement. Goods of foreign origin which are sent back to the country which produced them.

Repatriierung. Repatriation of overseas holdings, sometimes under official compulsion.

Replacement Cost. The company purchasing an asset should set on foot a depreciation programme, transferring yearly instalments to an investment fund so that at the end of the period estimated as the useful working life of the asset there is money to renew the asset. However, the effect of inflation in the period may have considerably raised the replacement cost, so that an additional sum must be provided to offset the inflationary increase. The asset may be written up yearly before depreciation is applied, or the additional sum may be allocated from some other source.

Report. (*Fr.*) On the Stock Exchange, but also on the foreign exchange market, an extension for a bull operator of the time of settlement; a carrying over, an amount brought forward.

Report Joué. A transaction whereby a bank buys spot on the exchange and sells at a term to another bank at a higher rate.

Report on Title. The borrower who offers title deeds as security must deposit them with the lending bank, if he has them. The banker will make a *prima facie* check of the deeds and then send them to a solicitor who will check and report on the title of the customer, and state in writing any points which are relevant to the title which is about to be acquired by the bank. However, the particular form of words which must appear in his report is that, after the title has been mortgaged, the bank will be in possession of a "good and marketable title" to the land. It is, of course, essential that the banker should be able to sell the security if he is so obliged.

Represent. To make out to be, to pretend to be, to pretend, to allege; to bring forward for payment a bill or cheque which has already been dishonoured.

Représentant. Representative.

Representation. Standing in the place of a deceased person, as an executor, etc.; a statement of facts; a protest; a statement made in the preliminary stages of the negotiation of a contract. In the latter sense, it is made by one of the parties to the contract to the other one, with the intention usually of persuading that other to enter into the contract. For the purposes of the Consumer Credit Act 1974, "representation" includes any condition or warranty, and any other statement or undertaking whether oral or in writing. *See also* Chain of Representation.

Representative. Fitting or qualified to represent, typical; an agent, deputy, delegate or substitute; one who stands in the place of another as heir, etc. *See also* Personal Representative.

Reprise. A hardening of a rate on the *Bourse* after a recession; a continuation of economic expansion after a temporary set back of industrial and commercial business.

Reputed Owner. A person who is in possession of property with the consent of the true owner, in circumstances which lead third parties to conclude that he is the owner of the property although in fact he is not. In bankruptcy law, the property of the bankrupt passing into the hands of the trustee includes such goods as are at the commencement of the bankruptcy in the possession, order or disposition of the bankrupt, in his trade or business, by the consent of the true owner, in such circumstances that he is the reputed owner thereof.

Requisition. A written order for materials or supplies, a formal demand; to seize.

Requisitions on Title. Questions framed

by the solicitor to an intending purchaser and addressed to the vendor's solicitor, referring to points in the chain of title of the property to be passed, on which he desires further enlightenment.

Requisitor. An official empowered by a court to investigate facts.

Res. A thing, things.

Resale Price Maintenance. The upholding of a fixed price for a product by a manufacturer or a group of manufacturers acting together. Concerted action of this kind by manufacturers was made illegal in 1964, unless they could show that it was in the public interest, but the right of an individual manufacturer to cut off supplies to a retailer selling at less than the fixed price has been upheld.

Res Angusta Domi. Pecuniary difficulties.

Res Angustae. Straitened circumstances.

Rescind. To annul, *e.g.*, a law or decision; to cancel, to revoke, to repeal, to reverse, to abrogate.

Rescission. The act of annulling or abrogating. An equitable remedy for the relief of a party to a contract where mistake has been a vital factor.

Rescissory Action. An action whereby deeds, etc., are declared void.

Rescriptions. Treasury bills; public authority loans.

Reservation. A clause or proviso in a conveyance or lease by which some right or easement is retained by the vendor or lessee.

Reserve. Funds set aside for possible contingencies (*see also* Provision); the minimum price acceptable to a vendor at an auction; the total of notes and coins shown on the assets side of the Bank of England return for the Banking Department. *See also* Hidden Reserve; Mindestreserve; Revenue Reserve; Specific Reserve.

Reserve Assets. These assets, to be held by banks and other financial institutions, are those which the Bank of England is ready to convert into cash, either directly or through the discount market. They comprise: (1) balances at the Bank of England (other than Special Deposits); (2) British and Northern Ireland government treasury bills; (3) money at call with the London money market; (4) British government stocks with one year or less to maturity; (5) local authority bills eligible for rediscount at the Bank of England; (6) commercial bills eligible for rediscount at the Bank of England (up to a maximum of 2 per cent of eligible liabilities).

Reserve Assets Ratio. The ratio between a bank's eligible liabilities and its reserve assets, fixed since 1971 at 12½%. *See* Competition and Credit Control.

Reserve Currency. Currencies of other countries held by a country as part of its central monetary reserves (*see* Reserves); a currency which is widely accepted as a means of settlement and finance of trade. The U.S. $ and sterling are the world's major reserve currencies.

Reserved Power. A reservation made in deeds, settlements, etc.

Reserve Fund. An allocation from profit in any business, to be set aside to meet unforeseen or unexpected expenses. The reserve fund should be invested outside the business.

Reserve Liability. That part of a company's share capital which it has resolved cannot be called up except in the case of the liquidation of the company.

Reserven Offene. Free reserves.

Reserven Stille. Secret reserves.

Reserve Price. A price below which no offer will be accepted.

Reserves. The U.K.'s reserves of gold and convertible currencies are held at the Bank of England and consist of varying amounts of gold bars, special drawing rights, convertible currencies of other countries and credits at the International Monetary Fund. These reserves are affected by deposits in London by overseas depositors, investments in British property or paper such as Treasury Bills, overseas borrowing by the Government and public enterprises, the balance of trade, and transfers made by the Bank of England in the course of stabilising the exchange rate of sterling.

Réserves Cachées. *See* Hidden Reserve.

Réserves Latentes. Reserves which do not figure in the balance sheet but which can nevertheless be approximately estimated on the basis of other indications in the balance sheet or annual report—for example, the difference between the book value and the value for insurance of fixed assets.

Réserves Liquides. Funds immediately available for investment when a favourable opportunity presents itself.

Réserves Minimales. Minimum amounts which a bank must deposit with the central bank, used as an instrument of financial policy. The amount is generally determined by that of the individual bank's short-term obligations.

Réserves Occultes. *See* Hidden Reserve.

Reserves Ouvertes. On the liabilities side of the balance sheet, the funds of the company other than the share capital.

Réserves Prises sur le Revenu. Revenue reserve.

Resettlement. *See* Settled Land.

Re-Shipment. The re-export of imported goods.

Residence. The act of dwelling in a place, the place where one resides; the basis in the U.K. for tax assessment of a British citizen; under the name of "domicile", the basis for succession duty.

Resident. For exchange control purposes, a person, firm or company dwelling or having a permanent place of business in the Scheduled Territories.

Residuary Devisee. The person who takes, under the terms of a will, all the real property remaining after the specific devises have been satisfied.

Residuary Legatee. The person to whom the residue of personal estate is bequeathed after all other claims are discharged.

Residue. That which remains after a part is taken, that which remains of an estate after payment of all charges, debts and particular bequests; the balance or remainder of a debt or account.

Residuum. The part of the estate of a testator which remains after payment of debts and legacies; the balance remaining of a bankrupt or trust estate after payment of preferred debts and claims; as a term in economics, the poorest stratum of a community.

Res Judicata. A thing already judged or settled.

Reskription. Short term acknowledgment of public debt, usually at three months, discounted by banks; a Treasury bond.

Resolution. The decision of a court or the vote of an assembly; motion, declaration; a proposition put before a meeting of company shareholders for discussion, passed by a majority. *See also* Extraordinary Resolution; Ordinary Resolution; Special Resolution.

Resolution to Borrow. Any application to borrow by a limited company should be supported by a copy of the resolution passed authorising such an application. The resolution should be certified by the secretary of the company as a true copy of the entry in the minute book. Whether this resolution is properly a resolution of the directors or whether it is one passed by the company in general or special meeting is a point to be checked by the bank with reference to the articles and memorandum of the company (*See* Borrowing Powers). The form of resolution should be satisfactory to the bank, and usually the bank will supply its own printed form for completion and return. Ideally the company should complete a resolution on each borrowing occasion to cover the sum required, for this ensures that all the members of the board know of the arrangements, and rules out a possible fraud by one director having power to sign alone on behalf of the company. However, a company requiring a series of overdrafts or loans is apt to resent having to complete a borrowing resolution each time accommodation is required, and therefore it is common practice to take an "*omnibus resolution*" for "such sums as the Company may require from time to time and the Bank be willing to lend". It should cover an overdraft, a loan, or both together. A resolution in support of the giving of a guarantee by the company should name the officials who will sign the guarantee on behalf of the company, authorise them to do so, and identify the guarantee. (One way to do this is to have the resolution typed out and signed on the back of the guarantee itself.)

Resolution to Wind Up. A company wishing to wind up voluntarily must pass a resolution to that effect. The type of resolution, whether ordinary, special or extraordinary, depends on the reason for winding-up—which may be unconnected with any financial difficulty (as, for example, if it wishes to amalgamate with another concern), or, on the other hand, on whether it cannot by reason of its liabilities continue in business, and that it is advisable to wind up. The commencement of the winding-up is the passing of the resolution for voluntary winding-up. The company must give notice of the resolution within fourteen days, by advertising it in the *Gazette*. *See also* Voluntary Liquidation.

Respondent. One who answers in certain proceedings, especially, in a chancery or divorce suit, the defendant.

Respondentia. A loan raised by the master of a ship upon its cargo, for which he is personally responsible; the instrument of hypothecation by which such a loan is raised. The money is repayable only if the ship safely reaches its port of destination, and the loan is for the purpose of paying for repairs to the ship urgently needed if it is to continue its voyage.

Resserrement. Contraction, credit squeeze.

Restanten. See Reliquat.

Restraint of Trade. A contract in restraint of trade, as between the buyer and seller of a business, is one which is intended to protect trade secrets and special proprietary rights or processes, or to maintain the goodwill of a business. Such a contract will be enforced only if it is no wider than is reasonably necessary to protect the party in whose interests it is imposed, is reasonable with reference to the party against whom it is made, and is reasonable from the point of view of the public at large. Contracts in restraint of trade are also found in the form of agreements between employers and employees. Such a contract will be enforced if it is necessary to protect the employer against the improper use by the employee of knowledge gained in the employer's service, but will not be upheld merely to stifle ordinary business competition or to prevent the employee using the personal skill and knowledge which he has acquired in his employment.

Restricted Circulation. An instruction to accompany any order, memorandum, or circular which is to be kept confidential among the more senior representatives of an organisation, *e.g.* the system of dealing with staff frauds, or the staffing policy of a large company, or the measures to be taken in the event of a strike of the work force.

Restricted-Use Credit Agreement. A regulated consumer credit agreement (1) to finance a transaction between the debtor and the creditor, whether forming part of that agreement or not; or (2) to finance a transaction between the debtor and a person (the "supplier") other than the creditor; or (3) to refinance any existing indebtedness of the debtor's, whether to the creditor or another person.

Restriction. A limitation, a confinement, a restraint; in the law of registered land, a notification to the Land Registrar to protect a minor interest, such as the necessity to pay the sale monies for land held upon trust for sale to two trustees. (*Fr.*) A limitation, for example in the granting of credit or in the flow of international payments.

Restrictions de Transfert. Limitations on the transfer of shares, as for example in a private company where any such proposed transfers must be approved by the directors.

Restrictive Covenant. A covenant by which the use of the covenantor's land is restricted for the benefit of the covenantee's land which adjoins it.

Restrictive Indorsement. One which prohibits any further negotiation of a bill of exchange; one which gives the indorsee authority to deal with the bill only as directed in the indorsement. A restrictive indorsement usually destroys the transferability of the bill (*e.g.* "pay John Smith only").

Resulting Trust. A trust which is not expressly created, but arises as a result of certain conduct of the donor from which it is concluded that he intended to create a trust. *See also* Protective Trust.

Retail. To sell in small quantities.

Retail Banking. The traditional course of business between a banker and his domestic customers, as opposed to "wholesale" banking. One of its principal distinguishing features is that it is conducted through a network of branches.

Retail Cost. The price of an article in the shop where it is sold.

Retail Price Index. *See* General Index of Retail Prices.

Retail Trade. The final stage of distribution, where goods are sold in shops to the people who are going to use or consume the goods.

Retaining Fee. A preliminary fee paid to a barrister or other professional man engaging his services.

Retention Money. Money held back for a

certain time—often six months—after a contract has been completed, while the work done proves itself. If in that time repairs are required, they are defrayed out of the retention moneys.

Retirement Pension. *See* Old-Age Pension.

Retiring a Bill. Payment of a bill of exchange at or before its maturity date, whether by an indorser who takes the bill up by paying the amount of it to a transferee, or by the drawer or acceptor who redeems it from the holder before maturity. Where the acceptor retires a bill at maturity it is in effect paid, and all the remedies on it are extinguished.

Retiring Partner. *See* Outgoing Partner.

Retrograd, Retrograde. Backwards; a method of calculating interest on current accounts.

Retrozession. The sharing by a bank of part of its commission with another bank or with an agent.

Return. To report officially; to yield a profit; the rendering back of a writ to the proper officer or court.

Return Day. The day on which a defendant is instructed to appear in court.

Returns. Cheques or bills unpaid for some reason.

Reugeld. A premium to be paid on retirement of business, a penalty clause.

Revalorisation. An increase in credit figures in compensation for losses in real terms by reason of the depreciating value of money, or any other unforeseeable cause; a revaluation of a balance sheet item which has previously been shown at below its effective value.

Revaluation. To put a fresh value on; the raising in value of a country's currency in terms of the currencies of other countries.

Revenue. Income derived from any source, especially the annual income of a state or institution; proceeds, receipts, profits. *See also* Inland Revenue.

Revenue Account. An account showing the income of a company and the expenditure chargeable against it.

Revenue Officer. An officer employed in the collection of excise or customs duties levied by the state.

Revenue Reserve. A sum which has been built up out of favourable profit and loss balances in previous years.

Revenu National. *See* Gross National Product.

Reverse. To turn the other way round, to give a contrary decision; to repeal, to revoke.

Reverse Annuity. A loophole in the tax laws of the U.K. which appeared in 1970–71, under which insurance companies and other financial institutions could grant a "reverse annuity" to a high taxpayer and he would repay by instalments in the form of an annuity spread over a period of years. The "annuity payments" were fully allowable against income tax and so the real cost to the taxpayer was very much reduced. The device was attractive to those paying tax at above 60% of income: the scope was therefore limited to the very wealthy. It was announced by the Chancellor of the Exchequer in March 1977 that he was proposing to introduce provisions to annul this system, such provisions to apply immediately.

Reverse Arbitrage. Borrowing from the market to clear off a bank overdraft when rates permit this.

Reverse Income Tax. *See* Negative Income Tax.

Reverse Takeover. A takeover of a larger company by a smaller one.

Reverse Yield Gap. When it became felt—at the end of the 1950s—that the future held nothing but steady progress, and that recessions were things of the past, it seemed evident that dividends on equities would go on rising, whereas fixed interest yields gave no protection against inflation. Consequently the yield on equities became less than that on fixed-interest securities and a "reverse yield gap" arose. In more recent years, however, the relationship between inflation, dividends and earnings appears to have broken down, and the reverse yield gap has widened to a record 9%.

Reversion. Land granted under a lease to a tenant for a number of years reverts to the lessor at the end of the time. A reversion is an interest arising by operation of law, as distinct from act of parties, whenever the owner of an estate grants a particular estate without disposing of the whole of his interest.

Reversionary Bonus. A bonus added to the value of a "with-profits" life policy on a periodic valuation of the profits made by the assurance company in the preceding period.

Reversionary Interest. *See* Remainder.

Révocable. According to the rules of the *Bourse*, an order is in principle valid until the end of the current month. A revocable order allows the operator to revoke at any time or to extend the order.

Revocable Credit. A credit which can be revoked or cancelled by the bank which opened it at any time during the period it is stated to remain in force. All credits are revocable, unless it is specifically stated that they are irrevocable. This type of credit offers no security to the exporter and is comparatively rare nowadays.

Revocation of Will. The annulment of a will by the testator, whether expressly or by implication. An express revocation has to be effected by an instrument which is executed with the same formality as a will requires. An implied revocation is effected: (1) by the making of a subsequent inconsistent formal testamentary document which disposes of the whole property mentioned in the original will; (2) by burning, tearing or otherwise destroying the will. There must be both physical destruction and the intention to destroy. The destruction must be carried out either by the testator or by someone in his presence acting with his authority; (3) by marriage. Subsequent marriage will revoke an existing will, whether made by a man or a woman, unless the will was expressed to be made in contemplation of marriage, and the marriage does take place as contemplated.

Revoke. To annul, to repeal, to reverse a decision.

Revolving Credit. A credit containing a clause for an automatic renewal of the credit on a roll-over basis. Thus any part of the credit used by the borrower (through the beneficiary utilising his power of availment) and reimbursed to the banker within the term of the credit becomes again available automatically upon such re-imbursement. There is therefore no limit to the total of turnover, although there is a stated limit to the amount of drafts which may be outstanding at any one time.

Rider. An addition to a manuscript or other document; an additional clause, as to a bill; a supplement tacked on to the original motion or verdict.

Riding. One of the three territorial divisions of the old county of Yorkshire. It is now divided into two Metropolitan Counties and three counties. Though no longer relevant for local government administrative purposes, the term still has some significance in Land Law.

Right. A just claim, a legal title.

Right *in Personam.* A right which can be enforced only against a limited number of persons.

Right *in Rem.* A right enforceable against the whole world.

Right of Action. A right to commence an action in court.

Right of Survivorship. The right of a surviving joint-tenant to own and enjoy the property, formerly held jointly, as against the personal representative of the deceased joint tenant.

Right of Way. A right, established by custom, to use a path over or through private property; such a path.

Rights Issue. The offer by a company of new shares direct to its existing members. The price is usually set below the market price of the existing shares, in order to make the offer attractive. The rights to subscribe, therefore, have themselves a market value, and can be sold. *See also* Open Offer.

Rights Letter. The document informing an existing shareholder of a company of his right to take up on favourable terms a number of newly-issued shares in the company. If the shareholder does not wish to exercise his right he may sell the letter of rights.

Rights of Holder of Bill. (1) He may sue on the bill in his own name. (2) Where he is a holder in due course, he holds the bill free from any defect of title of prior parties, and may enforce payment against all parties liable on the bill.

Rights of Unpaid Seller. The unpaid seller has by implication of law, and notwithstanding that the property in the goods may have passed to the buyer, (1) a lien on the goods or right to retain them for the price while he is in possession of them; (2) where the buyer is insolvent, a right of stopping the goods *in transitu* after he has parted with the possession of them; (3) a right of resale.

Rimesse. A consignment of shares, bonds or coupons, and particularly of bills of exchange.

Ring. A combination of persons to con-

Riparian trol prices within a trade; a term used to describe trading in various commodity markets, *e.g.* the Metal Exchange. (*Fr.*) In the *Bourse*, the circular bar round which the brokers are to be found transacting business when the *Bourse* is in session.

Riparian. Pertaining to, or situated on, the banks of a river; a dweller on, or a proprietor of, a river bank.

Risikoverteilung. Risk capital.

Risk. Danger, peril, hazard, chance of loss; amount covered by insurance; person or object insured.

Risk Capital. The ordinary shares of a company, dividends on which are poor or good according to the fortunes of the company. The term is also applied to a situation where a bank has lent money and can as yet recover neither capital instalment nor even an interest repayment. In such a case both capital and interest are "rolled over", *i.e.* capital repayments are postponed until such a time as the borrower can afford them, interest due is placed to a suspense account. There will be some special reason why this treatment is thought to be the appropriate one; normally the obvious solution would be to put the borrower in liquidation or make him bankrupt.

Rohstoffe. Raw material.

Roll-over. A term indicating a continuance of existing credit. A limit on a "roll-over" basis is renewed once it has been exhausted. If an interest rate is expressed to be on a roll-over basis it means that it will be re-negotiated at intervals, perhaps every three months. (In a time of rising interest rates a lender may not wish to commit himself for too long to a specific rate, when the chances are that he could get a better rate later on.)

Roll-over Loan. A loan for a fixed period but where the interest rate is reviewed at intervals throughout the term of the loan, based on a formula agreed at the time the loan is made (*e.g.* 1% over three months Inter Bank Offer Rate, usually abbreviated to I.B.O.R.).

Roman Law. The code of laws developed by the Romans, regarded as the basis of jurisprudence by the majority of European countries.

Rompu. (*Fr.*) An undersubscription of a new issue resulting in a taking-up of the unsold shares by underwriters; an amount short or over at the time of a balance.

Root of Title. *See* Good Root of Title.

Round Lot. The minimum number of shares acceptable for sale or purchase on the *Bourse*.

Roup. A sale of goods by auction.

Royal Mint. A government department responsible for the provision of coinage for circulation in the United Kingdom, and for the striking of coins for other Commonwealth and some foreign countries. Gold sovereigns are struck for use particularly in the Middle East, where the coin commands a universal respect. The Royal Mint also strikes medals and decorations, and seals for ministerial use. It is situated at Llantrisant, near Cardiff.

Royalty. Payment to an owner of land for the right to work minerals, or to an inventor for the use of his invention; payment to an author dependent upon the sales of his book. *See also* Redevance.

Rück. Back.

Rückdiskontierung. Re-discount.

Rückkaufswert. Surrender value of a life policy.

Rücknahmepreis. Redemption price.

Rückstellung. The allocation in advance in the balance sheet of a sum to off-set a future acquisition or a probable future loss.

Rückstellung, Rückgestellte Verbindlichkeit. Deferred liability.

Rückstellungskonto. Appropriation account.

Rugefrist. Period of time inside which the consignee of documents of title to goods, which show a dirty bill of lading, can raise an objection.

Rule Against Accumulations. When a settlor desires that the income from his property shall be accumulated and given to his descendants at some remote future date, some limit must be applied to the time in question, or at compound interest enormous sums will pile up. The modern rule was formulated in 1925, and refined in 1964. Any settlor with such an intention must choose one only of the following periods for the duration of the accumulation: (1) the life or lives of the settlor(s); (2) a term of twenty-one years from the death of the settlor; (3) the minority or respective minorities of any persons living or *en ventre sa mère* at the death of the settlor; (4) the minority or respective minorities only of any person(s) who, under the limitations of the settlement, would, if of full age, be entitled to the income directed to be accumulated; (5) a term of twenty-one years from the date of the settlement; (6) the duration of the minority or respective minorites of any person(s) in being at the date of the settlement.

Rule Against Perpetuities. In English land law, the rule that it is not permissible to suspend the vesting of interest in a piece of land for longer than a life in being plus twenty-one years. From 1964, a settlor may instead specify a fixed period of time not exceeding eighty years. The rule was designed to defeat the unbarrable entails by which families sought to keep their estates in perpetuity.

Rule in Clayton's Case. *See* Clayton's Case.

Run. To flee, to flow; to continue in operation; to continue without falling due, as a promissory note or bill; to have legal force; to manage (a business); a frantic rush on the part of depositors to withdraw their money from a bank believed to be in difficulties.

Running. Successive (Numbers); continuous (*e.g.* an order of account).

Running Account Credit. For the purposes of the Consumer Credit Act 1974, a facility whereby the debtor may continually obtain cash, goods or services up to an agreed limit, on a revolving basis, after allowing for payments made by or to the credit of the debtor, any limit agreed being at no time exceeded.

Running Broker. A bill broker who originally took bills from the merchant banks and financial institutions in the City of London, and disposed of them on a commission basis to banks and discount houses. The last two firms of running brokers now operate in a similar manner to the discount houses.

Running Days. Consecutive days, including Saturdays and Sundays, as opposed to business days.

Running Margin. A man who borrows money to invest it at interest both pays and earns interest. The difference between the interest he pays for his loan and the interest he gets from his investment is the running margin.

Running Yield. *See* Flat Yield.

S

Sachwert. Value-retaining capital investment, which ought to offer the most likely effective security against currency depreciation and falling off of purchasing power.

Safe Custody. Articles of value, locked boxes, wills, and many other things are left by customers in bank strongrooms for safety. Boxes should be locked and parcels sealed by the customer before handing them in to the bank. The banker will issue a receipt if so required. He must be careful to hand them back only against a signature by his customer or a properly-appointed agent who is known to the bank. Such a safe-keeping is a contract of bailment. If the banker makes a specific charge for the service, he is a paid bailee. If he does not, he is a gratuitous bailee. The paid bailee has to show a higher standard of care in dealing with the safe custody of articles than does a gratuitous bailee.

Safe Deposit. Some banks maintain a safe deposit service where the customer is taken into a strong room and himself puts his documents or articles of value into his box, or compartment, to which he alone has the key, or takes them out. The bank keeps duplicate keys in case of emergency, but does not use them except in the presence of the customer or by his express authority.

Saisie. Foreclosure, distraint.

Saisonkredit. Seasonal credit.

Salaire. Wages, pay, salary.

Salaried Partner. One whose status within the partnership is defined in the Partnership Deed. As far as the outside world is concerned, he is deemed to have held himself out as a partner and therefore to be fully liable with the other partners for the debts of the partnership. Whether or not his authority can be taken for instructions concerning the running of the banking account depends again on how it is defined in the terms of the Partnership Deed.

Salaries and Wages Accounts. *See* Wages and Salaries Accounts.

Sale. The act of selling, the exchange of a commodity for money or other equivalent; an auction. *See also* Bill of Sale.

Sale and Lease Back. The raising of immediate finance by a company by selling a capital asset, whether property or capital equipment, to a finance company or insurance company, and then leasing it back and continuing to use it as before. The ownership of the asset passes to the lessee, the finance company or insurance company. The leasing rental will contain an element of the cost of the asset purchased from the lessor company plus an interest charge to cover administrative and service charges. Sale and lease back arrangements are usually found only where the asset to be purchased is worth £25,000, or more. However, smaller figures may be found where a scheme exists for the purchase of houses from retired couples, widows or widowers, subject to an agreement allowing them to continue to live in the house for the rest of their lives at a nominal rental.

Sale by Auction. *See* Auction.

Sale by Description. Where there is a contract for the sale of goods by description, there is an implied condition that the goods shall correspond with the description.

Sale by Sample. In the case of a contract for sale by sample there is an implied condition: (1) that the bulk shall correspond with the sample in quality; (2) that the buyer shall have a reasonable opportunity of comparing the bulk with the sample; (3) that the goods shall be free from any defect, rendering them unmerchantable, which would not be apparent on reasonable examination of the sample.

Sales Ledger. A book of accounts of those persons to whom a firm sells goods on credit.

Salvage. The act of saving (a ship, goods, etc.) from shipwreck, capture, fire, etc.; compensation allowed for such saving; property so saved.

Sammeldepot. Documents of value deposited with a bank, where the securities of customers, and of the bank, are separated into their various categories and are looked after collectively, with no note as to the ownership of each individual title.

Sammelverwahrung. A rationalisation of safe custody deposit business, whereby all banks partaking in the scheme keep their securities in a centralised common centre.

Sample. A specimen of merchandise taken from the bulk for inspection, usually that of a prospective buyer, particularly important in the sales of tea and grains, etc., before an auction; a method of estimating public demand or reaction by postal enquiry of, or personal interview with, a representative number; a method of assessing the efficiency of a branch bank used by inspectors who select at random a number of administrative details for close checking—if these are satisfactory it is assumed that the generality of that particular activity is also satisfactorily carried out.

Sanction. Permission of the bank for an overdraft or loan; the amount of such sanction; ratification by a superior authority.

Sandwich Debenture. A common arrangement between banks and the Industrial & Commercial Finance Corporation, whereby the I.C.F.C. has first call on the fixed assets of a company to which both are lending, and the banks have first call on the floating assets, ranking second to the I.C.F.C. on the fixed assets. The arrangement also applies to insurance companies and some merchant banks.

Sanierung. A business reconstruction.

Sans Frais. An addition to the signature of the indorser of a bill, meaning that no expense is to be incurred on the bill.

Sans Garantie ni Responsabilité (s.g.n.r.). Without responsibility.

Sans Recours. An addition to the signature of a drawer or an indorser of a bill, meaning that the signatory will not accept any liability on the bill; literally, "without recourse".

Sauf Erreur et Omission (s.e.et o.). Errors and omissions excluded (E. & O.E.).

Sauvetage. Salvage.

Save. To keep from being spent, to keep untouched, to reserve, to lay by.

Save As You Earn (S.A.Y.E.). A government-backed scheme for savings made by regular monthly amounts. Introduced in 1969, it is administered both by the Department for National Savings and by the trustee savings banks and building societies. Savings may be made by deduction from pay (where the employer has agreed to co-operate) or by standing order on a bank, the National Giro, or a trustee savings bank. It enables all persons over the age of sixteen to save regular monthly amounts of anything between £1 and £20 in deposits with the Department for National Savings. An index-linked scheme came into operation in 1975. Under this scheme, contributions of between £4 and £20 may be made monthly over a period of five years. Periodical increases in value are made to the investment in step with any increase in the retail price index. Contributions stop after five years but if the capital is left for a further two years a bonus is paid. This scheme, for regular savers, is open to anyone who would be eligible for S.A.Y.E.

Savings Account. *See* Home Safe.

Savings Bank. A term covering the National Savings Bank and the Trustee Savings Banks. The National Savings Bank is administered through the Post Office and is designed to encourage small savers. Interest is allowed on deposits, but withdrawals on demand are limited to small sums, although larger amounts may be withdrawn at a few days' notice under special arrangements. Trustee Savings Banks were originally non-profit making bodies run for the benefit of their depositors, and were founded with the idea of promoting thrift and independence in old age. The Trustee Savings Banks have been restructured into eighteen regional institutions and are working their way towards the provision of a full banking service. They are linked together through the Trustee Savings Bank Association, of which they are all members. *See also* National Savings Bank.

Savings Bonds. *See* British Savings Bonds.

Savings Certificates. *See* National Savings Certificates.

Scalar Principle. The principle of hierarchy or grading according to a scale, whereby members of an enterprise have their duties graded according to degrees of responsibility and authority. In applying this principle to the business of banking, a superior higher in the "scalar chain" confers the right to exercise a lower degree of authority on a subordinate, to whom he assigns clearly specified and defined targets and duties. The subordinate (*e.g.* branch manager) then becomes responsible to the superior (*e.g.* area manager) for executing those duties and meeting those targets, and may indeed delegate some of the duties to further subordinates of his own.

Scarcity Value. The high price of a commodity in short supply.

Schatzanweisung, Schatzschein, Schatzwechsel. See Reskription.

Schätzung. Estimate.

Schedule. A smaller document forming part of the principal document, deed, bill, etc.; an appendix to an Act of Parliament; an official, tabulated list of goods and chattels; an inventory, a list of deeds; a timetable; in tax law, a heading under which is prescribed how a particular source of income is to be dealt with for the purpose of taxing that source.

Scheduled Territories. Formerly a list of countries whose currencies were linked to the £ sterling—since 1972 consisting only of the U.K., including the Channel Islands and the Isle of Man and Gibraltar.

Scheme of Arrangement. See Arrangement with Creditors or Members.

Schiffshypothekarkredit. A loan against the security of a registered mortgage over a ship.

Schlussdividende. Final dividend.

Schlusskurs. Closing rate.

Schuld. Debt.

Schuldner. Debtor.

Schuldschein. A document in which any person as debtor acknowledges a specified sum.

Schuldverscheibung. Bond, debenture.

Schwach. A downwards tendency on the stock exchange.

Schwebende Schuld. Unconsolidated short- or medium-term debts of the state, in the form of bonds, central bank issues, etc.

Schweizerische Bankiervereinigung, Case Postale 1155, Aeschenvorstadt 4, 4002 Basel. The Swiss Bankers' Association is an alliance of the bank, credit and finance sectors of the economy. It was founded in 1912, in Basle where it is based and where it maintains a permanent place of business. By its regulations it was excluded from any business activity, but its objects consist of the observation of the interests and rights of the Swiss banking industry and its representation; the preservation of its members from unfair competition; and the protection of Swiss investors, particularly in cases where savings capital is deposited in exchange for title documents. These objectives sought to harmonise banking habits and business with the patterns of state and cantonal law in all cases where the interests of the Swiss banking industry were affected, whether directly or indirectly, and to enlighten the public and its members through the dissemination of information on the situation of the banking industry and its function within the economy, through simplification and standardisation of business practice among the banks to improve and if possible cheapen their services to customers, and through the organisation of activities of a protective nature to safeguard the savings capital of the Swiss people. The organs of the bankers' association are the annual general meeting, the board of administrative management, and the committee. The board consists of a minimum of twenty members chosen for election from the general assembly. The Swiss Bankers' Association consists of a representative group from large banks, canton, regional and savings banks, domestic, foreign and private banks, and residual banks. It includes, moreover, stock exchange firms, organisations concerned with the transport of funds, and many finance and holding companies as well as numerous trustee and auditing concerns.

Schweres Papier. Share with a high exchange value.

Scrip. The document or provisional certificate which is given to a person who has agreed to take up bonds in connection with a government loan and has paid the first instalment. Scrip is principally associated with the issue of bonds or debentures.

Scrip Issue. A capitalisation of reserves by issuing fully paid-up shares free to present shareholders in proportion to their current holding. No cash changes hands. It is really a book-keeping transaction, designed primarily to bring the share capital more into line with the assets employed in the business. After a scrip issue, a shareholder owns more shares, but as the market price is adjusted accordingly, he is no better off. A scrip issue brings a high share price back to a more manageable sum and thus increases a share's marketability.

Scrivener. One who draws up contracts or other documents; one who places money at interest on behalf of clients; a public writer, a notary.

Scrutineer. One who examines votes cast at an election; one who computes the votes of members at a company meeting.

Seal. A die or stamp having a device for making an impression on wax or other plastic substance; a piece of wax, lead, or other material stamped with this and attached to a document as a mark of authenticity, etc., or to an envelope, package or box to prevent its being opened without detection; the impressions made thus on wax, lead, etc.; a stamped wafer or other mark affixed to a document *in lieu* of this. As deeds now require the signatures of the parties thereto, the seal has become a formality, and often an adhesive wafer is used. A company may use its seal to authenticate documents, but such documents are usually also signed by two directors and the company secretary to certify that the seal has been affixed in their presence. A contract under seal is valid because of the formality and does not require to be supported by consideration.

Seaman's Allotment Note. *See* Allotment Note.

Seaman's Advance Note. *See* Advance Note.

Searches. Enquiries made by an interested party, usually prior to concluding some contract. In Bankruptcy, a register of undischarged bankrupts is maintained in London at the Thomas More Buildings, Royal Courts of Justice, Strand, London W.C.2., for personal searches only. The information given consists of the number of the case, the name, occupation and last known address, together with the dates of various stages of past and present bankruptcy proceedings and their advertisement.

Searches Against a Limited Company are made personally at the Companies Registry on payment of a small fee, when the file of the company in which the searcher is interested will be produced for his inspection. Searches Against Unregistered Land Titles are usually carried out by the bank's solicitor, who will search against the customer's name on the Land Charges Register, using form L.C.11, stamped with the appropriate value in Land Registry stamps. The form is in duplicate and the Registrar will return one copy to the solicitor indicating on it the result of the search. Searches Against Registered Land Titles are carried out by (in the case of an equitable charge) the sending of the land certificate by the lender to the Land Registry in order that it may be written up to date, or (in the case of a registered charge) the completion and dispatch of Land Registry Form 94. This search form must be accompanied by the authorisation of the mortgagor or his solicitor. In the first case the lender can see, when the land certificate is returned to him, whether his title is clear, by looking at the copy of the Charges Register in the certificate. His own notice of deposit should be entered therein, and this should be the only charge outstanding. In the second case the duplicate of Form 94 is returned to the lender with the result of the search marked upon it. It is then known as the "official certificate of search". For searches on local land charges registers, *see* Local Land Charges Register. For searches on port registries, *see* Mortgage of Ship.

Seasonal. Occurring or done at the proper time, suitable to the season, opportune. A seasonal advance is one occurring regularly every year—such as to a farmer at the beginning of the season, repayment to be made from the produce of crops. There is a seasonal demand for cash in advance of Christmas each year to cover the heavy expenses of customers at this time; there is a seasonal demand on banks in the spring of each year for advances to pay taxes.

Secondary Market. Trading in stocks and shares after the closing of an issue. *See also* Certificate of Deposit.

Secondary Offering. The placing of parcels of shares held by individuals or by groups.

Secondary Risks. *See* Prime Risks.

Second Mortgage. A mortgage on a property which is already mortgaged to a first mortgagee. A second mortgage should be in legal form, and will comprise the grant of a term of years longer by one day than the term enjoyed by the first mortgagee. Notice should be given to the first mortgagee, who should be asked to confirm the amount due to him, whether he claims any right of consolidation, and whether he is under any obligation to make further advances. The second mortgage, if of unregistered land, should be registered with the Land Charges Department as a class C (i) charge. In the case of registered land, a second charge can be registered at the Land Registry, who will issue a certificate of second charge to the lender. *See also* Land Charges; Notice of Second Mortgage.

Second of Exchange. *See* Bill in a Set.

Secrecy. Concealment, the maintenance of confidentiality, the exercise of discretion. The duty of the banker to keep his customer's affairs secret is one of the terms of the banking contract. This confidential relationship is being progressively eroded by state measures, principally for checking tax evasion. Case law has authorised disclosure of information (1) under compulsion of law, (2) in pursuit of a public duty, (3) where the bank's interest requires disclosure, (4) where disclosure is made with the express or implied consent of the customer. All bank staff are required to sign an oath of secrecy on joining the bank staff. Banks and others are affected by powers given to officers of the Board of the Inland Revenue by the Finance Act 1976, to enter any premises and to search for and seize documents and other articles which they believe may be needed as evidence for proceedings in respect of an offence involving a tax fraud. Such a search can only be carried out if a warrant is issued by a judge, and is unlikely to be used against banks.

Secret Bancaire. *See* Secrecy.

Secret Commission. No agent may take for himself any consideration, whether by way of money, goods, services or favours, as inducement to act in a way prejudicial to the best interests of his principal, or to confer favour or preference to the third party offering the bribe or inducement. If this should happen, the secret commission or profit is the property of the principal, and the person offering the inducement, and the person accepting it, are both guilty of offences under the Prevention of Corruption Act 1906.

Secret Reserve. *See* Hidden Reserve.

Secundum. According to.

Secundum Legem. According to law.

Secundum Usum. According to established custom.

Secured Creditor. A person holding a mortgage, charge or lien on the property of the debtor, or any part thereof, as a security for a debt due to him by the debtor.

Secured Debenture. A debenture providing a fixed charge on specified company assets.

Securities. In a wider and less precise sense, a word meaning investments generally, *e.g.* "Stock Exchange securities".

Securities Management Trust Ltd. ("S.M.T. Money"). A wholly-owned subsidiary company of the Bank of England. It is used by the Bank as a nominee company for the placement of funds at market rates in the security and money markets on behalf of, and at the request of, Bank of England customers.

Security. The keeping of unauthorised persons out of bank premises, the supervision of cash in an office or strongroom, the guarding of a bank and its cash by day and by night; the valuable paper deposited at a bank by a borrowing customer, such as bearer bonds, stock exchange securities, life policies, guarantees or debentures, as an insurance against the possibility of default in repayment. For the purposes of the Consumer Credit Act 1974, "security", in relation to an actual or prospective consumer credit agreement or consumer hire agreement or any linked transaction, means a mortgage, charge, pledge, bond, debenture, indemnity, guarantee, bill, note or other right provided by the debtor or hirer, or at his request (express or implied), to secure the carrying out of the obligations of the debtor or hirer under the agreement.

Seigniorage. Anything claimed by a sovereign or feudal superior as a prerogative; a charge made by mints for coining ingots of gold or silver into currency; the difference between the bullion value of silver, copper, bronze and cupro-nickel coins and their face value; a share of the profits; a mining royalty.

Seisin. Possession of land under a freehold; the act of taking possession; the thing possessed.

Selbstfinanziering. Ploughing back profits.

Selbstschluss. Closing rates on the Stock Exchange.

Self-Liquidity. A characteristic of a loan which carries with it the seeds of its own repayment, *e.g.* a loan to a manufacturing company for the purchase of raw materials. These are worked up into the finished product, sold, and the loan repaid out of the proceeds of sale.

Self-Service. A response by management to the increasing cost of labour, whereby consumers help or serve themselves, whether or not with the aid of a machine of some kind installed by management, either initiating in the process a system which will eventually debit the consumer's account, or leading to a payment in cash at a check point. In banking the trend is observed in the installation of cash dispensers and developments such as "Cashpoint", "Servicetill", etc.

Sellers' Market. A condition of markets in which goods are scarce, and there is a great demand for them, so that the seller can make his own terms.

Selling Group. A group formed for the purpose of selling a new issue of stocks, shares or bonds to the investing public. It may or may not be identical with the group of underwriters who are acting for the issue. There is sometimes a smaller inner group which both manages the issue and organises the formation of a larger outer group to handle the disposal of the issue.

Selling Group Terms. The issue price minus the discount (usually 1¼%–1½%) allowed to the selling group. Out of this the selling group allows a commission or "re-allowance" of (usually) ½%, to authorised dealers.

Selling Out. Action taken by a seller on the Stock Exchange when the buyer fails to complete. This consists of an instruction to the Stock Exchange official broker to sell the securities in question, any loss arising being charged to the defaulting purchaser.

Send Direct. *See* Special Clearance.

Sensal. Broker, jobber.

Sequens (Seq.). The following; *(pl.) sequentes, sequentia.*

Sequestration. Confiscation, appropriation; the taking of some property from parties in dispute over it until some case is decided or some claim paid; a term used in relation to the benefice of a clergyman; under Scots law, a stage in bankruptcy proceedings. *See also* Writ of Sequestration.

Sequitur. He (she, it) follows.

Service. The act of serving; work done for an employer or for another; a benefit or advantage conferred on someone; willingness to work or act; use, assistance; formal legal delivery, posting up, or publication (*e.g.* a writ, summons, etc.).

Service Central des Risques. A list of borrowers from banks set up in France by the French National Credit Council, giving the names of borrowers, but not the amounts, for the benefit of banks only.

Service Centralisé des Paiements. Control and regulation of exchange with overseas countries where application has to be made for a decision to the appropriate Department.

Service Decentralisé des Paiements. Regulation of exchange with overseas countries where control is delegated to banks.

Service des Cheques Postaux. The French postal giro service.

Service Réglegmenté des Paiements. Exchange control.

Service Till. The name of a computerised cash dispenser which can also tell customers what their balances are, and take requests for new cheque books and statements. This machine operates from a Service card which bears a magnetised strip. This is returned to the customer at the time of operation. The service is controlled by a personal credit limit incorporated in the strip, arranged with the customer at the time of operation. Up to £100 can be issued at any one time in varying denominations of notes.

Set Off. The combining of debit and credit accounts so as to arrive at a partial or full repayment of a debt. A banker has the right to set off different accounts in the name of the same customer provided that he has not agreed to keep them separate and provided that the accounts are in the same right. It is not entirely certain that a banker has the right to set off balances *without notice* to his customer, especially where they are still on active running accounts. Therefore, it is common practice to take a letter of set-off from the customer giving such a right. A letter of set-off given by a limited company should be registered at Companies House as a measure of prudence.

Settled Land. Land which is subject to the terms of a settlement; land held under certain conditions by a tenant for life. A strict settlement was a device to preserve land in a family for as long as possible. This was done by the device of a conveyance of the land to trustees upon trust to hold it for the settlor for life, with remainder to the eldest son in tail and successive remainders, in the event of the death of this son without issue, to the younger sons in tail. On the attainment of majority by the son a re-settlement was made, whereby the land was reconveyed to the trustees on trust to hold it for the settlor for the remainder of his life, subject to an annual sum of money charged on the land in favour of the son, with remainder to the son for life and then to *his* eldest son in tail. A similar re-settlement was made every generation. The re-settlement, read together with the original settlement, was known as a *Compound Settlement*. A settlement taking effect by reference to another settlement was called a *Referential Settlement*. In this way land could be kept in the family, but it was so tied up that it could never be sold. In 1925, in pursuit of the principle of free alienation, it was provided by the Settled Land Act 1925 that after that year settlements must be made by two deeds. The trust instrument declares the trusts upon which the land is to be held. The vesting deed declares that the legal estate in the land is vested in the person who is for the time being entitled to the enjoyment of it as tenant for life. The latter is thus made the "estate owner" and entitled to sell the land. A purchaser is only permitted to examine the vesting deed and deals with the estate owner therein named. He has to pay the money, however, to the trustees, who must hold the money in place of the land, invest it, and apply the income according to the trusts of the settlement.

Settling Day. *See* Pay Day.

Seuil d'Imposition. The fiscal or customs figure below which a tax is not imposed. When this limit is exceeded, tax is levied on the total amount.

Sever. To part or divide by violence, to sunder, to cut or break off; to make a separation, to act independently of others in a joint law suit. *See also* Words of Severance.

Several Liability. *See* Joint and Several Liability.

Severalty. A freehold estate held solely by a tenant in his own right.

Share. The proportion of interest in the capital of a company which a shareholder has. *See also* Deferred Shares; Fully-Paid Shares; Growth Share; Incentive Share; Non-Voting Shares; Ordinary Shares; Partly-Paid Shares; Preference Shares; Private Company Shares; Redeemable Preference Shares; Subscription Shares; Unquoted Shares; Vendor's Shares.

Share Capital. The *Authorised* or *Nominal* or *Registered* capital is the amount of capital authorised in the Memorandum of Association of the company. The *Issued* capital is that part of the authorised capital which has in fact been issued. Money received from shareholders in exchange for issued shares is called the *Paid-up* capital and where the shares are fully paid up the issued capital and the paid-up capital are the same. But shares may be partly-paid, leaving a call perhaps to be made at some future time. This reservoir of capital is known as the *Uncalled* capital.

Share Certificate. A document issued by the company to its shareholders showing the numbers of shares held and the amount paid up.

Shareholder. One who has an interest in a joint property, particularly a member of a limited company.

Share Index. *See Indice des Actions.*

Share Option Scheme. A system to benefit employees of a company in that they may choose to buy shares of the company on a certain date at a price fixed in advance. Assessment for tax is on the excess of the market value of the shares at the time when the option was granted over the total cost of the option and the shares.

Share Pushing. The operations of fraudulent dealers who sell worthless stock, acting outside the recognised stock exchanges. *See also* Bucket Shop.

Share Register (or Register of Members). A book which a limited company is obliged to keep by law, containing the names and addresses of the members of the company. It must specify the numbers of shares held by each member, the date of purchase, the distinctive numbers of the shares, the amount per share and total amount of capital paid, and the date of sale. The register must be kept at the registered office of the company and be open for the inspection of members without fee and to any other person on payment of a fee.

Shares of No Par Value. *See* No Par Value.

Share Transfer (or Stock Transfer) Form. The instrument used when the holder of registered shares or stock transfers them to another person.

Share Warrant. Certificates issued by a limited company certifying that the bearer is entitled to the shares specified therein.

Sheriff. The chief officer of the Crown in every county, appointed annually and nominally entrusted with the execution of the laws and the maintenance of order. *See also* Under-Sheriff.

Shilling. The old name for a 5p piece.

Ship. Any vessel used for the carriage of goods and passengers by sea. A ship is divided into sixty-four parts for purposes of ownership and any person may own some or all of those shares. Individual shares may be jointly owned by up to five persons. A British ship is registered at any port in the U.K. where a register is maintained. A certificate of registry is issued to the ship to be used in the lawful navigation of the ship. Most ships are also registered at Lloyd's Register of Shipping.

Ship Bill of Sale. A bill of sale in the form prescribed by the Merchant Shipping Act 1894, evidencing the transfer to a purchaser of a ship or a share in a ship.

Ship-Broker. An agent for a shipping company who transacts business for a vessel lying in port; one who transacts marine insurance deals.

Shipment. The process of shipping; that which is shipped; a cargo. *See also* Groupage Shipment.

Ship Mortgage. *See* Mortgage of Ship.

Shipping Agent. One who arranges the shipment of goods or passengers.

Shipping Bill. An invoice of goods shipped; customs documents used where drawback is claimed.

Shipping Note. A document prepared by exporters and used to accompany goods to the dock, setting out the details of the ship, dock and the goods themselves.

Ship's Certificate of Registry. *See* Register of Ships.

Shopping List Credit. An Export Credits Guarantee Department-backed loan to a government or a foreign bank, often the central bank, who allocates portions of the loan on the same terms to buyers of British goods within their country; a type of transferable credit where the first beneficiary is the agent of, or principal supplier to, the applicant, for goods stated in the credit. These are usually issued for very large amounts and are sometimes known as "shopping bag" or "shopping list" credits. The first beneficiary will be responsible for distributing the portions of the credit to various suppliers, via the advising bank. Depending on the contractual relationship between the applicant and first beneficiary, the first beneficiary may be the commercial attaché of the applicant's country, or the principal supplier, or the applicant's representative agent or subsidiary company.

Short. Not long in space; not extended in time; wanting, deficient in cash, hard-up; the position of a foreign exchange dealer when his sales of currency exceed his purchases of that currency.

Short Bill. One which has only a few days to run to maturity, irrespective of the original tenor of the bill. It is also a term applied to any bill left at the branch for collection, irrespective of its maturity date.

Short-Dated Paper. Bills of exchange drawn at not more than three months.

Short End of the Market. That part of the money market which deals in short-dated government stocks. *See also* Short-Term Loan.

Short Exchange. On the foreign exchanges, bills payable within ten days.

Short Form Bill of Lading. A bill of lading which does not contain all the conditions of carriage.

Short Lease. A lease for not more than twenty-one years.

Short Rate. The price in one country at which a short-dated draft drawn on another country can be bought.

Shorts. Short-dated stocks, repayable inside five years.

Short Tap. Tap (*q.v.*) having, say, five years or less to maturity.

Short-Term Liabilities. *See* Current Liabilities.

Short-Term Loan. A loan for up to three years; Government stocks issued for a similar period.

Short-Term Money Market. A well-developed London money market providing for instant borrowing or instant placing of money. The short-term funds range from over-night borrowing to borrowing for periods of weeks or months up to one year. Anybody wishing to borrow for longer than this usually has to negotiate a term of say six or twelve months with an agreement, with an option, to re-negotiate the loan for a further period (rolling the loan over). The rate of interest payable when the re-negotiation takes place will be at the going rate at that time.

Short-Term Policy. An insurance policy which covers risks for a short period only, as where a businessman is taking a trip abroad.

Short-Term Rate of Interest. The rate of interest for loans of up to three months.

Short Ton. A unit of weight equal to 2,000 lb.

Sicherheit. Collateral.

Sicherungsgeschäft. *See Deckungsgeschäft.*

Sicherungswechsel. *See Depotwechsel.*

Sichtgelder, Sichtguthaben. Deposits repayable on demand.

Sight. A term used in connection with a bill of exchange, which may be payable "at sight" or on demand, *i.e.* immediately on presentation to the drawee. If a bill is payable after sight, *i.e.* at so many days/months after sight, it is a term bill, and in order to fix the maturity it is necessary to know when the drawee "sighted" it. For this purpose, therefore, he will add after his signature of acceptance the word "sighted" and the date on which he sighted it. The term of the bill will then run from that date.

Sight Bill. A bill payable as soon as the drawee sees it.

Sight Clause. *See* Exchange Clause.

Sight Credit. A credit where the beneficiary is to obtain payment immediately, either against a sight draft accompanied by documents of title, or against the documents only.

Sight Deposits. Current accounts, money deposited overnight, and money at call.

Signatory. One who is bound by his signature to the terms of an agreement; one who signs the Memorandum of Association of a limited company. A limited company may be bound by one or more of its officers signing in their official capacities for and on behalf of the company, or the seal of the company may be used. Any provision of the Consumer Credit Act 1974 requiring a document to be signed is complied with by a body corporate if the document is sealed by that body (but this does not apply in Scotland).

Signature. A sign, stamp or mark impressed, a person's name written by himself, the act of writing it. The signature of a customer on an instruction to his banker is the banker's authority to comply with the instruction and to debit the customer's account with the cost, *e.g.* a cheque. *See also* Forged Signature.

Simple. Single, not complex, entire, mere.

Simple Arbitrage. *See* Direct Arbitrage.

Simple Contract. One evidenced in writing, or formed orally.

Simple Debenture. Debentures which are unsecured.

Simple Interest. Money paid on the principal borrowed, but not on the accrued interest as in compound interest.

Sine. Without.

Sine Die. Without a day being set, indefinitely.

Sine Prole. Without issue, childless.

Sine Qua Non. An indispensable condition, an essential.

Single Costing. A system of quantifying cost where one commodity only is in question.

Single Entry. A system of book-keeping in which each item is entered once only in the ledger, etc.

Single Premium Policy. An insurance policy where one premium only, usually for a large sum, is payable at the time when the policy is taken out.

Sinking Fund. A fund created by sums

set aside at regular intervals and invested outside the business in order to provide for the replacement of an asset or the repayment of a particular liability at a known future date.

Sixpence. The old name for the 2½p piece. No new sixpences will be minted.

Skadenz. Period until maturity, period over which interest runs.

Skonto. A discount for prompt or early payment of an invoice amount.

Slander. The publication of defamatory matter in an ephemeral form, normally by means of an oral statement.

Sleeping Partner. *See* Dormant Partner.

Slip. (*Fr.*) A docket accompanying a document of title certifying that it complies with certain conditions, for example, that it is not enemy property, that it complies with an export licence, etc.

Slump. A long-term economic decline which manifests itself in high unemployment, increased bankruptcies and liquidations, falling production and low consumption. Slump conditions are usually world-wide, and are aggravated if countries in balance of payments difficulties impose restrictive actions on imports. This tends to decrease world trade even more and makes the existing conditions still worse.

Small Agreement. A regulated consumer credit agreement for credit not exceeding £30, other than a hire-purchase or conditional sale agreement; or a regulated consumer hire agreement which does not require the hirer to make payments exceeding £30, being an agreement which is either unsecured or secured by a guarantee or indemnity only (whether or not the guarantee or indemnity is itself secured).

Smithsonian Agreement. In December 1971, a meeting of the Group of Ten (the world's leading central bankers) at Washington resulted in an agreed realignment of currency parities. The Smithsonian agreement widened the limits of permissible fluctuations of one currency against another. The U.S. dollar was given the role of providing the "middle rates" around which the system revolved. *See also* Snake in the Tunnel.

"S.M.T. Money". *See* Securities Management Trust Ltd.

Snake in the Tunnel. Revised International Monetary Fund rules following the Smithsonian agreement allowed the currencies of the member countries to fluctuate around their new Smithsonian dollar parities, or middle rates, by 4½%, 2¼% on either side of the middle rate. Support operations, if needed, were to be used to keep the quotation or any particular currency within this permitted band. It came to be said that the "tunnel" was 4½%, but the maximum size of movements of any non-dollar currencies relative to each other was 9%. Thus if currency A fell from the highest quotation within the band, or tunnel, to the lowest, and currency B performed in a similar way but in the reverse direction, the two currencies would, in terms of each other, have fluctuated by 9%. The countries of the E.E.C., set on ultimately attaining complete monetary union, agreed amongst themselves to hold their currencies within a 2¼% tolerance of exchange fluctuations (1⅛% either side of parity relative to each other) as compared with the 4½% margin allowed under the revised I.M.F. rules. Changing movements within this narrower band allowed fluctuations up to 4½% as between the E.E.C. countries, these fluctuations being permitted anywhere inside the wider limits of the tunnel. While the latter was thought of as being composed of two straight lines (the "top" and "bottom" limits) at equal distances from the medium dollar parities, the movements of the E.E.C. currencies were described as the "snake", free to wriggle within the "tunnel", but never allowed to get outside it. If the top of the "snake" (the strongest European currency inside it) touched the top of the tunnel then the belly (the weakest currency) would be at the level of the par line with the U.S. dollar.

Social Accounting. The reporting of the cost incurred in complying with anti-pollution, safety and health and other socially beneficial requirements, and, more generally, the impact of the business entity on, and its endeavours to protect, society, its amenities and the environment.

Social Responsibility. The philosophy that a big organisation has duties not only to its shareholders and staff but also to society generally, which provides the environment in which the organisation flourishes, and which is affected by its actions. In recognition of this view big banks may associate themselves with sporting events by donations or give grants to encourage good citizenship in young people, etc. These activities also tend to improve the public image of the bank, which is an important factor in an increasingly critical and politically conscious society.

Société. Company, association.

Société Affiliée. Affiliated company.

Société Anonyme, Société à Responsibilité Limitée. Limited company.

Société Apparentée. Associated company.

Société de Gestion. Management company.

Société d'Investissement. Investment trust.

Société d'Investissement à Capital Variable. *See* Unit Trust.

Société Mère. Parent company.

Society. A number of persons unified by agreement, or incorporated by law, for some specific purpose; a company, an association, a club. The rules of a society may empower it to borrow and to provide securities held by trustees on its behalf. In the absence of security duly charged by properly-appointed trustees, however, a society has no power to borrow and, not being incorporated, has no separate entity to be made responsible for any borrowing. Any accommodation granted should be against the indemnity of a person interested in the society, who will be personally liable.

Society for Worldwide Interbank Financial Telecommunication (SWIFT). A co-operative society created under Belgian law and registered in Brussels. It is wholly owned by some 240 of the largest European and North American banks. The aims of SWIFT are to enable members to transmit between themselves international payments, statements and other messages connected with international banking. As 80% of international money transfers are carried out by mail transfers and the other 20% by cable transfers or telex, the SWIFT system has been able to speed up international settlements considerably. Messages previously sent by cable or telex are now transmitted by an "urgent SWIFT message": those formerly sent by mail transfer have become "SWIFT messages".

Soft Arbitrage. Switching between market and bank facilities to take advantage of interest rate differentials, or borrowing from banks while retaining readily realisable money market investments.

Soft Currency. The currency of any country which is in plentiful supply on the foreign exchanges, *i.e.* it is not hard to get.

Sola Bill. A bill consisting of one document only, as contrasted with a bill in a set.

Solawechsel. Promissory note.

Solde. Balance.

Solde Créditeur. Credit balance.

Solde Débiteur. Debit balance.

Sold Note. The contract note supplied by a stockbroker to his client, detailing the particulars of a sale made on his behalf.

Sole. Single, only, alone in its kind; unmarried.

Sole Proprietor. The owner of a one-man business.

Sole Trader. One who works in wholesale or retail trade for himself only.

Solicitor. A person legally qualified to represent another in a court of law, a lawyer, a law agent; a legal practitioner authorised to advise clients and prepare causes for barristers, but not to appear as an advocate in the higher courts.

Solicitor-General. A law officer of the Crown, ranking in England below the Attorney-General and in Scotland below the Lord Advocate.

Solicitors' Accounts. Because solicitors continually handle the money of their clients, it has been necessary to legislate as to the manner in which this money shall be dealt with. The conduct of solicitors in this regard is governed by a set of rules known as the Solicitors' Accounts rules. These provide that a solicitor holding money on behalf of a client shall pay such money into a current or deposit account in his own name with the word "client" included in the title. A solicitor will also need an "office" account for the running of his business, so that any solicitor will normally maintain at least two accounts. Solicitors are often appointed trustees for the funds and settlements of clients, or trustees under clients' wills, and a separate set of rules, called the Solicitors' Trust Accounts rules, provides for these. A solicitor-trustee must open a trust bank account in which the description "executor" or "trustee" must appear. No overdraft should appear on any "client" account.

Solicitor's Undertaking. A written promise, signed by a solicitor, to the effect that securities or deeds temporarily lent to him by the banker (against the written instruction of his customer) for inspection will be returned by him to the bank in the same state as that in which he received them; a similar promise that when funds are available, as for example in the case of a customer's house which is in process of sale, they will be forwarded by him to the banker for credit to the customer's account. A solicitor's undertaking is an essential factor in a bridging advance. The solicitor must be either known to the lending bank as reliable, or be favourably reported on by another bank. The terms of his undertaking must be unequivocal.

Solicitor-Trustee. A solicitor who is a sole trustee, or who is co-trustee only with a partner or employee of his.

Solid. *See* Swing.

Solidarbürge. A surety who can be forced to implement a pledge he has given on account of a principal debtor.

Solidarschuld. The proportions of a joint debt agreed by two or more debtors as their responsibilities. As against the creditor, however, each debtor is singly responsible for the total amount. The creditor may at his choice demand part or all of the sum from any of the joint debtors. *See also* Joint and Several Liability.

Solvency. The state of being able to pay all one's debts.

Solvency Ratio. The conventional relationship obtaining between a bank's own capital resources and its total deposit liabilities.

Sonderziehungsrechte. Special drawing rights.

Sorten. Foreign notes and currency.

Sorting. Arranging in kinds of classes, classifying, putting in order; the arrangement of customers' cheques into alphabetical or numerical order preparatory to posting them to the accounts or to filing them away; the division of cheques paid in during the day under the heads of various banks on which they are drawn, preparatory to machining them and dispatching them for collection; filing of customer's letters.

Sorting Code Number. A number placed on the face of a cheque to identify numerically the bank on which the cheque will be drawn. In the U.K. this consists of three groups of two figures each, the first group referring to the bank and the other two groups indicating the branch. It is also used in connection with credits, particularly dividends and all items distributed through the Bankers' Automated Clearing Services.

Souche. Cheque book counterfoil.

Soulte, Soulte de Conversion. On a conversion of shares, the difference between the repayment price of the old share and the issue price of the new share.

Souscription. Application for an allotment of a new issue; subscription.

Souscription Fictive. Stagging.

Souscription Préférentielle. The right of the members of an issuing syndicate to reserve for themselves a certain fraction of the issue being offered to the public.

Sous-Participation. The sharing in the placing of a loan by a bank which is not one of the syndicate floating the loan, but which takes a certain proportion of the issue.

Soutenu. A rate maintaining its level, a firm rate.

South Sea Bubble. The name given in the U.K. to an early example of widespread and reckless speculation. The South Sea Company was incorporated in 1710, and was given a monopoly of trade in the Pacific Ocean. The company was also engaged in various financial dealings at home: in particular the directors had worked out a scheme for taking over most of the National Debt from the government. Parliament was persuaded to agree to this, although there was strong opposition. The price of South Sea stock rose dramatically and people rushed to buy shares, recklessly investing all their life savings. When the share value reached ten times the nominal value people began to realise that the shares were not worth nearly as much as their quoted value, and confidence suddenly evaporated. There was a rush to sell and prices dropped catastrophically. Thousands of people were ruined.

Sovereign. The standard unit of the British coinage, a gold coin representing one pound sterling. Sovereigns are now minted only for export, particularly to the Middle and Far East. Internally the pound sterling is a banknote worth 100p. In some countries abroad sovereigns are named Kings or Queens according to the head of the sovereign portrayed.

Sozialprodukt. Total production of goods and services in a country, without deduction of indirect taxation.

Sparen. Savings.

Sparheft. The issue by the bank of a savings account book in the name of the holder, or bearer, giving particulars of withdrawals and other entries made which affect the balance.

Sparkasse. Savings bank.

Special. Particular, peculiar, designed for a particular purpose or occasion, uncommon, confined to a definite field of action or discussion.

Special Agent. One authorised to act only on a particular occasion or for a specific service, *e.g.* to bid at an auction on his principal's behalf.

Special Buyer. The Bank of England agent in the Discount Market.

Special Clearance, Special Collection. The accelerated clearance of a cheque for a customer, by posting the cheque direct to the branch on which it is drawn with a subsequent telephone call to ascertain fate.

Special Crossing. *See* Crossed Cheque.

Special Deposits. At the request of the Bank of England following agreement with the Treasury, banks may be asked to place Special Deposits with the Bank of England. The amount to be deposited by each bank will be a specified percentage of some or all of its eligible liabilities as reported to the Bank of England at the latest mid-monthly reporting date, the amount being rounded up to the nearest £5,000. The amount of each bank's Special Deposit will be adjusted as necessary to take account of changes in its eligible liabilities as subsequently reported, such adjustment normally taking place on the third Monday following the reporting date. Special Deposits bear interest at the average Treasury Bill Tender Rate rounded up or down to the nearest 1/16%. This rate is determined by the Treasury Bill Tender each Friday and is operative from the Monday following. Interest is paid weekly on a Monday. Banks may be called upon to make deposits on which no interest is paid, *e.g.* the "Corset" system.

Special Drawing Rights (S.D.R.s). A new type of international money devised in 1969, to try to assist world trade. S.D.R.s are lines of credit opened for countries by the I.M.F. to help them in settling their overseas debts, with the intent that temporary difficulties from payments deficits might be bridged over. The value of S.D.R. was fixed in terms of gold, although it was realised that the rate of increase in international trade might not always be paralleled by a similar growth in the outputs of the world's gold mines. This was a manifestation of the power of gold and the emotional reaction which it generates, that it still remains the only criterion of value. S.D.R.s were dubbed "paper gold". Special Drawing Rights are so denominated to distinguish them from the ordinary I.M.F. drawing rights available to all member countries. The S.D.R. has the widest range of the currencies of the major trading countries, consisting of a "basket" of fixed amounts of sixteen currencies, weighted broadly by their importance in international transactions.

Special Indorsement. One which specifies the person to whom, or to whose order, a bill or cheque is to be payable (*e.g.* "pay John Smith or order, Thomas Brown").

Special Investment Department. A department in the Trustee Savings Banks where customers maintain accounts which are subject to one month's notice of withdrawal, but which earn a rather higher rate of interest than deposits in the Ordinary Department.

Special Issue. A legal issue which denies the truth of parts only of the declaration or charge.

Special Manager. A person appointed by the Official Receiver, acting as liquidator of a company where he is satisfied that such an appointment is desirable because of the nature of the company's business, or in the interests of the creditors or shareholders. An application to the court by the liquidator is a necessary preliminary, and the court, if it agrees, will lay down what powers the special manager is to have and for how long he may exercise them.

Special Pleading. Unfair argument; bending the rules to suit one case.

Special Resolution. One passed by a majority of not less than three-fourths of such members as vote in person or by proxy, at a general meeting of which not less than twenty-one days' notice specifying the intention to propose the resolution as a special resolution has been duly given.

Specialty Contract. One executed under seal.

Specialty Debt. A debt which is acknowledged in a document under seal.

Special Verdict. A verdict stating the facts, but leaving the decision to be determined by the court.

Specie. Gold and silver coins, and bullion.

Specie Points. Where in currencies there is a fixed relationship to gold, fixed parities exist, and any movement of the rate away from the par of exchange would make it profitable to buy gold in one centre, send it to another, and sell it there. The cost of shipping and insurance sets margins on either side of the par of exchange to which the rate of exchange can vary before it becomes profitable to ship gold. These are the specie points.

Specification. A detailed statement of particulars, especially of materials, work to be undertaken or supplied by an architect, builder, manufacturer, etc.; the production of a new commodity out of materials belonging to another person.

Specific Performance. An equitable remedy sought where damages are not a satisfactory remedy, *e.g.* in cases of broken contracts concerning land or objects of art. Specific performance may be granted where the parties are on an equal footing, provided always that it is impossible for a money award to provide an agreeable solution.

Specific Reserve. A provision for a specific or contingent liability, such as tax or dividends shortly to be paid. Such provisions may be described as "reserves", but they should appear under the heading of a current liability and cannot be included in the fixed capital. Provisions linked directly with an asset, such as a provision for bad and doubtful debts or for depreciation of a fixed asset, should be shown as a deduction from the value of the asset.

Speculation. The purchase or sale of shares on an estimate of whether the share value will rise or fall, with the intention of making a quick profit, or avoiding a loss; a gamble on future price movements, whether in shares, land commodities or money. A speculator in stocks and shares buys a security without intending to pay for it on settling day, in the hope that he can sell it again at a higher price, in the same account. If he can successfully do this he will never have to pay for the security, but will receive the difference between the buying and selling prices, as his profit. On the foreign exchanges speculation against a currency may be purely in the hope of making a profit, but it is equally likely that it is the cautious placing of a company's money where it will be safest. If sterling is being sold on a large scale the reason is that the economy backing it is weak. International companies offset potential threats to their trading profits by hedging their currency commitments.

Spéculer à la Baisse. To speculate on a fall; to sell shares one does not possess for delivery at a term, in the hope of being able to buy them in later at a cheaper rate; to take part in a bear operation.

Spekulation. See Speculation.

Sperr, Sperrfrist. Embargo.

Sperrbestand. Earmarked stocks.

Sperrguthaben, Sperrkonto. Blocked account.

Sperrliste. List of articles lost, stolen or blocked for some reason.

Sperrstücke. Bond or share which is earmarked as not for payment at a specified term, or not to be disposed of under the issue price; valuable documents which appear on a cautionary list as lost, stolen or blocked for good delivery on some other ground.

Spesen. Expenses, charges.

Spitze. An error in calculation resulting in a balance over; a fraction arising from shareholder's rights to partake in a new issue on the basis of his existing holding, so that a further purchase is necessary to make up a whole share, or the fractional right must be sold.

Split-Level Trust. An investment trust where the greater part of the income passes to one class of shareholder, and the greater part of any capital gains to another.

Splitting. The division of shares in companies into units of smaller denomination in order to increase their marketability, or the division of stock units represented by an Allotment Letter or a Letter of Acceptance. In the last case splitting of the Allotment Letter is necessary where the holder wishes to dispose of some only of the stock units, or to dispose of all the stock units to more than one person. In such a case the holder completes the Form of Renunciation and forwards the Letter to the company by the appropriate time and date set out (varying as to whether the stock is partly or fully paid), specifying the number of stock units to be comprised in each split letter, whereupon the company will issue split letters as requested, which will be endorsed "original duty renounced".

Spot Against Forward. *See* Swap.

Spot, Spot Price. Cash price for immediate delivery.

Spot Rate. The normal rate of exchange quoted in the foreign exchange markets, *i.e.* the rate for transactions in which the funds are to be paid over in each centre two working days later.

Spread. Extended in length and breadth. Thus sundry debtors of a company should show a good spread, as opposed to having three or four big debtors, the failure of any one of whom would have a serious effect on the company. In the same way a bank seeks a good spread of its loans across a wide spectrum of borrowers, and a good spread for its investments over many different fields, in the case of government stocks having repayment staggered over a number of years. In the case of the secondary market for Eurobonds, the difference between a seller's asked and buyer's bid price, normally split between banks acting as market makers. Also used to describe the total of fees and commissions earned from the borrower by banks making a new issue; on the Stock Exchange, the difference between the higher and lower prices at which stock-jobbers are prepared to deal. The higher price is the price at which the jobber will sell stock to the broker; the lower is the jobber's buying price.

Staatschuld. National debt.

Stag. A Stock Exchange expression for a person who applies for shares in any new company, or any new issue, with the sole object of selling any allocation he may get as soon as a premium is obtainable, and never intending to hold or even fully subscribe for the shares.

Stale Cheque. *See* Antedated Cheque.

Stammaktie. Ordinary share.

Stammeinlage. The interest of an ordinary shareholder in the share capital of a limited liability company.

Stammgesellschaft. Parent company.

Stammkapital. Ordinary capital, ordinary share capital.

Stamping under Penalty. Stamping a legal document at an increased rate because the stamping has not been carried out in the time allowed by law.

Standard Contract. Where the contract is of a type which is constantly occurring a standard contract will emerge, which will have generally accepted terms which are normal and usual. Either or any of the parties to the contract may stipulate a variation to the standard form, but if they do not, they are bound by its terms.

Ständiger Auftrag. Standing order.

Standing. Fixed, established, permanent.

Standing Credit. *See* Credit Advice.

Standing Order. An order by a customer to his banker to make a regular payment to a named payee to the debit of his account.

Standing Orders. The statutory rules of any organisation, society, etc., governing the conduct of business at a meeting; orders made by a deliberative assembly as to the manner in which its business shall be conducted. *See also* Receiving Order.

Statement. A formal account, recital or narration; a declaration of fact or circumstance.

Statement *in lieu* **of Prospectus.** A company having a share capital which does not issue a prospectus, or which has issued a prospectus but has not allotted any shares to the public, must deliver to the Registrar of Companies for registration a statement *in lieu* of prospectus, signed by all directors, three days before proceeding to allot.

Statement of Affairs. The schedule of assets and liabilities provided by an insolvent person in his bankruptcy proceedings, or by a company in compulsory winding-up proceedings.

Statistics. Numerical facts or data collected systematically, summarised and tabulated; the science of collecting, studying and interpreting such information.

Status. (*Ger.*) An interim balance sheet as at any given day.

Status Enquiry. A bank will answer status enquiries on its customer and will make similar enquiries about other people's financial position on his behalf. For exporters it will obtain reports on traders abroad. To preserve the secrecy about the customer's affairs which banks must maintain, certain rules have been laid down. The bank will only answer enquiries which are put to it by other banks or reputable trade protection organisations and it will only answer to such groups. It will not answer private enquiries, nor disclose addresses. It seems likely that banker's confidential reports on customers supplied for the benefit of trade protection organisations will in future be expressed in very general terms. The reason is that legislation for the protection of consumers has given the latter the right of access to these files. Replies to all enquiries must be carefully considered and tactfully phrased. If a favourable reply cannot be given, a form of words should be used which conveys the right impression, without harming the customer's credit. The bank has a duty of care to the enquirer who is relying on the banker's special knowledge of his customer, and must make a true and faithful reply. He should always include in his opinion a clause disclaiming responsibility. *See also* Credit Rating.

Statut. Regulation, ordinance, statute, bye-law.

Statute. An Act of Parliament.

Statute-Barred. A debt which cannot be recovered at law, because more than six years has elapsed since the cause of action arose. *See* Limitation of Actions.

Statute Book. The complete record of legal enactments.

Statute Law. That law which originates in Acts passed by Parliament (also known as *Written Law*).

Statutory Books. Those books which companies must keep if they are registered under the Companies Acts. They are: a minute book, and registers of the members, directors and secretaries of the company.

Statutory Company. A company authorised by special Act of Parliament, *e.g.* a nationalised industry.

Statutory Declaration. A declaration by some person before a justice of the peace, notary public, or commissioner for oaths, as to some circumstance or fact of which he has knowledge; a declaration made by directors of a company in voluntary liquidation to the effect that they have made a full inquiry into the affairs of the company, and are of the opinion that the company will be able to pay its debts in full in a period not longer than twelve months from the commencement of the winding-up. This declaration must be made within the five weeks immediately preceding the date of the resolution for winding-up and it must be delivered to the registrar for registration before that same date. The declaration must include an up-to-date statement of the company's assets and liabilities. Where such a declaration has been made and delivered, the winding-up is known as a members' voluntary winding-up; where it is not made, the winding-up is known as a creditors' voluntary winding-up.

Statutory Legacy. The absolute right of the surviving spouse of a deceased intestate to receive a capital sum from the estate, as from time to time fixed by law, plus the personal chattels of the deceased.

Statutory Meeting. Every company limited by shares or by guarantee and having a share capital shall hold a general meeting of the members of the company between one and three months from the date from which the company is authorised to commence business. This is known as the statutory meeting.

Statutory Mortgage. As a special form of charge by way of legal mortgage, a mortgage of freehold or leasehold land may be made by a deed expressed to be made by way of statutory mortgage, being in one of the forms set out in the Fourth Schedule to the Law of Property Act 1925, with such variations and additions as the circumstances may require.

Statutory Owner. The trustees who take the legal fee simple in settled land when there is no person entitled to take it as tenant for life.

Statutory Receipt. A receipt indorsed on a mortgage deed, when the mortgage has been satisfied, which acts as a reconveyance. The receipt must be endorsed on, written at the foot of, or annexed to, a mortgage for all money secured. It must state the name of the person who pays the money and must be executed by the chargee by way of legal mortgage.

Statutory Report. The directors of a limited company shall, at least fourteen days before the date on which the statutory meeting is held, forward a report, referred to as the "statutory report", to every member of the company. The statutory report shall be certified by at least two directors of the company and shall state the total number of shares allotted; an abstract of the receipts and payments made up to seven days before the date of the report; and the names, addresses and descriptions of the directors, auditors, managers and secretary of the company. The report shall be certified as correct by the auditors of the company, and a copy shall be delivered to the registrar of companies for registration.

Statutory Restrictions on Company Loans. In the U.K. a company may not give direct or indirect financial assistance, whether by loan, guarantee, the provision of security, or in any other way, to any party for the purchase of, or subscription to, its own shares, or the shares of any holding company which it may have. Exceptions are allowed where lending money is part of the company's ordinary business, or where with the approval of the company in general meeting a loan is made to an officer of the company to be used in the furtherance of his duties. Similarly, a company may not make a loan to one of its directors, or to a director of its holding company, or provide a guarantee or any other form of security to another person on the terms that he will make the loan.

Statutory Trust for Sale. *See* Trust for Sale.

Stellage. A contract at a premium whereby an option-holder may at his choice on the day of expiry either receive or deliver the documents of value (shares, bonds, currency) stipulated.

Stellage-Geschäft. See Prämiengeschäft.

Stempelsteuer. Stamp duty.

Sterling. Pertaining to standard value, weight or purity, of solid worth; pure, genuine; British currency, generally used of the "pound sterling".

Sterling Area. *See* Scheduled Territories.

Sterling Bonds. Bonds of a foreign country payable in British currency.

Sterling Certificate of Deposit. (1) Prime Issues. A document evidencing receipt of a deposit by a bank for a fixed period at a fixed rate of interest. Certificates are issued in minimum denominations of £50,000 and thereafter in multiples of £10,000 to a maximum of £500,000 per certificate. The period of issue is from three months up to five years. Interest is paid gross on maturity for Certificates up to one year and thereafter on the anniversary of the issue date and on final maturity. Certificates are in bearer form and as such must be held by an Authorised Depositary. Additionally, payments of interest and final repayment may only be made on presentation of the certificate by an Authorised Bank. Certificates of deposit are fully negotiable and may be sold before maturity through the Secondary Market (*see below*).

(2) Secondary Sterling Certificate of Deposit. Certificates of deposit may be disposed of before maturity through the Secondary Market operated by banks and discount houses. A certificate is sold at a yield to maturity irrespective of the coupon rate at issue, the proceeds being calculated on the basis of the following formula:

$$\text{Proceeds} = \text{Principal} \times \frac{36{,}500 \text{ plus (issued rate} \times \text{tenor in days)}}{36{,}500 \text{ plus (quoted yield} \times \text{days to run)}}$$

See also "Straight" Deposit.

Sterling-Gebiet. See Scheduled Territories.

Sterling Securities. Any securities on which dividends are payable, and capital repayable, in sterling.

Stet. Let it stand.

Steuer. Tax.

Steuerwert. Tax due.

Steward. A person employed to manage the property or affairs of another, especially the paid manager of a large estate; one of the officials superintending the conduct of a public meeting.

Stichtag. Expiry date, settling day.

Stillhalten. In the case of option business, to wait until the expiry date of the option before taking a decision on whether to exercise it.

Stimmrechtsloseaktie. Non-voting share.

Stipend. Money paid for a person's services, an annual salary; the provision made for the support of a parish minister.

Stipendiary Magistrate. A paid magistrate.

Stipulation. A definite arrangement, a contract, a specified condition.

Stock. Capital, the money or goods invested in trade, manufacture, banking, etc., the supply of goods a trader has on hand; government securities; a share or shares in a national, municipal or other debt; the capital of a company.

Stockbroker. One whose business is to buy or sell stocks or shares for others.

Stock Certificate, Share Certificate. The document issued by a company to a share or stockholder specifying the number of shares or the amount of stock held by him. A registered certificate is evidence of the title of the person named therein and on a sale of the stock or shares the certificate must be sent with a completed stock transfer form to the company, which will then effect the necessary change of ownership on the register and issue a new certificate to the buyer.

Stock Dividends. Dividends paid by companies in further stock, instead of in cash. The purpose of stock dividends was partly to reduce tax payable by the recipients, and partly to retain cash within the company, thus raising, or at least maintaining, the level of working and investment capital. Since 5th April 1975, stock dividends are in the U.K. treated as income on which basic tax has been paid, so the notional gross amount now becomes liable for higher rate tax where appropriate. The effect has been the virtual cessation of dividend payments in the form of stock.

Stock Exchange. A London market for dealing in stocks and shares, handling gilt-edged and all kinds of commercial and industrial shares. Only members are admitted and business is transacted according to a prescribed set of rules. Anyone wishing to buy or sell shares must do so through a broker. Brokers are agents for the public, who deal with jobbers, dealers who specialise in certain kinds of stocks. They do not deal directly with the public. The Stock Exchange provides a value for quoted stocks and so allows securities to be valued on a daily basis in branch banks, to be compared with the accommodation outstanding.

Stock Exchange Daily Official List. The list of officially quoted prices of those securities which are considered sufficiently active to merit a daily quotation. A monthly supplement contains prices of securities for which markings are not frequently recorded.

Stock Exchange Indices. Figures calculated for a number of key share prices in order to give a general view of the movement of such prices and thus of the buoyancy of the market as a whole, e.g. the Financial Times Industrial Ordinary Share Index.

Stock-in-Trade. Goods and materials in stock, machinery, tools, fittings, etc., necessary to carry on a trade or business; the goods which a merchant, shopkeeper, etc., has on hand for supply to the public; resources, capabilities.

Stock-Jobber. See Jobber.

Stockpiling. The accumulation of reserves of essential raw materials for an emergency.

Stock Receipt. A receipt given by the seller of inscribed stocks to the purchaser. It has no value, and is no evidence of title. Where a customer produces a stock receipt as suggested security, the bank should check with the registering authority that the stock is still held. In many cases it will be found that the stock was sold years ago, or has been converted into registered stock.

Stock Relief. Born in November 1974, out of the need to ease the burden on the corporate sector of excessive inflation, stock relief was a device to mitigate the effects on company liquidity of taxation levied on profits which had been inflated by artificial appreciation in stock values. At first companies in the U.K. were allowed for tax purposes to reduce stock values by the amount by which the increase in book value of stocks exceeded 10% of trading profits, but in April 1976 this level was raised to 15%. The sums of money so saved were to be set aside as "deferred taxation", but the Chancellor said in March 1977 that "for the normal continuing business there is little or no risk that any substantial part of the deferred liability will arise". This encouraged the belief that companies will never have to pay these huge sums of money set aside. However, the deferred tax will become payable if the level of the individual company's activity is reduced, or if the value of stocks falls because commodity prices fall. The present stock relief scheme will in fact be continued, while a decision on inflation accounting is awaited, not only for 1977–1978, but also for 1978–1979. Thereafter a move would be initiated to introduce a permanent system with, if necessary, special provisions to ensure that any change does not lead to cash flow difficulties for individual companies.

Stock-Taking. The act of preparing an inventory or valuation of the goods on hand in a manufacturing, commercial or trading establishment. It is usual to value stock at the lower of cost or market price.

Stock Transfer Form. The form accompanying the certificate when shares are sold, both being sent to the company issuing the shares for registration and issue of a new certificate to the buyer. The form is in nearly all cases signed by the transferor only and includes the description of the security, the name of the undertaking, the consideration price, the number of shares or amount of stock sold, the names of the registered holder and the buyer and their addresses, and a request that such entries be made in the register as are necessary to give effect to the transfer. The stock transfer form is executed under hand, except in the rare cases where the articles of the company concerned require them to be under seal. Case law has established that a banker forwarding a stock transfer form to a company for registration is deemed to guarantee to the company the genuineness of the signature(s) on the stock transfer form.

Stop. To bring to a halt, to obstruct, to check, to suspend.

Stop-Go. A term for a period of opposing and contradictory monetary policies of government, whereby credit is alternately expanded and contracted, in the interests of containing inflation and yet maintaining full employment. The effect is that industry is encouraged to expand by borrowing, and then restricted by a drying-up of credit.

Stop Loss Order. To limit an eventual loss, an order to sell stock at the best rate obtainable when the price attains or exceeds a given level.

Stop Order. A notice by the customer to the bank that he wishes payment stopped on a cheque which he has drawn and issued. The customer should ideally state the number, date, and the amount of the cheque, and give the name of the payee. These details may be telephoned in the first instance, but should be confirmed in writing without delay. The banker's first action on receipt of the notice to stop should be to consult the customer's ledger (where this still exists), the day's vouchers, and the customer's paid vouchers to ensure that the cheque has not already been paid. Next the cashiers must be given the details so that the cheque is not paid if it should be presented over the counter. Finally, the ledger and statement must be marked with a warning note of some kind, or the computer programmed accordingly.

Stoppage *in Transitu.* An unpaid seller's right to stop the goods in transit and resume possession of them, after he has himself parted with them, in the event of the buyer becoming insolvent.

Stopped Account. *See* Clayton's Case.

Stopped Cheque. A cheque in respect of which the drawer has instructed the bank to refuse payment.

Storage. A charge for warehousing goods; the space occupied by them.

Storno. The cancellation of a transaction, a counter-entry.

Straddle. On the Stock Exchange, a contract in which a buyer of stock has the privilege of calling for or delivering it, at a pre-determined price. *See also* Marginal Risk *under* Margin, *Stellage.*

Straight. Passing from one point to another by the most direct route; direct, honest.

Straight Bill of Lading. One purporting to consign goods to a specified person.

Straight Bonds. Bonds having no right or option of conversion into any other form of shares, stock or bonds.

Straight Debt. A security without rights of conversion into a borrower's common stock.

"Straight" Deposit. A deposit accepted by a bank without the issue of a Sterling Certificate of Deposit.

Straight Line Method of Depreciation. *See* Depreciation.

Street Market. A continuation of Stock Exchange business in the street after the London Stock Exchange is closed for the day.

Street Prices. The prices established in the street market ($q.v.$).

Streifbanddepot. A deposit by a customer kept separately from other articles of a similar nature; deposit of a sealed packet for safe-keeping.

Stripping the Premium. *See* Premium Stripping.

Strohman. Nominee.

Stubbs Weekly Gazette. A weekly trade paper which collects and publishes details as to the bankruptcy proceedings of individuals and as to the liquidations of companies, together with other various matters connected with limited company mortgages and county court judgments. The paper has sections containing extracts from the Bills of Sale Registry, the Registry of Deeds of Arrangement, and the Registry of County Court judgments. In connection with bankruptcy there are notices to creditors as to the holding of meetings, petitions presented with the date of presentation in each case, details of receiving and adjudication orders, lists of principal creditors and, in some cases, details as to the appointment and discharge of trustees. Details are also given of orders made by the court on application for discharge from bankruptcy.

In connection with liquidation details are given of winding-up orders and dates, voluntary windings-up and the date of the appropriate resolutions, notices of the appointment of liquidators, notices to creditors relating to statutory meetings of company creditors, the appointments of Receivers and their dates, details of Receivers ceasing to act, and a list of declarations of solvency filed.

Under the heading Dissolution of Partnerships details are given of such dissolutions together with the appropriate dates, and under the heading Mortgages and Charges by Limited Companies are given details of such charges, taken from the registry at Companies House. From the same source there is a list of satisfactions of such mortgages and charges.

Some banks take *Stubbs Weekly Gazette* in each of the branches, and some only at Area Offices. It is the duty of a particular bank officer to go through the newspaper looking for the names of customers affected by county court judgments, bankruptcies or liquidations so that appropriate steps may be taken in connection with the customer's bank account.

Stückelung. The lower part of a bond consisting of detachable coupons.

Stückzins. The current rate.

Sub. Under, below, inferior.

Sub-Agent. One under the orders of an agent, a deputy agent, an agent's representative.

Sub-Branch. Small agencies or offices operated by a branch, known as the parent branch. Sub-branches may be open only for specified hours on certain weekdays. There may be a clerk travelling from the parent branch, or there may be a clerk-in-charge. If the business increases, the sub-branch may acquire a separate account at Head Office and be in time up-graded to the status of a full branch.

Sub-Charge. A charge on a charge certificate, that is, the owner of a charge on a piece of registered land has offered it as security to a lender. A banker deciding to accept the security may take an equitable sub-mortgage or a legal one. In the first case the banker will keep the charge certificate and give notice of its deposit to the registrar on Form 85A. The charge certificate must be written up to date to include the notice of deposit. The form of sub-mortgage to be signed by the sub-mortgagor may be drafted by the bank's solicitor, or an existing form of bank charge may be adapted. In the second case a search must be made, using Form 94A, and an official certificate of search obtained. An office copy of the form of sub-mortgage is prepared, and the charge certificate is the sent to the Registrar with the signed, sealed form of sub-mortgage, the office copy and the appropriate fee. The Registrar will keep the charge certificate and the copy form of sub-mortgage, and will issue to the banker as evidence of his title a certificate of sub-charge with the original form of sub-mortgage stitched inside it. This certificate will contain a reference to the head mortgage.

Subject to Contract. A phrase used by bargaining parties, especially where land is sold by private treaty, to indicate a general agreement on terms and conditions, but to prevent the actual formation of a contract, upon which action may be taken, until the parties' respective solicitors have drawn up a formal contract which has been agreed, signed and exchanged.

Sub judice. Under legal consideration.

Sub-Lease. The assignment by a tenant to a third person of his whole interest for part of the term, or the assignment by him of a part of his interest for part or the whole of the term. Landlords usually exact a covenant against assigning or underletting, usually without consent, such consent not to be unreasonably withheld. A sub-lease deposited as security should be accompanied by a certified copy of the head lease.

Sub-Mortgage. A mortgage of a mortgage. For example, A mortgages his property with B for £12,000. Later B needs to borrow, say, £2,000. He could get it by calling in the mortgage, but instead he goes to his bank, Bank C, and borrows the money from the bank against the security of the mortgage. The original mortgage then becomes the head mortgage and the newly created mortgage is a sub-mortgage, B being the sub-mortgagor and Bank C the sub-mortgagee. A legal sub-mortgage takes the form of a grant by the mortgagee (the sub-mortgagor), of a term of years a few days shorter than the term which he himself has. Alternatively, it may be done by a charge by way of legal mortgage. The form of charge may be drawn up by the bank's solicitor, or an existing form of charge by way of legal mortgage may be used. The bank's solicitor should examine the deeds and in his report on title should confirm that a good security is being obtained, bearing in mind the terms of the original mortgage. A search should be made at the Land Registry against the sub-mortgagor. A valuation of the security should be obtained and the insurance position checked. Notice must be given to the mortgagor and his acknowledgment received; he should confirm the amount of the debt. If he is making regular repayments of principal he should now send these direct to the bank in reduction of the mortgagee's debt. The equivalent of a sub-mortgage of unregistered land is a charge on a charge certificate. If a banker is offered a charge certificate as proposed security, the same general inquiries and acknowledgments must be made and obtained as in the case of a sub-mortgage of unregistered land. If the banker decides to accept the security he may take an equitable sub-mortgage or a legal one. In the first case the banker will keep the charge certificate and give notice of its deposit to the Registrar on Land Registry form 85A. The charge certificate must be written up to date to include the notice of deposit. If it is desired to take a legal sub-mortgage a search must be made, using Land Registry Form 94A, and an official certificate of search obtained. An office copy of the form of sub-mortgage is prepared, and the following documents are sent to the Registrar: (1) the charge certificate; (2) the signed, sealed form of sub-mortgage, with office copy. The Registrar will keep the charge certificate and the copy form of sub-mortgage, and will issue to the banker as evidence of his interest a certificate of sub-charge with the original form of sub-mortgage stitched inside. This certificate will contain a reference to the head mortgage.

Subpoena. A writ commanding a person's attendance in a court of law under a penalty; to serve with such a writ.

Subrogation. The substitution of one person for another, with succession to his rights and claims; the standing in the shoes of another.

Sub Rosa. Secretly.

Subscribed Capital. That part of the authorised capital which has been issued and taken up.

Subscription Shares. Shares in a building society, where an investor is allowed to purchase shares by instalments in return for an undertaking to subscribe a fixed sum regularly.

Subsidiary Company. A company which has another company, which controls the composition of its board of directors, as a member; or a company in which another company holds more than half in nominal value of its equity share capital.

Subsidy. Financial aid, a government

grant for some purpose such as keeping the cost of living down.

Sub Sigillo. Under the seal, confidentially.

Substantial Damages. Damages awarded to compensate for actual loss, whether large or small.

Substitutionsrecht. Delegated authority for a representative to act.

Sub-Underwriter. An issuing house which is to under-write the whole of a new issue may share out the liability among a number of sub-underwriters, each taking a fraction of the liability.

Subvention. *See* Subsidy.

Succursale. A branch office.

Sue. To seek justice by taking legal proceedings; to prosecute, to make application, to petition.

Suicide Clause. A clause in a life assurance policy providing that the policy would be void if the assured died by his own hand within a certain period, usually six or twelve months, of the date of the policy. "Suicide" was divided into "sane suicide" or "insane suicide". In the latter case the personal representatives had a right to the policy money except as modified by the clause. In the former case, where the life in question was thought to be fully in possession of all his faculties at the time of his death, and he killed himself as a deliberate act of policy (possibly so that the policy monies would repay his debts), a question of public policy intervened. Suicide was, in the U.K. before 1961, a crime, and no criminal is allowed to benefit from his crime. Therefore in these cases policies were always void. Since 1961, when the law was changed so that suicide is no longer a crime, it depends entirely on the terms of the policy whether or not policy monies are paid out after the suicide of the life assured.

Sui Generis. Of its own kind, peculiar, unique.

Sui Iuris. Fully able to sue and be sued, not subject to any legal disability.

Summary Administration. Where a petition in bankruptcy is presented by or against a debtor, if the court is satisfied that the property of the debtor is not likely to exceed £4,000 in value, the court may make an order that the debtor's estate be administered in a summary manner. If the debtor is adjudged bankrupt the Official Receiver shall be the trustee in bankruptcy. There shall be no committee of inspection. Other modifications to the usual procedure may be made with the view to saving expense and simplifying matters.

Summons. The act of summoning; an authoritative call or citation, especially to appear before a court or a judge.

Sum Payable. The sum payable by a bill of exchange is a sum certain within the meaning of the Bills of Exchange Act 1882, although it is required to be paid (1) with interest; (2) by stated instalments, with or without a provision that upon default in payment of any instalment the whole shall become due; (3) according to an indicated rate of exchange to be ascertained as directed by the bill.

Sundry Creditors. A heading on the liabilities side of a balance sheet to indicate money owed by the business on any particular day to trade and other creditors; the appellation of a bank account through which may be put isolated transactions not specifically referable to any particular customer's account.

Sundry Debtors. A heading on the assets side of a balance sheet to indicate the money owing to the business at a particular date by trade and other debtors; the appellation of a bank account through which may be put isolated transactions not specifically referable to any particular customer's account.

Superannuation. The pensioning off of an employee on the grounds of age or ill-health.

Superannuation Payment. A deduction from wages or salary towards a contributory pensions scheme; a regular contribution made by an employee towards his pension.

Supervision of Banks. The failures of the fringe banks in the U.K. and the resulting rescue operation by the Bank of England and the clearing banks, which came to be known as the "Lifeboat", raised from 1972 onwards the question of a stricter supervision of banks in a much more acute form. It was thought that the Bank of England, not the Department of Trade, should regulate and supervise the banking system. There was also the question of bringing the U.K. into line with the system in the other countries of the E.E.C., who have suggested that banks should be defined by law, licensed, and ought to be made to secure official approval for management and for existing and future plans. This question of supervision brought up again the need for a definition of a bank. It was announced in the House of Commons in October 1975, by the Paymaster General, that Britain is to have a basic banking law. This was followed by a White Paper, published in August 1976, describing the institutional framework proposed. The Bank of England is to be the licensing and supervising authority. There will be two groups of deposit-taking institutions. The first group will need a licence from the Bank of England. The criteria for obtaining a licence embrace a minimum figure for capital and reserves, trustworthy and qualified management, and a good past trading record. In assessing the record of a deposit-taking institution, the Bank will examine appropriate balance sheet relationships and ratios relating to the capital adequacy and the liquidity of the institution, the degree of risk attaching to various assets, the matching of liabilities and assets in both sterling and other currencies, the reliance on deposits from connected companies and the institution's lending to connected organisations, the distribution of its lending among economic sectors, and the provisions and profits that have been made. These licensed institutions will not be allowed to call themselves "banks". The second group need no licence. They will be granted a new statutory recognition as a "bank to certain deposit-taking institutions" and will generally be the major banking companies—the clearing banks, the merchant banks, the discount houses—which are recognised already under some existing legislation, notably the Exchange Control Act 1947. Exacting criteria for such recognition, covering such matters as minimum capital and reserves, the type or range of banking services required to be provided, and the reputation or status needed, will be determined by the Bank with the agreement of the Treasury. For the first group the Bank will have the power to demand management changes or the injection of additional capital as a condition for the granting or renewal of licences. Supervision over the second group will continue very much as it is now. In both cases there will be a right of appeal against an unfavourable decision by the Bank, to the Treasury, with the ultimate decision being made by the Chancellor, or to the courts on the grounds of a denial of natural justice. Overseas banks with offices in London will be supervised by their own authorities and will be free to use the title "Bank" if they commonly do so in the country in which they are registered, that country being a member of the E.E.C. A deposit protection scheme will be instituted and administered by the Bank, which will report annually on the exercise of its supervisory responsibilities, and these reports will be laid before Parliament. Representations from banks and other financial institutions on the proposed legislation have been called for. When these have been considered, a Bill will be presented to Parliament and should become law during the latter half of 1978. *See also* Protection of Depositors.

Supplement. Something added to fill up or supply a deficiency; an appendix, an extra charge.

Supplemental Instrument. An instrument containing provisions additional to those in a previous instrument, *e.g.* a codicil to a will. Any instrument expressed to be supplemental to a previous instrument shall be read and have effect as if the supplemental instrument contained a full recital of the previous instrument.

Supplementary Costs. Those costs of production which are fixed and do not vary with the output, including short-term administrative costs, as opposed to prime costs.

Supplier Credit. An arrangement whereby an exporter supplies goods to an overseas customer against a cash sum of up to 20% of the contract price, with promissory notes or sterling bills of exchange payable over a period, which are guaranteed by the Export Credits Guarantee Department, for the balance. The exporter then sells the instruments without recourse to his bank, the latter obtaining a separate guarantee from E.C.G.D. This arrangement is generally found in the case of contracts up to £2 million, the credit period being restricted to five years.

Supply. A sufficiency of things required, necessary stores; the amount of a product or commodity which will come on to the market.

Support. Used frequently in varying contexts. A bank supporting its customer is lending money to him. A "support operation" signifies financial backing by a strong lender to a weak borrower (*see* Lifeboat Operation). A central bank supports its own currency by spending its holdings of gold and foreign currencies (*see* Reserve) in buying the currency of its own country in an attempt through the laws of supply and demand to raise the value of the home currency. If the support required is heavy the central bank may find that the country's reserves are in danger of being drained away: the alternative is devaluation or, in the case of a floating rate, the further depreciation of the currency of the country in terms of the currencies of other countries.

Support Group. *See* Lifeboat Committee.

Supra **Protest.** After a bill of exchange has been protested for dishonour, in the case of dishonour by non-acceptance (provided the bill is not overdue) any person, not being a party already liable thereon, may, with the consent of the holder, intervene and accept the bill *supra* protest, for the honour of any party liable thereon, or for the honour of the person for whose account the bill is drawn. In the case of dishonour by non-payment, any person may intervene and pay it *supra* protest for the honour of any party liable thereon, or for the honour of the person for whose account the bill was drawn.

Surcharge. To make an additional charge; to impose extra words or figures; an excessive charge, load or burden; an item which an auditor will not allow to stand among a firm's liabilities, and must therefore be made good by the person responsible.

Surety. A guarantor (*q.v.*). For the purposes of the Consumer Credit Act 1974, a person by whom any security is provided, or the person to whom his rights and duties in relation to the security have passed by assignment or operation of law.

Surplus. Excess beyond what is wanted; excess of income over expenditure; the balance in hand after all liabilities are paid; the residuum of an estate after all debts and liabilities are paid; matter not relevant to a legal case which may therefore be rejected.

Surrender. To yield or hand over to the power of another, to deliver up possession of anything upon compulsion, to resign; to appear in court in discharge of bail; the giving up of a lease before the end of its term by a lessee to a lessor by mutual consent.

Surrender Value. The amount which an assurance company will pay on a life assurance policy if the policy-holder surrenders the policy to the company. There is usually no surrender value until two or three years' premiums have been paid. The surrender value is the basic security for an advance made against the security of a life policy. An assurance company will advise a lender on request of the surrender value of a policy, or there may be a table of surrender values incorporated in the policy.

Surviving Partner. A partner remaining to wind up the business. In doing this he has power to mortgage any of the partnership property to secure a debt in the name of the firm, as long as it is necessary for the winding up of the firm, and not intended for further trading.

Survivorship. *See* Joint Account; Presumption of Survivorship.

Survivorship Policy. A life assurance policy which is payable on the death of the last survivor of joint policy owners.

Suspense Account. An account to be used temporarily for items which for lack of detail or information at the time of posting cannot be placed to their regular accounts in the books. A review of such items should be made periodically to ensure that they are not overlooked.

Suspension of Payment. The cessation of payments to creditors because of shortage of cash. If a debtor gives notice to any of his creditors that he has suspended, or is about to suspend, payment of his debts, that is an act of bankruptcy.

Svenska Bankföreningen, Arsenalsgatan 2, Box 16 143 103 23, Stockholm 16. The Swedish Bankers' Association has as its main task to represent the Swedish commercial banks in questions concerning legislation and other government activities and enquiries. The Association also acts on behalf of the commercial banks in questions of mutual interest *vis-à-vis* the authorities, other credit institutions, etc. Finally, the Association administers research and development in the economic, legal and technical fields.

Swap. To exchange, to barter; an exchange. In foreign exchange operations, "swap" means a spot sale against a forward purchase, or a spot purchase against a forward sale. "Swap agreements" or "swap arrangements" are devices to increase international liquidity. One central bank agrees to lend its currency to another central bank in exchange for a loan from that bank of an equivalent sum in its country's currency. Each country thereby strengthens the backing for its own currency and improves its resources against speculative attacks. Britain has arrangements with twelve major industrialised countries on whom she can call in times of need.

Swing. The free movement of an account from one figure to another, or from credit to debit or *vice versa*, as opposed to a gradual and progressive reliance on a bank overdraft where the account becomes "solid", *i.e.* settles down at the maximum permitted level of debt. A good swing in an account is a healthy sign showing an active business. When applied to bilateral trade agreements, the limit for reciprocal credit.

Swiss Roundabout. A device to limit corporation tax liability arising as a result of foreign currency capital borrowings by a company, not necessarily being matched by fixed assets in the same foreign currency. In the case, for example, of a U.K. company borrowing through the medium of a loan stock (usually a dollar bond), then if dollar values increase the asset in dollars becomes liable for taxation, and the loan stock value liability increase is not tax deductible. To get over this, a subsidiary company in an offshore tax haven is established, to whom the U.K. company lends (as a capital loan), the funds being shunted back in the form of short-term working capital into the company's current assets. Besides providing protection on the exchange exposure creating a tax liability, the "Swiss roundabout" can also be used to provide a protection against tax liability on the earned income. Before entering into such an operation the U.K. company's tax advisers should be consulted to obtain Inland Revenue approval. Bank of England exchange control approval is also required as the transaction involves establishing a non-resident entity in a tax haven.

Switching. Changing from one form of investment to another, or from one foreign currency to another, according to the requirements of the time; raising money by issuing certificates of deposit and then on-lending these funds to borrowers on fixed deposit in order to make a turn.

Syndic. A legal representative chosen to act as agent for a corporation or company.

Syndicat, **Syndicate**, *Syndikat*. A number of persons associated to carry out some enterprise; an association of industrialists or financiers formed to carry out some industrial project, or to acquire a monopoly in certain goods; a group of Lloyd's underwriters; a banking consortium; a meeting of discount houses to decide on the bid to be offered each week for Treasury bills.

Syndicat d'Emission. The grouping together of several banks for the handling of a new issue or issues.

Synergy. Combined action (as in a consortium).

Systems Analysis. An enquiry into the cost of providing a particular service, or group of services. The enquiry should begin with a precise definition of the objective and should then evaluate the different possible ways of achieving it, estimating the cost of each. Any existing systems should be scrutinised for the information which they may yield, and conflicting priorities should be reviewed in connection with supplies (*e.g.* of labour) available and their cost and estimated future cost. *See also* Operational Research.

T

Table A. The first of a number of tables in the First Schedule to the Companies Act 1948. It sets out a series of model articles for a limited company. Some companies adopt Table A, but amend or re-write some of the articles, while keeping others in the form set out in the Act. A public company limited by shares need not write out its own special articles: it has three options. It may have its own special articles, or it may adopt Table A in its entirety, or it may have a combination of the two. Other Companies Acts also have Tables A which may apply to companies registered under those Acts. *See also* Articles of Association.

Tacking. The right of a mortgagee to priority of a subsequent mortgage over an intermediate one of which he had no notice. Tacking, except by a first mortgagee, was abolished in 1925. Since then a prospective mortgagee can ascertain if any prior charges not protected by deposit of the deeds are in existence. A first mortgagee can still tack if by the term of the mortgage he is obliged to make further advances, or if he has arranged to do so with the agreement of subsequent morgagees, or if he had no notice of any subsequent mortgage at the time he made a further advance. The right to tack is usually excluded under the conditions of a bank form of mortgage.

Tagesgeld. Money at call.

Take-over Bid. An offer by one company to purchase the shares of another, with a view to merging the two businesses so as to make for fuller and more economical use of assets and managerial skills. The offer will always be made to the shareholders of the company sought to be taken over, but in the case of agreement between the boards of the two companies, the directors of the company which is being taken over will recommend the bid. Consideration offered may be cash, shares in the bidding company, or a combination of both of these. As inside knowledge of a take-over can make a fortune for those unscrupulous enough to deal in the shares in advance of information being made public, a code has been devised to control such situations. It is known as the "City Code on Take-overs and Mergers" and it lays down general principles of conduct to be followed (*See* Panel on Take-overs & Mergers). Compliance with these terms is voluntary, but offences against the Code may be followed by suspension of a quotation on the Stock Exchange and/or withdrawal of a dealer's licence by the Department of Trade. Merchant banks are prominent in advising and participating in take-over bids. *See also* Reverse Take-over.

Tally. A stick in which notches are cut as a means of keeping account; such a notch or mark, a score, a reckoning, an account; anything made to correspond with something else, a counterpart, a duplicate; a label or tag for identification.

Tally System. The system of giving and receiving goods on credit, to be paid for by regular instalments; the system in some African banks whereby the holder of a cheque desiring encashment is given a numbered token while the cheque is compared with the ledger and the stop list before payment is authorised; a similar system in Companies House where those desirous of making a search against a company are allocated a number while the company's records are being fetched.

Tally Trade. A business arrangement, usually in the drapery trade, whereby customers are allowed to take articles on credit by agreement on a series of instalments to meet the price.

Talon. A slip issued along with the coupons attached to a bearer bond, to be used when further coupons are required.

Tangible Moveable Assets. Assets capable of realisation. If such an asset is disposed of for £1,000 or less, any gain made is not taxable. There is no liability on any gain made on the sale of a motor vehicle commonly used for private passenger travel, or on the sale of the owner's private dwelling house. *See also* Fictitious Asset.

Tantième. Royalty.

Tap. Government securities which are issued in unlimited quantities available direct from the issuing authority at any time. *See also* Long Tap; Short Tap.

Tap Bills. Treasury bills sold by the Treasury to other Government departments.

Tare. An allowance for the weight of boxes, wrapping, etc. in which goods are packed; an allowance for the weight of a container, such as a cask, crate, etc., in reckoning the price of dutiable goods; the weight of a vehicle when empty.

Tare Weight. The weight of an aircraft minus crew and cargo.

Target. A mark to aim at; a maximum sum of money aimed at in public subscription, *e.g.* "savings target"; the minimum consumption of fuel aimed at in an economy drive, *e.g.* "fuel target".

Target Population. A term used to describe any section of the population intended to be reached by any method of instruction, such as an advertising campaign.

Target Price. The fixing of farming prices in the E.E.C. which might be obtained in the open market. Imports may then be subjected to levies if they are below the target price. In particular areas where it is desirable to encourage production, a higher regional target may be set.

Tariff. A list of imported and exported goods on which duty is payable.

Tariff Company. An insurance company having a standard range of premiums.

Taux. Rate, scale.

Taux Bancaire. The official discount rate of the central bank.

Taux d'Escompte. The rate at which a bill of exchange is discounted.

Taux Lombard. The rate of interest charged on a loan which is covered by readily negotiable securities.

Taux Privé. The discount rate for first-class paper.

Tax. A compulsory contribution levied on persons, property or businesses to meet the expenses of government or other public services; to impose a tax on; to fix the amounts of costs, etc., in a legal action. *See also* Corporation Tax; Income Tax; Withholding Tax.

Taxable Income. The amount which is left after deducting personal and other allowances from total income (but not payments under deed of covenant, or life assurance relief). When taxable income exceeds a certain figure, the rate of tax mounts on an ascending scale in accordance with the amount of the total taxable income, up to the maximum rate (which varies from time to time) on any taxable income in excess of a figure currently in force.

Tax Avoidance. The act of claiming every allowance and relief which is available under the tax laws. Such avoidance, being allowable by law, is quite legal; failure to pay tax which is legally due is *tax evasion*.

Tax Certificate. A certificate by an issuing authority that tax on an interest payment has been deducted at source. A certificate of tax credit is issued in respect of dividends.

Tax Credit Scheme. *See* Negative Income Tax.

Taxe à Valeur Ajoutée (T.V.A.). *See* Value Added Tax (V.A.T.).

Taxe d'Émission. Stamp duty on new issues.

Tax Free. Any income received free of tax is regarded by the Inland Revenue as such a sum which, taxed at the basic rate, will leave the amount actually received. The recipient of the sum will also obtain from the payer a certificate in respect of the tax deducted to be submitted with his annual return to the Tax Inspector. Calculations of higher rate tax or investment income surcharge on the recipient will be based on the higher sum. *See also* Franco.

Teilhaber. Partner.

Teilzahlungsgeschäft. Hire purchase.

Telegraphic Transfer. A payment made in international commerce by a transfer of money by cable or telegraph from a bank account in one country to a beneficiary in another (also called *cable transfer*). The cost of the cable is charged to the customer who authorises the payment, unless he says that all charges are for the account of the payee. As with mail transfers, payment may be made in sterling or in currency, to the payee under advice, or on application and identification, or for credit to his account. The rate for the telegraphic transfer exceeds the rate for the mail transfer only by the cost for the cable, which may be at urgent, ordinary or deferred rate.

Telex. A system whereby a message sent by teleprinter is reproduced simultaneously at a distant point as it is typed.

Teller. A member of the House of Commons who counts votes; an officer at an election who performs a similar function; any person who counts votes at any voting meeting; a bank cashier.

Tel Quel Rate. An exchange rate calculated when buying a currency bill drawn on a foreign centre where the bill still has some time to run before maturity; a rate not taking interest into account: a flat rate.

Temporary Annuity. An annual payment for a fixed number of years, starting immediately.

Tenancy in Common. Two or more tenants having equal shares in the property of which they are tenants, usually land. On the death of one tenant, his share passes to his personal representative and not to his co-tenant(s). Tenancy in common is found in the case of partnership land (unless one partner is made sole owner as trustee for his co-partners), or under the terms of a will, *e.g.* where land is left to children equally. The tenancy in common has the disadvantage that on a sale of the whole land it is necessary to prove a separate title to each separate share. *See also* Joint Tenancy.

Tenant. One who has legal possession of real estate; one who pays rent for property which he occupies.

Tenant at Sufferance. A tenant of land whose original entry upon the land was lawful, but who wrongly continues in possession after his estate in the land has ended.

Tenant by the Curtesy. A widower entitled to a life interest in the land of which his wife dies seised in fee simple or in tail. Curtesy was abolished in 1925 with regard to all interests except an entailed interest and therefore now such a tenancy applies only when a female tenant in tail dies intestate.

Tenant-Farmer. One who occupies a farm on payment of rent to a landlord.

Tenant for Life. A person of full age who is for the time being beneficially entitled under a settlement to possession of settled land for his lifetime. If two or more persons are jointly entitled to possession, they together constitute the tenant for life.

Tenant *Pur Autre Vie*. A tenant holding an estate during the lifetime of another person. It is the lowest estate of freehold land known to the law.

Tenant Right. The legal right of a tenant to occupy property on regular payment of reasonable rent and to receive compensation if the contract is broken by the landlord; any right of the tenant of property, whether expressly stated or implied, such as a right to remove fixtures at the end of the tenancy, or to receive an allowance for seeds or fertiliser put on the land.

Tendance, *Tendenz*. The tendency of a market to follow one direction.

Tender. To offer in payment or for acceptance, to make an estimate; money proffered in payment of a debt; an offer to purchase Teasury bills. *See also* Legal Tender.

Tender Bills. Treasury bills offered for sale each week. Tenders must be submitted to the Bank of England before 1 p.m. on the Friday of issue.

Tender Guarantee. A guarantee given by a banker or an insurance company in support of a contractor tendering for a public works contract abroad. The guarantee is against the risk that the contractor, having gained the contract, will then fail to go on with the work. It is usually for 5% of the value of the contract.

Tenement. A dwelling-house; a building divided into separate flats and let to different tenants; any property which is permanently held by a tenant.

Tenor. The exact purport or meaning. Applied to a bill of exchange it means the purpose and intent of the bill on construction of the words and figures used in it.

Tenure. The act, manner or right of holding an office or property, especially real estate; the manner or conditions of holding; the period or term of holding.

Term. A boundary, a limit, especially of time; a period during which the law courts are sitting; a fixed day when rent is due to be paid.

Term Bill. A bill incorporating a period of credit and payable at the end of the term of credit.

Term (or Acceptance) Credit. A credit

where the beneficiary is to obtain payment upon the maturity of a bill of exchange drawn in compliance with the terms of the credit and accompanied by the relevant documents. Such a bill will usually be drawn upon the correspondent bank for the stipulated period of time and accepted by it. The drawer then has a credit instrument which he can discount or hold to maturity.

Term Days. The days on which rent falls due.

Term Deposits. Deposits which are repayable after a pre-determined time and not on demand; deposits in a Savings Bank for which a long period of notice for withdrawal is required.

Terminable Annuity. An annuity which will stop on a fixed date, or after a certain time, or on the beneficiary's death.

Terminating Building Society. *See* Building Societies.

Termingelder. Deposit at a fixed term.

Termingeschäft. See Lieferungsgeschäft.

Terminmarkt. Forward market.

Term of a Bill. The period of time for which a bill of exchange is drawn.

Term of Years. A period of years for which it is intended that an estate shall endure. Unless it satisfies the definition of a term of years absolute it is an equitable interest. A term of years absolute is a term which is to last for a certain fixed period, even though for one reason or another it may be liable to come to an end before the expiration of that period (*e.g.* by re-entry of the landlord, operation of law, etc.).

Termor. One who has an estate for a term of years or for life.

Terms, To Come to. To reach a compromise agreement.

Terms, Cash. Payment at time of purchase.

Term Shares. Money deposited with a building society on the basis that it cannot be withdrawn for a fixed period, normally from two to four years. In return the investor receives a higher rate of interest than on a normal share account.

Terms of Delivery. Indications as to whether sender or consignee shall pay delivery charges on a consignment of goods or whether the charges are to be divided between them, *e.g.* C.I.F., C. & F., F.O.B.

Terms of Payment. The conditions of payment associated with any particular sale of goods, *e.g.* cash with order, hire-purchase terms, credit card, monthly account, etc.

Terms of Reference. Points for discussion and settlement.

Terms of Trade. The comparison of the country's imports and exports by price. If the general price of imports rises faster than the price of exports, the terms of trade are becoming less favourable. In the U.K. the indicator is calculated by dividing the index of export prices by the index of import prices and multiplying by 100. Thus a fall in the final index indicates an adverse movement.

Term Transfer. The introduction of an indebtedness at a term into a market dealing with debts at shorter or longer terms, *e.g.* the introduction by banks of interbank deposits into the local authority market for a longer term.

Territorial Waters. The sea area around a country with a seaboard over which it claims exclusive rights for fishing, prospecting, sea farming, etc. Once set at three miles from land, this area has expanded as countries claimed more and more, a figure of 100 miles now being claimed in some cases. International agreement on these claims has not yet been achieved.

Tertiary Risks. *See* Prime Risks.

Theft. The act of dishonestly appropriating property belonging to another with the intention of permanently depriving that other of it.

Theory of Comparative Costs. The theory that even if one country has an absolute advantage in costs of producing all things, the world will still benefit if each country specialises in producing those goods in which it has the greatest relative cost advantage or least disadvantage.

Thesaurierung, Thésaurisation. Hoarding of precious metals, banknotes, coins or merchandise, sometimes with unfavourable effect on the economy.

Third of Exchange. *See* Bill in a Set.

Third Party. A person involved in some arrangement with a bank, who is neither the banker nor a customer (*see* Collateral); an insurance term for some person other than the insurance company and the person insured.

Through Bill of Lading. A bill of lading which covers shipment on more than one vessel or more than one type of transport.

Throughput Agreement. These agreements are used in, and associated with, the financing of oil and natural gas pipelines. A pipeline is constructed with the proceeds of a loan and the lender recognises that a high utilisation and continuous operation at a high capacity level is required to generate sufficient cash flow to service the debt and to make a profit. Including the lender, four parties are concerned. The other three are the pipeline owners, the source to which it is to be connected, and the output. The pipeline can link the primary producer to a utility company, a refiner, or a large industrial user. The lender must be satisfied that input to the line is insured by adequate oil or natural gas reserves to which the pipeline will be linked (the producer agrees to deliver a quantity which will be sufficient to service and repay the loan), that at the other end the purchaser has the financial ability to perform his obligations under the purchase agreement, and that the period required for the pipeline to maximise its profit potential (which may be up to twenty years) is satisfactory to him. Further protection may be afforded to the lender by obtaining a mortgage on the pipeline and an assignment of the payments due under the contract with the consumer.

Ticker Tape. A telegraphic installation which immediately transmits the rates ruling during a session of the stock exchange. It also transmits items of news.

Ticket Day. *See* Name Day.

Tick Up. The last resort procedure for finding an error in the day's work in a bank. In the case of an error in the debit side of the control it is necessary to call every debit item in the control list against the corresponding entry in the out-clearing sheets; in the case of an error in a ledger it is necessary to call back every item of the check ledger sheets day by day back to the day when the ledger was last known to be correct. (Procedures are somewhat different where computer accounting is in force.)

Tilgung. Redemption, amortisation.

Tilgungsanleihe. Bonds redeemable by lot.

Time. A particular moment, a period of duration, opportunity, occasion.

Time and Motion Study. A check on the time taken by an employee to do any particular task in order to see whether it can be done more efficiently.

Time Bargain. An agreement to contract business at a given time; a term applied to dealings on the Stock Exchange by "bulls" or "bears".

Time Charter. A charter party whereby the ship is chartered for a specific period.

Time Deposits. Deposits at a term (including certificates of deposit). *See also* Special Deposits.

Time Order. An order of the court defined in the Consumer Credit Act 1974 as follows: (1) If it appears to the court just to do so (*a*) on an application for an enforcement order, or (*b*) on an application made by a debtor or hirer under this paragraph after service on him of a default notice, or (*c*) in an action brought by a creditor or owner to enforce a regulated agreement or any security, or recover possession of any goods or land to which a regulated agreement relates, the court may make an order under this section (a "time order"). (2) A time order shall provide for one or both of the following, as the court considers just—(*a*) the payment by the debtor or hirer or any surety of any sum owed under a regulated agreement or a security by such instalments, payable at such times as the court, having regard to the means of the debtor or hirer and any surety, considers reasonable; (*b*) the remedying by the debtor or hirer of any breach of a regulated agreement (other than non-payment of money) within such period as the court may specify.

Time Policy. A marine policy extending cover for a fixed time only.

Tirage au Sort. Drawing by lot; repayment of bonds by this means.

Tiré. Drawee.

Tireur. Drawer.

Titel. Document of title, bill of exchange, bond, etc.

Titelkredit. See Lombardgeschäft.

Tithe. A tenth part; originally the tenth part of the produce of land and cattle allotted to the upkeep of the church and the clergy, later paid in the form of a tax.

Title. An inscription serving as a name or designation; the distinguishing formula at the head of a legal document, statute etc., including caption and text, as arranged for reference; the right to ownership of property, the legal evidence of this; an acknowledged claim, the grounds of this; fineness, especially of gold, expressed in carats.

Title Deed. A legal instrument giving the evidence of a person's right to property.

Titre. Evidence of a right; a document of title such as shares, stock or bonds, lending itself readily to dealing on a stock exchange.

Titres Bloqués. Bonds, shares, etc. carrying a condition—for example, that they shall not be sold before a certain time, or at a price below the issue price; securities which are included on a list of blocked bonds, shares, etc., which cannot be the subject of a good delivery because they have been lost, stolen, sequestrated, etc.

Titres de Placement. Securities particularly suitable for a long term investment, such as government bonds, but also first class industrial and commercial shares.

To Average Out. *See* Average.

Tochtergesellschaft. Subsidiary company.

To Indorse Over. *See* Indorse.

Token. A sign, a symbol; a coin or disc issued by a firm or company to be used by employees, *e.g.* in a canteen; a card issued with a stamp of a certain value and exchangeable for goods in a shop, *e.g.* book token, record token.

Token Money. Coins where the value of the metal in them is less than the value attached to them by law, such as the cupro-nickel and bronze coins of the U.K.

Token Payment. A deposit paid as token of later payment of full debt; earnest money.

Toll. A tax or duty charged for some privilege or service, especially for the use of a road, bridge, or tunnel.

Tombstone. The list of underwriters advertised as acting in connection with a new issue. These names are placed one after another vertically and as there are usually enough of them to form a more or less solid block of print there can be said to be a reference to a "tombstone", a reference perhaps strengthened by the resemblance between the words "underwriter" and "undertaker". "Tombstone" is therefore a short way of alluding to the members of the underwriting group.

Tontine. A form of joint assurance whereby the sum received by the subscribers increases as their number decreases, until with the death of the last survivor the tontine completely lapses.

Tontine Annuity. A form of joint annuity whereby the sum received by the subscribers increases as their number decreases, until with the death of the last survivor the tontine completely lapses. *See also* Reverse Annuity.

Tontine Policy. A life assurance policy under the terms of which no bonus is payable if the death of the policy holder occurs before the end of a specified period, usually about twenty years. During that time the policy has no surrender value. At the end of the period the bonus vests in the maturing policy. The barren period is called the Tontine period. *See also* Tontine Annuity.

Topping-Up Clause. Where in a form of charge a borrowing customer agrees to maintain a margin of security at all times, a clause recording his agreement to deposit further security if the lending bank asks for it.

To put a Premium on. *See* Premium.

Tort. A private or civil wrong, an injury to person or property for which damages may be claimed in a court of law. It has been said that in tort the banker is on the defensive. He is not likely to be bringing an action himself, but will be looking for a good defence to an action being brought against him by someone else. The most likely grounds are for conversion or negligence.

Town and Country Planning. For the checking of haphazard and ribbon development the government imposed, in a series of Acts from 1947 onwards, rules for planning the future way in which the country's land is to be used, and decreed that consent must be obtained for any development. "Development" was defined as "the carrying out of building, engineering, mining or other operations in, on, over and under land, or the making of any material change in the use of buildings or land". Under planning law, local planning authorities have decided upon development plans for their areas, and the details of these plans are to be found in the register of districts, borough and county councils. Here will be found such information as road charges, town planning schemes, demolition orders and building-preservation orders. *See also* Local Land Charges Register.

Town Clearing. Deals with articles of £5,000 and over drawn on and paid into the banks and branches in the "Town Clearing", all within the City of London and therefore within easy walking distance of the Clearing House. By using this clearing large cheques can be paid in up to the close of business each day and still be cleared, or returned unpaid, the same day. All other cheques drawn on branches of the clearing banks are passed through the General Clearing.

Trade. The business of buying and selling, commerce, barter, shopkeeping; occupation (in industry); the purchase or sale of goods or services at home (*domestic trade*) or abroad (*foreign trade*).

Trade Balance. *See* Balance of Trade.

Trade Bill. A bill drawn by one trader on another against an actual trade transaction, but not bearing a bank indorsement.

Trade Board. A board of representatives of employers and employees, nominated by the Department of Trade to settle trade disputes, etc.

Trade Credit. Credit granted by one trader to another who has bought goods from him.

Trade Cycle. The alternately recurring periods of prosperity and depression affecting world commerce; the tendency of business activity to fluctuate regularly between periods of boom and depression.

Trade Discount. An allowance made by wholesalers to traders who buy goods for the purpose of re-sale: an allowance on a quantity or number of articles.

Trade Gap. The excess of visible imports over visible exports.

Trade Investments. In a balance sheet, the sum representing the total of the company's investments in affiliated companies or associated organisations.

Trade Mark. A registered name or device marked on goods to show that they have been produced by a certain manufacturer.

Trade Name. A registered name given by a manufacturer to a proprietary article; a name used among traders and manufacturers for a certain commodity; a name under which an individual or company trades.

Trade Protection Society. An organisation which supplies information as to the credit standing of companies, firms and individuals, primarily those engaged in trade.

Traders' Credit. A system of settlement for traders offered by banks, whereby the trader hands the bank a list of amounts to be paid with names, bank, branch and sorting code number of each bank keeping each of the accounts, with a separate bank giro credit slip for each one. The bank supplies the printed blank credit forms and a book with the sorting code numbers of all the banks. The trader gives the bank one cheque for the total and the bank distributes the credits. This system is now part of the credit clearing.

Trade Union. A legally recognised association of clerks, workmen, etc. for the purpose of securing their rights, safeguarding wage scales, and preventing exploitation by employers. Any property of the union should be vested in trustees, to whom a banker must make any advance. Any borrowing must be covered by the rules of the union.

Trade-Weighted Depreciation. The introduction of floating currencies has replaced occasional devaluations by a constant creeping loss in the exchange value of the pound sterling. This has come to be called trade-weighted depreciation, and is a measure of the value of the pound against other currencies rated by their importance to U.K. overseas trade. The average depreciation is calculated daily by the Bank of England and is adjusted to account for differences in seasonal trade.

Trading Account. The account of a business concern which shows how the gross profit has been arrived at.

Trading Certificate. The certificate issued by the Registrar of Companies, on receipt of which the company is authorised to commence business.

Trading Cheques. Vouchers issued by clothing clubs which can be exchanged at designated local shops for articles of clothing, members repaying the club by instalments over a period, usually about twenty weeks.

Trading Company. A company formed for the purpose of carrying on trade and making a profit.

Trading Partnership. A partnership in which any partner has authority to bind the firm in drawing, accepting or indorsing bills of exchange, in making agreements, and generally in contracting debts on the firm's behalf.

Trading Profit. Gross profit.

Trading Stamps. Stamps given by retailers to their customers in proportion to their purchases, which can be exchanged with the company supplying the stamps for a range of attractive goods.

Traite Documentaire. A bill of exchange drawn by an exporter or importer and to be accepted or paid by him. *See also* Bill for Collection.

Traitement. Salary.

Tranche. A slice, an instalment. A phrase used where wholesale finance is concerned and where the sums in question are substantial, to indicate the taking or "drawing down" of an instalment or tranche of the sum agreed. Also often used to indicate a borrowing by a country from the I.M.F., which consists of a part of an agreed sum.

Transaction. The act of carrying through or negotiating a piece of business; an affair, a proceeding; the adjustment of a dispute by mutual concessions.

Transaction. (*Fr.*) Bargain, compromise, arrangement.

Transaction au Comptant. Cash transaction.

Transfer. To move from one place to another; to convey property to another; the document authorising this. *See also* Term Transfer.

Transferability of Cheque. A cheque is transferable when it circulates quite freely. It may or may not be negotiable also. A transferable cheque gives each successive transferee a good title, provided that the title is good in the first place and that it does not become defective while in the course of passing from hand to hand. *See also* Not Transferable.

Transferable Account. An account maintained in this country by a non-resident on which sterling is freely convertible into any other currency.

Transferable Credit. A credit where the benefit of a credit opened in favour of a middle-man by the importer is transferred to the exporter of the goods. This is a convenient way for the middle-man to pay the actual supplier of the goods without having himself to find temporary finance or arrange a credit. The credit opened by the negotiating bank in favour of the exporter will be for a lesser sum than that shown on the original transferable credit (the difference being the middle-man's profit) and will show the middle-man as the buyer. It may stipulate for an earlier shipment date. The name of the exporter should not be divulged to the importer (and *vice versa*), nor should the importer be able to find out what the original price of the goods was. When the exporter's documents are to hand, the middle-man's invoices are substituted for his and sent with the other documents of title to the importer, whose bank will re-imburse the exporter's bank. The procedure is similar to that in a back-to-back credit, the main difference being that in that case the second credit is opened only on the strength of the first one, whereas with a transferable credit the benefit of the original credit is transferred to the exporters; there must therefore be a provision in the credit for the transfer.

Transfer Agent. The office (very often a bank department) which handles transfers of registered shares and delivers the certificates in the names of new purchasers.

Transfer Certificate. Where, exceptionally, a company does not issue a new share certificate to a new shareholder, it may issue a transfer certificate authenticating the transfer, which should be held by the buyer together with the old certificate(s).

Transfer Days. Days set aside by companies for registering the transfers of registered stock; the official days at the Bank of England for the transfer of Government stocks.

Transfer Deed. The instrument transferring the ownership of securities from one person to another; a stock transfer form.

Transfer Fee. A fee charged by a company upon registration of a change of ownership of shares

Transferkredit. *See* Rahmenkredit.

Transfer of Mortgage. The conveyance of mortgaged property from one owner to another. This may happen where a banker takes over such a security from another bank which has been lending, against repayment by the banker. Such a new lending must be by way of loan with permanent reductions to defeat the operation of the "Rule in Clayton's Case". Normally a banker will take a new form of mortgage in such a case. A transfer of a mortgage may also occur where the customer requests the lending banker, who is about to be repaid, to reconvey the property, not to him, but to a third party. The method of transfer is by a deed which declares that the mortgagee transfers the benefit of the mortgage. Such a deed vests in the transferee all the rights under the mortgage formerly enjoyed by the transferor. The mortgagor should join in the deed of transfer. Alternatively, a statutory receipt may be prepared for the moneys due under the mortgage, endorsed on or annexed to it, stating the name of the person paying the money and executed by the chargee by way of legal mortgage.

Transfer of Shares. *See* Register of Transfers, Share Transfer.

Transferor by Delivery. The holder of a bill payable to bearer who negotiates it by delivery without indorsing it. He is not liable on the instrument (because he has not indorsed it) but he warrants to his immediate transferee being a holder for value, that the bill is what it purports to be, that he has a right to transfer it, and that at the time of transfer he is not aware of any fact which renders it valueless.

Transfer Order. An order addressed by a bank holding a warehousekeeper's certificate or receipt in its own name, to the warehousekeeper, requesting him to transfer the goods into the name of another, usually his customer.

Transfer Receipt. The receipt given by a company when a document for the transfer of stocks and shares is presented for registration.

Transfer Register. *See* Register of Transfers.

Transfert. Payment; a transaction between two monetary zones; an indorsement of an instrument payable to order.

Transit Trade. *See* Re-Export.

Trassant. The drawer of a bill of exchange.

Trassat. Drawn.

Tratte. A bill of exchange drawn but not yet accepted.

Travel Agent. An agent who arranges tickets and reservations for road, sea, rail or air transport for persons desirous of travelling from one place to another, whether within a country or overseas, on business or holiday. He acts on behalf of his principal, the carrier company.

Travel Cheques (Traveller's Cheques). Cheques issued in sterling or in certain other currencies by banks to their customers wishing to travel abroad. Each cheque has a space for the customer to sign immediately he gets the cheques, and another space for him to sign in the presence of the paying agent at the time he is cashing the cheque. The customer pays for the cheques in full (plus the bank's commission) when he is issued with them, and must then keep them in a safe place. If he loses them or has them stolen through no fault of his own, the bank when notified will usually replace them free.

Traveller's Letter of Credit. *See* Letter of Credit.

Treasure Trove. Any money, plate or bullion of unknown ownership found buried in the ground. It becomes the property of the Crown.

Treasury Bills. Obligations of the British Government issued on a weekly basis by the Bank of England. Issued in denominations of £5,000, £10,000, £25,000, £50,000, £100,000 and £250,000, they are normally repayable ninety-one days after issue. Treasury Bills are issued at a discount and in bearer form. Application for the issue of Treasury Bills is by tender, allotment being made at the highest tender rate and downwards, until the whole issue has been allotted. Treasury Bills qualify as reserve assets for United Kingdom banks. *See also* Tap Bills; Tender Bills.

Treasury Directive. When the Bank of England was nationalised in 1946 by the Bank of England Act, section 4 of that Act gave powers to the Treasury to give from time to time such directions to the Bank as, after consultation with the Governor of the Bank, they think necessary in the public interest. The bank, in turn, is empowered to make requests of, and issue directives to, the clearing bankers and other financial institutions. In the past these directives have been concerned with the purpose for which loans were being granted (qualitative) or with the volume of lending (quantitative). When Competition and Credit Control was adopted, quantitative directives were supposed to end, but the new system of non-interest-bearing special deposits related to increases in the banks' interest-bearing eligible liabilities, introduced in December 1973, was a quantitative control in all but name.

Trésor. Safe, strongroom.

Trésor Public. Treasury.

Treuhänder. Trustee.

Treuhänderisch. Fiduciary.

Treuhandgeschäft. A transaction in which a trustee, very often a bank, acts in its own name, but on the instructions of, and at the risk of and for the account of, the principals; in a wider sense, any business arising out of the trust connection, such as auditing, giving expert opinions, re-organising businesses, dealing with tax questions or liquidation, or making specialised knowledge available.

Treuhandgesellschäft. A trust company.

Trial Balance. In double-entry bookkeeping, the extraction of debit and credit balances from a ledger, the totals of which should agree.

Triptique. A document for Customs inspection in connection with cars touring abroad.

True Owner. The true owner of a bill of exchange is the person rightfully in possession of it; first the drawer who draws it, then the payee, then the endorsee, if any. When theft or fraud enters into such a series of operations, however, the true owner becomes someone different from the person in possession of it, and may sue either the possessor, or the banker collecting the bill, for conversion. The true owner is the person rightfully entitled at any particular time to the proceeds of the bill.

Trust. Confidence, reliance, implicit faith; property used for the benefit of another; a combine of business companies in which the shareholders turn over their holdings to a board of trustees; a business combine to restrict competition and establish a monopoly. In regard to land, a trust arises where any person who is the legal owner of property is bound to hold and administer that property on behalf of another. *See also* Breach of Trust; Charitable Trust; Constructive Trust; Express Trust; Flexible Trust; Implied Trust; Investment Trust; Management Trust; Open-Ended Trust; Precatory Trust; Private Trust; Protective Trust; Resulting Trust; Split-Level Trust.

Trust Corporation. The Public Trustee or a corporation either appointed by the court to be a trustee or entitled by rules made under the Public Trustee Act 1906 to act as custodian trustee. A Trust Corporation is an alternative in many statutes to "not less than two trustees". Thus money arising from the sale of land formerly subject to a trust for sale must be paid over to at least two trustees, or to a trust corporation. A trustee delegating his powers, where he is entitled to do so, may delegate to any person except to his only other co-trustee, unless a trust corporation. The banks' executor and trustee corporations come under his head.

Trust de Valeurs. An investment trust of which the capital is invested in easily negotiable securities.

Trust d'Investissement. See Investment Trust.

Trustee. One to whom property is committed for the benefit of others; one of a body of men, often elective, managing the affairs of an institution. *See also* Appointment of New Trustee; Custodian Trustee; Naked Trustee; Public Trustee.

Trustee Clause. A clause in an equitable mortgage of land by means of which the lending banker can obtain a legal title as a preliminary to the sale of the security, in cases where the customer has failed to repay, and has also failed to keep his promise to sign any documents which the bank may require him to sign (where such a clause has also been incorporated in the form of mortgage). The Trustee clause may run as follows:

"I will hold the mortgaged property in trust for the bank as mortgagee and the bank may at any time remove me and appoint another person to be trustee, and the mortgaged property shall vest in the person so appointed." If the customer will not sign, the bank can appoint someone else who will.

Trustee for Sale. The person, including a personal representative, holding land on trust for sale.

Trustee in Bankruptcy. A person appointed by the creditors of an insolvent person who has been adjudicated bankrupt to take charge of the bankrupt's estate and to liquidate it for the benefit of the creditors. He may be assisted by a Committee of Inspection, formed from the creditors themselves. The trustee's title to the property of the bankrupt relates back to the beginning of the bankruptcy, that is, the date of the earliest act of bankruptcy in the three months preceding the date of the receiving order. The trustee's remuneration is by way of a percentage of the value of the realised assets. When the trustee has realised all the assets and has distributed a final dividend to the creditors he obtains his release by an order of the Department of Trade.

Trustee Savings Bank. *See* Savings Bank.

Trustee Securities. Securities declared by law to be suitable and authorised for the investment of money held on trust.

Trust Estate. An estate managed by trustees.

Trust for Sale. Property established in a trust for the beneficiaries, with the intention that the property shall be sold, whether immediately or eventually. In relation to land, "trust for sale" means an immediate binding trust for sale, whether or not exercisable at the request or with the consent of any person, and with or without a power of discretion to postpone the sale.

Trust Immobilier. A trust whose capital funds are invested in real property or in the shares of property companies.

Trust Instrument. An instrument, whether a will or deed, setting up a trust, naming trustees, specifying the objects of the trust, and indicating the trust property. With regard to settled land, the trust instrument shall declare the trusts affecting the land, appoint trustees of the settlement, contain any power to appoint new trustees, set out any powers intended to be conveyed by the settlement over and above those conferred by the Settled Land Act 1925, and bear the appropriate stamp duty. Under this Act, every settlement of a legal estate in land *inter vivos* must be effected by two deeds, a "vesting deed" and a "trust instrument". The first operates to vest the land in the tenant for life, and the second declares the trusts on which the settled land is to be held.

Trust Letter, Trust Receipt. A document signed by a customer of a banker where goods have been pledged as security for an advance. To repay the advance it is necessary for the customer to get the goods and sell them, but the documents of title which would enable him to get them are in the possession of the bank. The bank therefore releases the documents of title to the customer against his signature on a trust receipt, by the terms of which the customer undertakes to deal with the goods as an agent for the banker for the purpose of getting delivery of the goods and then selling or warehousing them. He undertakes to effect any necessary insurance and to hold the proceeds of sale on behalf of the banker until the loan is repaid. The trust letter protects the rights of the banker as pledgee, which he would otherwise lose when he gave up the documents of title, and protects him in the case of the customer's bankruptcy, by taking the relative goods out of the operation of the reputed ownership clause. The bank's books must show that the documents of title actually came into the hands of the bank before the trust receipt relating to those same goods was signed. This shows that the pledge was created by the deposit of the documents, and was extended by the terms of the trust receipt.

Trustzertifikat. A document representing a stated share in the capital of a co-operative society; not a document of title, but merely evidencing ownership.

Turn. A difference between buying and selling prices or the bid and offered prices, as quoted by foreign exchange dealers, or by jobbers on the London Stock Exchange.

Turn-Key Contract. Where a large or complex building or industrial plant is being erected, the phrase signifies that when everything is finished and work can begin, the contractor will so inform the client (by analogy, he hands the "key" over and says "Turn it and begin"), from which moment production should proceed without trouble. The trial period before "the key is handed over" will include tests of machinery in action and may include training the client's work force.

Turnover. The total sales of a business in a trading period. *See also* Rate of Turnover.

Tutor. In Scotland, the guardian of a pupil, having control of the person and the estates of his ward (usually the father, or if there is no father, the mother alone or with tutors appointed by the father during his lifetime, or by the court).

Two-Tier Systems. Differentials in price costings to various classes of consumers or users, *e.g.* first and second class mail, tourist and par exchange rates, investment and par exchange rate, interest rates for loans intended for differing purposes (*e.g.* farm investment and property speculations), gold prices where transfers of officially held gold between monetary authorities are made at an official price, while other transfers are made at prices determined entirely by supply and demand.

Types of Life Policy. *See* Policy.

U

Überbrückungshilfe. Bridging loan.

Übernahmeangebot. The offer price, to be accepted inside a fixed time, of a takeover bid.

Übernahmevertrag. A term used on the occasion of a new issue to refer to the agreement between the issuing company and the group handling the issue.

Uberrimae Fidei. Of the utmost good faith. A description of a type of contract where one party has in the nature of things information which only he can know, but which is vital to the contract. In such a case there is a duty on him to supply this information truthfully and to make a full disclosure. If he does not, the contract may be voided at the option of the other party. The prime example of this type of contract is the contract of life assurance, where the previous medical history of the assured, and that of his family, is clearly of great importance to the question of whether a contract shall be entertained and, if it is, what the premium shall be.

Überschuss. Surplus, profit.

Übertragungsangebot. Transfer offer.

Übertragungsurkunde. Transfer deed.

Überziehen. To overdraw.

Ullage Certificate. One showing the measurement of the liquid or semi-liquid removed from a tanker.

Ultimate Balance. A phrase used in a form of guarantee to describe the sum owing to the bank on the last day of notice given by the guarantor, or on the day the bank calls upon the guarantor. On that day the overdrawn account of the principal debtor should be ruled off and subsequent credits may be posted to another account, newly opened if necessary, where they will have no effect on the final debt. The ultimate balance is arrived at by combining all accounts.

Ultimo. The last day of the commercial or *Bourse* month.

Ultra Vires. Beyond the (legal) powers of. The phrase is applied in particular to limited companies, whose legal powers are defined in the objects clause of their memorandum of association. Any act not covered in the objects clause is said to be *"ultra vires"* the company, and any debt thus incurred is irrecoverable at law. In Europe a different view has been taken. There it is enacted that a contract entered into in good faith by a person dealing with a company should not be set on one side on the ground that it is *ultra vires* the company. The phrase is also used in connection with the powers, particularly the borrowing powers, of company directors. The usual provision in the Articles of Association is that the directors may exercise the company's powers. Often, however, the company imposes a top limit beyond which the directors may not commit the company without the prior sanction of members in general or special meeting. Where Table A has been adopted, the directors' powers will be set out in the Table A clause appropriate to the company. According to the date of its incorporation, the company will be governed by the Table A of the Companies Act 1908 (article 71), the Companies Act 1929 (article 67) or the Companies Act 1948 (article 79). The effect of these articles is that on or before 30 September 1906, the company's borrowing powers are fully exercisable by the directors. After that date, the directors may borrow only up to a sum equal to the amount of the issued capital of the company. (After June 1948 the directors are still limited to this same figure of issued share capital, but in the 1948 Act there appeared for the first time a provision that temporary loans obtained from the company's bankers in the ordinary course of business need not be taken into consideration when calculating the amount that has been borrowed.) Directors who exceed any of these limits are acting *ultra vires.* See also Articles of Association.

Umlaufvermögen. Assets which at the date of the balance sheet are in a liquid state or capable of being realised in a short time, current assets.

Umsatz. Turnover.

Umsatzprovision. Bank commission levied on the turnover of an account.

Unauthorised Signature. *See* Forged Signature.

Unbestätigtes Akkreditiv. Unconfirmed credit.

Uncalled Capital. *See* Share Capital.

Unclaimed Balance. *See* Dormant Account.

Uncleared Effects. The total of cheques collected for a customer, which is credited to his account on the day he pays them in. The proceeds remain uncleared for three days, or five if a week-end intervenes. During this time the bank is presenting the cheques to the paying banks through the clearing house. If they are unpaid they should be received back through the post on the morning of the fourth (or sixth) day. (Town clearing cheques are cleared more quickly.) Whether or not the customer is allowed to draw against the proceeds of these cheques before they are cleared is a question of fact in each case, but the banker does not have to pay against uncleared effects unless he so wishes. If he does do so, however, he may encourage the customer to think that similar concessions may be made on future occasions, and an implied permission may be construed.

Unconnected Depositor. A depositor in a deposit-taking institution whose only business connection with the institution is that he has invested money in it. The relationship may become important in the event of the liquidation of the deposit-taking institution, in which case the liquidator may look upon an unconnected depositor with more favour than a depositor who has other business interests with the liquidated company, some of which may have gained him an interest other than the mere payment of interest on deposit.

Undated Stock. Gilt-edged security issued by the government on a perpetual basis and having therefore no date by which it will be redeemed.

Under. Below, beneath, lower than, subordinate.

Under Bond. Imported goods stored in a Customs bonded warehouse until such time as the duty is paid or they are re-exported.

Under-Lease. The granting by a lessee of a part of his interest in a lease to another person, whether part of the property for any or all of the term, or all the property for part of the term.

Under-Sheriff. An English sheriff's deputy who performs the execution of writs.

Undertaking. A business enterprise; a stipulation, promise or guarantee, given to or by a bank in various connections, *e.g.* an undertaking to review conditions of service. *See* Solicitor's Undertaking; Deed of Postponement.

Under the Counter. *See* Counter.

Underwriter. A person who in the seventeenth century wrote his name under the wording on an insurance policy, which provided cover on a limited and personal basis for merchants' undertakings. These were almost wholly concerned with ship voyages and cargoes. In modern times an underwriter may be concerned with marine insurance policies, issued by Lloyd's, where the underwriting members are formed into syndicates which are represented at Lloyd's by underwriting agents, or on the Stock Exchange with the taking up of capital issues. In the latter case the underwriters engage to buy and pay for any shares issued by a company which are not taken up by the public. *See also* Insurance; Issuing House; Selling Group.

Undischarged Bankrupt. The legal state of a bankrupt person from the time of his adjudication as bankrupt until his application to the court for an order of discharge is successful. This will be more readily forthcoming if the bankrupt has co-operated well with his trustee and done all he can in the matter of making full disclosure of his assets. Until his discharge the bankrupt has very few legal powers or rights. He is entitled to the tools of his trade and the necessary wearing apparel of himself, his wife and children, to an inclusive value of not more than £250. In addition, the trustee may from time to time make such allowance as he thinks just to the bankrupt out of his earnings for the support of the bankrupt and his family. The undischarged bankrupt may not (1) maintain a banking account without the knowledge of his trustee or the Department of Trade; (2) either alone or jointly with another obtain credit to the value of £50 or more without disclosing his disability; (3) engage in any trade or business under a name different from the one under which he was adjudicated bankrupt, without disclosing that name to all with whom he does business; (4) obtain credit under false pretences, make any gift or transfer of any of his property or any charge on it with intent to defraud his creditors, or conceal or remove any part of his property with a similar intention; (5) act as a company director or take part in the management of any company except by leave of the court.

Undisclosed Principal. Where an agent contracts on behalf of his principal without disclosing the fact that there is a principal, but nevertheless contracting within the powers given to him by his principal, the third party may think that he is contracting with another principal. If he wishes to sue on the contract, and has in the meantime discovered the true state of affairs, he has the choice of suing either the principal or the agent.

Undue Influence. An influence which excludes free consent to a contract. Where no special relationship exists between the parties, the party seeking to avoid the contract must prove the undue influence as a fact. But where a fiduciary relationship exists between the parties, undue influence will be presumed and must be disproved by the party sued.

Unearned Income. For the purposes of tax, income derived from investment.

Unearned Increment. An increase in the value of an asset due to increased demand rather than to any improvement in the asset carried out by the owner; increased bank profits due to an increase in the minimum lending rate.

Unemployment. Lack of paid work. In Britain, the estimate of unemployed persons is based on the number drawing unemployment benefit. As this figure includes those retired early, those disabled, students on holiday, and the unemployable, some inaccuracy is inevitable. In the U.S.A. unemployment is measured by surveys which determine the number of people who are looking for employment.

Unexecuted Agreement. This means a document embodying the terms of a prospective regulated agreement, or such of them as it is intended to reduce to writing.

Unfunded Debt. Short-term government debt.

Ungesichert. Unsecured.

Uniform Customs and Practice for Documentary Credits. A code of uniform practice formulated by the International Chamber of Commerce with which the U.K. complies. *See Appendix I.*

Unilateral. One-sided.

Unilateral Contract. One which is binding on one of the parties only.

Unilateral Relief. Where income arises from an overseas country to a taxpayer resident in the U.K., unilateral relief is the credit which will be given against U.K. tax liabilities for any overseas tax suffered on such income. In the majority of cases there is a reciprocal agreement between the countries concerned.

Unincorporated Association. An association of persons grouped together for a non-commercial purpose, such as a social, sports, or literary and dramatic club. Such groups are managed by officers and committees elected from their own number. The banking account is usually opened in the name of the society and operated by the treasurer and one or more members of the committee. There is no legal entity which can be sued for repayment of any borrowing where accommodation is requested, therefore there must be a firm undertaking by an individual or individuals to be personally responsible for any debt.

Unit. A single person, thing or group, regarded as one for the purposes of calculation.

Unit Assurance. *See* Unit-Linked Policy.

Unit Costing. A method of costing used where manufacture is continuous and units are identical.

Unité de Compte. *See* Unit of Account.

Unit-Linked Policy. A type of life assurance policy where a part of the premium is invested on behalf of the assured in a unit trust. There are two basically different types of unit-linked policy. Where the emphasis is placed on the life assurance aspect, a small part of the premiums only is invested in units, the remainder being kept by the assurance company in order to provide assurance benefits. The income earned by the policy-holder's units is retained by the company and paid out in the form of regular bonuses. Where the emphasis is placed on the investment aspect, the major part of the premiums is invested in units. The company keeps a small proportion to meet the cost of the life assurance cover. The income earned on the units is re-invested in more units on the policy-holder's behalf.

Unit of Account. A unit used by the E.E.C. as a kind of international currency. Its value has been fixed at 0·88867088 grains of fine gold, which was the value of the gold-pegged dollar in the Bretton Woods system. Because the Common Market is unlikely to have a common currency for some considerable time the unit has persisted, although it is now said to have up to sixteen different definitions. The unit of account is the "currency" for all E.E.C. transactions such as the calculations for the common agricultural policy, loans to Britain and so on.

Unit Trust. A method of investment whereby money subscribed by many people is pooled in a fund, the investment and management of which is subject to the legal provisions of a trust deed. The fund is invested in securities on behalf of the subscribers by a management company. The investments so acquired are held by a trustee. The management company and the trustee must be quite independent of each other. The advantages claimed for the unit trust idea of investment are a good yield, security, regular income distribution, the benefit of professional management, regular reviews of portfolios and, above all, spread of risk. The units are not quoted on the Stock Exchange, but are bought and sold by the management company which works out purchase and sale prices ("bid" and "offer") based on the market value of the underlying securities.

Universalbank. (*Ger.*) A bank, usually a large one, which can offer a variety of services to its customers under one and the same roof.

Unlimited Company. A company where there is no limitation to the liability of the shareholders for the debts of the company.

Unpaid Seller. One to whom the whole of the price has not been paid or tendered, or one who has taken a bill of exchange or other negotiable instrument as conditional payment, and the condition on which it was received has not been fulfilled by reason of the dishonour of the instrument or otherwise.

Unpaid Seller's Lien. The unpaid seller of goods who is in possession of them is entitled to retain possession of them until payment or tender of the price if (1) the goods have been sold without any stipulation as to credit; (2) the goods have been sold on credit, but the term of credit has expired; (3) the buyer becomes insolvent.

Unquoted Shares. Shares of a public limited company which has not applied, or has not yet applied, for a quotation on the Stock Exchange; and shares of a private limited company. *See also* Private Company Shares.

Unregistered Company. A company not registered in any part of the U.K. under the Companies Acts. Any Trustee Savings Bank certified under the Trustee Savings Banks Act 1863.

Unregistered Land. That system of land ownership where title is evidenced by a set of deeds and documents, as opposed to *Registered Land*, where title is evidenced by a registered land certificate.

Unsecured Creditor. A creditor whose only claim is against the general assets of the debtor; one who has no specific security. Such a creditor may, however, be a preferential creditor if he falls into one of the statutory classes.

Unterbeteiligung. Participation by a bank not represented in an issue syndicate through taking over a part of the business and handling it for a member of the syndicate.

Unternehmerkredit. An advance to a builder whereby he will have a fixed sum at his disposal, the advance being secured by an assignment of a building agreement.

Unwiderrufliche Akkreditive. Unconfirmed credit.

Unwritten Law. Any law not originating in Parliament; the common law. *See also* Common Law; Equity; Gresham's Law; International Law.

Upper Chamber. In a bicameral legislature, the House that is the more restricted in terms of membership, *e.g.* the House of Lords, the Senate of the United States of America and some others.

Upset Price. The lowest fixed price at an auction sale at which, by agreement of the vendor, the property will be in the first instance offered, and at which it will be sold if no better offers are forthcoming.

Ursprungszeugnis. Certificate of origin.

Usance, *Usanz.* The usual time allowed for payment of bills of exchange, particularly in connection with foreign trade. Thus bills are drawn upon differing centres at different terms, according to the custom in that trade and between those centres.

Usance Bill. A bill drawn at a term governed by the custom in the trade, for example three months' date for bills on Paris, thirty days' sight for bills on Bombay, or ninety days' date for bill on Lisbon. *See also* Pig on Pork; Treasury Bill; Bill Broker; Bill for Collection; Bill for Negotiation.

User. *See* Change of User.

Usufruct. The right of using and enjoying the produce, benefit or profits of another's property provided that the property remains undamaged.

Usure. See Usury.

Usury. Lending at an exorbitant rate of interest. From the time of Henry VIII onwards many statutes were passed to regulate the rate of interest. The Usury Laws were repealed in 1854 to provide a greater flow of capital to industry, and a new Moneylenders Act was passed which enacted that a rate of anything over 48% per annum was *prima facie* unreasonable and would be set aside unless the lender could satisfy the burden of proof on him that in the circumstances the rate he had charged was justifiable. The Moneylenders Act was repealed by the Credit Consumer Act 1974, by which the courts are given wide powers to adjust or re-open transactions where a borrower who considers the terms of an agreement are extortionate has obtained a court ruling. On the continent *"usure"* is also a civil contract instancing an evident disproportion between the position of the parties, in that the dominant party has exploited the need, weakness or lack of experience of the other.

Utter. To put into circulation, *e.g.* to utter a false cheque, to put forged notes, base coins, etc. into circulation.

V

Vacant Possession. Property available for purchase with no tenant in possession, and therefore able to command a higher price, is said to be "for sale with vacant possession".

Valeur, Valor. *See* Value.

Valeur à Revenu Fixe. Fixed interest stock, etc.

Valeur à Revenu Variable. Variable interest stock, etc. The U.K. Treasury as an innovation introduced £400 m to the market in May 1977. The rate of interest on the stock varies in line with the rate on three months' Treasury Bills. Interest is payable at a rate half a percentage point above Treasury Bill rate, calculated weekly. The stock thus provides much the same characteristic as a money market deposit renewable every seven days.

Valeur Commerciale. Consideration.

Valeur Compensée Risk. A capital risk in a foreign exchange transaction arising from the possibility that the bank will have to part, at maturity of the contract, with the sterling or currency involved in the deal before it can be certain of receiving the counterpart. This risk is represented by the highest aggregate figure of "boughts and solds" maturing on any one day. *Valeur compensée* risks disappear on maturity of the relative contract. *Valeur compensée* lines are granted only to banks of very good standing.

Valeur Comptable. Book value.

Valeur de Liquidation. Break-up value.

Valeur de Rendement. A value calculated on the basis of actual or expected profits; a capitalised value.

Valeur Marginale. Marginal value.

Valeur Nominale. The amount indicated on a share certificate, etc., not necessarily corresponding with the market or real value; nominal value.

Valeur Réelle. All kinds of negotiable securities, deeds, precious metals, real property, etc. An investment in such securities offers in principle the greatest safeguard against a fall in the purchasing power of money.

Valeurs de Premier Order. Gilt-edged securities.

Valeurs de Tout Repos, Valeurs de Père de Famille. Obligations of the State considered particularly safe from an investment point of view, but not incorporating a gold clause.

Valid. Well-grounded, cogent, logical; legally sound, sufficient, effective binding.

Validate. To make valid, to ratify.

Validation de Titres. The process of revalidating to their original owners securities which have been lost, destroyed, or seized during war-time.

Validity. Legal force; soundness; power to convince.

Valor. *See* Value.

Valorisation. A general rise in balance sheet figures which have hitherto been recorded at under their real worth.

Valuable Consideration. "Some right, interest, profit or benefit accruing to one party, or some forbearance, detriment, loss, or responsibility given, suffered or undertaken by the other." Any contract not under seal must be supported by valuable consideration if it is to be enforceable at law. Valuable consideration for a bill may be constituted by (1) any consideration sufficient to support a simple contract; (2) an antecedent debt or liability. Such a debt or liability is deemed valuable consideration whether the bill is payable on demand or at a future time.

Valuation. The act of valuing or appraising; in banking, the value placed upon security offered by a borrowing customer. In the case of real property, valuation is effected by a branch manager who physically inspects the property; in the case of Stock Exchange security, valuation is taken from the daily Stock Exchange list of quotations; in the case of unquoted or private company shares, valuation is estimated from the company balance sheet or by application to the secretary of the company; in the case of a life assurance policy, valuation is obtained from the assurance company who, upon request, will state the surrender value of a policy. Valuation of a company's stock for balance sheet purposes will be made by the company directors. Valuation of Stock Exchange securities of a deceased person's estate for probate is effected by taking a figure one-quarter of the difference between the buying and selling prices, and adding it to the buying price (one quarter up).

Value. Worth; the desirability of anything; the qualities that are the basis of this; worth estimated in money or other equivalent; the market price, estimation, appreciation of worth; to place a value upon, to estimate the worth of. See also Presumption of Value.

Value Added Tax (V.A.T.). A form of turnover or sales tax, introduced in the U.K. in 1973. It is a tax on final consumer expenditure in the domestic economy. V.A.T. is collected in instalments: liability to tax arises at each stage in the chain, whenever taxable transactions are carried out by taxable persons, on all goods and services except those which are specifically exempted or zero rated. V.A.T. replaced S.E.T. and purchase tax. It falls on imports and exports of goods; in the latter case V.A.T. is not only charged directly but also provides machinery for rebating tax entering indirectly into export costs.

Value Date. The date on which funds are actually available for use by a bank in foreign currency accounts maintained by the bank abroad.

Valued Policy. A marine policy having the value of the ship or freight insured stated in the policy.

Value in Account. A term used in bills of exchange to indicate that there remains a balance in the drawer's favour.

Value Received. A term used in bills of exchange to indicate that the drawee has received either money or goods from the drawer of the bill. It is not legally necessary in the U.K. to include these words, for every party whose signature appears on a bill is *prima facie* deemed to have become a party thereto for value, but the law is different on the continent of Europe.

Valuta. Rate of exchange, value, currency; entries in bank books which fix charges to be made or interest charges due, such as the determination of opening and closing dates for the relative periods.

Valutaklausel. A protective clause in foreign business designed to offset the possible loss following a devaluation of currency.

Variable Cost. A cost of production varying with output.

Variable Rate Stock. See *Valeur à Revenu Variable*.

Variance. An accounting term for the difference between a budget, any estimate and actual performance. See also Adverse Variance; Favourable Variance.

Velocity of Circulation. The average number of times each unit of money is used in a given time.

Vend. To sell, to dispose of by sale.

Vendee. The person to whom anything is sold.

Vendor. The seller.

Vendre. To sell, to market.

Vendue. An auction.

Vente. Sale. See also *Frais de Vente*.

Vente à Découvert. See *Spéculer à la Baisse*.

Vente à Perte. See Loss Leader.

Vente à Tempérament. Sale by hire purchase.

Verbindlichkeit. Liability.

Verbraucher. Consumer.

Verbrauchsgüter. Consumer goods.

Verbrauchssteuer. Indirect tax, excise.

Verfall. Maturity.

Verjährung. The point in time at which a debt due can no longer be enforced at law. See also Limitation.

Verkauf. Sale.

Verkaufskosten. Selling costs.

Verkaufsöfferte. Offer for sale.

Verkaufsstätte. Market, outlet.

Verkehrswert. Market value.

Verluste. Losses.

Verlustschein. A certificate issued on the occasion of an insolvency, in respect of an outstanding debt; this does not qualify for interest.

Vermögenssteuer. Property Tax.

Vermögenswerte. Asset, stock.

Verpfändung. The right held by the pledgee, in case of non-payment, to realise the security.

Verpflichtungskredit. A credit in which a bank advances no money to its customer, but gives its guarantee on his behalf.

Versement. Instalment, deposit.

Versicherer. Underwriter, insurer.
Versicherung. Insurance.
Verstaatlichung. Nationalisation.
Vertical Combination. An amalgamation of companies at different stages of production.
Vertrag. Agreement.
Verwaltungsrat. Board of Directors.
Verzugszins. The rate charged on an overdue debt, from the date of default to the date of eventual settlement.
Vested. Placed in possession of; that which cannot be transferred to another, or taken away.
Vested Interest. An interest which passes unreservedly to the beneficiary, so that if he dies before receiving it, it will when it is due pass to his estate.
Vested Remainder. An interest which passes eventually to a remainderman if he is alive; if he is dead, it passes to his estate.
Vesting Assent. *See* Assent.
Vesting Deed. *See* Trust Instrument.
Veterinary Certificate. A certificate required to indicate live stock as free from specified diseases.
Via. By way of.
Viable. Capable of maintaining independent existence. Applied to a company which is insolvent, but whose work staff have formed a co-operative with government support.
Vidimer. To certify that a document is a true copy of the original.
Vindictive Damages. *See* Exemplary Damages.
Vinkulieren. (Of shares) non-transferable without the consent of the directors.
Virement. Payment by means of a book entry.
Visa. An official endorsement, as on a passport, to show that the document has been examined and found correct.
Visible Exports. Goods and commodities exported from one country to another, as opposed to services rendered by one country to another. *See also* Invisible Exports.
Void. Destitute of all legal effect.
Void *ab Initio*. Of no binding importance at any time from the beginning (of the supposed contract).
Voidable. Legal and binding, but capable of being set on one side by one party to the contract at his option.
Volkseinrommen. *See* Gross National Product (G.N.P.).
Volksvermögen. The total stock of goods in a national economy.
Volkswirtschäft. *See* Economics.
Voluntary. Proceeding from choice or free will, unrestrained, spontaneous.
Voluntary Conveyance. A conveyance of property against no valuable consideration; a deed of gift. A voluntary settlement by a debtor subsequently becoming bankrupt is an act of bankruptcy. If the settlor becomes bankrupt within two years of the date of the settlement, it is void as against the trustee in bankruptcy; if subsequently but within ten years from the date of the settlement, it is void as against the trustee unless the parties claiming under the settlement can prove that the settlor was, at the time of making the settlement, able to pay all his debts without the aid of the property comprised in the settlement. *See also* Fraudulent Conveyance.
Voluntary Liquidation, Voluntary Winding-Up. The winding-up of a company following a resolution to that effect. The winding-up may be because of difficulty in paying its debts, or it may be for quite a different reason, such as an amalgamation with another company, or because the company's existence may have served the purpose for which it was formed. A company may be wound up voluntarily (1) when the period, if any, fixed for the duration of the company by the articles expires, or the event, if any, occurs, on the occurrence of which the articles provide that the company is to be dissolved, and the company in general meeting has passed a resolution requiring the company to be wound up voluntarily; (2) if the company resolves by special resolution that the company be wound up voluntarily; (3) if the company resolves by extraordinary resolution to the effect that it cannot by reason of its liabilities continue its business, and that it is advisable to wind up. Where a statutory declaration has been made, the winding-up is a members' voluntary winding-up; otherwise it is a creditors' voluntary winding-up. *See also* Statutory Declaration.
Voluntary Patient. *See* Mental Illness of Customer.
Voluntary Waste. A wrong of commission amounting to a positive act of injury to the inheritance, such as pulling down or altering houses, digging for

gravel, clay etc., converting wood or pasture into arable land or cutting timber. *See also* Equitable Waste.

Voluntary Winding-Up. *See* Voluntary Liquidation.

Voranschlag. Budget, estimate.

Vorbörslicher Handel. Business done on the *Börse* before the beginning of the daily session, not officially quoted.

Vorlegen. Short-term borrowing among banks against bills, for a commission payment.

Vorrangsbelastung. Prior charge.

Vorstand. Board of directors.

Vorstandsmitglied. Director.

Vorzugsaktie. Preference share.

Vostro* Account,** ***Vostro Konto. Accounts maintained abroad by a bank in the currency of the country where the account is, usually in the capital of the foreign country.

Voucher. A paper or document that serves to vouch for the corrections of accounts, or to establish facts; a receipt; a cheque; a paying-in slip; office debit or credit.

Vowel Index. An index whereby items are sorted first under the letter of the alphabet with which the title of the item begins, and then under the vowel which first occurs in the spelling of the title of the item.

Voyage Charter. A charter party whereby the ship is chartered for a single voyage.

Voyage Policy. A marine policy for a particular voyage only.

W

Wachstumswerte. Growth stock.

Wadset. A mortgage or bond in security for a debt in Scotland.

Wage Drift. The term used to describe the tendency for employers who are short of labour to bid against each other, thus forcing wages higher than the normal rates.

Wage Freeze. An attempt to restrain inflationary wage increases by holding them at their existing levels, by force of law, for a period of time. A small increase in actual or percentage terms may be allowed. Such attempts, which have to be made against the interests of the trade unions, give a temporary relief only and are liable, when control is relaxed, to give way to a "wages explosion". (Also known as a *Pay Pause*.)

Wages and Salaries Account. Special accounts opened by companies at the request of lending banks where the company is in danger of liquidation. The purpose is to segregate the amount of money lent by banks for the purpose of paying wages, in order to acquire a preferential claim in the event of liquidation. In such a case the bank can take over the claim which the clerk, workman, servant or labourer would have had, had he not been paid out of money advanced by the bank for that purpose. The claim is limited to £800 per man in the four months preceding the liquidation.

Währung. The stable order of currency in a country with adequate reserves, steady resources for payment and firm international valuations in terms of gold and foreign currencies.

Waiter. An attendant at the London Stock Exchange, or one in the Room of Lloyd's of London.

Waiver. A forgoing, a renunciation.

Waiver Clause. A clause in a contract which enables an obligation to be avoided in certain circumstances.

Walks Department. Cheques drawn on non-clearing banks, mostly in London, are presented by clerks or messengers from the clearing banks, which maintain a "Walks Department" for this purpose.

Wandelobligation. *See* Convertible Bond.

Wandelparität. The price at which shares may be exchanged for bonds, or *vice versa*, as quoted on the Stock Exchange.

Wandelpreis. Quoted price for the conversion of convertible bonds into shares.

Ward. Guardianship, control; a pupil, minor or person under guardianship.

Ward in Chancery. A minor under the protection of the court.

Wardship. The office of a guardian; the state of being under a guardian.

Warehousekeeper's Certificate, Warehousekeeper's Receipt. An acknowledgment by a warehousekeeper that he has received certain goods which are stored in his warehouse. Such an instrument is not a document of title, nor is it transferable. The goods are not deliverable against its production. If a bank is asked to lend against goods already held in an independent warehouse the customer will be in possession of such a receipt. Because it is only a receipt its deposit with a bank will not create a pledge in the bank's favour.

Warehousekeeper's Lien. The right of a warehousekeeper to retain possession of property left with him for storage until payment for the service is made to him. Such a lien may be particular or general. (*See* General Lien; Particular Lien.) A warehousekeeper's lien may be of special importance to a banker who has taken a charge over his customer's goods in warehouse. It may be necessary for the banker to try to get the warehousekeeper to release a general lien so as to allow the particular goods to be made available for sale. Naturally the particular charge will have to be paid first.

Warehousekeeper's Receipt. *See* Warehousekeeper's Lien.

Warehousekeeper's Warrant. A document of the title transferable by indorsement, if it is issued by a recognised warehousekeeper having power under an Act of Parliament to issue transferable warrants. Warrants issued by other warehousekeepers not having statutory powers are not transferable, and a pledge can only be obtained by returning the warrant to the warehousekeeper together with a delivery or transfer order signed by the customer, which will result in the issue of a new warrant in favour of the bank.

Warehousing. The use of money invested in an insurance company or in a unit trust to buy and hold shares which would otherwise have fallen sharply in price; the use of such money to build up a concealed takeover stake; the building up of a significant stake by spreading purchases of shares over a group of people acting in concert and sometimes as nominees for one person. The Companies Act 1976, sought to control this practice by requiring disclosure when acquisitions take the stake to 5% or more of the company's issued capital.

Warenkredit. Credit granted against the security of goods, produce lending.

Warenzeichen. See Trade Mark.

Warrandice. A clause in a deed binding the grantor to make good to the grantee any loss arising out of obligations antecedent to the date of the conveyance; the right conveyed; warranty.

Warrant. An instrument which justifies an act which otherwise would not be permissible nor legal; a negotiable writing, which authorises a person to receive money, as a warrant in repayment of Savings Bank balances issued in favour of a beneficiary by the Director of Savings and cashable at a Post Office. A crossed warrant may be passed through a bank account, but it is not a negotiable instrument. *See also* Dock Warrant; Warehousekeeper's Warrant.

Warrant for Goods. Any document or writing evidencing the title of any person named therein, or his assignees, or the holder thereof, to the property in any goods, wares or merchandise lying in any warehouse or dock, or upon any wharf, and signed or certified by or on behalf of the person having the custody of the goods, etc.

Warranty. An assurance that a thing is as represented, security; a term for a guarantee that an article is free from defective workmanship; an agreement with reference to goods which are the subject of a contract of sale, but collateral to the main purpose of such contract, the breach of which gives rise to a claim for damages, but not to a right to reject the goods and treat the contract as repudiated. As regards Scotland, a breach of warranty is deemed to be a failure to perform a material part of the contract.

War Risks Insurance. Ship insurance is in three parts; marine, war risks, and club or mutual insurance. A marine policy protects the insured against loss by perils of the sea. The policy has standard clauses, but leaves a number of contingencies unprovided for, or only partially provided for. Among these contingencies is that of war risks cover. The risk of war is sometimes covered, subject to an additional premium. Some discrepancies may be expected as to what war risks are. A policy may cover damage as a result of an outbreak of war while the ship is at sea, but may not cover damage by collision with an old mine left over from the last war. Such remote contingencies remain to be covered by club insurance.

Wartung. Maintenance, servicing.

Waste. Such damage to houses or lands as tends to the permanent and lasting loss of the person entitled to the inheritance. It falls into two classes; *permissive waste* and *voluntary waste. See also* Permissive Waste; Voluntary Waste.

Wasting Assets. Assets which become used up in the course of time as they are worked, *e.g.* mines or quarries. This progressive depreciation should be provided for by an annual allocation out of profits.

Waybill. A list of passengers or articles carried by a vehicle. *See also* Air Waybill.

Wayleave. A right of way granted by a landowner for some specific purpose in consideration of payment.

Ways and Means Advances. Advances made by the Bank of England to the Treasury to pay for the annual supply services.

Weak. A term applied to a currency which has become worth less in terms of another currency.

Wechsel. Charge, bill of exchange, exchange, draft.

Wechselbürgschaft. See. Aval.

Wechselkurs. Exchange rate.

Wechselnehmer. The person or firm for

whose account a bill of exchange is made out, and who is entitled to the proceeds on indorsement.

Wechselpension. Lending against the security of readily negotiable instruments.

Wechselprotest. *See* Protest.

Wechselstrenger. A shortened procedure of liquidation registered against the debtor on a cheque or bill of exchange.

Weekly Return. The weekly balance sheet of the Bank of England.

Weiche Währung. Weak currency.

Weighting. An adjustment on a banking charge in recognition of an exceptional service given to a customer; the giving of a greater importance to certain items in the construction of an index number.

Weight Note. In trade, a note issued by an independent third party evidencing gross and net weights of goods.

Weiterverpfändung. Second mortgage.

Wert. Worth, value.

Wertberichtigung. Rectification of property asset figures under the Liabilities side of the balance sheet.

Wertpapier, Wertschrift. Valuable paper, documents of title.

Wertschriftentrust. Investment trust, unit trust.

Wertsteigerung. Stock, appreciation.

Wertzuwachsteuer. Value added tax (V.A.T.).

White Paper. An official statement of government policy on an issue of the day.

Whole Life Policy. A life assurance policy under the terms of which a fixed sum is payable on the death of the life assured, passing into his estate for the benefit of his heirs.

Wholesale. Sale of goods in bulk to retailers; selling or buying in large quantities; extensive; indiscriminate.

Wholesale Banking. Borrowing or lending, usually in large sums, by big banks amongst themselves through the medium of the interbank market; dealing with other financial institutions, as opposed to retail banking, which consists of the traditional course of business between a bank and its customers.

Wholesale Cost. The cost to the retailer of buying goods in bulk from the producer or wholesaler.

Widerrufliche Akkreditive. Confirmed credit.

Will. A declaration made in writing by a person of full age, showing how he wishes his property to be disposed of after his death. The person making the will is called a testator. His signature must be witnessed by two persons, both present at the same time, who attest that in the testator's presence and at his request and in the presence of each other they have signed as witnesses.

Windbill. An accommodation bill accepted by the drawee to oblige the drawer, without consideration for so doing; a "kite".

Winding-Up of a Company. *See* Compulsory Liquidation or Winding-Up; Voluntary Liquidation.

Window Dressing. Specious manipulation of accounts of a company or one's assets to produce a more favourable impression than the circumstances actually warrant.

Wire Fate. *See* Special Clearance.

Wirtschaft. Economy.

Wirtschaftsprüfer. Chartered accountant.

Withdrawal of Bill. *See* Retiring a Bill.

Withholding Tax. A tax imposed by some countries on interest and/or dividends remitted abroad to residents outside that country. If a double taxation agreement exists between the U.K. and a country which levies a withholding tax, it is possible for the tax on the interest payable on a loan from the U.K. to the country imposing the tax to be largely deductible against the U.K. lender's tax liability, *e.g.* a part of the interest receivable by an U.K. firm is "withheld" abroad as a "tax", and part of this sum may be offset against U.K. tax liabilities. More generally, a tax deduction at source.

Without Engagement. A term used when quoting prices of articles liable to fluctuate suddenly; the price quoted is the market price at the moment, but the quotation is not binding on the one who gives it.

Without Prejudice. Without abandoning a claim or right; without impairing any pre-existing right.

Without Recourse. A party to a bill of exchange may negative his liability on the bill by adding these words (or the words *sans recours*) after his signature on the bill. Such a clause will make the bill less easily negotiable.

Without Reserve. At an auction, an indication of complete freedom as to bidding and a guarantee that goods will be sold at whatever price is bid.

"With Profits" Policy. A life assurance policy, whether endowment or whole life, which provides that in return for an increased premium the policy holder will share in the profits made by the assurance company. Bonuses are declared usually at three-year revaluations. (Also known as a *Participating Policy*.)

With Recourse. Where a bank discounts or negotiates a bill of exchange for a customer it does so "with recourse", that is, if the bill is dishonoured at maturity the bank is able to claim the amount of the bill from the customer.

Witness. Attestation of a fact, testimony, evidence; a thing that serves as evidence or proof; one who gives evidence in a law court or for judicial purposes, especially on oath; one who affixes his name to a document to testify to the genuineness of the signature; to sign as a witness, to attest, to state in evidence.

Words of Severance. When land is conveyed or devised to two or more persons in such a way as to show that they are to take distinct and separate shares, they take as tenants in common and not as joint tenants. Words of severance show that the beneficiaries are to take "equally", in equal shares, etc.

Work. Labour, toil, an undertaking, a task, employment as a means of livelihood, occupation, deed, performance, achievement.

Working Capital. What is left out of the paid-up capital after all the fixed and fictitious assets have been paid for. It should be sufficient to provide all the circulating capital and to cover the day-to-day running of the business. Another way of arriving at the working capital is to subtract the current liabilities from the floating assets.

Working Day. For the purposes of the Consumer Credit Act 1974, any day other than (1) Saturday or Sunday; (2) Christmas Day or Good Friday; (3) a bank holiday within the meaning given by section 1 of the Banking and Financial Dealings Act 1971.

Working Expenses. All expenses necessarily incurred in the running of a business (*e.g.* rent, rates, wages, etc.) and entered in the profit and loss account.

Working Partner. *See* Active Partner.

Working Party. A group appointed in an advisory capacity, to study methods of obtaining maximum efficiency in industry; a group appointed to undertake an enquiry and report their findings.

Work-in-Progress. The state of raw materials, to which some work has been done in the manufacturing stage, but which have not yet been completed to the point of being regarded as stock.

Works Oncost. Production overheads: the cost of the expenses of production.

Work Study. *See* Time and Motion Study.

World Bank. *See* International Bank for Reconstruction and Development.

World-Wide Letter of Credit. *See* Letter of Credit.

Writ. A written command or precept issued by a court, *e.g.* one requiring the attendance of a defendant in a civil or criminal action; an order to a person commanding him to do or refrain from doing some particular act therein specified.

Writ of *Distringas*. *See Distringas*.

Writ of *Elegit*. A writ by means of which a judgment creditor sought to obtain satisfaction of his debt out of the proceeds of land belonging to the debtor. Its place is now taken by a charging order.

Writ of Execution. A writ directed to the sheriff, commanding him to take certain compulsory proceedings for the purpose of carrying into effect a judgment of the court.

Writ of *Fieri Facias*. *See Fieri Facias*.

Writ of Possession. An order directing a sheriff to put a person in possession.

Writ of Sequestration. A process available against a person who is in contempt for disobedience of the court. Following the issue of the writ, those on whose behalf it was issued (the sequestrators) may demand information and transfer of property from the third party. Once a bank knows that a writ has been issued against a customer, the account should be conducted normally until demand for payment is made. The bank must act upon this, and must also give up any articles held on safe custody if demanded by the sequestrators. The fullest information must be given on request—the bank's normal duty of secrecy is over-ridden—and this would even extend to give information of any attempts by the customer to avoid sequestration, such as transferring sums out of the account.

Writ of Summons. The formal document by which a High Court action is commenced.

Write Down. To reduce the book value of an asset.

Write Off. To remove entirely from the asset book values, as with a bad debt which it has proved impossible to recover; to cancel; to dismiss from consideration.

Written Law. *See* Statute Law.

Wrongly Delivered. Cheques which by mistake are presented for payment to branches different from the ones on which they are drawn. Such a cheque must be presented to the correct paying bank branch on the same day, if possible; if not, it must be sent direct to the paying branch by post, and an adjustment made in the Clearing House total. Articles wrongly delivered at the Clearing House itself are to be returned to the presenting bank at the Clearing House on the following day. The bank will then present it again, correctly. The totals of all articles wrongly delivered in this way are agreed by representatives of all the clearing banks meeting at the Clearing House on the next day; adjustments between the banks in respect of them are then made.

Wrong Post. The placing of a debit or a credit amount to a wrong account.

Wucherzing. Usurious rate of interest. *See* Usury.

Wuchsaktie. Growth share.

Y

Yearling Bond. *See* Local Authority Bonds.

Yearly Tenancy. A tenancy from year to year. Notice to terminate, whether from landlord or tenant, must be given to expire just before an anniversary of the commencing date of the tenancy. The notice must be in unmistakable terms. Not less than half a year's notice is necessary, unless a different agreement has been made by the parties.

Years' Purchase. A method of expressing the value of real property as equal to the rent over a certain number of years.

Yield. That which is produced to give a return or profit; a measure of the income which an investor gets from holding a repayable loan stock expressed as a percentage. *See also* Dividend Yields; Earnings Yield; Flat (or Running) Yield; Grossed-Up Redemption Yield; Gross Yield; Net Yield; Redemption Yield.

Yield Gap. In the past the dividend yield on equities has been higher than the gross yield on long-dated Government stocks because the income from equities has been considered less assured. The difference between them—the yield gap—has usually been taken to be the difference between the return on $2\frac{1}{2}\%$ Consols (which have no redemption date) and the yield on the shares making up the Financial Times Ordinary Share Index. *See also* Reverse Yield Gap.

Yours. A phrase used by foreign exchange dealers to indicate that they are sellers of the currency in question.

Z

Zahlung. An accounting, a payment.
Zahlungsabkommen. See *Clearingabkommen.*
Zahlungsanweisung. Money order.
Zahlungsaufschub. Delay in payment.
Zahlungsbilanz. The balance of payments of a country.
Zahlungseinstellung. Suspension of payment.
Zahlungsfähig. Solvent.
Zahlungsunfähig. Insolvent.
Zedent. See *Abtretung.*
Zeichnung. Subscription for a new issue.
Zeichnungspreis. Issue price.
Zeitgeschäft. See *Lieferungsgeschäft.*
Zero Budgeting. Considering a period of expenditure, and how it is to be financed, on the basis that no present commitments exist, and no balance is carried forward (used in public expenditure in the U.S.A. where it is known as the "sunset law"), as opposed to the conception, as is done with the annual review of public expenditure in this country, of an examination of new programmes and the increases in current programmes. Zero budgeting aims at starting each annual spending budget from nought, and looking at the whole range of public spending. It puts a definite term to each spending programme with the onus on the spenders to justify continuation.
Zertifikat. See *Certificate.*
Zession. Assignment.
Zessionskredit. An advance against the security of an assignment of book debts.
Ziehungen. Redemption of bonds by lot.
Zins. Interest; payment for the use of capital.
Zinsen. Tax, duty, interest.
Zinsfuss, Zinsrate, Zinssatz. Interest-rate.
Zinsschein. Coupon.
Zinsspanne. The range of interest costs; the difference between the rate of interest charged on freely negotiable security, and that charged on real property; the difference between what a bank has to pay to attract deposits, and the rate it charges for granting loans.

Zirka-Auftrag. A stock exchange order with a limit attached.
Zirkularkreditbrief. See *Kreditbrief*; Circular Letter of Credit.
Zoll. Customs duty.
Zollverein. A customs union. In 1818 Prussia agreed with the independent German states to abolish all tariffs between them and to erect instead an external tariff wall which would be common to all of them. Similar considerations created, more than a century later, the Common Market and the European Free Trade Association.
Zone Sterling. See *Scheduled Territories.*
Zoning. Enclosing, dividing into belts or sub-divisions; the divisions of a country into regional areas, *e.g.* for the distribution of commodities, for the control of bank branches by a regional manager, etc; the allocation of use for a particular area under Town and Country Planning regulations.
Zoological Certificate. Also known as a health certificate. A certificate required to indicate hides and certain foodstuffs as free from contamination.
Zusammenlegung von Aktien. The reduction of share capital of a business by the lowering of the nominal value of the shares and their equation with or replacement by a new share issue.
Zusammenschluss. See *Amalgamation; Merger.*
Zuteilung. See *Repartierung.*
Zuteilungsschein. See *Allotment Letter.*
Zwangskonversion. The compulsory conversion of a bond issued under which the bond holder has no chance of electing for repayment.
Zwangssparen. Compulsory saving on a large scale by a state-imposed limitation of consumption expenditure, carried out in such a way that the money "saved" is directed into channels which place it at the disposal of the state (usually by way of a consumption tax) or direct it towards a specific end (as finance for an old people's pension fund).

APPENDICES

APPENDIX I

Uniform Customs and Practice for Documentary Credits

Copyright © International Chamber of Commerce

This publication is available from the British National Committee of the International Chamber of Commerce (6/14, Dean Farrar Street, London SW1H ODT) or from the International Chamber of Commerce (38, Cours Albert-1er, 75008, Paris) or from other National Committees of the International Chamber of Commerce.

The Uniform Customs and Practice for Documentary Credits were first published in 1933. Revised versions were issued in 1951 and 1962.
This Revision was adopted by the ICC Executive Committee in December 1974, and first published as Publication No 290 in March and July 1975.

GENERAL PROVISIONS AND DEFINITIONS

(*a*) These provisions and definitions and the following articles apply to all documentary credits and are binding upon all parties thereto unless otherwise expressly agreed.

(*b*) For the purposes of such provisions, definitions and articles the expressions "documentary credit(s)" and "credit(s)" used therein mean any arrangement, however named or described, whereby a bank (the issuing bank), acting at the request and in accordance with the instructions of a customer (the applicant for the credit),

(*i*) is to make payment to or to the order of a third party (the beneficiary), or is to pay, accept or negotiate bills of exchange (drafts) drawn by the beneficiary, or

(*ii*) authorises such payments to be made or such drafts to be paid, accepted or negotiated by another bank,

against stipulated documents, provided that the terms and conditions of the credit are complied with.

(*c*) Credits, by their nature, are separate transactions from the sales or other contracts on which they may be based and banks are in no way concerned with or bound by such contracts.

(*d*) Credit instructions and the credits themselves must be complete and precise.

In order to guard against confusion and misunderstanding, issuing banks should discourage any attempt by the applicant for the credit to include excessive detail.

(*e*) The bank first entitled to exercise the option available under Article 32(*b*) shall be the bank authorised to pay, accept or negotiate under a credit. The decision of such bank shall bind all parties concerned.

A bank is authorised to pay or accept under a credit by being specifically nominated in the credit.

A bank is authorised to negotiate under a credit either
   (i) by being specifically nominated in the credit, or
   (ii) by the credit being freely negotiable by any bank.
(f) A beneficiary can in no case avail himself of the contractual relationships existing between banks or between the applicant for the credit and the issuing bank.

A. FORM AND NOTIFICATION OF CREDITS

Article 1

(a) Credits may be either
   (i) revocable, or
   (ii) irrevocable.
(b) All credits, therefore, should clearly indicate whether they are revocable or irrevocable.
(c) In the absence of such indication the credit shall be deemed to be revocable.

Article 2

A revocable credit may be amended or cancelled at any moment without prior notice to the beneficiary. However, the issuing bank is bound to reimburse a branch or other bank to which such a credit has been transmitted and made available for payment, acceptance or negotiation, for any payment, acceptance or negotiation complying with the terms and conditions of the credit and any amendments received up to the time of payment, acceptance or negotiation made by such branch or other bank prior to receipt by it of notice of amendment or of cancellation.

Article 3

(a) An irrevocable credit constitutes a definite undertaking of the issuing bank, provided that the terms and conditions of the credit are complied with:
   (i) to pay, or that payment will be made, if the credit provides for payment, whether against a draft or not;
   (ii) to accept drafts if the credit provides for acceptance by the issuing bank or to be responsible for their acceptance and payment at maturity if the credit provides for the acceptance of drafts drawn on the applicant for the credit or any other drawee specified in the credit;
   (iii) to purchase/negotiate, without recourse to drawers and/or bona fide holders, drafts drawn by the beneficiary, at sight or at a tenor, on the applicant for the credit or on any other drawee specified in the credit, or to provide for purchase/negotiation by another bank, if the credit provides for purchase/negotiation.
(b) An irrevocable credit may be advised to a beneficiary through another bank (the advising bank) without engagement on the part of that bank, but when an issuing bank authorises or requests another bank to confirm its irrevocable credit and the latter does so, such confirmation constitutes a definite undertaking of the confirming bank in addition to the undertaking of the issuing bank, provided that the terms and conditions of the credit are complied with:
   (i) to pay, if the credit is payable at its own counters, whether

against a draft or not, or that payment will be made if the credit provides for payment elsewhere;
  (*ii*) to accept drafts if the credit provides for acceptance by the confirming bank, at its own counters, or to be responsible for their acceptance and payment at maturity if the credit provides for the acceptance of drafts drawn on the applicant for the credit or any other drawee specified in the credit;
  (*iii*) to purchase/negotiate, without recourse to drawers and/or bona fide holders, drafts drawn by the beneficiary, at sight or at a tenor, on the issuing bank, or on the applicant for the credit or on any other drawee specified in the credit, if the credit provides for purchase/negotiation.
(*c*) Such undertakings can neither be amended nor cancelled without the agreement of all parties thereto. Partial acceptance of amendments is not effective without the agreement of all parties thereto.

Article 4
(*a*) When an issuing bank instructs a bank by cable, telegram or telex to advise a credit, and intends the mail confirmation to be the operative credit instrument, the cable, telegram or telex must state that the credit will only be effective on receipt of such mail confirmation. In this event, the issuing bank must send the operative credit instrument (mail confirmation) and any subsequent amendments to the credit to the beneficiary through the advising bank.
(*b*) The issuing bank will be responsible for any consequences arising from its failure to follow the procedure set out in the preceding paragraph.
(*c*) Unless a cable, telegram or telex states "details to follow" (or words of similar effect), or states that the mail confirmation is to be the operative credit instrument, the cable, telegram or telex will be deemed to be the operative credit instrument and the issuing bank need not send the mail confirmation to the advising bank.

Article 5
When a bank is instructed by cable, telegram or telex to issue, confirm or advise a credit similar in terms to one previously established and which has been the subject of amendments, it shall be understood that the details of the credit being issued, confirmed or advised will be transmitted to the beneficiary excluding the amendments, unless the instructions specify clearly any amendments which are to apply.

Article 6
If incomplete or unclear instructions are received to issue, confirm or advise a credit, the bank requested to act on such instructions may give preliminary notification of the credit to the beneficiary for information only and without responsibility; in this event the credit will be issued, confirmed or advised only when the necessary information has been received.

B. LIABILITIES AND RESPONSIBILITIES

Article 7
Banks must examine all documents with reasonable care to ascertain that they appear on their face to be in accordance with the terms and conditions

of the credit. Documents which appear on their face to be inconsistent with one another will be considered as not appearing on their face to be in accordance with the terms and conditions of the credit.

Article 8

(a) In documentary credit operations all parties concerned deal in documents and not in goods.

(b) Payment, acceptance or negotiation against documents which appear on their face to be in accordance with the terms and conditions of a credit by a bank authorised to do so, binds the party giving the authorisation to take up the documents and reimburse the bank which has effected the payment, acceptance or negotiation.

(c) If, upon receipt of the documents, the issuing bank considers that they appear on their face not to be in accordance with the terms and conditions of the credit, that bank must determine, on the basis of the documents alone, whether to claim that payment, acceptance or negotiation was not effected in accordance with the terms and conditions of the credit.

(d) The issuing bank shall have a reasonable time to examine the documents and to determine as above whether to make such a claim.

(e) If such claim is to be made, notice to that effect, stating the reasons therefore, must, without delay, be given by cable or other expeditious means to the bank from which the documents have been received (the remitting bank) and such notice must state that the documents are being held at the disposal of such bank or are being returned thereto.

(f) If the issuing bank fails to hold the documents at the disposal of the remitting bank, or fails to return the documents to such bank, the issuing bank shall be precluded from claiming that the relative payment, acceptance or negotiations was not effected in accordance with the terms and conditions of the credit.

(g) If the remitting bank draws the attention of the issuing bank to any irregularities in the documents or advises such bank that it has paid, accepted or negotiated under reserve or against a guarantee in respect of such irregularities, the issuing bank shall not thereby be relieved from any of its obligations under this article. Such guarantee or reserve concerns only the relations between the remitting bank and the beneficiary.

Article 9

Banks assume no liability or responsibility for the form, sufficiency, accuracy, genuineness, falsification or legal effect of any documents, or for the general and/or particular conditions stipulated in the documents or superimposed thereon; nor do they assume any liability or responsibility for the description, quantity, weight, quality, condition, packing, delivery, value or existence of the goods represented thereby, or for the good faith or acts and/or omissions, solvency, performance or standing of the consignor, the carriers or the insurers of the goods or any other person whomsoever.

Article 10

Banks assume no liability or responsibility for the consequences arising out of delay and/or loss in transit of any messages, letters or documents, or for delay, mutilation or other errors arising in the transmission of cables, telegrams or telex. Banks assume no liability or responsibility for errors in translation or interpretation of technical terms, and reserve the right to transmit credit terms without translating them.

Article 11
Banks assume no liability or responsibility for consequences arising out of the interruption of their business by Acts of God, riots, civil commotions, insurrections, wars or any other causes beyond their control or by any strikes or lockouts. Unless specifically authorised, banks will not effect payment, acceptance or negotiation after expiration under credits expiring during such interruption of business.

Article 12
   (a) Banks utilising the services of another bank for the purpose of giving effect to the instructions of the applicant for the credit do so for the account and at the risk of the latter.
   (b) Banks assume no liability or responsibility should the instructions they transmit not be carried out, even if they have themselves taken the initiative in the choice of such other bank.
   (c) The applicant for the credit shall be bound by and liable to indemnify the banks against all obligations and responsibilities imposed by foreign laws and usages.

Article 13
A paying or negotiating bank which has been authorised to claim reimbursement from a third bank nominated by the issuing bank and which has effected such payment or negotiation shall not be required to confirm to the third bank that it has done so in accordance with the terms and conditions of the credit.

C. DOCUMENTS

Article 14
   (a) All instructions to issue, confirm or advise a credit must state precisely the documents against which payment, acceptance or negotiation is to be made.
   (b) Terms such as "first class", "well known", "qualified" and the like shall not be used to describe the issuers of any documents called for under credits and if they are incorporated in the credit terms banks will accept documents as tendered.

C. 1 Documents evidencing shipment or dispatch or taking in charge (shipping documents).

Article 15
Except as stated in Article 20, the date of the Bill of Lading, or the date of any other document evidencing shipment or dispatch or taking in charge, or the date indicated in the reception stamp or by notation on any such document, will be taken in each case to be the date of shipment or dispatch or taking in charge of the goods.

Article 16

(a) If words clearly indicating payment or prepayment of freight, however named or described, appear by stamp or otherwise on documents evidencing shipment or dispatch or taking in charge they will be accepted as constituting evidence of payment of freight.

(b) If the words "freight pre-payable" or "freight to be prepaid" or words of similar effect appear by stamp or otherwise on such documents they will not be accepted as constituting evidence of the payment of freight.

(c) Unless otherwise specified in the credit or inconsistent with any of the documents presented under the credit, banks will accept documents stating that freight or transportation charges are payable on delivery.

(d) Banks will accept shipping documents bearing reference by stamp or otherwise to costs additional to the freight charges, such as costs of, or disbursements incurred in connection with, loading, unloading or similar operations, unless the conditions of the credit specifically prohibit such reference.

Article 17

Shipping documents which bear a clause on the face thereof such as "shipper's load and count" or "said by shipper to contain" or words of similar effect, will be accepted unless otherwise specified in the credit.

Article 18

(a) A clean shipping document is one which bears no superimposed clause or notation which expressly declares a defective condition of the goods and/or the packaging.

(b) Banks will refuse shipping documents bearing such clauses or notations unless the credit expressly states the clauses or notations which may be accepted.

C. 1.1 Marine Bills of Lading.

Article 19

(a) Unless specifically authorised in the credit, Bills of Lading of the following nature will be rejected:
   (i) Bills of Lading issued by forwarding agents.
   (ii) Bills of Lading which are issued under and are subject to the conditions of a Charter-Party.
   (iii) Bills of Lading covering shipment by sailing vessels.

(b) However, subject to the above and unless otherwise specified in the credit, Bills of Lading of the following nature will be accepted:
   (i) "Through" Bills of Lading issued by shipping companies or their agents even though they cover several modes of transport.
   (ii) Short Form Bills of Lading (i.e. Bills of Lading issued by shipping companies or their agents which indicate some or all of the conditions of carriage by reference to a source or documents other than the Bill of Lading).
   (iii) Bills of Lading issued by shipping companies or their agents covering unitised cargoes, such as those on pallets or in containers.

Article 20

(a) Unless otherwise specified in the credit, Bills of Lading must show that the goods are loaded on board a named vessel or shipped on a named vessel.

(b) Loading on board a named vessel or shipment on a named vessel may be evidenced either by a Bill of Lading bearing wording indicating loading on board a named vessel or shipment on a named vessel, or by means of a notation to that effect on the Bill of Lading signed or initialled and dated by the carrier or his agent, and the date of this notation shall be regarded as the date of loading on board the named vessel or shipment on the named vessel.

Article 21

(a) Unless transhipment is prohibited by the terms of the credit, Bills of Lading will be accepted which indicate that the goods will be transhipped en route, provided the entire voyage is covered by one and the same Bill of Lading.

(b) Bills of Lading incorporating printed clauses stating that the carriers have the right to tranship will be accepted notwithstanding the fact that the credit prohibits transhipment.

Article 22

(a) Banks will refuse a Bill of Lading stating that the goods are loaded on deck, unless specifically authorised in the credit.

(b) Banks will not refuse a Bill of Lading which contains a provision that the goods may be carried on deck, provided it does not specifically state that they are loaded on deck.

C. 1.2 Combined transport documents.

Article 23

(a) If the credit calls for a combined transport document, *i.e.* one which provides for a combined transport by at least two different modes of transport, from a place at which the goods are taken in charge to a place designated for delivery, or if the credit provides for a combined transport, but in either case does not specify the form of document required and/or the issuer of such document, banks will accept such documents as tendered.

(b) If the combined transport includes transport by sea the document will be accepted although it does not indicate that the goods are on board a named vessel, and although it contains a provision that the goods, if packed in a Container, may be carried on deck, provided it does not specifically state that they are loaded on deck.

C. 1.3 Other shipping documents, etc.

Article 24

Banks will consider a Railway or Inland Waterway Bill of Lading or Consignment Note, Counterfoil Waybill, Postal Receipt, Certificate of Mailing, Air Mail Receipt, Air Waybill, Air Consignment Note or Air Receipt, Trucking Company Bill of Lading or any other similar documents as regular when such document bears the reception stamp of the carrier or his agent, or when it bears a signature purporting to be that of the carrier or his agent.

Article 25

Where a credit calls for an attestation or certification of weight in the case of transport other than by sea, banks will accept a weight stamp or declaration of weight superimposed by the carrier on the shipping document unless the credit calls for a separate or independent certificate of weight.

C. 2 Insurance documents.

Article 26
(a) Insurance documents must be as specified in the credit, and must be issued and/or signed by insurance companies or their agents or by underwriters.
(b) Cover notes issued by brokers will not be accepted, unless specifically authorised in the credit.

Article 27

Unless otherwise specifed in the credit, or unless the insurance documents presented establish that the cover is effective at the latest from the date of shipment or dispatch or, in the case of combined transport, the date of taking the goods in charge, banks will refuse insurance documents presented which bear a date later than the date of shipment or dispatch or, in the case of combined transport, the date of taking the goods in charge, as evidenced by the shipping documents.

Article 28
(a) Unless otherwise specified in the credit, the insurance document must be expressed in the same currency as the credit.
(b) The minimum amount for which insurance must be effected is the CIF value of the goods concerned. However, when the CIF value of the goods cannot be determined from the documents on their face, banks will accept as such minimum amount the amount of the drawing under the credit or the amount of the relative commercial invoice, whichever is the greater.

Article 29
(a) Credits should expressly state the type of insurance required and, if any, the additional risks which are to be covered. Imprecise terms such as "usual risks" or "customary risks" should not be used; however, if such imprecise terms are used, banks will accept insurance documents as tendered.
(b) Failing specific instructions, banks will accept insurance cover as tendered.

Article 30

Where a credit stipulates "insurance against all risks", banks will accept an insurance document which contains any "all risks" notation or clause, and will assume no responsibility if any particular risk is not covered.

Article 31

Banks will accept an insurance document which indicates that the cover is subject to a franchise or an excess (deductible), unless it is specifically stated in the credit that the insurance must be issued irrespective of percentage.

C. 3 Commercial invoices.

Article 32
   (*a*) Unless otherwise specified in the credit, commercial invoices must be made out in the name of the applicant for the credit.
   (*b*) Unless otherwise specified in the credit, banks may refuse commercial invoices issued for amounts in excess of the amount permitted by the credit.
   (*c*) The description of the goods in the commercial invoice must correspond with the description in the credit. In all other documents the goods may be described in general terms not inconsistent with the description of the goods in the credit.

C. 4 Other documents.

Article 33

When other documents are required such as Warehouse Receipts, Delivery Orders, Consular Invoices, Certificates of Origin, of Weight, of Quality or of Analysis, etc. and when no further definition is given, banks will accept such documents as tendered.

D. MISCELLANEOUS PROVISIONS

Quantity and amount.

Article 34
   (*a*) The words "about", "circa" or similar expressions used in connection with the amount of the credit or the quantity or the unit price of the goods are to be construed as allowing a difference not to exceed 10% more or 10% less.
   (*b*) Unless a credit stipulates that the quantity of the goods specified must not be exceeded or reduced a tolerance of 3% more or 3% less will be permissible, always provided that the total amount of the drawings does not exceed the amount of the credit. This tolerance does not apply when the credit specifies quantity in terms of a stated number of packing units or individual items.

Partial shipments.

Article 35
   (*a*) Partial shipments are allowed, unless the credit specifically states otherwise.

(b) Shipments made on the same ship and for the same voyage, even if the Bills of Lading evidencing shipment "on board" bear different dates and/or indicate different ports of shipment, will not be regarded as partial shipments.

Article 36

If shipment by instalments within given periods is stipulated and any instalment is not shipped within the period allowed for that instalment, the credit ceases to be available for that or any subsequent instalments, unless otherwise specified in the credit.

Expiry date.

Article 37

All credits, whether revocable or irrevocable, must stipulate an expiry date for presentation of documents for payment, acceptance or negotiation, notwithstanding the stipulation of a latest date for shipment.

Article 38

The words "to", "until", "till", and words of similar import applying to the stipulated expiry date for presentation of documents for payment, acceptance or negotiation, or to the stipulated latest date for shipment, will be understood to include the date mentioned.

Article 39

(a) When the stipulated expiry date falls on a day on which banks are closed for reasons other than those mentioned in Article 11, the expiry date will be extended until the first following business day.

(b) The latest date for shipment shall not be extended by reason of the extension of the expiry date in accordance with this Article. Where the credit stipulates a latest date for shipment, shipping documents dated later than such stipulated date will not be accepted. If no latest date for shipment is stipulated in the credit, shipping documents dated later than the expiry date stipulated in the credit or amendments thereto will not be accepted. Documents other than the shipping documents may, however, be dated up to and including the extended expiry date.

(c) Banks paying, accepting or negotiating on such extended expiry date must add to the documents their certification in the following wording:

"Presented for payment (or acceptance or negotiation as the case may be) within the expiry date extended in accordance with Article 39 of the Uniform Customs."

Shipment, loading or dispatch.

Article 40

(a) Unless the terms of the credit indicate otherwise, the words "departure", "dispatch", "loading" or "sailing" used in stipulating the latest date for shipment of the goods will be understood to be synonymous with "shipment".

(b) Expressions such as "prompt", "immediately", "as soon as possible" and the like should not be used. If they are used, banks will interpret them as a request for shipment within thirty days from the date on the advice of the credit to the beneficiary by the issuing bank or by and advising bank, as the case may be.

(c) The expression "on or about" and similar expressions will be interpreted as a request for shipment during the period from five days before to five days after the specified date, both end days included.

Presentation.

Article 41

Notwithstanding the requirement of Article 37 that every credit must stipulate an expiry date for presentation of documents, credits must also stipulate a specified period of time after the date of issuance of the Bills of Lading or other shipping documents during which presentation of documents for payment, acceptance or negotiation must be made. If no such period of time is stipulated in the credit, banks will refuse documents presented to them later than 21 days after the date of issuance of the Bills of Lading or other shipping documents.

Article 42

Banks are under no obligation to accept presentation of documents outside their banking hours.

Date terms.

Article 43

The terms "first half", "second half" of a month shall be construed respectively as from the 1st to the 15th, and the 16th to the last day of each month, inclusive.

Article 44

The terms "beginning", "middle", or "end" of a month shall be construed respectively as from the 1st to the 10th, the 11th to the 20th, and the 21st to the last day of each month, inclusive.

Article 45

When a bank issuing a credit instructs that the credit be confirmed or advised as available "for one month", "for six months" or the like, but does not specify the date from which the time is to run, the confirming or advising bank will confirm or advise the credit as expiring at the end of such indicated period from the date of its confirmation or advice.

E. Transfer

Article 46

(a) A transferable credit is a credit under which the beneficiary has the right to give instructions to the bank called upon to effect payment or acceptance or to any bank entitled to effect negotiation to make the credit available in whole or in part to one or more third parties (second beneficiaries).

(b) The bank requested to effect the transfer, whether it has confirmed the credit or not, shall be under no obligation to effect such transfer except

to the extent and in the manner expressly consented to by such bank, and until such bank's charges in respect of transfer are paid.
(c) Bank charges in respect of transfers are payable by the first beneficiary unless otherwise specified.
(d) A credit can be transferred only if it is expressly designated as "transferable" by the issuing bank. Terms such as "divisible", "fractionable", "assignable", and "transmissible" add nothing to the meaning of the term "transferable" and shall not be used.
(e) A transferable credit can be transferred once only. Fractions of a transferable credit (not exceeding in the aggregate the amount of the credit) can be transferred separately, provided partial shipments are not prohibited, and the aggregate of such transfers will be considered as constituting only one transfer of the credit. The credit can be transferred only on the terms and conditions specified in the original credit, with the exception of the amount of the credit, of any unit prices stated therein, and of the period of validity or period for shipment, any or all of which may be reduced or curtailed.

Additionally, the name of the first beneficiary can be substituted for that of the applicant for the credit, but if the name of the applicant for the credit is specifically required by the original credit to appear in any document other than the invoice, such requirement must be fulfilled.
(f) The first beneficiary has the right to substitute his own invoices for those of the second beneficiary, for amounts not in excess of the original amount stipulated in the credit and for the original unit prices if stipulated in the credit, and upon such substitution of invoices the first beneficiary can draw under the credit for the difference, if any, between his invoices and the second beneficiary's invoices. When a credit has been transferred and the first beneficiary is to supply his own invoices in exchange for the second beneficiary's invoices but fails to do so on first demand, the paying, accepting or negotiating bank has the right to deliver to the issuing bank the documents received under the credit, including the second beneficiary's invoices, without further responsibility to the first beneficiary.
(g) The first beneficiary of a transferable credit can transfer the credit to a second beneficiary in the same country or in another country unless the credit specifically states otherwise. The first beneficiary shall have the right to request that payment or negotiation be effected to the second beneficiary at the place to which the credit has been transferred, up to and including the expiry date of the original credit, and without prejudice to the first beneficiary's right subsequently to substitute his own invoices for those of the second beneficiary and to claim any difference due to him.

Article 47

The fact that a credit is not stated to be transferable shall not affect the beneficiary's rights to assign the proceeds of such credit in accordance with the provisions of the applicable law.

APPENDIX II

Uniform Rules for Collections

Copyright © International Chamber of Commerce

This publication is available from the British National Committee of the International Chamber of Commerce (6/14, Dean Farrar Street, London SW1 0DT) or from the International Chamber of Commerce (38, Cours Albert-1er, 75008, Paris) or from other National Committees of the International Chamber of Commerce.

The International Chamber of Commerce published its "Uniform Rules for the Collection of Commercial Paper" for the first time in 1956. They were revised in 1967, the revision being effective from 1st January 1968, as Publication No 254.

The present revision was approved by the Council of the ICC in June 1978 to be in force from 1st January 1979. It is being issued with the title "Uniform Rules for Collections" as Publication No 322.

GENERAL PROVISIONS AND DEFINITIONS

(A) These provisions and definitions and the following articles apply to all collections as defined in (B) below and are binding upon all parties thereto unless otherwise expressly agreed or unless contrary to the provisions of a national, state or local law and/or regulation which cannot be departed from.

(B) For the purpose of such provisions, definitions and articles:
1. (*i*) "Collection" means the handling by banks, on instructions received, of documents as defined in (*ii*) below, in order to
    (*a*) obtain acceptance and/or, as the case may be, payment, or
    (*b*) deliver commercial documents against acceptance and/or, as the case may be, against payment, or
    (*c*) deliver documents on other terms and conditions.
  (*ii*) "Documents" means financial documents and/or commercial documents:
    (*a*) "financial documents" means bills of exchange, promissory notes, cheques, payment receipts or other similar instruments used for obtaining the payment of money;
    (*b*) "commercial documents" means invoices, shipping documents, documents of title or other similar documents, or any other documents whatsoever, not being financial documents.
  (*iii*) "Clean collection" means collection of financial documents not accompanied by commercial documents.
  (*iv*) "Documentary collection" means collection of
    (*a*) financial documents accompanied by commercial documents;
    (*b*) commercial documents not accompanied by financial documents.
2. The "parties thereto" are:
  (*i*) the "principal" who is the customer entrusting the operation of collection to his bank;
  (*ii*) the "remitting bank" which is the bank to which the principal has entrusted the operation of collection;

(*iii*) the "collecting bank" which is any bank, other than the remitting bank, involved in processing the collection order;
(*iv*) the "presenting bank" which is the collecting bank making presentation to the drawee.
3. The "drawee" is the one to whom presentation is to be made according to the collection order.

(C) All documents sent for collection must be accompanied by a collection order giving complete and precise instructions. Banks are only permitted to act upon the instructions given in such collection order, and in accordance with these Rules.

If any bank cannot, for any reason, comply with the instructions given in the collection order received by it, it must immediately advise the party from whom it received the collection order.

LIABILITIES AND RESPONSIBILITIES

Article 1
Banks will act in good faith and exercise reasonable care.

Article 2
Banks must verify that the documents received appear to be as listed in the collection order and must immediately advise the party from whom the collection order was received of any documents missing.

Banks have no further obligation to examine the documents.

Article 3
For the purpose of giving effect to the instructions of the principal, the remitting bank will utilise as the collecting bank:
(*i*) the collecting bank nominated by the principal, or, in the absence of such nomination,
(*ii*) any bank, of its own or another bank's choice, in the country of payment or acceptance, as the case may be.

The documents and the collection order may be sent to the collecting bank directly or through another bank as intermediary.

Banks utilising the services of other banks for the purpose of giving effect to the instructions of the principal do so for account of and at the risk of the latter.

The principal shall be bound by and liable to indemnify the banks against all obligations and responsibilities imposed by foreign laws or usages.

Article 4
Banks concerned with a collection assume no liability or responsibility for the consequences arising out of delay and/or loss in transit of any messages, letters or documents, or for delay, mutilation or other errors arising in the transmissions of cables, telegrams, telex, or communication by electronic systems, or for errors in translation or interpretation of technical terms.

Article 5
Banks concerned with a collection assume no liability or responsibility for consequences arising out of the interruption of their business by Acts of God,

riots, civil commotions, insurrections, wars, or any other causes beyond their control or by strikes or lockouts.

Article 6
Goods should not be dispatched direct to the address of a bank or consigned to a bank without prior agreement on the part of that bank.
In the event of goods being dispatched direct to the address of a bank or consigned to a bank for delivery to a drawee against payment or acceptance or upon other terms without prior agreement on the part of that bank, the bank has no obligation to take delivery of the goods, which remain at the risk and responsibility of the party dispatching the goods.

PRESENTATION

Article 7
Documents are to be presented to the drawee in the form in which they are received, except that remitting and collecting banks are authorised to affix any necessary stamps, at the expense of the principal unless otherwise instructed, and to make any necessary endorsements or place any rubber stamps or other identifying marks or symbols customary to or required for the collection operation.

Article 8
Collection orders should bear the complete address of the drawee or of the domicile at which presentation is to be made. If the address is incomplete or incorrect, the collecting bank may, without obligation and responsibility on its part, endeavour to ascertain the proper address.

Article 9
In the case of documents payable at sight the presenting bank must make presentation for payment without delay.
In the case of documents payable at a tenor other than sight the presenting bank must, where acceptance is called for, make presentation for acceptance without delay, and where payment is called for, make presentation for payment not later than the appropriate maturity date.

Article 10
In respect of a documentary collection including a bill of exchange payable at a future date, the collection order should state whether the commercial documents are to be released to the drawee against acceptance (D/A) or against payment (D/P).
In the absence of such statement, the commercial documents will be released only against payment.

PAYMENT

Article 11
In the case of documents payable in the currency of the country of payment (local currency), the presenting bank must, unless otherwise instructed in the collection order, only release the documents to the drawee

against payment in local currency which is immediately available for disposal in the manner specified in the collection order.

Article 12

In the case of documents payable in a currency other than that of the country of payment (foreign currency), the presenting bank must, unless otherwise instructed in the collection order, only release the documents to the drawee against payment in the relative foreign currency which can immediately be remitted in accordance with the instructions given in the collection order.

Article 13

In respect of clean collections partial payments may be accepted if and to the extent to which and on the conditions on which partial payments are authorised by the law in force in the place of payment. The documents will only be released to the drawee when full payment thereof has been received.

In respect of documentary collections partial payments will only be accepted if specifically authorised in the collection order. However, unless otherwise instructed, the presenting bank will only release the documents to the drawee after full payment has been received.

In all cases partial payments will only be accepted subject to compliance with the provisions of either Article 11 or Article 12 as appropriate.

Partial payment, if accepted, will be dealt with in accordance with the provisions of Article 14.

Article 14

Amounts collected (less charges and/or disbursements and/or expenses where applicable) must be made available without delay to the bank from which the collection order was received in accordance with the instructions contained in the collection order.

ACCEPTANCE

Article 15

The presenting bank is responsible for seeing that the form of the acceptance of a bill of exchange appears to be complete and correct, but is not responsible for the genuineness of any signature or for the authority of any signatory to sign the acceptance.

PROMISSORY NOTES, RECEIPTS AND OTHER SIMILAR INSTRUMENTS

Article 16

The presenting bank is not responsible for the genuineness of any signature or for the authority of any signatory to sign a promissory note, receipt or other similar instrument.

PROTEST

Article 17
The collection order should give specific instructions regarding protest (or other legal process in lieu thereof), in the event of non-acceptance or non-payment.

In the absence of such specific instructions the banks concerned with the collection have no obligation to have the documents protested (or subjected to other legal process in lieu thereof) for non-payment or non-acceptance.

Any charges and/or expenses incurred by banks in connection with such protest or other legal process will be for the account of the principal.

CASE-OF-NEED (PRINCIPAL'S REPRESENTATIVE) AND PROTECTION OF GOODS

Article 18
If the principal nominates a representative to act as case-of-need in the event of non-acceptance and/or non-payment the collection order should clearly and fully indicate the powers of such case-of-need.

In the absence of such indication banks will not accept any instructions from the case-of-need.

Article 19
Banks have no obligation to take any action in respect of the goods to which a documentary collection relates.

Nevertheless in the case that banks take action for the protection of the goods, whether instructed or not, they assume no liability or responsibility with regard to the fate and/or condition of the goods and/or for any acts and/or omissions on the part of any third parties entrusted with the custody and/or protection of the goods. However, collecting bank(s) must immediately advise the bank from which the collection order was received of any such action taken.

Any charges and/or expenses incurred by banks in connection with any action for the protection of the goods will be for the account of the principal.

ADVICE OF FATE, ETC.

Article 20
Collecting banks are to advise fate in accordance with the following rules:
(i) *Form of advice.* All advices or information from the collecting bank to the bank from which the collection order was received, must bear appropriate detail including, in all cases, the latter bank's reference number of the collection order.
(ii) *Method of advice.* In the absence of specific instructions, the collecting bank must send all advices to the bank from which the collection order was received by quickest mail but, if the collecting bank considers the matter to be urgent, quicker methods such as cable, telegram, telex or

communication by electronic systems, etc. may be used at the expense of the principal.

(*iii*)(*a*) *Advice of payment.* The collecting bank must send without delay advice of payment to the bank from which the collection order was received, detailing the amount or amounts collected, charges and/or disbursements and/or expenses deducted, where appropriate, and method of disposal of the funds.

(*b*) *Advice of acceptance.* The collecting bank must send without delay advice of acceptance to the bank from which the collection order was received.

(*c*) *Advice of non-payment or non-acceptance.* The collecting bank must send without delay advice of non-payment or advice of non-acceptance to the bank from which the collection order was received.

The presenting bank should endeavour to ascertain the reasons for such non-payment or non-acceptance and advise accordingly the bank from which the collection order was received.

On receipt of such advice the remitting bank must, within a reasonable time, give appropriate instructions as to the further handling of the documents. If such instructions are not received by the presenting bank within 90 days from its advice of non-payment or non-acceptance, the documents may be returned to the bank from which the collection order was received.

INTEREST, CHARGES AND EXPENSES

Article 21

If the collection order includes an instruction to collect interest which is not embodied in the accompanying financial document(s), if any, and the drawee refuses to pay such interest, the presenting bank may deliver the documents against payment or acceptance as the case may be without collecting such interest, unless the collection order expressly states that such interest may not be waived. Where such interest is to be collected the collection order must bear an indication of the rate of interest and the period covered. When payment of interest has been refused the presenting bank must inform the bank from which the collection order was received accordingly.

If the documents include a financial document containing an unconditional and definitive interest clause the interest amount is deemed to form part of the amount of the documents to be collected. Accordingly, the interest amount is payable in addition to the principal amount shown in the financial document and may not be waived unless the collection order so authorises.

Article 22

If the collection order includes an instruction that collection charges and/or expenses are to be for account of the drawee and the drawee refuses to pay them, the presenting bank may deliver the document(s) against payment or acceptance as the case may be without collecting charges and/or expenses unless the collection order expressly states that such charges and/or expenses may not be waived. When payment of collection charges and/or expenses has been refused the presenting bank must inform the bank from which the collection order was received accordingly. Whenever collection charges and/or expenses are so waived they will be for the account of the principal, and may be deducted from the proceeds.

Should a collection order specifically prohibit the waiving of collection charges and/or expenses then neither the remitting nor collecting nor presenting bank shall be responsible for any costs or delays resulting from this prohibition.

Article 23

In all cases where in the express terms of a collection order, or under these Rules, disbursements and/or expenses and/or collection charges are to be borne by the principal, the collecting bank(s) shall be entitled promptly to recover outlays in respect of disbursements and expenses and charges from the bank from which the collection order was received and the remitting bank shall have the right promptly to recover from the principal any amount so paid out by it, together with its own disbursements, expenses and charges, regardless of the fate of the collection.